The Field of
Adult Services

THE FIELD OF

ADULT SERVICES

Social Work Practice and Administration

GARY M. NELSON, DSW
ANN C. ELLER, MSW
DENNIS W. STREETS, MA, MPH
MARGARET L. MORSE, PhD
EDITORS

NASW PRESS

National Association of Social Workers
Washington, DC

Ann A. Abbott, PhD, ACSW, President
Sheldon R. Goldstein, ACSW, LISW, Executive Director

Nancy A. Winchester, *Editorial Services Director*
Patricia D. Wolf, Wolf Publications, Inc., *Project Manager*
Ronald W. Wolf, Wolf Publications, Inc., *Copyeditor*
Louise Goines, *Proofreader*
Annette Hansen, *Proofreader*
Wm. H. Long, *Indexer*

Library of Congress Cataloging-in-Publication Data
The field of adult services : social work practice and administration
   / Gary M. Nelson ... [et al.], editors.
      p.   cm.
   Includes bibliographic references and index.
   ISBN 0-87101-250-2
   1. Social service--United States.   I. Nelson, Gary M.
II. National Association of Social Workers.
HV91.F49   1995
361.3'0973--dc20
                                                        95-9331
                                                          CIP

Printed in the United States of America

CONTENTS

Part 3: Specialized Fields of Practice

Part 4: Leadership and Management

What constitutes the field of adult social services, and what represents excellence among those working in it? Such questions spurred the production of *The Field of Adult Services: Social Work Practice and Administration*. Thousands of social workers and hundreds of supervisors and managers assist adults with disabilities and older adults each year through a variety of services. These social workers come from varied backgrounds of education and experience to do this important work and, with supervisors and administrators, have accepted their responsibilities without a well-defined set of principles or methods for achieving excellence in their work. This book was written to define the field and to give social work professionals a framework on which to base their practice.

Defining adult services as a field of social work practice is long overdue. Social work is a thinking and doing profession, and as such it has an intellectual content and a set of practice methods. Adult services social work draws on the principles of social work generally, but it is also a specialized branch of the profession with its own values, knowledge, and skills. Formal recognition of this field is important for the professional self-esteem of adult services practitioners and vital to the well-being of their clients. Without greater understanding and recognition, resources will continue to lag behind the needs of social workers and administrators in this challenging area. *The Field of Adult Services: Social Work Practice and Administration* intends to redress this situation by identifying and describing the field as it is relevant to adult services programs in the United States.

As those involved in this book discovered, there is much that is exemplary about the current practices of adult services social workers and managers. The book represents a collaborative effort to identify, develop, and promote these many good practices; to supplement them with new ideas gathered from a variety of sources; and, most important, to organize this information in such a way that it represents a clear model for the field. In doing this the book draws extensively on the experience of adult services social workers, supervisors, and administrators in North Carolina and around the nation.

The focus of this book on administration, supervision, and social work practice recognizes that excellence depends on the quality of each. The book reflects a consensus on themes and represents a collection of thoughts about excellence in adult services. It provides an overview of key skills and issues essential to effective practice, supervision, and administration. It also presents these skills and issues in the context of a family-centered assessment and change method for practice. As an overview, this book represents a beginning, not a conclusion, to the process of defining the field. The ideas, principles, and approaches outlined in this book will need further application and testing to ensure their usefulness in improving the day-to-day practice of adult services programs.

Content

This book has four parts. The first, "The Field and Mission of Adult Services Social Work," considers the history of public services to adults and endorses the value of clear mission statements. A major theme introduced in part 1 that runs throughout the book is that empowerment is the ultimate goal for adult services management and workers as well as for clients and their families.

Part 2, "Principles and Methods of Adult Services Social Work Practice," introduces the basis for excellence in adult services practice. It presents a method for change and problem solving—beginning with intake and ending with closing or transferring the case—that can serve social workers as a way of thinking about their work with adult clients and their families. In its stages are a sequence of activities that focus on supporting, enabling, and empowering adult clients and their families to achieve optimal functioning in six basic dimensions: (1) social, (2) economic, (3) mental health, (4) physical health, (5) activities of daily living, and (6) home and community environment.

Using the family assessment and change method, the social worker considers the strengths, preferences, and needs of clients. The social worker uses two basic types of skills. The first, clinical skills, includes interviewing and relationship development, counseling, and crisis intervention. The second type of skill, resource development and coordination, includes case management, advocacy, and development of community resources. Clinical skills are important because through them the social worker helps clients mobilize their internal resources to solve problems. Resource development and coordination skills make it possible for the social worker to help clients obtain needed material resources. This approach to change applies to social work in general and to the specialized areas of adult services practice presented in part 3, "Specialized Fields of Practice."

Part 3 examines the major practice areas common to many adult services programs. These include adult protective services, guardianship, in-home services, placement, adult day care and day health, and monitoring board and care. Each chapter in part 3 outlines the purpose of the service, reviews the application of the family assessment and change method, and discusses special practice considerations. The authors acknowledge that social workers also use other services beyond those in this model to serve adult clients. In general, the family assessment and change method can be used with any adult client, regardless of the service being offered.

The fourth part of the book, "Leadership and Management," considers basic supervisory and administrative functions essential to achieve excellence in adult services. These functions are strategic planning and management, program development, and staff development; we call the professionals who perform these functions "managers" throughout this book. This is not a comprehensive discussion of the knowledge, skills, and attitudes important to effective leadership and management, but it does introduce many elements of the structure and support necessary for excellence in adult services. Other areas, such as working effectively with boards and commissions, remain to be examined.

Process

From the beginning this was a collaborative project, and at every stage in the development of the model there was a spirit of cooperation and joint ownership among the parties involved. The adult services programs throughout North Carolina were a central source of expertise and experience that helped shape this book. In particular the staff of the Adult Services Branch and the Adult Programs Representatives of the North Carolina Division of Social Services and staff members from adult services programs in Alexander, Catawba, Halifax, and Mecklenburg county departments of social services contributed to the development of this book.

In addition to the North Carolina perspective, state social services agencies and schools of social work around the country were contacted and asked to share any information that would be useful to this book, and many states and schools did so. In addition to the direct experiences of state adult services programs, we drew on the professional and research literature to prepare each chapter. Responsibility for interpretations of those experiences and applications of professional and research literature are those of the authors. The goals used to guide us in our writing were

- to optimize outcomes for adult clients and their families by identifying and promoting excellent social work practice and effective supervision and administration
- to define a body of values, knowledge, and skills essential to social work practice with adults
- to maximize job satisfaction and self-confidence of adult services social workers by recognizing and encouraging excellent practice and practitioners
- to identify barriers to excellent practice and seek to remove or reduce these barriers
- to develop a common language and understanding among practitioners that reflects standards of excellent practice
- to identify how line workers, supervisors, and administrators must work in concert to achieve excellence
- to enable agencies to assess for themselves how well they are providing services to produce the outcomes clients need and desire.

Several things have been done to facilitate the use of this book. Chapters are written to stand alone, if necessary, but they include cross-references to aid the reader in making comparisons across service areas and to find discussions of related topics. Case examples are used when possible to illustrate ideas and suggested approaches. Each chapter concludes with a summary of key points, typically drawn from the discussion in the chapter but sometimes introducing ideas to foster new thinking and future initiatives.

Implementation and Future Development

The people who participated in developing this book hope that the adult services social workers, supervisors, and administrators for whom it was written will find it to be a useful reference and tool. Most readers will focus first on those chapters most immediately relevant to them, but one of the purposes of the book is to assist in cross-training and to encourage adult services personnel to appreciate more fully the work of their colleagues. For an adult services program to make maximum use of the book, an active exchange of ideas and questions among its personnel is vital. An adult services staff, for instance, might share responsibility for reviewing and leading discussion of chapters, using a focus group or seminar format. Three key questions that might be considered for each chapter and for the book as a whole are

1. What are its most important ideas?
2. How do these ideas fit with current practice?
3. How can these ideas be put into practice in an adult services program?

The developers of this book hope that one of its outcomes will be the sharing of ideas and debate about how to achieve excellence in adult services. Although this review and discussion will take time, it is an effort that should be rewarded with empowered adult services personnel and clients and, subsequently, better-focused and more efficient services. Ultimately, the usefulness of this book will be measured by its part in creating a workable model for administrators, supervisors, and line social workers that improves services to clients and their families and increases staff effectiveness and satisfaction.

There will be barriers to the achievement of excellence, given the increasing complexity of issues in adult services and the constrained resources available to address these issues. This realization, though, makes the identification and promotion of excellent social work practice and effective administration and supervision that much more important. Those who developed this model hope that all the adult services practitioners and administrators who read it will learn new and exciting ways of developing their skills and will feel themselves confirmed in the importance of their professional roles.

ACKNOWLEDGMENTS

Many people contributed to this book. In listing them, no doubt we will leave out someone, to whom we offer our sincere apologies. We extend our thanks to Nan Campbell, Andrea Benfield, Harriet Sederholm, Emily Hale, and Beverly Patnaik from county adult services programs in North Carolina. The personnel at the state Division of Social Services at the time the book was first developed—Adult Programs Representatives Miriam Davis, the late John Flemming, Joye McLean, Peggy Plater, JoAnn Smith, and Susan Southard, and the Adult Services Branch staff, Suzanne Merrill, Ann DeMaine, Ann Eller, Vicki Kryk, Rosalyn Pettyford, Alan Richmond, Geoffrey Santoliquido, and Kathy Woodcock—were instrumental in preparing this book, and it has profited from their contributions and support. Special thanks go to Suzanne Merrill, head of the Adult Services Branch, and John Tanner, chief of the Adult and Family Services Section of the Division of Social Services, for their unfailing support of this book. Finally, thanks go to staff members of the Center for Aging Research and Educational Services (CARES) at the School of Social Work, University of North Carolina–Chapel Hill, many of whom are authors of individual chapters. We also thank Gael Hallenbeck, program coordinator at CARES during its first years, and the students who worked with us while the book was being developed—Janice Braxton, Kara Richards, and Sarah Rous (who is now a staff member at CARES).

PART 1

The Field and Mission of Adult Services Social Work

CHAPTER 1

The Field of Adult Services

GARY M. NELSON

Historically the needs and problems of younger and older adults with disabilities have been the concern and responsibility of public social services agencies. However, rarely has systematic attention been given to the needs of the administrators, supervisors, and direct social work practitioners who provide these services in the public sector. Unlike child welfare, which has a long history, well-developed practice methodologies, and a well-documented repertory of social interventions designed to address the needs of children, adult services lacks a similar historical documentation and cataloging of appropriate methodologies and interventions.

This book seeks to remedy this deficiency. It is addressed to professionals engaged in serving adults in the country's public social services system. The book is divided into four sections: (1) the history and structure of social work in adult services; (2) the family assessment and change method proposed as the basis for excellent practice; (3) what we believe should be excellent social work practice in specific adult services program areas; and (4) a discussion of excellence in administrative and supervisory support.

To set the stage for understanding the nation's adult services programs, this chapter establishes their historical and organizational context. The first section of this chapter provides a perspective on the development of adult services programs throughout the states, with a description of the primary adult services populations they serve. The chapter continues with a brief description of key attributes and characteristics of adult services programs and a description of the jurisdictional overlap with other agencies and then touches on adult services roles in a changing environment and the contribution of a collaborative planning approach toward shaping and redefining those roles. It outlines emerging adult services program models that address issues of collaboration and summarizes key points.

National Perspective on Adult Services

Community concern and provision for adults in need is as old as the country itself. The needs of infirm people and those people made destitute in old age were addressed by the earliest European settlers, who brought with them from England the concepts of government assistance based on the Elizabethan Poor Laws (Trattner, 1989). However, as might be expected, the role of public social services agencies in meeting the needs of adults has changed with the times and circumstances.

Currently, states operate adult services programs within the public welfare or public social services arm of state, regional, or local government. In some states (for example, Louisiana and Massachusetts) adult services programs are limited primarily to providing protective services, whereas aging network and other community-based programs assume responsibility for such essential supportive services as adult day care and in-home services. In other states, such as North Carolina, New York, and Texas, county adult services programs in local departments of social services provide an array of in-home and community services (for example, in-home aide services, adult day care, and placement) as well as protective services.

Primary Service Populations

The organizational and systems issues that adult services administrators, supervisors, and social work practitioners address are often as complex as the problems of their adult clients. Excellent services for adult clients, whether young or old, call for understanding both the service needs and organizational and systems issues that accompany this service population. The organizational structure for service delivery, which varies from state to state, is discussed later in this chapter. To some degree that organizational structure determines who adult services clients are. For this book they are clients who are considered adults under state law, who have some physical or mental disability, and who qualify (for example, on account of income, age, or disability) for assistance through a public social services program.

There is a paucity of national data on the characteristics of adult services clients as well as reasonable concern about who to include in any sample. We conducted a survey of adult services programs administered through North Carolina's county departments of social services (Center for Aging Research and Educational Services [CARES], 1990) that can shed some light on the subject. Of the social workers with clienteles made up exclusively of adults, 72 percent said that more than half of their clients were over age 60. These social workers estimated the proportions of their clients with special problems, and on average more than 50 percent had physical disabilities; nearly 20 percent had dementia or other cognitive impairments; and about 10 percent had visual impairments, developmental disabilities, or chronic mental illness. Although some workers may carry specialized caseloads, for instance in the areas of in-home services or adult protective services, most workers generally deal with a cross-section of cases representing the range of problems and issues.

SERVING OLDER ADULTS

Although older adults have always been one of the target populations of public social services policy and effort, the demand in the past has never been what it is likely to become in the next 50 years. This is because there have never been as many older people in the United States, both in absolute numbers and in proportion to the total population, as there will be in the next half-century. Some of this increase is the result of greater longevity, but most comes from increased survival in the first years of life. The extraordinary increase in births after World War II (the baby boom generation) will result in an unprecedented number of people who turn 65 between 2011 and 2028 and survive perhaps another 20 years.

In chapter 3 we suggest that the functional status of any individual may be related to but is not dictated by diagnosis. Similarly, functional status and the resulting need for social services are related to age, but age does not immediately imply disability. However, the risk of disability rises sharply with age. Some 8 percent of people ages 65 to 74 have at least one impairment in carrying out the activities of daily living (self-care, eating, bathing, moving from bed to some other location, and using the toilet), whereas the rate for those ages 75 to 84 is 14 percent and for those ages 85 and over, 21 percent.

Although age and diagnosis do not predict disability for individuals, they do provide a way to foresee the needs of populations as a whole. It is likely then that in the future more older people will need assistance from their families and from providers of social services (whether private or public) to compensate for losses in functioning. For this reason, adult services social work is a growing field.

ADULTS AGES 18 TO 59

Although little has been written about public social services for older adults, even less is available concerning younger adults, those ages 18 to 59. Several possible explanations for this exist. Because the prevailing assumption about adults in this middle-age group is that they are at their most independent and productive life stage, society neither expects nor understands dependency and need among them, as it might for children and older adults. Access to services is more likely to be based on unanticipated circumstances such as sudden illness or unemployment or on more permanent disabling conditions (for example, mental illness, developmental disabilities, physical or mental disabilities arising from accidents, or chronic or progressive diseases). Other potential adult services clients between the ages of 18 and 59 (for example, homeless people, people with acquired immune deficiency syndrome [AIDS], and unemployed people) have clear needs but no specialized agency to address them. This may be because the public, policymakers, and the public social services sector hold deep-seated assumptions that adults in this age group should be independent, with the result that the service community does little to reach out to them or encourage them to make their needs known. Additionally, because of the diversity of needs and interests, these adults have no ready focus around which to assemble advocacy groups.

Other reasons for a lack of coherence in programs for younger adults may result from overlapping jurisdictions among public social services and other segments of the health and human services community with regard to this population. Services for clients with persistent mental disorders furnish a prime example. Although mental health programs are available to people who have mental illnesses in our states and communities, a typical adult services caseload will frequently include substantial proportions of clients who have cognitive impairments, chronic mental illnesses, or developmental disabilities (CARES, 1990). Some of this overlap results from a lack of clarity about service populations for specific agencies and some from an overburdened and underfunded mental health system.

An additional area in the adult services in which there is a growing younger population involves home and community long-term care. Younger adults with disabilities, whether from head injuries or, increasingly, from chronic illnesses such as AIDS, are becoming a major in-home service population for adult services programs. Although much of the early history of in-home and community care has centered on services for older adults, there is growing pressure to serve adults with disabilities regardless of age. In part, this pressure results from the increasing presence of Medicaid funding for personal care and home and community care in adult services programs. Medicaid, unlike the Older Americans Act of 1965 (OAA), pays for home and community care on the basis of income and medical need and not age.

Adult Services as a Field of Study

Given the long, rich history of public social services for adults, it is surprising that so little has been written about adult services and the provision of a varied array of services through the public sector. Only Adult Protective Services (APS) has been covered (National Aging Resource Center on Elder Abuse [NARCEA], 1990; Quinn & Tomita, 1986; Tatara, 1993). Consequently, some people look at adult services narrowly.

The two notable exceptions to this narrow treatment of adult services as only or primarily APS occurred in the 1950s and early 1960s. A grant from the Doris Duke Foundation to the American Public Welfare Association (APWA) in the early 1950s resulted in the 1953 publication *The Needs of Older Adults and Public Welfare Services to Meet Them*, by Elizabeth Wickenden. In Fall 1958 and again in Spring 1962, the Ford Foundation granted funds to APWA to identify the training needs of social workers serving older adults in the public sector (APWA, 1971).

Although these efforts recognized the need for new models and training programs for those working in adult services, especially in light of the growing population of older adults, only Wickenden's book provided a published, comprehensive description and analysis of the public welfare experience with older clients. Then, as now, the primary role of public social services for adults was to share with the family the provision of aid and social protection for members who, because of illness, external circumstances, or some temporary misfortune, were unable to meet their own needs. Wickenden's book dealt with the needs of certain adults for assistance in the areas of employment, housing, health care, institutional care, and family and individual support and counseling. The Ford Foundation's later initiatives (APWA, 1971) resulted in a series of national training and technical assistance workshops for providers of adult services, but none of the written materials, mostly monographs and technical notes, were formally published and therefore never became readily accessible to those workers who did not take part in the training.

Government Support for Adult Services Programs

FEDERAL INVOLVEMENT

Until the early 1960s public responsibility for providing any type of social services lay primarily with state and local government. Social services first gained significant federal financial support and recognition with the 1962 amendments to the Social Security Act, whose goal was to use intensive social services as a method for reducing the public assistance rolls. The 1967 amendments to the Social Security Act provided the states with increased latitude in targeting social services both to individuals currently receiving public assistance and to those at risk of needing it.

The Title XX Social Service Amendments of 1974 further broadened social services entitlements. States had the option of providing older adults with eligibility as a group, without regard to income. Information and referral, child protective services, and APS were provided in all states on this basis. Although the Title XX amendments broadened entitlements, they also capped federal expenditures in this area and so limited access to federally supported public social services (Gilbert, Specht, & Terrell, 1993).

Title XX, amended in 1982 as the Social Services Block Grant (SSBG), broadly articulated the purpose of social services for both adults and children in public-sector programs (Omnibus Budget Reconciliation Act, amended 1982). These goals still capture the purpose and direction that guide adult services programs across the country and include

1. *to help people become or remain economically self-supporting*
2. *to help people become or remain able to take care of themselves*
3. *to protect children and adults who cannot protect themselves from abuse, neglect, and exploitation and to keep families together, preserve family life, or rehabilitate families*
4. *to prevent or reduce inappropriate institutional care as much as possible by making home and community services available*
5. *to help place people in appropriate institutions when placement is in their best interest and strengthening services in institutions.* (Thomas & Mason, 1989, pp. 56–57)

Although Title XX (SSBG) has been the prime funding source of adult services programs across the country, adult services administrators, workers, and clients and their families function in a complex world of multiple sources of funding for social and health services. Supplemental Security Income benefits, veterans' benefits, housing, food stamps, and Medicare represent a short list of other important federal resources that adult services administrators draw on to serve their constituency. State and local resources, as well as private nonprofit agency resources, also help to weave together the support system for adults with disabilities and for older adults.

Two sources of federal funding of particular importance to adult services include OAA and Medicaid. OAA and its associated network of state units on aging and community-based area agencies on aging in many states share an overlapping mission with departments of social services in providing assistance to adults with impairments. OAA has grown from a fledgling planning and advocacy program in 1965 to a well-established planning and service network with a budget greater than $1 billion in 1992 (Torres-Gil, 1992).

A number of state units on aging and social services programs for adults have structurally integrated their service networks and missions over the past several decades into a common network and mission. Others that remain structurally separate collaborate extensively at the state and local levels in planning and service delivery (APWA and National Association of State Units on Aging [APWA/NASUA], 1988, 1989). An additional example of close collaboration between these two systems can be found in the Administration on Aging's funding of NARCEA in 1988 (Stein, 1991). The Administration on Aging is the federal agency responsible for overseeing the implementation of the OAA. NARCEA, a strong advocate for effective adult protective services programs throughout the nation, is a joint project of APWA, NASUA, the National Committee for the Prevention of Elder Abuse, and the University of Delaware.

Medicaid, also established in 1965, provides resources for both acute and long-term care for younger and older adults. Its budget was $120 billion in 1992. People over age 60 with disabilities accounted for nearly one-fourth of all Medicaid enrollees but for two-thirds of program spending (Feder, Rowland, Holahan, Salganicoff, & Heslam, 1993). Medicaid is a vital source of funding for clients of adult services programs. It provides community-based long-term care (for example, personal care, Medicaid waiver programs, and case management services), as well as nursing home and acute care coverage.

ADULT SERVICES AT THE STATE LEVEL

Adult services programs across the country come in a number of configurations. To piece together a picture of these programs, no two of which are exactly alike, we looked at two publications from APWA/NASUA (1988, 1989) and we conducted a national telephone survey of adult services programs (CARES, 1991) to provide some answers. In addition, in 1990 CARES reported on a survey of the adult services workforce in North Carolina, which illuminates some of the characteristics of adult services social workers and their clients.

The picture that emerges should be seen for what it is, a national "snapshot" of adult services characteristics, service patterns, and issues. Parts are fuzzy, lacking the detail that would come from a more comprehensive survey of the field. However, enough detail exists to provide a brief description of administrative structures for adult services programs, service offerings by various state and local programs, the number and professional qualifications of adult services social workers, and some of the critical practice issues.

Administrative Structures

The administrative structures selected by various states and communities to implement adult services programs reflect different approaches to the issue of how best to coordinate services provided through public welfare agencies and through aging network programs. The study by APWA/NASUA (1988) found that 14 states administered SSBG and OAA funds through one department administered by a single agency. For example, in Arizona both programs were administered by one director through the Aging and Adult Administration within the Department of Economic Security.

Twelve states administered these two programs under separate units within the same department. In North Carolina, the Division of Aging administers OAA programs, whereas the Division of Social Services administers adult services programs. Both divisions are part of the state's Department of Human Resources.

In the remaining 24 states and the District of Columbia, these programs were administered through two different cabinet-level offices. Massachusetts' Older Americans Programs were housed in a department-level Executive Office of Older Affairs, whereas adult services programs, primarily APS, were administered through the Department of Social Services in the Executive Office of Human Services (APWA/NASUA, 1988).

Most states support state-level coordinating groups, variously labeled aging and adult services or long-term-care coordinating councils and committees, to foster collaborative approaches to serve adults with impairments. Activities and program areas tackled by such councils include planning and provision of long-term care, APS, case management, and training. Research on adult services and aging programs at the local level finds as much or more collaboration, including joint planning, funding, and delivery of services. The degree and nature of the collaboration varies according to state and local administrative structure and agreements (APWA/NASUA, 1989). For example, even in North Carolina, where adult services and aging network programs are administered in two parallel structures at the state and local level, nearly 45 percent of the state's 100 county adult services programs had OAA resources in their budgets, and all worked either directly or indirectly with their aging network counterparts. In addition, 96 percent of the local adult services programs had other state resources in their budget, in addition to federal

SSBG and OAA funds. Ninety percent of the programs also had county funds, and 80 percent had Medicaid funds in their adult services budgets (CARES, 1990).

Service Offerings

Information on service expenditures and offerings through SSBG funding and adult services networks is poor. When Title XX was consolidated with SSBG during the Reagan administration, requirements for state plans and planning data were eliminated. National data on expenditures using SSBG and adult services funds are limited and inferential. Although there is some national information on services provided to older adults, it barely exists for younger adults with disabilities.

The most recent national estimate for how many recipients of SSBG-funded services were age 60 and over ranged from zero percent in Montana and Wyoming to 79 percent in California, where much of this funding is devoted to providing in-home services. Nationally, an estimated 22.8 percent of SSBG recipients were age 60 or older, accounting for 17.4 percent of SSBG allocations in 1987 (APWA/ NASUA, 1988). States with no or small commitments of SSBG funds to older adults are generally those where adult services are limited to protective services; those states with larger commitments generally have a broader array of services available to older adults. No recent estimates are available regarding SSBG commitments to younger adults with disabilities.

Of services reported, the one receiving the highest level of SSBG support was homemaker services, followed by case management and APS. Adult day care, transportation services, and home-delivered meals were ranked relatively high in a number of states. A number of states offered such services as counseling, health screening, legal services, respite care, foster care, and personal care services, although these services had lower levels of support (APWA/ NASUA, 1988).

In 1991 we conducted a telephone survey of state adult services programs (CARES, 1991) and tabulated nine services likely to be offered directly by adult services programs: (1) adult day care, (2) adult foster care, (3) case management, (4) guardianship, (5) in-home services, (6) intake, (7) payee, (8) APS, and (9) placement services. Of the 46 responding states, 10 offered all nine services, and 26 offered eight or more. The most frequently offered service was APS.

The information on service patterns and expenditures for adult services programs points to great variation among states and communities. Much of the difference seems related to whether SSBG adult services and OAA resources and networks have been integrated, to the degree of collaboration between parallel yet complementary adult services and aging networks, and to the administrative structure of social services programs, whether state or locally administered. Yet even in those states that focus almost entirely on APS, adult services agencies must work collaboratively with other providers in the community to secure the broad range of services and protections that APS clients and their families require.

Adult Services Social Workers

PREPARATION AND CASELOAD CHARACTERISTICS

The 1991 CARES telephone survey suggested that there are more than 12,000 adult services social workers nationally. The average number of adult services social workers in a state was 243, ranging from 17 in the state-administered program in sparsely populated Idaho to 960 in New York's county-administered program.

The professional preparation of these social workers is a vexing situation. No national estimates are available of the proportion who have bachelor's (BSW) or master's degrees (MSW) in social work. Some states have made estimates, and of them, Maryland appears to have the workforce with the highest rates of professional training—an estimated 60 percent of 245 adult services social workers held MSWs. In contrast, in South Carolina an estimated 5 percent of 184 adult services social workers had a BSW and 2 percent had an MSW. The professional training of the 960 adult services workers in New York was unknown.

In 1988 the authors surveyed the workforce in county departments of social services in North Carolina and determined that of the nearly 600 adult services social workers, 16 percent held BSWs and 5 percent held MSWs. Another 9 percent held a master's degree in another field. Small rural counties in North Carolina were more likely than large ones to employ social workers with BSWs, but none employed a social worker with an MSW. One-quarter of those workers were interested in going back to a university full-time to obtain an advanced degree. Of those wanting more formal education, three-quarters selected social work with a concentration in aging (51 percent), followed by administration (17 percent) and children and family (14.1 percent) (CARES, 1990).

In some respects, the volume of work for North Carolina's adult services social workers may match those for states with similar county-administered programs, including New York and California and a number of southern states. In other ways, however, because North Carolina is rural, the issues may be similar to other rural states such as Ohio and Alabama. The average caseload for an adult services social worker in North Carolina in 1988 was 54, but in the smallest counties the average rose to 68. Nearly one-third of adult services social workers also had children and families in their caseload. When adult services social workers identified the service areas in which they spent most of their time, most claimed "general social work," followed by in-home services, intake, and APS (CARES, 1990).

PRACTICE ISSUES

In the 1991 national telephone survey, the authors asked 42 adult services program representatives to identify the three most critical practice issues facing adult services workers in their state. The leading issues identified by 42 responding states related to APS, followed by more-general issues of service coordination and integration and caseload size and staffing (CARES, 1991).

The practice issues pertaining to APS included better-developed methods for investigating allegations; cross-training with other involved professionals such as law enforcement personnel; methods of treatment for victims of abuse and neglect; how better to handle legal aspects, including appearance in court; and how to secure guardians for clients when necessary. For coordination and integration of services, the issues included improved access and continuity for community-based long-term-care services; increased funding, particularly for in-home services; and training on issues of ethics and values for community-based care. Finally, it is not surprising that a number of states wanted improved staffing and workload standards in response to shortages of workers and large caseloads.

Adult Services Roles in a Changing Environment

Adult services programs operate in environments that are often turbulent and constantly changing. A volatile economy, demographic changes, the return of federal and state mandates to communities, competition among service systems and service providers, and shifts in values and philosophies regarding human services programs are a few of the trends and developments that shape and reshape the roles of state and local adult services programs. In view of the changes, collaborative planning at both state and county levels is often used as a tool for understanding and responding to the various trends and needs in the community and creating a vision of how best to achieve a fit between the role and function of adult services programs and the needs of a changing adult services constituency.

At the state level, adult services programs are constantly reevaluating agency missions against state and community trends and possible collaborative partnerships to serve adults with disabilities. The process of collaborative partnership calls for individual systems and professionals to swallow differences and set aside notions of where personal, professional, and system responsibilities begin and end. Adult services programs must be concerned with a wide array of preventive and supportive services that focus on the whole family and ensure that those people in need are served and empowered.

OVERLAPPING SYSTEM ROLES

The consumers served by community adult services programs have problems that often do not fall neatly into the province of only one service system. Excellent adult services social work involves sharing responsibility for clients with other health and social services systems. For example, clients who need in-home services also need access to physicians for general medical care and perhaps to the home health system for skilled in-home care. Adult services clients with behavioral problems may need both concrete support services and counseling from adult services social workers as well as short- or long-term treatment from the mental health system. Older adult services clients may receive transportation services from a social services agency to enable them to attend a congregate nutrition program or senior center operated by an area agency on aging.

Individual social workers located in community social services programs may find the lines of administrative accountability blurred or multiple. For example, social workers serving clients with developmental disabilities or visual impairments through public social services agencies may need to be aware of and able to work with other programs and agencies established to serve these specific populations. Adult services workers obtaining Medicaid services for their clients or counseling clients with chronic mental illness must be aware both of their own practice role and accountability to the client and family as well as their place and accountability in the overall service system.

EMERGING ADULT SERVICES PROGRAM MODELS

Partly to address issues of overlap with other state human services networks, state adult services programs nationally have evolved into three organizational models: (1) a unified model, (2) a coordinated parallel model, and (3) a restricted model. In the unified model, states such as Arizona have combined the planning, administrative, and service functions of their aging and adult services programs. In other states, including North Carolina, these programs remain separate and parallel, with the focus being on coordinating policy and services when there is significant overlap. Restricted state models can be found in Louisiana, Oregon, and Massachusetts, where adult services programs provide APS only, whereas the state's aging program is responsible for offering a range of services to adults with disabilities, increasingly regardless of age.

With the unified model, many state and local adult services programs have assumed collaborative roles in planning and managing adult services and aging programs for individuals and families in need. In these communities younger and older adults with disabilities have access to a wide range of services, and workers operate under a common mission. The collaborative role of adult social services in the unified model helps to ensure that its historical constituency of disadvantaged younger adults and older adults with disabilities has access to the broadest possible array of appropriate and high-quality services. The blend of responsibilities under this model does and will vary from state to state and community to community, but the mission and commitment to serve both younger and older adults is jointly embraced.

In the coordinated parallel model, state and local adult social services programs join with other agencies in providing needed home and community care services. In such a model, state and local adult social services programs engage in parallel and coordinated planning activities with state units on aging and local area agencies on aging. Collaborative leadership and commitment to a common vision for older adults with disabilities can be effective when the various systems communicate openly and fully with each other. In the parallel model, adult social services programs serve as both key service providers for younger and older adults with disabilities and as major stakeholders in state and local planning activities.

In restricted models of adult social services, in which the primary or only service is APS, the challenge of providing needed services to high-risk adults and their families is probably the greatest. Suspected abuse or neglect cases are also an indicator of need for other services within the community. Timely access to preventive services, treatment and counseling, and respite and in-home services might moderate or eliminate the need for protective services.

In states where APS workers are structurally isolated from directly accessing needed home and community services, many adults and their families are at risk. The recent changes in the OAA to include a focus on elder abuse will help address this issue. Elder abuse and neglect services, particularly in those states where adult social services includes only or primarily APS, must be fully integrated into the adult and aging services home and community care network.

Adult services programs have a long and rich history. The goals of these programs are to support clients' self-determination and empowerment through judicious and compassionate use of community-based services. Younger and older adults in need of assistance often must seek help from a complex, overlapping system of public, nonprofit, and proprietary social and health services. Adult public social services programs are an essential element of this larger system of care. Adult services programs based on excellent social work practice, directed by effective program management, and informed by strategic planning help ensure that those in need obtain timely access to quality assistance both within the public social services and in the broader community.

Key Points

Excellent adult services social workers
- are aware of the national and state history of adult services programs
- know and are committed to the overriding goals of adult services programs.

Excellent adult services managers
- know the implications of various adult services roles and models for planning and administration
- know the implications of home and community care services for adult services programs.

Excellent leaders
- take into account and try to harmonize the efforts of the various systems of services for adults
- support collaborative planning as a method for achieving a fit between the role and function of adult services programs and the needs of adult services clients.

References

American Public Welfare Association. (1971, Fall). The Public Welfare Project on Aging. *Public Welfare,* pp. 439–446.

American Public Welfare Association and National Association of State Units on Aging. (1988). *The relationship between Title III of the Older Americans Act and the Social Services Block Grant. Phase I report: State-level relationships.* Washington, DC: Authors.

American Public Welfare Association and National Association of State Units on Aging. (1989). *The relationship between Title III of the Older Americans Act and the Social Services Block Grant. Phase II report: Local-level relationships.* Washington, DC: Authors.

Center for Aging Research and Educational Services. (1990). *Manpower in county departments of social services. Executive summary and full report.* Chapel Hill, NC: Author.

Center for Aging Research and Educational Services. (1991). *National telephone survey of state adult services programs.* Unpublished data, Chapel Hill, NC.

Feder, J., Rowland, D., Holahan, J., Salganicoff, A., & Heslam, D. (1993). *The Kaiser commission on the future of Medicaid. The Medicaid cost explosion: Causes and consequences.* Baltimore: Henry J. Kaiser Family Foundation.

Gilbert, N., Specht, H., & Terrell, P. (1993). *Dimensions of social welfare policy.* Englewood Cliffs, NJ: Prentice Hall.

National Aging Resource Center on Elder Abuse. (1990). *Elder abuse: A decade of shame and inaction* (Report for the Subcommittee on Health and Long-Term Care of the Select Committee on Aging of the U.S. House of Representatives). Washington, DC: U.S. Government Printing Office.

Older Americans Act of 1965. P.L. 89-73, 79 Stat. 218.

Omnibus Budget Reconciliation Act Amendment of 1982. P.L. 97-253, 96 Stat. 763.

Quinn, J. J., & Tomita, S. T. (1986). Elder abuse and neglect: Written protocol for identification and assessment. In M. M. Quinn & S. T. Tomita (Eds.), *Elder abuse and neglect* (pp. 267–274). New York: Springer.

Social Security Act Amendments of 1962. P.L. 87-543, 76 Stat. 173 and P.L. 87-878, 76 Stat. 1202.

Social Security Act Amendments of 1967. P.L. 90-248, 81 Stat. 821.

Social Security Act Amendments of 1974. P.L. 93-647, 88 Stat. 2337.

Stein, K. F. (1991). A national agenda for elder abuse and neglect research: Issues and recommendations. *Journal of Elder Abuse and Neglect, 3*(3), 91–108.

Tatara, T. (1993). Understanding the nature and scope of domestic elder abuse with the use of state aggregate data: Summaries of the key findings of a national survey of state APS and aging agencies. *Journal of Elder Abuse and Neglect, 5*(4), 350–357.

Thomas, M. P., Jr., & Mason, J. (1989). *A guidebook to social services in North Carolina* (4th ed.). Chapel Hill, NC: Institute of Government.

Torres-Gil, F. M. (1992). *The new aging: Politics and change in America.* New York: Auburn House.

Trattner, W. I. (1989). *From poor law to welfare state.* New York: Free Press.

Wickenden, E. (1953). *The needs of older adults and public welfare services to meet them.* Chicago: American Public Welfare Association.

CHAPTER 2

Adult Services: An Empowered Learning Community

GARY M. NELSON

To demonstrate excellence in adult services, the adult services community—state, regional, and local—must share a commitment to empowerment and to working in a learning community. Because adult services professionals are committed to bringing about change that enhances the well-being of adults with functional impairments, as well as their families, the principles and values associated with empowerment, continual learning, and change make it possible to shape and reshape the organizational mission and purpose to serve this clientele best. Mission and purpose provide direction to planning, policy, and social work administration and practice. Mission represents a shared vision of what adult services practice will look like when it works well for both adult services personnel and their clients.

This chapter explores two concepts, and the values and principles related to them, that are central to effective adult services practice: (1) empowerment and (2) continual learning. After the discussion of these concepts, the related attributes of an empowered learning community are identified and a case study of a state and local perspective on mission to illustrate these attributes is presented. The chapter concludes with an exploration of how empowerment and continual learning benefit line workers, managers, and consumers.

Empowerment

Empowerment is often written and talked about in social work practice, administration, and policy. Rappaport (1985) explored the power of empowerment language and Hasenfeld and Chesler (1989) examined client empowerment from a personal and professional perspective. Solomon (1982) and Gutiérrez (1990) viewed empowerment issues from the vantage point of gender and race. More recent slants on the concept of empowerment introduce the notions of client as well as community strengths and assets (Cowger, 1994; Saleebey, 1992). Rapp and Poertner (1992) discussed the implications of empowerment and a strengths perspective for management in social services.

All of these perspectives on empowerment are important, yet perhaps no one presents a more balanced and intriguing view than Block (1991, 1993). Block recognized that empowerment is an interdependent process involving an exchange between those with power and control in their lives and those without. It is an exchange and a partnership in which entitlements and rights are "paid" for by responsible and accountable action on the part of the party being empowered, whether it is the consumer, line worker, manager, or organization.

Power and empowerment allow control of one's own circumstances and fate. People and organizations are self-determining and self-organizing entities and phenomena. A social worker cannot empower a client nor can a manager empower a social worker. Manager and social worker can, however, together create the social architecture and practices that support partnership and offer individuals choices and opportunities for empowerment (Block, 1993). Nevertheless, such choices, entitlements, or rights (for example, the right to a service or the rights associated with a professional position) that are not met with responsible action on the part of clients and families or workers and managers can undermine freedom, self-esteem, and empowerment.

When some managers and workers in adult services programs think of empowerment, they think of larger budgets, more employees, greater personal recognition, and freedom from failure, disappointment, and risk. Similarly, some consumers may think greater empowerment is the right to more services, the resolution of all problems, and life in a risk-free environment. Empowerment, however, does not mean that people get everything they ask for or that they are protected from every threat (Block, 1993). It does mean more choices and an enhanced capacity to determine for oneself, whether that "self" is an organization, program, employee, or client, how one will respond to challenges and problems.

Social work has a long tradition of emphasizing the rights of individuals, both for workers and clients. The record is shorter, though, with respect to responsibility for change and for seeking empowerment.

Almost all people have a thirst for independence, more rights, and greater freedom. At times, however, almost all people also demonstrate an inclination for dependence and freedom from exercising choice. Entitlements and rights without responsibility for making choices and bearing their consequences fosters dependence, caretaking, and paternalism (Block, 1993). Entitlements balanced with responsible action for self-determination, and independence over dependence, equals empowerment. Entitlement to services or a professional position, without responsibility, is claiming rights that have not been earned. For example, individuals who avail themselves of job training and seek, obtain, and hold a job are empowered.

Adult services social workers who obtain training, exercise improved decision making, and manage the outcomes associated with their decisions are empowered.

Learning Organizations

Recently there has been a boom in interest in building organizations that emphasize continuous learning (Handy, 1993; Pinchot & Pinchot, 1993; Senge, 1990a, 1990b). We recognize in adult services programs and elsewhere that the complex, dynamic nature of issues facing clients and organizations alike demand flexible, adaptive, and intelligent organizational structures and workforces. "The old model, 'the top thinks and the local acts,' must now give way to integrated thinking and acting at all levels" (Senge, 1990a, p. 7).

Our traditional bureaucratic organizations, premised on command and control, not only disempower workers, they also disempower the clients and families they are supposed to serve. Workers who do not think for themselves but instead focus on complying with rules and regulations cannot effectively model or teach self-determination and self-control to their clients. Traditional organizations distrust both workers and clients and, in the absence of trust, tighten control over workers' discretion and consumers' choices.

To foster effective adult services programs marked by continuous learning and experimentation, we must understand two things: (1) a paradox and (2) a corollary belief that accompanies that paradox. The paradox can be simply stated that, if we are to achieve more control and satisfy a mission, we must give up control (Handy, 1994). Thinking and acting must be integrated at all levels of the organization, rather than concentrated at the top. The authority to think and act must be located where the work gets done (Block, 1993). This translates into empowerment, that is, more freedom of action for supervisors and line workers. It also means a greater reliance on teams and collaborative community partnerships to capture the complexity of problems and the necessary interdependence of those people trying to solve them.

The corollary to this paradox concerns the issue of trust and the impulse of people to learn and act in their own and their community's best interest. In the absence of controls, managers worry about how workers will behave, and for this reason, many organizations exert controls to take out as much guesswork as possible. However, there is another perspective, best captured by W. Edwards Deming, one of the more persuasive of its exponents. Deming, the leader and originator of the quality movement, said "People are born with intrinsic motivation, self-esteem, dignity, curiosity to learn, joy in learning" (quoted in Senge, 1990a, p. 7). If this natural motivation is harnessed to a common mission and set of goals, people will make a positive difference in their family, organization, and community. Agency leaders, middle management, and line workers must believe that if they are given the flexibility to learn and experiment, people will work for positive change.

Superior performance, whether of an agency, family, or individual, depends on superior learning. This link between the concepts of empowerment and continuous learning is shown in the distinction between adaptive and generative learning. Both concepts are discussed in chapter 3 in the context of adopting a family assessment and change method rather than a problem-solving approach to client and family needs.

Adaptive learning is coping and problem solving in the present only, whereas generative learning is creating solutions and approaches that go to the heart of the problem rather than just responding to and treating its symptoms (Argyris & Schön, 1978; Senge, 1990a). Generative learning calls for a new way of looking at the world. It also calls for adult services programs both to analyze current reality and to develop a compelling vision of a desired future. Likewise, to produce the best possible outcome for themselves, adult services clients and their families, with the support and facilitation of line workers, must envision a desired future.

Adult services managers who rely on adaptive learning (that is, analyzing only the current situation and developing coping strategies to deal with it) are managing change and reacting to change, rather than managing for change in keeping with a desired picture of the future. For line workers, using adaptive learning alone results in a coping or problem-solving approach that minimally satisfies needs in the present, rather than optimizing a possible future for adult clients and their families.

The fundamental distinction between the two modes of learning, adaptive or creative, lies in the question of empowerment. In the case of problem solving and adaptive learning, the motivation for change is extrinsic (Senge, 1990a). The motivation for change is not fully embraced or directed by the party in question, whether it is the worker or the client. The control of the change process lies with an outside agent. With creative learning, the motivation is intrinsic. The individual, team, or organization is empowered to shape its own future with the assistance of others. Those who are empowered steer the change process, continually learning and optimizing as they go along.

Adult Services: An Empowered Learning Community

Effective adult services programs are family and performance centered. Such programs find their measure of effectiveness in their ability to maintain or improve the functioning and quality of life of adult services clients. Effective practice relies on the concepts of empowerment and continuous learning. Just as the well-being of adult services clients relies on their access to resources and control over their circumstances and future (their problems often stem from lack of access and control), the well-being and effectiveness of administrators and social workers are likewise affected by the resources they possess and the control they have over their circumstances and future.

In addition to the principles discussed earlier in this chapter, there are related values and associated behaviors (Rapp & Poertner, 1992) that are important to effective practice in adult services. They include supporting clients, practitioners, and administrators; honoring the client; developing family- and client-centered performance outcomes; relying on a family assessment and change method; and honoring the public servant. These behaviors, along with the concepts of empowerment and continuous learning, are reflected throughout this book.

Values and Behaviors for Adult Services

SUPPORTING PERSONNEL AND CLIENTS

Support is an important factor in the development of empowerment and continuous learning and so figures in the well-being of clients as well as administrators and social workers. Support can be found in choices and opportunities for clients and workers, often as concrete resources in the form of services for clients and adequate conditions of employment for practitioners. Material support permits both staff members and clients to achieve greater control over their environment (for example, transportation to medical care for a client or training for and access to up-to-date technology for a worker). Adult services administrators, supervisors, and social workers need a certain level of basic resources from the community and the agency to demonstrate excellent and effective practice. Clients, in turn, need the supportive services, including information about their choices, that empowered and effective social work programs can offer them.

For example, to initiate a home and community care program supported by Medicaid, whether through personal care services or a waiver program, a local adult services agency may need to obtain the support of the county commissioners and county manager. Obtaining this support from the community in turn enables social workers to offer adults with disabilities in-home services that allow them to remain in the community. Achieving this desired outcome—maintaining adults with disabilities in the community—requires forging a link between the different players in the process and the adult services client.

The concept of support also may take on a less tangible form and involve issues of facilitation or access to information as avenues to empowerment. Training and education are good examples of methods that can support and empower both workers and clients. An adult services supervisor who identifies training needs in consultation with his or her staff members and arranges training is supporting them to master their work. Opportunities to gain knowledge and skills for workers and consumers are essential components of empowerment. Social workers who provide information to clients concerning courses of action to address a challenge are providing them with an opportunity, based on more-complete information and a greater sense of choice, to fashion solutions to problems for themselves.

HONORING THE CLIENT

Fundamental to the notion of empowering adult clients is the manner in which administrators and social workers consciously or unconsciously view and treat people served by the program. It is important to see adult services clients as individuals complete in themselves, who have independent lives, interests, families, and histories outside of their involvement with the program and not as stereotypes of poor people, older individuals, people with mental disabilities, or any other category.

In writing about client-centered management, Rapp and Poertner (1992) would have agency employees "venerate" clients. Although perhaps this term is too strong, their point is that adult services clients deserve the assistance they seek and need. Practitioners should acknowledge and personalize their clients' histories, celebrate their achievements in the face of obstacles and barriers, and confirm their right to control their own destinies with the support and assistance of others.

FAMILY- AND CLIENT-CENTERED PERFORMANCE OUTCOMES

The philosophical linchpin of practice in adult services is the focus on performance outcomes for clients and families. That is, does the intervention the social worker, client, and family develop effectively and efficiently meet the goals they have set? This returns us to the earlier observation that the principal function of adult services interventions is to improve the quality of clients' lives. Do these interventions foster self-determination in clients and families? Do such services help clients and their families achieve the futures they desire?

Stated in more clinical and functional terms, outcomes for clients include the following five categories: (1) maintenance of the client's functional levels; (2) palliation of the client's distress, whether the result of physical or psychological pain; (3) improved family outcomes, such as decreased burden on a caregiver; (4) prevention of new or further functional impairment; and (5) rehabilitation of lost functional abilities and, when possible, development of new abilities. Watchful monitoring of performance outcomes for clients provides a baseline measure of the effectiveness of practice in adult services and gives clients a clear picture of their own progress.

USING A FAMILY ASSESSMENT AND CHANGE METHOD

Reliance on a family assessment and change method for adult services amounts to the development of a global approach to practice that adult services agency administrators, supervisors, and social workers can use with some modification for specialized areas. The principle behind the development and use of such a method is a commitment to the notion that barriers to client and family functioning can be surmounted or minimized through an organized approach. Use of this method shows optimism and hope in the face of what appear to be intractable challenges. It should help empower clients and their families by instilling in them the belief that they themselves can identify problems, set goals, mobilize resources, develop strategies, and overcome barriers to optimal functioning and thus exert more control over their lives.

HONORING THE PUBLIC SERVANT

The fundamental wealth and true assets of a social services agency are its staff members. If they are not treated with respect and rewarded for excellent performance, this most important resource can be squandered and lost. Furthermore, a social services agency cannot expect to treat its clients with respect and courtesy unless it treats its own staff members in a similar fashion. Creating agency procedures that invest in personnel through training and research, establishing and promoting working conditions that allow them to aim for and demonstrate excellence, and rewarding and celebrating individual and team contributions to the organization and its clients are ways of honoring the public servant. Celebrating workers' achievements is essential to maintaining high morale and motivation, which in turn are essential to excellence in adult services.

The Agency's Mission and Purpose

Empowerment is at the heart of the process that adult services agencies use to attain their aspirations, and agency mission statements capture both a sense of those aspirations and their central guiding principles and values.

Mission statements provide direction to the organizational planning process and motivation to individual employees, who are committed to realizing the objectives and values incorporated in the mission statement. Lacking mission statements, organizations and their employees make the mistake of assuming that they are what they do, rather than understanding their purpose. Mission statements set forth what an organization aspires to be: A vision of success that is made manifest in the day-to-day work plans of individual employees, in the organization and function of working groups, and in the long-term strategic plan for the agency as a whole.

Adult services programs operate in changing environments. To remain healthy and keep organizational missions responsive, programs must stay in touch with their community, their primary constituencies, and their stakeholders. Left to their own devices, many organizations will primarily talk internally, not to those outside (Wilensky, 1967). Human services programs, however, operate in a competitive environment in which different groups and organizations contend for the attention of principal stakeholders and constituencies and the resources they can provide. To be effective, to demonstrate excellence, and to be empowered to achieve organizational goals, adult services programs must continually pay attention to the needs of both service constituencies and their primary community stakeholders. Such constant attention to external needs and problems will prompt continuing innovations in product or service mix, costs, financing, and management practices essential for adult services programs to remain effective.

As Bryson (1988) suggested, mission statements can generally be captured in one-page documents that address six basic questions: (1) Who are we as an organization? (2) What are the basic social needs we exist to fill or social problems we exist to address? (3) What must we do to recognize or anticipate and respond to those needs or problems? (4) How should we respond to our key stakeholders and constituencies? (5) What is our philosophy and what are our core values? (6) What makes us unique and distinctive? State and local adult services programs need mission statements that capture these essential points of purpose, direction, and underlying values.

CASE EXAMPLE

North Carolina provides a good illustration of state and local missions, principles, and goals that provide direction to its social services and adult services programs. Public social services in North Carolina are administered at the county level and supervised at the state level. At the state level, the Division of Social Services, located in the state's Department of Human Resources (DHR), administers both child and adult services programs, whereas local programs are housed in the 100 county departments of social services.

State Perspective on Mission and Purpose

In 1989 the North Carolina General Assembly called on DHR to develop a state social services plan that would provide a core set of social services and public assistance programs uniformly to all citizens of the state. To support this effort, DHR and the Division of Social Services adopted new mission statements to inspire direction of public social services in the 1990s. The state also developed a social services plan (North Carolina Department of Human Resources, Division of Social Services [NCDHR/DSS], 1991), which links the mission statements with more-explicit goals, purposes, and principles.

Although DHR's mission enunciates the state's mandate to promote the well-being of all its citizens, the division's mission addressed specifically the needs of disadvantaged people. This mission, which provides direction to state and local services for adults and children, embraces the fundamental concept of empowerment and self-determination:

> *The Division of Social Services is dedicated to assisting and providing opportunities for individuals and families in need of basic economic support and services to become self-supporting and self-reliant. We advocate for and encourage individuals' rights to select actions appropriate to their needs. Furthermore, we recognize our responsibility through teamwork and professional effort to assist in this process. Toward this end, in cooperation with local departments of social services and other public and private entities, we seek to identify needs, devise and focus resources, and deliver services responsively and compassionately.* (NCDHR/DSS, 1991, p. 1)

The goals and principles identified for North Carolina's social services plan build on the federal goals originally outlined in Title XX of the Social Security Act Amendments of 1974 and elaborate on them in the context of complex state and local, public and private, human services delivery systems. These goals and principles are

- *to ensure that children and adults are protected from abuse, neglect, and exploitation*
- *to enable citizens in order to maintain or achieve maximum self-sufficiency and personal independence through employment, if possible*
- *to strengthen family life to nurture children so they may become productive, healthy, and responsible adults*
- *to assist disabled and dependent adults, while ensuring that they live in the most independent setting feasible with the least possible intrusion from public agencies*
- *to ensure that every family and individual has sufficient economic resources to obtain the basic necessities of life.* (NCDHR/DSS, 1991, p. 1)

The successful accomplishment of these goals is conditioned on an effective coordination of efforts among public and private entities. Effective coordination is in turn predicated on the acceptance of certain principles of financing, administration, and decision making. The ultimate aim of the North Carolina social services plan, and subsequent planning for adult services clients at the county level, is the creation of a "proactive planning environment which allows for the constant evaluation of the system's response to a changing environment of needs and constraints," based on the following principles:

- *The department acknowledges the benefits derived from administration closest to the source of service/benefit provision, while recognizing that there is a need to establish clearer standards and to strengthen state supervision of program operations.*
- *The department understands that both the state and counties' ability to raise revenues is finite. Shared responsibility for financing must be established in such a manner as to distribute the burden as equally as possible based on ability to contribute.*
- *The department recognizes that the appropriate balance of shared decision-making responsibility will be constrained, in part, by federal and state statutes and regulations. Within these constraints or limitations, the plan envisions a sharing of decision-making responsibilities that maximizes the capabilities of counties to respond efficiently to local needs.* (NCDHR/DSS, 1991, p. 3)

County Perspective on Mission and Purpose

In North Carolina there would appear to be agreement as to what should go into a mission statement for local adult services programs. When talking about the mission of adult services programs in counties, adult services managers (administrators and supervisors) speak of clients' self-determination, self-sufficiency, enhanced quality of life, and increased ability to remain in their own homes. They express values such as freedom of choice, family- and client-centered services, empowerment, confidentiality, and respect when they outline the philosophy that underlies their mission, vision, and programs.

An excellent example can be found in Mecklenburg County's Older and Disabled Adult Services (ODAS) unit, which operates in accordance with both a mission and a vision statement. The mission statement captures broad organizational purpose and intent, and its vision statement depicts how the organization "will work together" to successfully implement its mission. The ODAS mission statement says

> *Our purpose is to advocate for and provide services to older and/or disabled people 18 years old or older in order to preserve their dignity, enhance independence, and assure them an optimum level of physical and emotional well-being in a safe, secure, noninstitutional setting as long as possible.* (Older and Disabled Adults Services Unit of the Mecklenberg County Department of Social Services, circa 1990)

The unit's vision statement outlines in greater detail how the organization will proceed to accomplish its mission. It links the processes by which workers perform their jobs and the way in which the unit works with the community to produce quality services for adults with disabilities and older adults.

> *ODAS is an organization of caring individuals who are committed to improving the quality of life for the people it services, for the Charlotte-Mecklenburg community, and for its employees by*
> - *enhancing the human potential by recognizing the value and dignity of each individual and encouraging autonomy and innovation*
> - *being a leader in the community by providing high-quality services to the people we serve*
> - *being responsive to issues affecting the constituency, the community, its employees, and working to meet identified needs*
> - *creating a team environment with clients, staff, and other community or-ganizations.* (Older and Disabled Adults Services Unit of the Mecklenberg County Department of Social Services, circa 1990)

Lessons for Adult Services

Many adult services administrators and supervisors across the country see their service population as adults who are vulnerable, frail, and have disabilities, with particular attention focused on those age 60 and older. If North Carolina is indicative of what is happening in other states and communities, adult services programs are generally clear about the priority of services for adults with disabilities, whether old or young, who are abused, neglected, or exploited. The goals for other adults (those between ages 18 and 59 and those age 60 and older who are not abused or neglected) are less well-defined. Some adult services supervisors and administrators may identify adults of any age and income with unmet needs as a priority population. Others hold that the client who calls with a need is the priority for that day. Given an environment of scarce resources, mounting unmet needs, and overlapping service jurisdictions, the ability to set priorities, identify groups of potential clients with the highest levels of need, and target services to them is essential to an effective program.

Because words can be empowering, written mission statements are important. The translation, understanding, and acceptance of the driving values and purposes in the mission statement by the organization's staff and by external constituencies and stakeholders are critical to the success of the adult services program. Adult services administrators and supervisors can bring the mission to life by modeling its supporting philosophy and values in their behavior toward the staff and in the community. Internally, group staff meetings, in-service training for team building, educational memorandums, individual conferences, and performance appraisals are mechanisms for conveying and supporting the adult services mission. Speeches delivered to civic groups, participation in interagency committees, use of the media, and sponsorship of and participation in service fairs are ways of informing the community about the program's mission.

Adult services administrators and supervisors at the state or local level believe it is important to keep agency committees and boards, state and local political decision makers, legislators, county commissioners, and mayors informed about the adult services mission and related programs. Involvement of adult services staff members in program planning and special projects and as members of both committees and boards is particularly effective. Personalizing adult services programs by inviting committee and board members and elected officials to visit or through presentations of case histories is as important to keeping them informed as regular updates with formal reports and written presentations.

"Celebrations" of successful individual cases as well as programs (for example, declaring an "adult services week") can infuse life and meaning into otherwise impersonal data and programs. Getting the message out, getting it endorsed, and getting it accepted within the agency and in the community are all important. Equally important is putting into operation the mission and vision statements for adult services by developing and matching annual program statements of purpose with related service objectives and strategies.

Empowering Social Workers and Administrators

The level of empowerment and effectiveness of a state or local adult services program depends on its environment and on the capability of administrators and social workers to put state and community resources to work for adult services clients while motivating clients to work for themselves. The economic, political, and cultural contexts of the state and communities affects the agency's ability to gain access to needed resources. Those same contexts within the agency itself affect the ability of the adult services program to obtain resources from within the agency and from the community. The ability of adult services administrators and social workers to persuade key groups in their environment, both inside and outside the agency, to endorse the mission, values, and goals of the agency and their program will largely determine which resources and influence they can muster on behalf of clients and families.

Empowered aging and social services agencies and their adult services programs are more able to create the conditions necessary for the provision of quality services to adult clients. For example, empowered agencies are more effective at obtaining well-trained personnel and other resources essential to support their mission and work. Empowered workers can control the conditions of their work better and have greater access to sources of knowledge and expertise essential to that work. They take responsibility for their work and continue to learn and grow from their experiences. Empowered clients are more likely to obtain the services they need and want. Disempowered agencies have insufficient and poorly trained personnel and lack other necessary resources to support their work. Disempowered workers lack control over their working conditions and products, face overwhelming caseloads, and lack basic training and expertise. Disempowered clients remain dependent on the system rather than developing their own coping skills and resources to the fullest.

How, then, do adult services social workers and managers within state and local programs gain empowerment? How do they bring to life the principles and values that underlie the concept of empowerment? How do they bring life, energy, and commitment to agency and adult services mission statements? Many people who write about empowerment assert that it is the collective effect of leadership at all levels of the organization (Bennis, 1989; Block, 1991; Hasenfeld, 1987; Rapp & Poertner, 1992).

Many people who write about issues of empowerment and leadership use different concepts to reinforce similar messages about what works and what makes organizations effective in meeting the needs of clients. These concepts are elaborated in part 4 of this book in the chapters on planning and program and staff development, but some are important to mention here. Bennis (1989) described what he calls "truisms" about fostering leadership throughout a workforce. The essence of Bennis's truisms is that empowerment is evident in organizations where employees feel significant and part of a community, where learning and competence are rewarded, and where work is exciting. Empowered administrators and social workers are those who feel that what they do has meaning and is recognized as valuable. Empowered adult services workers are those for whom mistakes are not seen as failures but rather as opportunities for feedback and improved mastery and competence. Empowered workers in an adult services program have a sense of team effort and belonging. Social workers take pride in the accomplishments of the organization as well as the accomplishments of individual members. Empowered adult services programs are those whose employees believe their work is exciting. In empowered programs, organizational leadership pulls others to excellence by example rather than by trying to push them through administrative directives.

Block (1991) wrote that empowered managers (this should hold for empowered social workers as well) use what he calls an "entrepreneurial cycle" that can invigorate and empower an organization rather than a "bureaucratic cycle" of practice. Bureaucratic organizations practice top-down, high-control patriarchal orientations toward work, narrow definitions of self-interest, and manipulative strategies that promote hierarchical dependency within the organization. Block suggested that human services entrepreneurs, in contrast, should act with autonomy and compassion in service to a mission or vision for the agency.

Block would say that empowered adult services administrators and social workers are those who form an "entrepreneurial contract" with the agency, based on the notion that the most trustworthy source of authority comes from within individuals who are committed to the mission and values represented by the agency. Workers hold an enlightened sense of self-interest, and they measure success by contributions and service to clients and other departments within the agency and community. A social worker who, with the support of administration, initiates and leads the development of a free medication program for indigent people in the community exemplifies the spirit of an "entrepreneurial" worker. An entrepreneur is someone who demonstrates initiative in developing new and needed programs for adult clients. Block (1991) also said that empowered administrators and workers use authentic tactics in relating to one another, that is, letting people know where they stand, sharing as much information as possible about what is going on, sharing control, and taking reasonable risks. Finally, an entrepreneurial approach to empowerment supports administrators and social workers in developing and claiming autonomy within a framework of commitment to the service mission of the agency and adult services program.

Empowering Adult Services Clients through Quality Services

Empowerment is that process by which managers and social workers, and thus clients, obtain the concrete and interpersonal resources that enable them to secure greater control over their environment and attain their aspirations (Hasenfeld, 1987). Quality adult services that create environments of empowerment for clients are forged link by link in a chain of interconnected episodes of adult services practice. Services may begin with a phone call to an adult services intake worker, but they are backed by leadership, empowerment, and advocacy on all levels of the agency.

Donabedian (1980) suggested that evidence of quality in adult services can be identified in three general domains: (1) the technical, scientific aspect of practice; (2) the interpersonal art of care; and (3) the amenities of care. The technical aspect of practice can be found in the specific theories, knowledge, and skills that inform different aspects of the model of excellence, whether in the area of case management or counseling or strategic planning or managerial techniques. For example, training in the knowledge and skills associated with the family assessment and change method is essential for the worker who is expected to use it to help adult services clients become empowered. The chapters in part 4 address administrative practice in adult services and outline theory, knowledge, and skills associated with excellence in these areas.

The art of quality adult services practice can be found in the management of the interpersonal aspects—in the worker–client relationship as well as in the relationships between social worker and manager and manager and community. Studies of clinical effectiveness have demonstrated that a major determinant of effective practice lies in the quality of the relationship between social worker and client (Orlinsky, Grawe, & Parks, 1994; Siebolt et al., 1986). Likewise, the diplomatic, administrative, and political skills exercised by administrators and social workers alike with representatives of the broader community are also essential to the empowerment of the adult services client. Chapters in this book address to different degrees the interpersonal components of excellent practice in the adult services.

The last element of quality adult services practice involves what are often called the amenities of that practice. These amenities may be such things as a pleasant waiting room and the availability of private, comfortable interviewing rooms. It also refers to such matters as courtesy, promptness, privacy, respect, and acceptance. Adult services clients can obtain a sense of empowerment simply from being treated with respect and courtesy and made to feel and understand that they have a right to assistance. Just as the empowerment of clients is linked to the empowerment of workers and managers, the respect and sense of autonomy afforded an adult services social worker by her or his supervisor and the respect and autonomy afforded to the supervisor by the agency's service administrator or director contributes to the quality of services.

The challenge of demonstrating excellence in adult services can be met by individuals who share a common mission. This sense of mission in turn derives its direction from a set of principles and values that emphasize client-centered practice and empowerment and continual learning for workers and clients alike. Empowerment and excellence in adult services programs demand that workers and clients accept the challenges and risks associated with gaining greater control over the work environment, in the case of managers and social workers, or personal life, in the case of clients. The demonstration of excellence is an evolving continual learning process through which new methods are proposed, adopted, evaluated, and revised or refined. The demonstration of excellence requires a partnership among social services departments, programs for adult services and aging individuals, and community constituencies that is committed to excellent service for adult clients.

Key Points

Excellent adult services social workers
- see and honor adult clients as people with personal lives, histories, hopes, and dreams
- demonstrate a commitment to client-centered practice that emphasizes accountability in maintaining or improving clients' functioning
- understand the connection between empowered, skilled, and knowledgeable social workers and empowered clients.

Excellent adult services managers
- understand the importance of developing a mission for adult services programs that emphasizes empowerment and clients' well-being
- treat and respect employees at all levels as the key to quality services for adults
- honor and celebrate the success experienced by adult services staff members in serving their clients
- demonstrate a commitment to continuous learning.

Excellent leaders
- develop a mission statement to motivate and guide the development of state policy and practice in adult services
- foster empowerment, creativity, and entrepreneurship in county adult services programs.

References

Argyris, C., & Schön, D. (1978). *Organizational learning: A theory-in-action perspective*. Reading, MA: Addison-Wesley.

Bennis, W. (1989). *Why leaders can't lead*. San Francisco: Jossey-Bass.

Block, P. (1991). *The empowered manager*. San Francisco: Jossey-Bass.

Block, P. (1993). *Stewardship: Choosing service over self-interest*. San Francisco: Berrett-Koehler.

Bryson, J. M. (1988). *Strategic planning for public and nonprofit organizations*. San Francisco: Jossey-Bass.

Cowger, D. C. (1994). Assessing client strengths: Clinical assessment for client empowerment. *Social Work, 39*, 262–268.

Donabedian, A. (1980). *Explorations in quality assessment and monitoring. Volume 1. The definition of quality and approaches to its assessment*. Ann Arbor, MI: Health Administration Press.

Gutiérrez, L. M. (1990). Working with women of color: An empowerment perspective. *Social Work, 35*, 149–153.

Handy, C. (1993). *Understanding organizations*. New York: Oxford University Press.

Handy, C. (1994). *The age of paradox.* Boston: Harvard Business School Press.

Hasenfeld, Y. (1987, September). Power in social work. *Social Service Review, 61,* 469–483.

Hasenfeld, Y., & Chesler, M. A. (1989). Client empowerment in the human services: Personal and professional agenda. *Journal of Applied Behavioral Science, 25*(4), 499–521.

North Carolina Department of Human Resources, Division of Social Services. (1991). *The North Carolina social services plan: A road map for change.* Raleigh: Author.

Older and Disabled Adult Services Unit of the Mecklenberg County Department of Social Services. (circa 1990). *Mission statement.* Unpublished manuscript, Charlotte, NC.

Orlinsky, D. E., Grawe, K., & Parks, B. K. (1994). Process and outcome in psychotherapy. In S. Garfield & A. Bergin (Eds.), *Handbook of psychotherapy and behavior change* (4th ed., pp. 270–376). New York: John Wiley & Sons.

Pinchot, G., & Pinchot, E. (1993). *The end of bureaucracy and the rise of the intelligent organization.* San Francisco: Berrett-Koehler.

Rapp, C. A., & Poertner, J. (1992). *Social administration: A client-centered approach.* New York: Longman.

Rappaport, J. (1985). The power of empowerment language. *Social Policy, 17*(2), 15–21.

Saleebey, D. (1992). *The strengths perspective in social work practice.* New York: Longman.

Senge, P. M. (1990a, Fall). The leader's new work: Building learning organizations. *Sloan Management Review,* pp. 7–23.

Senge, P. M. (1990b). *The fifth discipline: The art and practice of the learning organization.* New York: Doubleday/Currency.

Siebolt, A. F., Allen, J. G., Colson, D. B., Coyne, L. F., Gobbard, G. O., Horowitz, L., & Newman, G. (1986, February). Therapeutic alliance: Its place as a process and outcome variable in dynamic psychotherapy research. *Journal of Consulting and Clinical Psychology, 54,* 32–38.

Social Security Act Amendments of 1974. P.L. 93-647, 88 Stat. 2337.

Solomon, B. (1982). Empowering women: A matter of values. In A. Weick & S. T. Vandiver (Eds.), *Women, power and change* (pp. 206–214). Silver Spring, MD: National Association of Social Workers.

Wilensky, H. L. (1967). *Organizational intelligence.* New York: Basic Books.

PART 2

Principles and Methods of Adult Services Social Work Practice

CHAPTER 3

Adult Services Social Work: The Family Assessment and Change Method

GARY M. NELSON

Adult services can be defined as a specialized area of social work practice in a number of ways. One approach is to gain an understanding of the history, mission, and principles of empowerment that underlie adult services programs and to recognize the challenges presented to workers by their diverse clientele. Chapters 1 and 2 have provided that overview. Another approach to defining adult services is to conceptualize a method—the family assessment and change method—that can be used to guide practice and then describe the primary skill areas that support that method, which is the goal of this chapter.

Three assumptions are central to the family assessment and change method. (1) The purpose of adult services practice is to help bring about change. Adult services social workers are dedicated to making a positive difference in the lives of clients and their families. (2) Individuals are best helped to change when assessments and social interventions are family centered. The most effective interventions have an influence on the family system. (3) In bringing about change, adult clients and their families should be empowered to assume as much control of their circumstances as possible. Change comes about from the inside out. Empowered individuals are marked by self-control.

These three assumptions regarding change, family-centered practice, and empowerment provide the foundation on which the skill areas central to adult services practice rest. Central skill areas include intake and screening, comprehensive functional assessment, identification of problems and goals, service planning, implementation, monitoring and reassessment, and service termination. These steps in the method are supported in the larger context of practice by expertise and skills in clinical and therapeutic relationships, community development, and case management, as well as knowledge specific to the services the agency provides to adults. These components of the model and their contribution to excellence in adult services social work are described in this chapter.

Principles Underlying the Family Assessment and Change Method

Change is a constant in all of our lives. It represents a dynamic interplay between current circumstances and our aspirations for the future. In working with adults and their families, social workers serve as guides, coaches, and facilitators for the change process. When successful, this process involves overcoming current barriers or problems that stand between the individual and family and their aspirations for the future. The family assessment and change method combines two perspectives, problem solving and clients' strengths, to overcome current realities and shape a new, more acceptable future.

CHANGE PROCESS

The family assessment and change method combines the best of past and emerging social work approaches: problem solving, first outlined by Perlman (1957), and strengths, described by Saleebey (1992). Perlman identified the central tasks of helping people deal with their problems. Her analysis recognized that clients' problems in functioning often result from a combination of external (environmental) and internal (social or psychological) constraints. Although problems are most often what lead individuals to seek help, building on individual, family, and community strengths is the route to overcoming current problems and preventing future ones. Clients are more than a catalog of problems and failures: They hold ideas about change, possess a capacity to learn, and can do many things well (Saleebey, 1992). They can create a vision of a better future with the assistance of the adult services social worker.

From juxtaposing the current situation and a vision of a better future, a "creative tension" for change is created (Senge, 1990). It is this integrative principle of creative tension on which change or learning is based. In an approach that focuses solely on problem solving, the energy for change comes from attempting to avoid undesirable aspects of current reality. This energy is reactive, negative, and characterized by fear. A positive vision of the future developed by the individual and family is proactive and generative. Aspiration is a much stronger motivator for change than the fear that attends a focus on problems. Assessing and respecting the client's strengths, and assessing and identifying problems and barriers that stand between the client and a better future, represent the necessary foundation on which the client can begin to learn and change.

FAMILY-CENTERED PRACTICE

The importance of family cannot be underestimated. Judith Viorst (1986), in *Necessary Losses*, wrote about the centrality of the family in our lives:

We cannot detach ourselves so easily from our first, our original family, from that intricate web of relationships which connects us, albeit imperfectly, to each other. . . . For our family, our first family, was the setting in which we became a separate self. It was also the first social unit in which we lived. And when we walked away we carried along its many central, shaping lessons. (p. 248)

Not only do we carry the family's shaping lessons with us, but the family continues to be a resource into which a person may dip for direction, meaning, and style throughout his or her life (Moore, 1994). The past and the future meet in the life of the family for both children and older people as their identities, values, worldviews, and life habits build and extend through time.

The family-centered approach to practice has a basic premise that "human beings can be understood and helped only in the context of the intimate and powerful human systems of which they are a part" (Hartman & Laird, 1983, p. 4). This is consistent with Perlman's recognition that the client brings unseen people and circumstances into the helping process, some of whom are family members, both current and historical. Recognition of the family, first as a system and also as the unit of choice for intervention, is central to effective adult services social work practice (Nelson, 1992). Recognition of the importance of family is also central to social work practice with older adults (Bumagin & Hirn, 1990; Greene, 1986; Silverstone & Burack-Weiss, 1983).

Family members are defined by the client, perhaps following traditional notions of nuclear or extended families but also perhaps including people not related by blood or marriage. As Moore (1994) put it,

a family is not an abstract cultural ideal: a man, a woman, and children living blissfully in a mortgaged house on a quiet neighborhood street. The family the soul wants is a felt network of relationship, an evocation of a certain kind of interconnection that grounds, roots, and nestles. (p. 19)

Adult services practice involves assessment and intervention within whatever family system or network of relationships the client identifies. This involves determining the quality of communication and the nature of the role relationships within the family that may affect its ability or willingness to assist the client or that may be affected by interventions in the family system.

The social worker's actual involvement with the family varies widely. Some clients choose not to include family members in the process, and some clients do not have family members available. In these circumstances, even the absence of family members is a critical factor in assessment and service planning. Those unseen people and circumstances are still a critical part of the client's life, even though not physically present. The client's values, behavior patterns, physical propensities, and beliefs about life are based historically on what was learned in the family of origin and modified through the years by interaction with other significant people. These factors affect the client in the present. Even when the social worker is involved only with the designated client, the family is the conceptual context in which the social work process is carried out.

For many clients who are dependent or frail, however, the family becomes a major player in the process and a major provider of services to the client. This is even more critical when clients are incompetent or incapacitated and need people to act on their behalf. In these circumstances, the designated client's role is limited by his or her capabilities, and the social worker may of necessity work primarily with the family. It is important for the social worker to assess carefully each client's functional capabilities, work directly with the client as much as possible to maximize strengths the client may still have, and ensure the client's wishes are being carried out to the extent the client can comprehend and express them.

In some circumstances, the entire family becomes "the client." Especially in families with many competing interests, complex dynamics, multiple problems, or limited resources, effective assessments and interventions may involve all family members. The social worker helps the entire family assess its needs, develop goals, and plan and implement strategies. This type of social work makes use of systems theory, with its understanding that a change in one part of the system creates change in other parts of the system. Interventions are made that will strengthen the entire family system.

The family assessment and change method described in this book can be used in any of the possible variations of involvement with the family. When we use the word "client," the underlying assumption is that "client" is being discussed within the context of family and that the process will involve family members to whatever extent is advisable in the client's situation. Whenever appropriate, work with adult clients involves the family in the decision-making process and actively includes the family in planning services and activities, so as not to disrupt this vital informal support system. When the client's needs and preferences come into conflict with the family's, the excellent social worker offers counseling and mediation to enable the client and family members to reach the most acceptable solution.

MOVING TOWARD EMPOWERMENT

The principles of empowerment, identified in chapter 2 as the basis of practice and administrative approaches to adult services programs, are demonstrated in an attitude toward practice that stresses the client's right and responsibility for autonomous change (Gutiérrez, 1990; Hasenfeld, 1987; Rappaport, 1985; Solomon, 1982). According to Reid (1978), the individual is neither as much a prisoner of unconscious drives as psychological theories might suggest nor so much the pawn of environmental contingencies as behavioral theories would have it. Social work practice in adult services holds that clients are not at the mercy of external or internal circumstances but rather have will and choice. The challenge for adult services social workers is to tap clients' capacities for change through effective use of relationship and counseling.

The principal objective of an adult services social work intervention is to assist clients in preventing, ameliorating, or overcoming barriers to more-positive functioning. A constructive change experience that leads to empowerment is one in which the client's attitude toward joining with potential helpers in a team is enhanced and the client's ability to address future problems is successfully increased. In cultivating the clients' willingness to accept help, social workers must acknowledge and demonstrate respect for what clients want, even when the clients' preferences are strongly at odds with the workers'. In this case workers suggest alternative courses of action and make their own feelings known, but they do not try to impose their own goals. As the client's agent, workers should demonstrate competence in helping the client to identify barriers to optimal functioning under current circumstances, envision a better state, and identify possible steps for achieving that future state.

Another benefit of a constructive change experience is that clients learn skills and reshape beliefs so they can handle future situations themselves. It must be the social worker's fundamental conviction that clients can learn to change. By mastering the change method outlined here, the social worker demonstrates its various steps in a clear and logical way so the client can comprehend and duplicate the process. Through listening, teaching, role playing, and counseling, the social worker helps the client develop new, or awaken old, strategies for independent change. Empowerment of adults through involvement in the family assessment and change method is a constant feature of the adult services practice model.

COMPONENTS OF THE FAMILY ASSESSMENT AND CHANGE METHOD

Adult services systems and models of intervention rest on a body of theory, which in turn relies on a set of assumptions about human behavior and life circumstances and how to improve them best. A major cornerstone of the approach presented in this book is its focus on the functioning of adult services clients, and specifically, the problems in functioning that jeopardize the quality of their lives.

This focus is drawn largely from the literature and research in the field of aging, in which there is increasing agreement that functional status, rather than diagnosis, best predicts the future well-being of adults (Campbell & Thompson, 1990; Fillenbaum, 1984; Ivry, 1992; Kane & Kane, 1981). Although the sources of this function-oriented approach relate to the care of older adults, the theory behind it is generalizable and can be appropriately applied to adults of all ages whose functioning is impaired in some way. Interventions that focus on prevention of new loss in functioning, maintenance, or rehabilitation are the best route to improving the client's well-being. The family assessment and change method does not attempt to deal with remote or historical origins of a problem in functioning (Reid, 1978) but rather with those factors both internal and external to the individual that are currently causing the problem. Social workers concentrate on those factors that they and the client together can change.

Obstacles to functioning often are found at the intersection of the client's personal actions and beliefs and the environment in which the client lives. The amelioration or resolution of problems often lies in optimizing the fit between the person and his or her environment by addressing clients' dysfunctional beliefs, tapping their internal resources and strengths, helping them gain access to needed resources, and sometimes changing or modifying the actual physical environment. Skills central to the family assessment and change method include the ability to pinpoint the source of barriers to functioning, whether internal or external to the client, through a comprehensive functional assessment and to plan appropriate interventions to reduce those barriers.

This method incorporates a core of clinical and program skills, introduced in this chapter and elaborated in later chapters, necessary to excellent social work practice. The therapeutic relationship, examined in chapter 7, is an integral element in the family assessment and change method. When a client seeks help from a social worker, a "helping relationship" is established. Clients, however, are not asking for a "personal relationship," nor is one appropriate; rather they are asking for change. When such a relationship is established with warmth, empathy, and genuineness, the client feels recognized as a person with strengths, capacities, and motivation for change and not just as the bearer of problems. A helping relationship, established around a shared concern and supported by enabling and facilitative behaviors, can free the client's energies and motivation for change and the attainment of goals.

Necessary Skills for Adult Services Social Work Practice

There are three types of skills central to this practice model: (1) the core skills, which entail using the family assessment and change method as the basis for problem solving; (2) the clinical skills; and (3) the resource development and coordination skills (Figure 3-1). The core skills encompass a process for engagement with the client, assessment of problems and strengths, identification of goals that capture a preferred future state of functioning, and the development and monitoring of interventions to bring about that state. The core skills begin with intake and screening, followed by a comprehensive functional assessment, development of a list of areas for change and strengths, setting goals, planning for interventions and services, implementing the services planned, monitoring and reassessment, and terminating services. Sometimes emergency interventions (interventions to keep the client from immediate harm) must be offered before a comprehensive assessment begins. Clinical skills include crisis intervention and counseling as well as interviewing and relationship development. Resource coordination includes case management, either through a centralized or brokerage approach, and resource development, which involves advocacy with and for clients and efforts to generate community resources of general benefit to them.

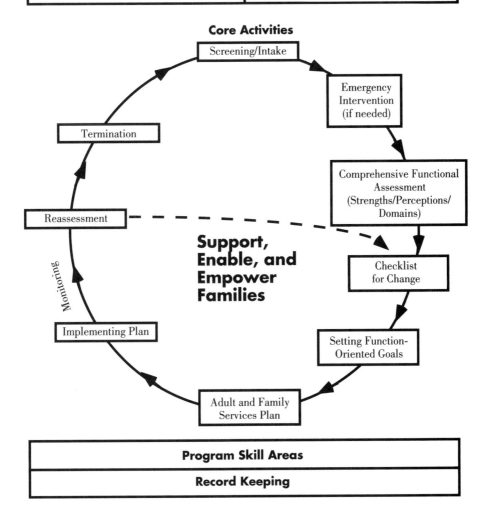

Clinical Skills	Resource Development and
(Interviewing and Relationship Development, Crisis Intervention Counseling)	Coordination Skills (Advocacy, Community Development, Case Management)

Core Activities

Screening/Intake

Emergency Intervention (if needed)

Termination

Comprehensive Functional Assessment (Strengths/Perceptions/ Domains)

Reassessment

Support, Enable, and Empower Families

Checklist for Change

Monitoring

Setting Function-Oriented Goals

Implementing Plan

Adult and Family Services Plan

Program Skill Areas

Record Keeping

Figure 3-1 _____

THE FAMILY ASSESSMENT AND CHANGE PROCESS FOR ADULT SERVICES.

Adapted from Family and Children's Resource Program. (1992). *A model for excellence in adult services administration and social work practice* (p. 37). Reprinted by permission of Family Forum, School of Social Work, University of North Carolina–Chapel Hill.

CORE SKILLS

The core skills associated with the family assessment and change method are a logical way of thinking about and organizing work with clients. These skills enable the social worker to determine why the client came or was referred to the agency and whether the agency has the resources to assist the client. The method prompts the worker to do a thorough assessment to help the client identify functional problems and strengths. Then, worker and client together set reasonable goals and develop strategies to meet those goals, often including services the agency can provide or arrange. The social worker monitors implementation of strategies and delivery of services and evaluates with the client how effective the intervention is. Because practice grounded in the empowerment of clients seeks to return responsibility for managing their own lives to them, all of the core skills aim at this goal.

Access to the Agency

Adults in need of assistance gain access to the agency as a result of the agency's outreach activities and through referrals from other agencies. Another name for these activities that emphasizes their proactive nature is *case finding,* a process by which the adult services program and social workers identify and establish contact with individuals and families who need the services provided by the agency (Moore, 1992; Rothman, 1991; Steinberg & Carter, 1983). Limited resources make it important for adult services programs to be clear about the target populations they are designed to serve. Clear guidelines about these populations, which should be one of the by-products of a well-formulated mission statement, assist workers in conducting outreach activities or informing referral sources about the sorts of services the agency can provide. Clear guidelines also help the agency to direct resources where they will do the most good. Without clear guidelines regarding access to the agency, programs become reactive, because they are defined by those who seek services rather than defining for themselves which clients they can best serve.

Intake and Screening

Intake is often conceptualized as starting a new case record or reactivating an old one, with the consent of the adult client (Rothman, 1991; Steinberg & Carter, 1983). For adult services programs, intake occurs when the client or someone acting on the client's behalf makes contact with the agency. Intake is important because this may be the client's first contact with the agency. Impressions formed about the respect and professionalism shown at intake set a tone for the client's future dealings with the agency. Intake begins the client's involvement with the system, and case accountability begins with intake.

Screening, which is often a part of intake, is the process by which adult services programs make preliminary determinations regarding the suitability of the agency's services for the potential client. Screening is a brief assessment procedure that results in a referral to another agency or program or in an assessment by a social worker to determine whether the adult services program can provide assistance. Screening is brief and is not meant to replace the thorough functional assessment that is the next step of the process. Screening should be thorough enough, however, to have a high probability of starting the client in the right place. Referral to the wrong program because of inadequate screening frustrates the client, takes valuable time from the social worker, and may result in services being provided inappropriately.

For example, a client who expresses a need for housing may be referred to a housing referral service in the community or to a particular worker in the agency who specializes in housing services. A frail older person or a family member seeking assistance for a client who is having difficulty functioning at home should be referred to a social worker familiar with a range of possible interventions—in-home services, day care, and placement—who can then carry out a full assessment to determine the best alternatives. Agencies may want to consider establishing screening criteria that are sensitive enough to pick up the possible need for a service but specific enough to exclude those who do not need to be assessed further for that problem.

Functional Assessment

The cornerstone of adult services social work is the functional assessment. Because disabilities and the medical diagnoses that may accompany them are not necessarily a reliable guide to functioning, a multidimensional functional assessment, rather than a diagnosis, can best be used to determine which strategies and interventions are most likely to benefit clients. Kane and Kane (1981) and Bernstein (1992) have demonstrated that measures of functional status that assess the individual's ability to live independently are substantially better predictors of the types and amounts of services any individual will require than are medical diagnoses. Furthermore, a standardized assessment format helps to organize the process of identifying problems and strengths for the worker, serving as a checklist for items or issues that might be overlooked or forgotten.

Although an assessment begins as the response to stated problems, it also must identify the client's strengths and resources and the client's and family's perception of their problems and strengths. This further empowers clients to meet their needs. It also supports the notion of family-centered practice, because the family is often an invaluable resource, and in a time of scarce agency resources, the more clients can provide for themselves, the more agencies can provide for clients.

George and Fillenbaum (1985) proposed—and it has become accepted—that clients' functioning should be assessed in multiple dimensions. Furthermore, there is substantial agreement about which dimensions of functioning should be assessed (Ivry, 1992; Kane & Kane, 1981). These include social functioning, economic functioning, physical health, mental health, and the ability to perform the physical and instrumental activities of daily living. Beyond this, the individual's home and community environment should be considered.

A family-centered assessment must take into account the life experience and changes to which most adults and, particularly, older adults have successfully adapted. Life cycle experiences associated with work, marriage, child rearing, and illness all engender various coping skills and adaptive strengths. For example, the multiple roles of mother, daughter, grandmother, wife, and sister bring with them an additional reservoir of experiences, skills, and strengths that can be drawn on in difficult times. Families have traditions that keep them strong and stable over time. All of these strengths should be assessed and accounted for in developing a complete picture of the client and situation (Cowger, 1994).

Developing a Checklist for Change

The functional assessment is designed to help clients identify first how they and their families are functioning and then to mobilize abilities, resources, and motivations to make changes that resolve or ameliorate any problems identified. Before the adult services social worker helps the client identify goals or service interventions, the two must jointly develop a list of problems and strengths and a checklist of areas in which the client and family would like to see change occur. This list is function-oriented, that is, it identifies what the client wishes to do but cannot and what strengths the client has to begin improving the situation. Because the list is based on assessment findings, which provide a picture of the client's situation at the beginning of the relationship with the agency, it serves as a baseline for measuring progress. The use of a structured checklist for change helps prevent the worker from overlooking areas of concern to the client and from jumping to solutions too early.

Once the checklist is developed, the client and social worker assign each item a priority. Bloom and Fischer (1982) suggested the following questions to assist in this process. The relevance of these questions depends on the circumstances of each particular case.

- *Is it [a problem] that the client and the client's family prefers to start with or about which they are most concerned?*
- *Does it have the greatest likelihood of being changed?*
- *Is it relatively concrete and specific?*
- *Can you work on it readily, given your resources?*
- *Does it have the greatest chance of producing the most negative consequences if not handled?*
- *Does it have to be handled before other problems or barriers can be tackled?*
- *Will changes in this problem or barrier result in tangible, observable changes for those involved, thereby perhaps increasing the client or the family's motivation to work on other problems or barriers?* (pp. 59–60)

Setting Goals

Helping the client formulate goals is an integral part of the service-planning process. The goals for all service interventions, including counseling, should be clearly stated in the client's record. They should be set out in terms of the functional problem or barrier and responsive to the changes identified in the client's checklist for change. Each should include a positive statement of what change in the client's circumstance will indicate progress and when progress will be evaluated. It is important that all goals be clearly stated in clients' records, because implicit or inferred goals can lead to confusion among those involved in care of clients, including clients themselves. Setting goals can be empowering for both the social worker and the client, because this step reinforces the notion that change is possible and inspires the development of strategies to bring that change about.

When possible, goals should be developed with the client's family, or at a minimum, with the family in mind. In a family-centered approach, each family member may have goals, and there also may be familial goals, such as keeping everyone in the same community or continuing family traditions. It is important that the identified client's goals be developed in the context of those other spoken or unspoken goals. When a client's and family's goals are at odds with one another, the challenge is to help the client address his or her goals in the family system.

The Joint Commission on Accreditation of Hospitals (1981) specified three types of goals: (1) crisis stabilization, (2) growth, and (3) sustenance or maintenance goals. Additional categories of goals that fit with adult services social work practice include prevention, rehabilitation, and palliation. Crisis stabilization focuses on the reduction of stress or hazardous circumstances that pose a threat to the client or family member. Goals aimed at ending abuse or neglect fit into this category. Growth goals are aimed at enhancing the intellectual, interpersonal, or instrumental skills and functioning of an adult. Participation in job training or an educational program through a community college fit in this category, as might counseling to reduce disruptive behavior. Prevention goals may respond to risks produced by certain lifestyles or personal practices that jeopardize the individual's present or future well-being. Smoking cessation or compliance with prescribed medication regimens are examples of prevention goals. Rehabilitation goals may address recapturing lost or impaired functioning (for example, the survivor of a stroke who regains the ability to speak through speech therapy or to walk with a cane through physical therapy). Sustenance or maintenance goals are focused on maintaining a present level of functioning (for example, helping a socially active older person maintain his or her contacts with family and friends after placement in a board-and-care home). Finally, palliative goals acknowledge that there are some problems that cannot be improved or resolved directly (for example, chronic or terminal illness, or loss of a loved one) but that it is possible to manage the pain associated with these problems.

Goals should focus on achieving outcomes that are open to observation by the adult services social worker, the client, and the client's family. Such goals must first and foremost be responsive to changes sought by clients and their families. In addition, goals for clients should be quantifiable, time-limited statements of planned results (Altman, 1979). That is, they should be formulated in terms that are measurable at predetermined intervals (Rothman, 1991). To the degree possible, they should address specific, discrete functional problems that currently impair or are likely to impair the client in the future. Goal statements should address five points: (1) who or what will change (the client, the family system, or the environment); (2) in what way the client, family system, or environment is expected to change; (3) how much change is expected; (4) under what conditions the change will take place; and (5) in what time frame the change should be observable (based on Altman, 1979).

Planning Services

Service plans and interventions are designed to achieve the optimal fit between the client's need to improve, regain, or sustain functioning and the amount of self-care or services the client needs to achieve the outcomes specified in the goal statements. Key features of service planning involve determining the level and type of assistance compatible with achieving goals; determining what kind of external resources, if any, are needed and appropriate; and discovering what beliefs, concerns, or values the client may have about the plan of action that may affect its success. It also involves determining activities that can be carried out by family members and the effect those activities will have on the family system.

A tool that can help facilitate the process of service planning between social workers, clients, and families is the service agreement. A service agreement or plan is a written statement of goals, tasks, and responsibilities that client, family, and social worker have negotiated. Service agreements should identify all involved parties; specify major service goals for the client, including those associated with counseling; identify the responsibilities and tasks that the client, family, social worker, and any others agree to undertake; identify a time frame for reassessment; contain signatures of the involved parties; and record the date from which it is in force (Gambrill, 1983). A written service agreement facilitates practice because it causes all parties to focus their attention on the service plan and demands some accountability from all who agree to it.

Implementing Plans

The process of providing services and linking clients to agencies or to informal providers such as families and friends is an integral part of the adult services family assessment and change method. In implementing intervention plans, the social worker's task is twofold. In instances in which tangible resources are needed and unavailable to the client and family, the worker may need to arrange for a referral to an appropriate source or provide services directly. In other instances, the proposed social intervention may be accomplished by drawing on or bolstering resources and strengths within the client and family system. The adult services social worker in such cases may more appropriately serve as a facilitator or coach in helping the client to overcome barriers to functioning. Finally, in many cases, the proposed social intervention will be a combination of tangible services and more intangible capacity building within the existing family or community network.

Monitoring and Reassessment

Monitoring allows the social worker to determine at regular intervals whether the service plan is being carried out as specified, how well goals are being met, and whether changes are necessary. An essential tool for monitoring is the function-oriented progress note—sometimes done as "dictation" in the client's record or entered on a contact log and summarized on the quarterly review—that captures both qualitative and quantitative data about the success of the plan.

Reassessment is an extensive procedure whereby the social worker and client evaluate the success of all current plans and determine whether there are new problems that must be addressed. Reassessment completes the cycle envisaged in the family assessment and change method because it measures the effect of the client's and social worker's actions against the client's initial circumstances and, depending on the results, reinitiates the process of identifying problems and strengths, prioritizing the problems, specifying goals, developing and implementing a revised service plan, and monitoring the client's change or response.

Monitoring can often be done through brief contacts by telephoning service providers and others involved in the case and through visits or phone calls to the client. Reassessment requires more-extensive contact with the client and family, because the social worker should review the client's status using an assessment format like the one used when the case began but focusing specifically on change since the first meeting. The reassessment also offers the social worker, client, and family the opportunity to step back and look at the client's situation as if for the first time, to see better whether time has altered the situation and the areas in which they want change. The frequency of both monitoring and reassessment depends on setting reasonable time frames over which change may be expected to take place, on recognition of the severity of the client's functional problems, on the stability or instability of the client's condition, and on the cost of the service plan. Clients with more-severe functional problems, unstable conditions, or more-costly service plans should be reassessed more frequently than those whose situation is stable and likely to stay that way.

Termination of Services

The inclusion of termination of services in the family assessment and change method underscores the concept of appropriate care. Clients who receive too little or too much care are not well served. Too much care fosters dependence, undermines competence and the ability for self-care, and, in a system of publicly funded services, leads to unnecessary expenditures and denial of service to other clients who could benefit. Clients should receive care that is compatible with successful management of a problem or maintenance of functioning. The emphasis in this model on empowerment and consequently on goals that aim at restoration of functioning and growth also demands that social workers be able to judge when services should end.

Services for clients may be terminated for a number of reasons: Services are no longer necessary because goals have been met; different services not offered by the agency (or program area) are deemed more appropriate to address the client's goals; services are no longer desired; or the client no longer meets eligibility requirements, has moved from the area, or has died. The decision to terminate services to a client or transfer the client to another level of care calls on the worker to record why services are being ended, whose choice it was to end them, a review of the service plan and client's progress, and whether and why follow-up is being proposed. This termination summary can be passed on to any new provider of services.

CLINICAL SKILL AREAS

Clinical skills, as defined here and as opposed to resource development and coordination skills, specifically address problems in desired functioning that result from the client's internal barriers—perhaps psychological beliefs or cognitive responses to social circumstances or external barriers such as lack of material resources. They also capitalize on the client's strengths in problem solving. The social worker's clinical skills in the areas of interviewing and relationship development, crisis intervention, and counseling help the client examine personal, internal barriers to functioning and strengths for overcoming those barriers.

Interviewing and Relationship Development

Effective communication and relationship building provide an essential foundation for all subsequent change, and they require both skill and art (Rogers & Roethlisberger, 1991). The interview is the professional medium by which the social worker communicates with adult services clients and their families or representatives. As a skill, interviewing requires a knowledge of techniques that ensure the receipt of important and reliable assessment information and properly convey service intervention and treatment plans. Interviewing plays a part in all phases of the family assessment and change method. With the use of interviewing, the social worker obtains basic identifying data from the client and family at intake, learns their reason for seeking help, obtains a case history, conducts an initial screening, directs the comprehensive assessment, identifies goals and plans service interventions, monitors interventions, reassesses achievement of goals, and helps clients adjust to ending services when that is necessary. Social workers must be attentive to issues of who should be present during interviews, the pacing of the interview, and any circumstances that may influence the interviewing process (for example, the client's sensory deficits or particular cultural influences).

Interviewing is a means by which the worker establishes a professional relationship with the client and family, which is distinct from a personal relationship (Bumagin & Hirn, 1990). As Perlman (1957) stated, the client "will not be asking you for a [personal] relationship. He is likely to be asking for some plain, ordinary, necessary life-sustaining thing like money, like medicine, like advice, like action on his behalf" (p. 19). Nonetheless, a good professional relationship has personal benefits for clients and families, because it can enable them to feel valued and free to assert and celebrate their self-worth and realize their potential. Good professional relationships require from the social worker warmth, empathy, and genuineness.

Crisis Intervention

In simple terms, a *crisis* can be seen as an event in a client's normal living situation when usual problem-solving approaches, skills, and resources are inadequate. The client or family perceives the changed situation as a loss, a threat, or a challenge to continued well-being. Lack of an effective change response results in an intolerable situation, often marked by stress, anxiety, and depression (Sherman, 1985). On the other hand, an effective response to crisis can create an opportunity for positive change. Crises are time limited in nature, in contrast to chronic or ongoing problems that produce stress, anxiety, or depression.

Responses on the part of social workers that can lead to a healthy resolution of the crisis draw again on the principles associated with the family assessment and change approach. First, the worker accepts the client's often negative, irrational feelings in response to what seems to be an overwhelming situation. It is important not to label the client's affect and response as inappropriate. Having accepted that response with a measure of empathy and understanding, the worker then sets about isolating and restructuring what has happened as an initial step to change.

Working with the client and family, the social worker is able to isolate factors—both objective circumstances and subjective responses to those changed circumstances—that have led to the serious disruption in functioning. The worker and client seek to frame the problem or issue in a manner that will suggest a way to reestablish the previous equilibrium or find a new stability. In demonstrating this approach to change, the worker points out and helps the client draw on internal and external resources that can be brought to bear on the problem. Crisis intervention places exceptional but realizable demands on the worker for effective interviewing and communication skills and focused short-term counseling and problem solving.

Counseling

Adult services social workers do engage in counseling with clients and their families. Rothman (1991) made a useful distinction between counseling and therapy. He characterized counseling as an approach that is not as highly intrapsychic as traditional therapy, but which does deal with internal beliefs and concerns associated with change, reality testing, socialization skills, and accepting practical help. He goes on to suggest that effective counseling uses such abilities as teaching basic living skills, using role playing, and modeling desirable behavior. It also involves communicating information and providing consultation to clients and their families: for example, helping clients and families to identify and assess facilities when placement in a nursing or board-and-care home is necessary or negotiating such legal issues as establishing guardianship.

Counseling skills also include short-term, task-centered approaches to clients' aspirations for improved functioning. In counseling clients, adult services social workers do not attempt to identify or deal with the remote, historical origins of a problem except as they currently have a bearing on the efforts to improve functioning. They do not engage in long-term therapy. Working with individuals and families around difficult placement issues, working with families to protect members from abusive situations, or providing supportive counseling to a client coping with loss of a loved one or adjusting to an impairment that cannot otherwise be remedied are just a few examples of situations when adult services social workers might engage in counseling. Counseling in adult services draws on the steps and activities outlined in this chapter in identifying counseling needs, setting goals, and maintaining progress toward them.

RESOURCE DEVELOPMENT AND COORDINATION SKILLS

Resource development and coordination skills associated with the family assessment and change method represent a recognition of both the agency setting and the larger community in which social workers function. In this environment, workers must often act as advocates for adult clients to break down community and organizational barriers to services; as program developers who use input from clients to identify, initiate, plan, and implement new service programs or modify old ones; and as organizational reformers who seek to change community and organizational processes that reduce the effectiveness of services. Here workers are engaged with change efforts on behalf of the adult client to obtain needed resources from the external environment, that is, the larger community and the social services system itself. Skills used by workers to assist adult clients in accessing needed resources include advocacy, community development, and case management.

Advocacy

An *advocate* is someone who pleads the cause of another. In their role as advocate for their clients, adult services social workers assume the perspective that a major component of clients' impaired functioning and threats to future functioning stem from the lack of fit between the clients' needs and the larger environment. Clients turn to workers because their own efforts at change and at locating resources and support have been ineffective. In assessing clients' circumstances, workers must be able to identify which aspect of the agency or community must be targeted to become more responsive to the clients' and families' needs.

Advocacy can occur on two levels. The first level, case-by-case advocacy, is a familiar role for social workers. Here they negotiate with agencies to accept a referral, reconsider a previous denial of services, or work within the agency to modify practices to meet the needs of a client. Advocacy is not a passive process of referral to community agencies. Advocacy is commitment to stand shoulder to shoulder with the client in dealing with agency and community resources until the client's need is met. It is a willingness to be persistent and at times confrontational on behalf of a client.

Advocacy also occurs at the level of the program, system, or community. A social worker may need to act on behalf of a class of clients when he or she identifies agency practices or gaps in services that systematically affect them. A worker who recognizes a gap in available services in the community (for example, in-home assistance for people with acquired immune deficiency syndrome [AIDS] or Alzheimer's disease) might set about assisting interested parties in developing community programs to respond to such unmet needs. Case management is the method or set of skills for case-by-case advocacy, whereas community development skills address issues of system or community advocacy.

Community Development

Community development or community organization consists of social planning and social action (Mizrahi & Morrison, 1993; Rothman, 1979). In their role as change agents and advocates for clients, adult services social workers frequently assume the role of community worker.

Community development is primarily concerned with capacity building and self-help, that is, developing the knowledge of community leaders concerning the needs of adult clients and fostering self-help groups within the affected population. Developing and disseminating information about the needs of adult services clients is a step toward making visible an often invisible population to promote community support for their needs. An example of community development could be providing information about the Medicaid-waiver programs for adults with disabilities in a community without this resource and pulling together a group of interested individuals to set about planning for such a program.

Social planning involves a systematic process of identifying needs, building consensus, setting goals, and identifying strategies, a process similar in many respects to the family assessment and change method used with individual clients. Social workers may exhibit a willingness to assume a leadership role (for example, in the efforts of an adult services program to develop a mission statement and an overall plan). Because of their close day-to-day involvement with clients, adult services workers are one of the best sources of input into agency or community planning processes.

Social action represents a second class of community development activities in which workers may involve themselves. Social action on behalf of adult services clients involves collaboration with various parties, including consumers, around a particular issue. One area of recent social action involves the concept of assisted living, a service-infused housing alternative to traditional public housing or nursing and board-and-care homes, which has increasing appeal to many adults with functional impairments. Adult services social workers, either formally through their agencies or through voluntary independent involvement, may choose to participate in such a social action movement.

Case Management

"Case management is a service function directed at coordinating existing resources to assure appropriate and continuous care for individuals on a case-by-case basis" (White, 1987, p. 92). Usually it involves securing resources from the community. Two general models of case management exist: (1) the brokerage model and (2) the centralized model. The brokerage model, which typifies most adult services case management activity, is one in which social workers seek to enlist the assistance of other community agencies in providing resources for clients. In this model, social workers have no direct authority over those resources. In the centralized model, the worker can authorize service expenditures. Medicaid-waiver programs, which exist in most states, are based on this model. Case managers work with a defined budget from which they can secure certain services needed to assist the individual in remaining in the community.

Grisham, White, and Miller (1983); Rothman (1991); and White (1987) acknowledged case management as a method of resource provision that relies on a basic problem solving and change approach to the needs of adults and draws on a long-established tradition in social work. The steps, activities, and tasks that are used to identify clients' needs for resources and to secure and monitor the use of these resources are reflected in the family assessment and change method presented in this chapter.

RECORD KEEPING

Record keeping is an area that is necessary to all aspects of the family assessment and change method. Adult services social work records should provide a concise, usable account and documentation of why the client came to the agency; what problems were identified; what goals were set; what interventions were planned and implemented; how well the interventions worked; and what subsequent interventions, if any, were provided. The case record should parallel, support, and reinforce the basic change method outlined for adult services practice. Supervisors use case records as teaching tools for improving practice and as administrative tools for monitoring program performance and compliance (Kagle, 1984, 1991, 1993).

PROGRAM SKILL AREAS

In addition to being familiar with the basic family assessment and change method outlined in this chapter, social workers must be knowledgeable and skilled in their particular fields of practice within adult services. The term *field of practice* is used here to refer to the various service areas in which workers find themselves, including adult protective services, guardianship, in-home services, placement, board-and-care monitoring, and adult day care. In addition, they may need special expertise for working with clients with such specific problems as visual or hearing impairment or chronic degenerative diseases (for example, multiple sclerosis or AIDS).

Each of these service areas requires its own set of skills and knowledge. APS workers must be able to identify accurately instances of abuse, neglect, and exploitation; understand the legal ramifications of substantiating the need for protective services; and be skilled at finding the least intrusive ways to remedy such situations. Placement and in-home services workers alike must be able to differentiate between clients who are able to remain in their homes and those whose needs make placement in a protected setting preferable. Adult services social workers need a detailed knowledge of their own areas of responsibility, but they also must know other service areas to which their clients may need referral.

Sensitivity to Diversity

Adult services social workers encounter diverse client populations. Working with clients whose age, race, ethnicity, religion, and values are different from the social worker's requires the worker to engage in a process of discovery—exploring the world as the client constructs it, rather than as the worker believes it to be (Proctor & Davis, 1994). Because the interview process is the source of most of the social worker's information about clients, discovering the client's world relies on language and communication.

In writing about social workers who are competent in working with diverse populations, Sue and Sue (1990) identified three characteristics of culturally competent practitioners: (1) awareness of one's assumptions, values, and biases; (2) understanding of differences in worldviews that are governed by culture; and (3) ability to develop and use appropriate intervention strategies and techniques. Knowledge of and skill in handling racial, ethnic, cultural, geographic, and social class characteristics of clients are essential for excellence in adult services.

Summary

This chapter has provided an introduction to a family assessment and change method basic to excellence in adult services social work. It has touched on the central core of procedures, the clinical skills that support them, and the case management and community development skills that make resources available. Subsequent chapters will treat these skills in greater detail.

The use of a family assessment and change method in adult services emphasizes the partnership involved in this enterprise. Client, family, and social worker engage in a process of discovery—clarifying needs, developing plans, and monitoring their implementation and effectiveness. The goal of improving the well-being of the client, often through a combination of concrete supportive services and facilitative counseling, empowers clients and their families to assume increased control of their circumstances. The combination of specific change skills and a detailed knowledge of the needs and the diversity of the adult services population enables social workers to demonstrate excellence in their work and take pride in their successes.

Key Points

Excellent adult services social workers
- use a family assessment and change method to address their clients' needs
- seek to empower clients through a combination of resource development, coordination skills, and clinical skills

- demonstrate detailed knowledge and skill in adult services fields for which they are responsible while maintaining a working knowledge of allied service areas
- possess the knowledge and skills to handle issues of diversity.

Excellent adult services managers
- know and support the family assessment and change method through their supervisory and administrative activities
- provide and support basic training for the family assessment and change method and cross-training within the various service areas and fields of practice
- model cultural sensitivity and support training for their staff members in this area.

Excellent leaders
- incorporate the basic elements of the family assessment and change method into policy and procedure
- support statewide competency-based training in the use of the family assessment and change method
- acknowledge diversity and support related training for social services workers at all levels.

References

Altman, S. (1979). Performance monitoring systems for public managers. *Public Administration Review, 39*(1), 31–35.

Bernstein, L. H. (1992, December). A public health approach to functional assessment. *CARING Magazine*, pp. 32–38.

Bloom, M., & Fischer, J. (1982). *Evaluating practice: Guidelines for the accountable professional.* Englewood Cliffs, NJ: Prentice Hall.

Bumagin, V. E., & Hirn, K. F. (1990). *Helping the aging family: A guide for professionals.* Glenview, IL: Scott, Foresman.

Campbell, L. A., & Thompson, B. L. (1990, August). Evaluating elderly patients: A critique of comprehensive functional assessment tools. *Nurse Practitioner*, pp. 11–18.

Cowger, C. D. (1994). Assessing client strengths: Clinical assessment for client empowerment. *Social Work, 39,* 262–268.

Family and Children's Resource Program. (1992). *A model for excellence in adult services administration and social work practice.* Chapel Hill: Family Forum, School of Social Work, University of North Carolina.

Fillenbaum, G. G. (1984). *The well-being of the elderly: Approaches to multidimensional assessment* (World Health Organization publication no. 84). Geneva: World Health Organization.

Gambrill, E. (1983). *Casework: A competency-based approach.* Englewood Cliffs, NJ: Prentice Hall.

George, L., & Fillenbaum, G. G. (1985). OARS methodology: A decade of experience in geriatric assessment. *Journal of American Geriatrics Society, 33*(9), 607–615.

Greene, R. R. (1986). *Social work with the aged and their families.* Hawthorne, NY: Aldine de Gruyter.

Grisham, M., White, M., & Miller, L. S. (1983). Case management as a problem-solving strategy. *PRIDE Institute Journal of Long Term Home Health Care, 2*(4), 22–28.

Gutiérrez, L. M. (1990). Working with women of color: An empowerment perspective. *Social Work, 35,* 149–153.

Hartman, A., & Laird, J. (1983). *Family-centered social work practice.* New York: Free Press.

Hasenfeld, Y. (1987, September). Power in social work practice. *Social Service Review,* pp. 469–483.

Ivry, J. (1992). Teaching geriatric assessment. In M. J. Mellor & R. Solomon (Eds.), *Geriatric social work education* (pp. 3–22). New York: Haworth.

Joint Commission on Accreditation of Hospitals. (Eds.). (1981). *Accreditation manual for hospitals 1982.* Chicago: Author.

Kagle, J. D. (1984). *Social work records* (1st ed.). Homewood, IL: Dorsey Press.

Kagle, J. D. (1991). *Social work records* (2nd ed.). Belmont, CA: Wadsworth.

Kagle, J. D. (1993). Record keeping: Directions for the 1990s. *Social Work, 38,* 190–196.

Kane, R. A., & Kane, R. L. (1981). *Assessing the elderly: A practical guide to measurement.* Lexington, MA: Lexington Books.

Mizrahi, T., & Morrison, J. D. (1993). *Community organization and social administration.* New York: Haworth.

Moore, S. (1992). Case management and the integration of services: How service delivery systems shape case management. *Social Work, 37,* 418–423.

Moore, T. (1994). *Soul mates.* New York: Harper Collins.

Nelson, G. M. (1992). Training adult service social workers in the public sector: A core curriculum for effective geriatric social work practice. *Educational Gerontology, 18,* 163–176.

Perlman, H. H. (1957). *Social casework: A problem-solving process.* Chicago: University of Chicago Press.

Proctor, E. K., & Davis, L. E. (1994). The challenge of racial difference: Skills for clinical practice. *Social Work, 39,* 314–323.

Rappaport, J. (1985). The power of empowerment language. *Social Policy, 17*(2), 15–21.

Reid, W. J. (1978). *The task-centered system.* New York: Columbia University Press.

Rogers, C. R., & Roethlisberger, F. J. (1991, November/December). Barriers and gateways to communication. *Harvard Business Review*, pp. 105–111.

Rothman, J. (1979). *Planning and organizing for social change: Action principles from science research.* New York: Columbia University Press.

Rothman, J. (1991). A model of case management: Toward empirically based practice. *Social Work, 36,* 520–528.

Saleebey, D. (1992). *The strengths perspective in social work practice.* New York: Longman.

Senge, P. M. (1990). *The fifth discipline: The art and practice of the learning organization.* New York: Doubleday Currency.

Sherman, E. (1985). Casework services. In A. Monk (Ed.), *Handbook of gerontological services* (pp. 142–168). New York: Van Nostrand Reinhold.

Silverstone, B., & Burack-Weiss, A. (1983). *Social work practice with the frail elderly and their families.* Springfield, IL: Charles C Thomas.

Solomon, B. (1982). Empowering women: A matter of values. In A. Weick & S. T. Vandiver (Eds.), *Women, power, and change* (pp. 206–214). Silver Spring, MD: National Association of Social Workers.

Steinberg, R., & Carter, G. (1983). *Case management and the elderly.* Lexington, MA: Lexington Books.

Sue, D. W., & Sue, D. (1990). *Counseling the culturally different: Theory and practice* (2nd ed.). New York: John Wiley & Sons.

Viorst, J. (1986). *Necessary losses.* New York: Ballantine Books.

White, M. (1987). Case management. In G. Maddox (Ed.), *The encyclopedia of aging* (pp. 92–96). New York: Springer.

CHAPTER 4

Access and Intake

GARY M. NELSON

The way in which potential clients gain access to adult services programs not only determines what assistance they will receive but also colors their initial perception of the agency and their subsequent relationships with individual social workers and programs. Intake is a process and not a single event. It may begin with a telephone call from the client to an intake worker, an adult services social worker, or the agency's receptionist. It may start as an inquiry on the part of a concerned family member, neighbor, physician, or home health worker. This chapter examines access to the agency and the intake process for adult services.

Intake begins with the inquiry and ends when an official case record is opened (or reopened) and the client is referred to an adult services social worker for assessment, when the client is referred to some other program operated by another agency, or when the client's problem is handled during the intake process and the client needs no further assistance.

Access to the agency, which reflects the agency's interaction with other human services providers and the community, is considered here because it influences the intake process. A social services agency that defines its mission clearly and publicizes it within the community will find that potential clients and concerned others acting on their behalf can make clearer judgments of what the agency has to offer. Access is tied to the adult services agency's role in community planning, which is covered in greater detail in chapter 18.

This chapter also examines the intake process for adult services social work as one part of the family assessment and change method. It outlines the knowledge and skills essential for excellence in this area, including an awareness of the cultural and ethnic diversity of the client population, interviewing and communication skills, screening techniques and emergency intervention, knowledge of resources within the agency and the community, and the ability to work well in an organizational context.

Access to the Agency

Social services help individuals and families bring about change and overcome problems. However, gaining access to a social services system dedicated to helping and change is the most important and the most difficult hurdle for potential adult services clients to overcome. The nature of clients' presenting problems and the changes they seek may make asking for help difficult or impossible. For many clients, asking for help is an admission of inadequacy and involves swallowing a large measure of pride, particularly among an older generation for whom taking public "welfare" may be seen as shameful. For other clients, the barrier may be unfamiliarity with what assistance adult services can offer.

Social services departments in many communities are seen as the primary source of information for a range of questions from housing and day care to social security and Medicare. This may be the function of a poorly articulated and understood mission or the perception that the agency will handle all service requests and turn no one away. On the other hand, it may be the outgrowth of a strong, highly visible agency with a clear mission and an excellent information and referral capacity. The issue here, as in so many other aspects of adult services, is that agencies must exercise a conscious choice regarding functions they want to undertake in providing adult services.

Access to adult services and the intake process can be made easier. First, a clear and well-publicized mission statement that spells out the role and function of the agency will increase the likelihood of appropriate self-referrals and referrals from other service providers. In addition to publicizing the mission and services, agencies may engage in an active campaign of outreach to those in need, a process called case finding or service targeting (Rothman, 1991; Steinberg & Carter, 1983).

Client-specific case-finding strategies require that adult services programs have clear written guidelines for intake workers that identify criteria for determining referrals for both agency- and community-based services. Such guidelines should be updated at least annually. Regular use of case staffings to discuss clients whose needs raise difficulties can help clarify the application of the agency's service-targeting standards. Such standards should help intake workers distinguish among the possibilities for referral and serve as the basis of screening tools and procedures developed by the agency (see more about this in the section on Screening in this chapter). In-house intake workers, as well as those based in the community, should use common criteria in targeting agency services.

Organizational case-finding strategies depend largely on how well the agency informs potential sources of referrals about available services. This can be done either through information campaigns or through formal and informal interagency agreements. Adult services programs that use community awareness campaigns to sensitize the public and human services agencies about abuse of adults with disabilities are an excellent example of the use of publicity to enhance service targeting and promote more appropriate use of adult protective services.

Because home and community Medicaid-waiver programs target services to adults at risk of nursing home placement, adult services programs managing this program may establish formal or informal ties with hospitals, home health agencies, and community physicians to secure appropriate referrals.

Another strategy for active case finding is to locate social workers directly in the community, rather than in a centralized office. The Mecklenberg County, North Carolina, Department of Social Services uses this approach to extend services to the residents of a senior housing complex. Here the social worker can become familiar with residents and detect and respond to problems before they become serious. Access to services is available for people who might otherwise have difficulty coming to the central office. Recently, a number of state and local adult services programs across the country have experimented with active case-finding efforts to identify people who might qualify for Supplemental Security Income (SSI) benefits. As local adult services programs become more involved in strategic planning for community services, case finding in long-term care, income assistance, or APS is likely to grow in importance.

Role of the Intake Social Worker

Once potential clients have arrived at the agency, what is the role of intake social workers and what special expertise do they need to do their jobs well? The process of initiating potential clients into a helping relationship and a service system requires an extensive knowledge base and a clear set of skills. Those mentioned in this chapter include interviewing and communication skills, familiarity with screening criteria, and knowledge of resources and the ability to work in an organizational context. Because intake is so challenging and requires such a diverse set of abilities, agencies are well advised to put some of their most experienced and talented workers in these positions.

Although specific definitions of adult services intake vary from state to state and community to community, intake can generally be described as the function of designated staff members whose responsibility it is to initiate clients to the agency's service delivery system. Activities associated with the process include receiving and exploring requests for services, taking applications, establishing eligibility, beginning a record containing information about the client, and certifying clients for purchased services. This process also may include a brief assessment of the applicant's circumstances and provision of information or referral to other appropriate community agencies.

Although the description of the intake process can be straightforward, the practice varies across agencies and communities. In larger adult services programs, intake is a specialized function for designated staff members, with separate sections for adult and child services. In other agencies, intake workers handle this function for both adult and children's services. Elsewhere, no one worker specializes in intake; rather, all the social workers may do intake in rotation. In some cases, the adult services program's receptionist may gather basic information, receive referrals, and channel requests for services to an intake worker or directly to a service unit.

Whatever the adult services program's method for handling intake, it is an important social work activity and the first step in the family assessment and change method. For this reason, the circumstances under which clients make contact with the agency deserve close attention, as does the professional training of the personnel whose responsibility it is to begin the relationship with clients. Such things as the appearance of the agency's lobby and the courtesy of staff members on the telephone or in person set the stage for the client's successful or unsuccessful relationship with the adult services program. In more sensitive areas, such as the evaluation of protective services cases, when clients often do not refer themselves voluntarily, deft handling of initial contact can make the intervention more effective and the social worker's job easier.

Intake requires of its practitioners a specialized knowledge and a particular temperament that not all social workers possess. Intake is a reactive service in that workers must see every person who walks in and answer every phone call. Intake workers must be prepared to address any situation, often within a single hectic workday. Intake workers are the social work equivalent of emergency department physicians. The successful intake worker must be someone with a knack for getting a brief account of the client's desire for change, who enjoys being a generalist and knowing about the programs and services offered at the agency and in the community, and who is satisfied with and finds meaning in offering short-term services, because in many cases the client will be referred to another worker for a longer-term intervention.

Successful intake workers assist people requesting services with help in problem solving and identifying desired changes at the point of inquiry, either by reframing the questions or issues, providing essential information, or referring clients to another agency or community service provider. One of the most important tasks of the intake worker, however, is to begin establishing for clients a favorable environment in which they feel comfortable asking for and receiving help.

GIVING AND RECEIVING HELP: ROLE OF RELATIONSHIP

One definition of *help* is something tangible or intangible offered by one person or group to another person or group to achieve resolution of a problem. To help someone is to facilitate change. Compton and Gallaway (1989) suggested that help has two important elements: "(1) what is given and (2) how it is given and used. To be helpful, what is given must be something of value or use to the recipients, and it must be given in such a way as to leave the recipient free to use it in their own way without paying the penalty of loss of self-esteem or a loss of control over their own lives." (p. 416)

Because the United States has a culture that values individualism, people in this country often believe that most problems originate with the individual and that responsibility for change lies first with individuals and then with their families. Because problems often are seen as faults, people may construe asking for help both as an admission of fault and as an admission of weakness. Thus, for many people, seeking and receiving help may represent a threat to their sense of self, adequacy, and control. For these reasons, social workers (and other "helping" professionals) must respect the difficult circumstances in which clients find themselves and the constraints they may experience in asking for and receiving help. As the providers of assistance, social workers also must recognize the limits of their ability to alter the circumstances of clients and the importance of handling the helping relationship constructively (Bumagin & Hirn, 1990).

To accept help, clients must accept that something in their situation needs changing, be able to talk about the nature of the problem, accord the intake worker a limited right either to tell them what to do or to do something for them, and be willing to change (Keith-Lucas, 1972). For their part, intake workers—whether receptionists, formally designated intake workers, or other social workers—must understand the importance of empathy, warmth, and genuineness in establishing a helping relationship during the intake process. Through empathic listening, which is marked by attention focused on the speaker and responses that reflect understanding, the intake worker establishes a rapport with the potential client. The demonstration of empathy allows and encourages potential clients to express their feelings about the problems that brought them to the agency (Bumagin & Hirn, 1990; Gambrill, 1983). The worker communicates warmth by hearing the person's story without making judgmental statements, through comments that demonstrate positive regard, and by expressing a commitment to be of assistance (Lambert, De Julio, & Stein, 1978). Intake workers demonstrate genuineness through responses to potential clients that convey sincerity and respect for their concerns. This includes trying not to be defensive when confronted with clients who are angry or hostile and diffusing negative emotions by acknowledging their validity.

The process of intake is the initial step in establishing a helping and a change-based relationship. The intake worker and the potential client must deal with the subtle and often unspoken difficulties of entering into that relationship, begin to explore the issues, and identify and agree on the worker's and the service system's boundaries (including the individual's, family's, and community's), strengths, capacity, and resources for helping. The intake worker first should make clear what the process will entail so clients can decide whether they are willing to proceed, either through referral to one of the adult services social workers for further assessment or to a more appropriate agency in the community.

The spoken word is the medium through which clients and social workers begin to identify and assess issues and opportunities for change and through which they agree to enter into a helping relationship. Intake interviews, either over the telephone or in the office, require that the worker obtain essential information while letting clients communicate the facts and the emotions associated with the presenting problems. The challenge to the intake worker is to "follow and lead" the discussion, so as to obtain the necessary information yet not be sidetracked. Chapter 7, on counseling, reviews interviewing in greater detail. Of the most important points, perhaps the first is that an intake interview is more than a conversation—it is a purposeful use of self in obtaining important information and establishing a helping relationship. With this in mind, workers must understand professional closeness and through it, how to express warmth, empathy, and genuineness. Intake workers also must be aware of their styles of interaction. Clients who feel that their lives are in crisis risk becoming overdependent. Intake workers must help them avoid this learned helplessness to forge a style of interaction that promotes clients' self-reliance in conjunction with the willingness to accept help.

Beyond this, intake workers must be skilled in identifying potential barriers to communication and overcoming them. Particularly among older clients, sensory loss may be an issue, and intake workers must know how to make communication as easy as possible. Cultural and ethnic diversity also may contribute to possible misunderstandings, so although every worker in the agency must be alert to this issue, it is particularly important for intake workers to recognize how it can affect the abilities of potential clients to ask for help and the manner in which they do so. Finally, much of the content of communication is unvoiced. Observant intake workers hear not only the words but also register the messages conveyed by the body language of potential clients and use this information in their understanding of clients' situations.

CULTURAL AND ETHNIC DIVERSITY

Intake workers are confronted daily with a wide array of problems and people from diverse backgrounds and circumstances. One minute an intake worker may be interviewing a homeless person and the next responding to a telephone call from a bank president concerned about a family member or friend. The ability to see human worth through the apparent frailty and confusion of an older person, the unkempt attire of a homeless person, the anger of a daughter who believes that her parent is not receiving appropriate care, or the shame of a recently unemployed father is a challenge for the intake worker.

The ability to accept and respond appropriately to diversity, whether cultural, ethnic, racial, religious, or in other areas, while also according each individual respect is something that is only in part inherent (Proctor & Davis, 1994). An understanding of and respect for diversity and skills for interviewing and communication with individuals from diverse backgrounds also can be learned. Sensitivity and empathy for the circumstances of the client whose hardship is compounded by limited ability to speak English may lead the social worker to know how and where to find interpreters or even to gain a rudimentary knowledge of another language (Castex, 1994). Although most people require a measure of privacy and confidentiality, the social worker must know how these ideas are constituted for individuals of different social and ethnic backgrounds. Being prepared to recognize and respond appropriately to diversity and being able to listen with a "third ear" for differences and sensitivities are essential for effective intake workers.

Screening: Brief Assessment of Need and Risk

The primary purpose of the intake process is to achieve a match between potential clients' requests for help and the most appropriate sources of that help. The agency may be the best resource or another provider may be, but in many instances, the most appropriate source of change and problem solving will be the potential clients themselves. Because many adult services cases are handled at intake, it seems likely that providing basic information or laying out alternative courses of action may be all that is needed to reinvigorate some of these clients' own problem-solving skills and abilities to change. Consistent with this thinking, in some instances adult services intake workers should engage in short-term direct services (generally a visit or two as part of their case finding and outreach activities), rather than referring clients, when that seems to be the best solution.

In other instances, when more help is needed and appropriate, the task of the intake worker is to gather sufficient information to make an appropriate referral. Such preliminary information gathering should include basic identifying data, the presenting problem, the client's and family's strengths, and a brief case history, so the intake worker can apply screening criteria to determine how the client's needs can be met best. The intake worker provides a sound beginning for the family assessment and change process.

IDENTIFYING DATA

Identifying data include such important information as the client's name, address (perhaps with directions on how to get there), telephone number, and involved others, such as family members, physicians, other helping professionals, and insurance providers. Additional information recorded at this stage includes date of initial service application, name of the intake worker, referral source, and a checklist noting any subsequent referral for services. The identifying data constitute the first element of any subsequent assessment process and case record.

PRESENTING PROBLEM

Some potential clients or concerned others who contact the agency on their behalf present specific requests for services, whereas others may contact the agency with global, nonspecific problems or requests for assistance in changing their circumstances. It is important to focus on the range of attributes, including individual and family strengths, to capture fully the context within which problems are presented and overcome (Mattaini & Kirk, 1991). In all cases, the intake worker must strive to obtain a statement of both the desired change and underlying problems that have brought the client to request assistance, rather than focusing on the particular service requested. This is because requesting a specific service may be the only way the client knows to ask for help. The service requested may not be the best or most efficient solution to the problems and issues at hand. It is important for intake workers to ask such questions as "What brings you to adult services today?" and "How do you believe that coming here can help you?"

CASE HISTORY

To clarify the presenting problem and request for assistance in bringing about change, the intake worker should ask the client for a brief case history, that is, a description of the antecedents, onset, implications, and seriousness of the problems that caused the client to come to adult services and what efforts the client has made to change and overcome these problems. Questions about antecedents and onset might include "When did this problem begin?" "What do you think caused it?" "What else was going on in your life when the problem began?" Questions about implications might include "What effect is this problem having on your life now?" "How much trouble is this problem causing you right now?" "How do you see it affecting your future?" Questions exploring previous self-initiated change efforts to deal with the problem might include "What have you done to solve this problem yourself?" "What has worked and why?" "What hasn't worked and why?" The intake worker also might ask at this time what sort of help the client believes the adult services agency can offer (Ryback, 1974). Helping clients clarify requests in this way demonstrates the intake worker's engagement in the helping process and helps clients to reformulate their change efforts and identify new strategies for overcoming their problems. It also offers hope, because the process suggests that there are avenues for overcoming problems.

CASE SCREENING

After obtaining the client's basic identifying data and an understanding and statement of his or her perception of the desired changes, in many cases the intake worker will need to make a recommendation for referral based on screening criteria that the agency has developed to help workers decide how to respond to specific presenting problems. Case screenings are brief, standardized procedures for identifying variables and risk factors that indicate the need for referral and help identify the level at which any service intervention should begin. Screening is a form of triage, that is, a procedure for matching individuals with possible interventions and determining how quickly action is needed. Assessment, which is part of the next step in the family assessment and change method, involves a more thorough and detailed review of the client's functioning. Assessment may be performed by social workers in different service programs within the adult services agency or by other providers in the community (for example, a hospital, home health agency, or nursing home).

The types of screening procedures, questions, and instruments used by the intake worker depend on the presenting problem and desired changes articulated by clients or their family members. For example, Williams and Williams (1982) developed a useful screening sequence for referring older adults or individuals with disabilities to different levels of care for further assessment and follow-up. In its simple but logical sequence, clients whose condition is unstable enough medically or mentally that they pose a danger to themselves or others are referred to an acute care hospital setting. If the client meets neither of these criteria, the worker uses a second set of brief questions to decide whether assessment for nursing home, board-and-care facility, or home care might be the best starting point for the client. Many tools already are available to assess risk in different areas (for example, for APS and suicide prevention). For each client, intake workers should have in mind—if not actually written down—a series of questions they can ask and on the basis of which they can refer clients to appropriate service units within the agency or to other programs in the community.

EMERGENCY AND CRISIS INTERVENTION

Emergencies and crises are situations faced by clients and families that adult services social workers must be prepared to address. Emergencies occur when the health, safety, or security of clients is at serious risk in the absence of immediate relief (Parad, 1965). Obvious emergency situations occur after a natural disaster or an accident that results in serious bodily harm. Similarly, a client in imminent danger of eviction, faced with the loss of heating or cooling during extreme weather, or whose primary caregiver is suddenly disabled is experiencing an emergency. In these situations, the social worker's immediate task is to help provide or arrange for the necessary material assistance, whether it be financial, medical, or something else.

Emergencies often result in a state of crisis for clients, that is, clients can no longer cope emotionally with the situation. Clients in crisis find that their usual problem-solving approaches, skills, and resources are inadequate, and as a result, they feel overwhelmed. The social worker intervenes through short-term counseling and problem solving to help the client find stability. Chapter 7 describes the steps of crisis intervention.

Emergencies sometimes occur without resulting in a crisis, and similarly, crises are not necessarily based on an emergency situation. A client who faces eviction, for example, may have the necessary coping skills to deal emotionally with this prospect and be able to identify sources of support, including the adult services agency. Still, the risk of suddenly having nowhere to live constitutes an emergency. On the other hand, a client whose spouse dies may not have any material needs that require emergency relief, yet this client may be in crisis if he or she cannot cope with the grief resulting from the loss.

Just as the agency develops criteria to distinguish among clients who might benefit from home care as opposed to a board-and-care or nursing home placement, agencies should develop criteria to help intake workers distinguish between emergencies and crises. Situations inappropriately treated as emergencies take time and attention away from other cases and may jeopardize workers' abilities to respond promptly to other situations that are critical. Serious situations mislabeled as emergencies also may result in inappropriate interventions because emergency-based assessment and service planning short-circuits a more deliberate and careful family assessment and change process.

Emergencies do occur and should be remedied as quickly as possible. However, the process should not end when the immediate threat to the client's well-being has been reduced. Once emergency assistance is provided, the agency must support a process whereby clients are referred to services that can address underlying problems, identify desired changes, and result in lasting solutions.

Knowledge of Resources and Their Match with Needs

CONTINUUM OF CARE

State, regional, and local adult services agencies are major providers of services to both younger and older adults. Their services and those of proprietary or nonprofit care providers can be conceptualized as falling on a continuum that ranges from institutional interventions, which can markedly restrict the individual's control of his or her environment and circumstances, to less-restrictive interventions involving community-based and in-home services. Depending on the agency's decision about its mission and target populations, it may provide services either directly or indirectly by purchasing or arranging for them from other providers. In other instances, the client may be linked to a service provider or service setting through a referral and placement process, perhaps to a community mental health center or to a nursing or board-and-care home.

Intake workers must have an understanding not only of the needs of their clients but also of the available service interventions that might best fit those needs. Beyond the options available within the agency, services in the community that are of immediate relevance include mental health, home health, hospital, family planning, housing, transportation, and the array of services and programs that fall under the aging network of the Older Americans Act of 1965. In addition, intake workers must have a working understanding of major financial programs—Medicaid, Medicare, social security, SSI, and veterans' benefits—and the overlapping and often conflicting eligibility guidelines that govern access to them. Effective adult services intake requires specialization and ongoing training in the area of adult and aging services, and this need will become more pressing as the population of older adults increases.

Like other social workers within adult services agencies, intake workers must do their job effectively in a complex organizational context. Effectiveness in intake is in good measure determined by the degree to which workers are able to understand and work with other agencies and organizational representatives. As the gatekeepers for services provided to potential clients who come for help, intake workers must be familiar on a number of levels with other gatekeepers within the social services agency and the community. Having established an initial database and conducted a preliminary screening to determine the best fit between the client's presenting problem, individual and family strengths, and agency or community resources, the worker must initiate a match between the client and those resources. An effective intake process is one in which clients not only receive appropriate referrals for services but are successful at gaining help.

As gatekeepers, intake workers who form collegial and informal working relationships with their peers in the service community can overcome many of the barriers to access that clients encounter. In examining the coordination of community-based services for older adults in a number of Alabama counties, Bolland and Wilson (1991) found that much of the universally decried service fragmentation was overcome by the informal networking of service gatekeepers and providers. To return to the agency's role in case finding and service targeting, formal agreements and screening guidelines established among service providers can lighten the intake worker's task. Similarly, cross-training of workers within the agency and the community can improve coordination. One of the uses we envisioned for the chapters on services in this book is to serve as a springboard for such cross-training.

Summary

The agency's mission is vital to the intake worker's practice in that it specifies the agency's goals in serving the community. Screening criteria developed in light of this mission make the intake worker's job easier because potential clients can be more efficiently directed to sources of help. Intake is a vital social work activity. The process of helping people—some of whom are experiencing emergencies—to overcome difficulties in asking for help while promoting self-reliance, combined with a talent for matching needs with resources, requires a highly competent professional. As part of the family assessment and change method, intake is the first stage of the relationship between the client and helping professional. The knowledge, care, and sensitivity with which intake workers perform their complex responsibilities shape all subsequent interactions, and thus are critical to the success of any intervention.

Key Points

Excellent intake workers

- are among the agency's most capable and experienced workers
- understand the difficulties inherent in asking for and receiving help
- are adept at interviewing skills, aware of cultural diversity and how it shapes communication, and able to focus the potential client's attention on the problem at hand while allowing expression of associated emotions

- follow consistent methods for screening potential clients to see whether the agency has appropriate help to offer
- have a working knowledge of the agency's resources and a familiarity with eligibility guidelines
- can develop relationships with and know the mission of other human services providers within the community
- are prepared to handle diverse short-term cases, yet turn them over readily to other workers for longer-term interventions.

Excellent adult services managers

- acknowledge and support the professional nature of the intake function
- support the development of training in aging and aging services for intake workers
- ensure that intake workers have access to necessary training and supervision in interviewing, screening, crisis intervention and emergency services, agency and community resources, and cultural diversity
- develop interagency agreements that clarify the mission and target service populations of community service providers and support the development and dissemination of screening criteria to make it easier for clients to be directed to appropriate sources of assistance
- support necessary training for intake workers and develop or adopt appropriate screening tools for their use.

Excellent leaders

- support the classification of intake as a professional social work function that promotes the most efficient and effective use of agency and community resources
- support specialized training for intake workers in aging and aging-related services.

References

Bolland, J. M., & Wilson, J. V. (1991). *A network approach to the assessment and development of comprehensive coordination in the delivery of community-based services to the elderly.* Tuscaloosa: Institute for Social Science Research, University of Alabama.

Bumagin, V. E., & Hirn, K. F. (1990). *Helping the aging family: A guide for professionals.* Glenview, IL: Scott, Foresman.

Castex, G. M. (1994). Providing services to Hispanic/Latino populations: Profiles in diversity. *Social Work, 39,* 288–296.

Compton, B. R., & Gallaway, B. (1989). *Social work processes* (4th ed.). Belmont, CA: Wadsworth.

Gambrill, E. (1983). *Casework: A competency-based approach.* Englewood Cliffs, NJ: Prentice Hall.

Keith-Lucas, A. (1972). *Giving and taking help*. Chapel Hill: University of North Carolina Press.

Lambert, M. J., De Julio, S. S., & Stein, D. M. (1978). Therapist interpersonal skills: Process, outcome, methodological considerations, and recommendations for future research. *Psychological Bulletin, 85*, 467–489.

Mattaini, M. A., & Kirk, S. A. (1991). Assessing assessment in social work. *Social Work, 36*, 260–266.

Older Americans Act of 1965. P.L. 89-73, 79 Stat. 218.

Parad, H. J. (Ed.). (1965). *Crisis intervention: Selected readings*. New York: Family Service Association of America.

Proctor, E. K., & Davis, L. E. (1994). The challenge of racial difference: Skills in clinical practice. *Social Work, 39*, 314–323.

Rothman, J. (1991). A model of case management: Toward empirically based practice. *Social Work, 36*, 520–528.

Ryback, R. S. (1974). *The problem-oriented record in psychiatry and mental care*. New York: Grune & Stratton.

Steinberg, R., & Carter, G. (1983). *Case management and the elderly*. Lexington, MA: Lexington Books.

Williams, T. F., & Williams, M. (1982). Assessment of the elderly for long-term care. *Journal of the American Geriatrics Society, 30*(1), 71–75.

CHAPTER 5

Functional Assessment for Adult Clients

GARY M. NELSON

A multidimensional functional assessment is the cornerstone of the family assessment and change method outlined in chapter 3. The purpose of the assessment is to serve clients and their families by helping to ensure that they receive high-quality, appropriate care that facilitates positive change. In this sense, an assessment is a decision-making tool. To help clients collaborate in the design of good service plans, the social worker must help them identify their functional capacities and incapacities, strengths and problems in functioning, and the onset and history of any changes. The information gathered through the assessment is used to help make decisions about the types and amounts of services, if any, that clients require and the activities they can undertake to produce desired changes. Social workers make periodic reassessments to determine whether the service plan is working and whether the initial services and other interventions should be continued, changed, or discontinued (Bernstein, 1992; Kane, 1985).

Because functional assessment is critical to the family assessment and change method, this chapter reviews its major aspects. It identifies the purpose of formal assessments and highlights the reasons for basing assessment on function rather than diagnosis. During the intake process, as elaborated in chapter 4, the intake worker records, for each client, identifying data, a presenting problem and strengths, and a brief case history; performs screening activities; and initiates an emergency intervention, if needed. This chapter examines how that information is used as the beginning point for a functional assessment. It continues with a detailed discussion of the major elements of a comprehensive functional assessment, including each of six dimensions (environmental, social, economic, physical, mental, and activities of daily living [ADL] and instrumental activities of daily living [IADL]), and notes some tools that can be used in the process. Because clients and their families are often their own best resource, a thorough assessment takes into account the determination of clients' and families' strengths, values, and preferences, as well as what assistance or services they have already managed to arrange or provide for themselves. Finally, because clients' problems are often complex, the chapter concludes with a discussion of the role of multidisciplinary teams in assessment.

Why Make a Formal Assessment?

Properly made and used, assessments represent a major investment of social workers' time and resources, to say nothing of the clients' and families' time. Uniform, systematic assessments are essential to ensuring effective and high-quality services for clients (Gallo, Reichel, & Andersen, 1988; Kane & Kane, 1981). They help the social worker and client and families alike to reach decisions on appropriate levels of care, services, and treatments.

Without the information gathered through assessment, clients, families, and social workers have a limited basis for decision making, and the consequences of poor decisions have serious implications for clients individually, families as a whole, and for the system of care itself. Foley, Menar, and Schneider (1980) suggested some of these implications:

- *If more service is provided than is needed, the client may become more dependent.*
- *If less service is provided than needed, the client may suffer the consequences of inadequate care.*
- *Most service programs are demand-based; in the absence of good assessment information and guidelines about the allocation of services, inappropriate decisions tend to be self-perpetuating.*
- *Service or placement decisions that are more intensive than needed lead to unnecessary costs to the system.* (p. 1152)

Properly developed and implemented assessment tools offer many benefits. First, they help organize the worker's efforts and provide a checklist of items to address what otherwise might be overlooked. Second, assessments also provide a baseline against which the worker can observe improvement or deterioration in clients' functioning. The checklist for change, which captures the client's and family's current problems and aspirations for change, their goals, and their baseline functioning as recorded in the assessment, serves as a basis for accountability. Third, comprehensive assessments also can help social workers and managers address program and system objectives. Clearly documented in written case records and designed for incorporation in automated information systems or other compiled databases, assessments can help address and answer broader questions about the effectiveness and quality of programs and systems of care. For example, one way to measure effectiveness of adult protective services programs could be to examine recidivism rates associated with abuse and neglect cases according to the interventions used to remedy them.

Why Make a Functional Assessment?

The comprehensive assessment of clients' functional status and family context provides a clear basis for deciding on interventions and services because it examines the interaction between clients' abilities, motivation, and environment. All three of these factors are important to outcomes for clients. Identification of abilities requires a clear look at what an individual can realistically be expected to accomplish. The client's perception of whether a situation is problematic and his or her motivation to change determines how likely the client is to overcome what others might identify as obstacles. The client's environment—whether the physical setting or the social network of family, friends, and community—all figure in the client's ability to perceive and change problems.

Functional status may be influenced by medical or psychiatric diagnoses, but diagnoses do not predict functional status. Two adults with diabetes or heart conditions can and often do have different abilities to remain in the community and perform basic personal care and social functions. Adults with severe and persistent mental disorders may likewise demonstrate different abilities to remain in the community even when they have similar diagnoses.

Although adult services clients often experience chronic physical or mental health problems, what brings them to the adult services program for help is difficulty in functioning. Sometimes the assistance they need includes more or better medical or psychiatric care, and the adult services worker may be able to help them obtain it. However, the social worker's professional expertise is in helping clients eliminate or reduce problems in functioning by building on individual and family strengths as well as appropriate social interventions. Such an approach has implications for clients' well-being, whether their problems result from physical or mental health issues or from social, economic, or environmental factors in their lives. Therefore, decisions on interventions with adult clients and the monitoring of services provided must focus on changes and improvements in functioning rather than on the elimination of medical or psychiatric diagnoses. A functional assessment that captures the interplay between individual abilities, motivations, family context, and the social environment can provide the necessary data for making decisions about how to increase functional capacity through educational, social, medical, economic, or environmental interventions.

COMPREHENSIVE DATABASE FOR FUNCTIONAL ASSESSMENT

The foundation of the family assessment and change method and social work practice in adult services is development of a database for each client that includes the information from a comprehensive functional assessment. In many cases, central elements of that database may be gathered at intake (the client's identifying information, presenting problems and strengths, brief case history, and case screening), but this information also may be obtained or clarified during the comprehensive functional assessment.

To review the scope of the preliminary information (see chapter 4 for a more detailed description), the client's identifying data include important demographic information (name, address, telephone number, age, education, gender); source of the referral; basic information on family structure and caregivers, including medical and other services; and insurance and economic status. Some or all of this information should be in the documentation begun at intake, and the remainder should be added during the initial stages of the assessment process. The statement of the client's presenting problem (that is, the problem that brought the client to the agency) should be captured in a brief narrative. The presenting problem, however, may not be the problem that will ultimately be the focus of the service intervention.

The information gathered at intake also includes a brief case history that identifies the antecedents, onset, and implications or seriousness of the stated problems for the client's ability to function, as identified by clients or their families. Using a brief format for documentation, the adult services social worker records when the problem first began, what events triggered it, what the client's circumstances were when the problem began, and what the client and family have done to solve the problem. The importance of this last piece of information is that it helps the social worker gauge the client's and family's perception of the problem and the level of informal support for coping with it (Ryback, 1974).

Finally, there is case screening, which is a brief, standardized determination of the client's risk factors and needs. It identifies the potential clients who come to the agency who should be referred to other services in the community and those who can benefit from the agency's own programs and services. Additionally, screening should suggest to the intake worker which of the agency's programs is the most likely starting place. If the agency is large enough to have a specialized intake process, the social worker to whom the client has been referred may not need to perform a second screening. When there has been no screening, or when it has been too general, the social worker who receives the referral will probably want to make a screening, as it suggests the direction and emphasis of the assessment. The assessment is a detailed review of the client's functional status that leads directly to conclusions about impairments to be remedied and possible intervention strategies (Bernstein, 1992; Campbell & Thompson, 1990; Gallo et al., 1988; Ivry, 1992; Kane & Kane, 1981). For the adult services social worker, screening is a form of case finding or case confirmation, identifying individuals who could benefit from specific services or levels of care.

Screening procedures, processes, and assumptions are shaped by the agency's mission for its services and programs. Williams and Williams (1982) devised a screening method to sort individuals by level of care (see chapter 4). Fillenbaum (1985) developed a five-item IADL screening list that is easy to administer and answer and that can identify those individuals who need a more extensive assessment for community-based services. Responses to Fillenbaum's questions have been found to have a high correlation with the individual's physical and mental health. Such a screening might be conducted at intake, and depending on the answers, the client might be referred to a social worker who manages in-home services. If this screening, or one like it, was not performed at intake, the in-home services social worker might do it before deciding to proceed with a comprehensive assessment.

Comprehensive Functional Assessments

A comprehensive functional assessment is by definition multidimensional. The various dimensions or domains that must be assessed are environmental, social, economic, mental health, physical health, and capacity for self-care as assessed by ability to perform ADLs and IADLs (Gallo et al., 1988; Kane & Kane, 1981). Although these dimensions are assessed separately, they are often related and overlap. Capacity or impairment in any one dimension is likely to affect functioning in the others. For example, a person with Alzheimer's disease has a problem that is primarily one of physical health, but the individual will increasingly exhibit impairments in social and mental functioning and ADLs and IADLs as the disease progresses.

SOCIAL ASSESSMENT

An assessment of social functioning addresses both the quantity and the quality of the client's interpersonal ties and community involvement, as well as the possible burden on his or her informal support system. As the result of an extensive survey of the literature on social health, Donald (1982) identified four primary areas in which social interaction and participation take place: (1) family and home, (2) social friendships, (3) community involvement and participation, and (4) work. For most older people, the primary focus of a social assessment will involve the quality and quantity of ties with the informal support network outside of work (although according to the U.S. Department of Commerce [1990] approximately 12.1 percent of people over age 65 are in the workforce), whereas for younger clients work may play a bigger role in their social life and support system. For both younger and older adults, the informal support network of family and friends is central to well-being. One useful tool to assess family adaptation, partnership, growth, affection, and resolve, the family APGAR, measures social functioning in these dimensions (Smilkstein, Ashworth, & Montano, 1982).

Although it is important to note the number of people clients identify as part of their social environment, as well as the availability and the frequency of contact with them, it is the quality of the social support network and the presence of a confidant that often is most important for personal well-being and physical health status (Antonucci, 1985; Donald, 1983). An understanding of the client's family network and broader social support system can be gained from a combination of standardized questions as well as a genogram and an ecomap (Garvin & Seabury, 1984). The genogram identifies an individual's family network, and the ecomap outlines the individual's social network, including active familial and community relationships.

The genogram is a useful tool for gathering and making a graphic representation of family composition and history. Genograms also can capture major changes in health status, family events (births, deaths, marriages, relocations), and occupations. By using different mapping techniques, such as solid, dotted, or hatched lines, the strength, tenuousness, or stress associated with different relationships can be represented. Drawing a genogram can be a useful technique for identifying the family support system and for understanding the health and social history of the family as it relates to current relationships and problems. Assessments of caregiver burden should supplement an assessment of family functioning. Such assessment tools (Biegel & Blum, 1990; Gallo et al., 1988) can help capture both caregivers' strengths as well as burdens associated with caring for adults with disabilities (Figure 5-1).

The ecomap is a useful tool for mapping clients' degree of connectedness with the community and social supports, as well as with families. One could use a

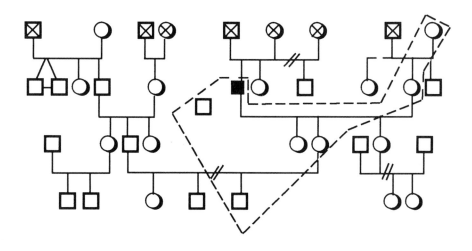

Figure 5-1

A SAMPLE GENOGRAM INTERPRETATION

This male client has been married once and lives with his wife, mother-in-law, his eldest daughter who is single, his middle divorced daughter and her younger son, and his male friend. Outside the home he has a living sister and half brother, a youngest daughter and her second husband, two granddaughters by his youngest daughter and another granddaughter and grandson by his middle daughter and her divorced husband. His parents are not living. His wife has a living brother and an out-of-wedlock stepsister.

ready-made tool with preset circles (Figure 5-2) or a blank piece of paper to draw a schematic diagram of the client's social world, identifying potential friendships and involvements in recreational and cultural activities, work, church, and health and human services agencies. Different types of lines (for example, solid, dotted, and hatched) and the proximity of elements can represent the nature of the relationship between the client and others in his or her social environment. Having clients draw and explain their own ecomaps or having the social worker make the drawing as clients describe their social world can elicit a remarkable amount of information relevant to this and other areas of the assessment in a short time.

Just as computerization has eased production of spreadsheets in business applications, it also can help produce graphics for clinical practice. A number of commercially available software programs can produce family trees and genograms, and the Visual EcoScan (Mattaini, 1993) produces graphics for examining cases at multiple systemic levels.

To assess the depth of an individual's social support network, more specific questions may be needed. These might address not only whom the client can call on for support but also for how long and in what circumstances. For example, a client who needs some support to live at home might have a neighbor who has been helpful in the past. In planning services, it would be useful to know whether that neighbor might be willing to telephone the client daily, visit, fix an occasional meal, or spend several hours per day doing little jobs around the house.

ECONOMIC ASSESSMENT

Economic assessment examines the adequacy of clients' income and economic resources, as well as the determination of eligibility for additional assistance. Establishing the adequacy of financial resources involves assessing whether the client has sufficient resources to obtain food, shelter, clothing, medical care, and other necessities (Gallo et al., 1988). Eligibility for additional resources involves knowing and assessing whether the client is aware of rights to and possible eligibility for such health, social, or economic resources as Medicaid, respite services, Supplemental Security Income (SSI), or special employment programs.

Establishing the adequacy of an individual's economic resources involves asking questions that identify income, assets, and expenditures of the client to assess whether income and resources are adequate and also whether the client has disproportionate expenses in any given area that jeopardize other needs. For example, a client who spends all of his or her resources for rent and food may have no money for medication.

Economic assessment involves looking at and beyond income. It may be easy for the social worker to identify resources directly available to the individual (for example, a monthly social security check, paycheck, or the balance of a savings account). Clients also may have indirect resources (for example, financial assistance that could include "in-kind" contributions such as regular meals pro-

Name: Mrs. E.
Date: 1/28/95

Brief History: Recently widowed, Mrs. E. becomes frightened at night and calls her son late and repeatedly, which makes it difficult for him to work. Son says that she has left bills unpaid, wears dirty clothing even though she has a washer, seems not to be eating (she has lost weight). This eco-map shows real and potential resources, areas in which Mrs. E. earlier made contributions, domains in which to seek out new resources.

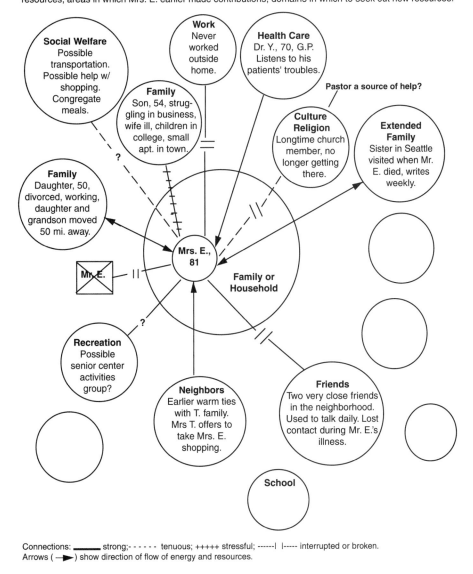

Connections: _____ strong; - - - - - tenuous; +++++ stressful; ------| |----- interrupted or broken.
Arrows (➤) show direction of flow of energy and resources.

Figure 5-2 ———————————————————

A SAMPLE ECOMAP

vided by a family member) or possibly the conversion of home equity into a monthly income annuity that can be used for ongoing expenses. Beyond accounting for the client's assets, though, the social worker also must consider such subjective concerns as the client's values concerning budgeting and money management. Because this is an area in which people hold different values, social workers should be aware of their own values when it comes to identifying clients' resources and assessing financial need or difficulties in managing money.

Determining eligibility for a range of health, social, and economic benefits requires that the worker have some knowledge of the basic eligibility requirements and limits for various federal, state, and local programs to which clients may be entitled as a result of their income, age, or functional disability. The Job Opportunities and Basic Skills Training (JOBS) program for families who qualify for Aid to Families with Dependent Children, food stamps, Medicaid and Medicare, the mental health system, and the aging services network all may offer meaningful benefits and opportunities for eligible adult services clients and families. However, the health and human services system is a complex and confusing maze for those trying to gain access to it. Through assessment, social workers can help clients learn about programs, interpret regulations, and benefit from available resources.

MENTAL HEALTH

Mental health status assessments for adult services clients focus on behavioral and psychological problems that impair individual functioning in one or more areas. The social worker must consider two areas of mental health in particular, cognitive functioning and emotional well-being (Hinrichsen, 1990; Turner, 1992). There are few assessment protocols whose goal is to identify good mental health. Rather, assessments in this area focus on self-reports and observation for symptoms of cognitive incapacity, psychiatric disorders, or other risks. Most assessment instruments ask the client (and in some cases a caregiver) to identify either the presence or absence of impairment. A number of short mental health status questionnaires have been developed and used for many years for assessing older clients (Folstein, Folstein, & McHugh, 1975; Kahn, Goldfarb, Pollack, & Peck, 1960; Pfeiffer, 1975). A more recent test, the six-item short blessed test (Katzman et al., 1983), also has proved reliable.

Emotional health refers to an absence or remission of affective disorders that reduce functioning. Social workers should be familiar with the symptoms and manifestations of the major affective disorders. They also should recognize anxiety, depression, loneliness, and the risk factors associated with suicide and with alcohol and substance abuse (Hinrichsen, 1990; Turner, 1992). The modified Beck, Ward, Mendelson, Mock, and Erbaugh (1961) depression inventory and Yesavage and Brink's (1983) geriatric depression scale are frequently used with older clients. Workers who have questions about clients' cognitive or emotional functioning should consult with experts qualified in those areas.

PHYSICAL HEALTH

Three tools exist that social workers may use to evaluate clients' physical health status: (1) clients' self-assessment of health, (2) checklists of symptoms and illnesses, and (3) reviews of clients' use of medications. Bernstein (1992) provided a descriptive overview for health care providers of common health problems and their implications for intervention with individuals with disabilities and older adults.

Although self-assessments and checklists of symptoms may suggest needed medical services, they do not necessarily predict impaired functioning. By assessing risks to physical health, social workers may uncover evidence of untreated conditions that need follow-up or noncompliance with current medical regimens that threaten the client's well-being. For example, the social worker who learns that an older client is experiencing frequent falls must discuss arranging a medical appointment for the client and possibly accompany the client. Similarly, if the social worker reviews medications with a client who has chronic mental illness and learns that he or she has stopped taking prescribed medication, the social worker must encourage the client to see a mental health worker or psychiatrist and discuss the consequences of not taking medications.

Health Self-Assessments

Self-assessment of health is a good indicator of health status and the use of health-related services in a population, but Maddox (1962) expressed some reservations about how well self-assessments capture health status for the individual. One purpose of this type of assessment is to screen for potential health problems or decline in health status. The Philadelphia Geriatric Center's multidimensional functional assessment instrument (Lawton, Moss, Fulcomer, & Kleban, 1982) is useful for older adults. It asks, "How would you rate your overall health at the present time? Excellent (3), good (2), fair (1), or poor (0)?" This or similar wording may be used to obtain a measure of self-assessed health.

Symptoms Approach to Health Assessment

The first symptoms approach to physical health assessment was developed in the late 1940s, and since then other checklists have been developed to correspond to different assessment protocols. Symptom checklists identify health risk factors that warrant medical attention. The tool used by the World Health Organization focuses on four key symptoms to identify health risk factors: (1) phlegm, (2) pain or pressure, (3) joint pain, and (4) shortness of breath (Fillenbaum, 1984). The comprehensive assessment and referral evaluation (CARE), developed for a long-term-care population, has been used to identify other health risk factors such as malnutrition, visual problems, and arthritis (Gurland et al., 1977).

Another way to assess physical health status is by inquiring about chronic conditions and diagnosed illnesses, using a structured rather than an open-ended form for greater reliability. The listing of conditions and diagnosed illnesses is more likely to ensure that certain important health items, such as dental, nutrition, and hearing problems, are not left out. Research into the accuracy of such assessments, however, tends to find underreports of chronic health problems and illnesses (Fillenbaum, 1984). Not all clients have regular contact with medical services or understand the diagnostic terminology used to describe their condition. Findings may point to the need for more routine health assessments and check-ups by qualified health professionals.

Thornton's (1989) handbook is a useful and easily understood guide to common health problems and treatments for older adults. This and similar lay health and medical handbooks can provide guidance to the practice of adult services social workers, as well as serving as valuable informational aids to clients and their families.

Use of Medications

Another important area to assess is the client's use of medications, including a comprehensive listing of medications taken, including when, how, and the dosage of each. It is important to ask about use of over-the-counter drugs and home remedies as well as prescriptions. Issues that may arise around medication usage include multiple prescription of drugs, dose-related complications, and compliance with medication regimens (Giannetti, 1983; Libow & Sherman, 1981). Some clients with memory impairments (often older people) make significant errors in compliance with medication regimens and risk adverse drug reactions. Illiteracy can complicate this matter.

Other factors that may lead to noncompliance include lack of clear written instructions, the cost of medications, or emotional problems such as depression that result in a refusal to acknowledge an illness and take medications properly. Additionally, clients may have religious reasons for not taking medications, or significant side effects may discourage them from complying. A social worker who finds that a client takes three or more medications (prescription and over the counter) should have an appropriate health care professional review the regimen. Additionally, unexplained changes in physiological status such as confusion, depression, irritability, vomiting, or diarrhea may result from drug interactions or inappropriate self-medication (Giannetti, 1983).

ASSESSING ADLS AND IADLS

Of all the dimensions of personal functioning, the ability to carry out ADLs is probably the most important. Performance in basic self-care activities is necessary to maintain independent functioning and is often related to the individual's physical, mental, and social well-being. Beyond the measure of ADLs is the related assessment of IADLs, which contribute to the client's ability to function in the community. General health assessments have limited value in predicting how independent the client can be, whereas measures of ADL and IADL functioning give a good picture of a client's ability to be self-sufficient.

Significant agreement exists about what constitutes ADLs. Almost all scales include some combination of bathing, toileting, dressing, transfer (that is, getting from bed to chair), and eating (Gallo et al., 1988; Kane & Kane, 1981). The best known, most valid and reliable measure is the Katz Index of ADLs (Katz, Ford, Moskowitz, Jackson, & Jaffee, 1963), which asks whether the client can perform the five above-mentioned activities, as well as whether the client is incontinent. Although the final rating focuses on whether the client can manage these activities (yes or no), the form allows for differentiation of those who can do them with human assistance and those who can do them independently (without supervision, direction, or active personal assistance). More easily applied versions of the form assign points: 0 for no help needed; 1, uses a device; 2, needs human assistance; 3, completely dependent (Kane & Kane, 1981).

Less agreement exists on what constitutes an appropriate assessment of IADLs. The IADL assessment addresses a range of activities more complex than those having to do with self-care and maintenance. Items typically included are activities and tasks performed in the home or immediate social environment. Capacity for performing them is broadly construed as being related to the individual's social competence (Fillenbaum, 1985; Katz et al., 1963).

An example of an IADL assessment form is the one used by the Suncoast Gerontology Center. It covers six areas: (1) ability to use the telephone, (2) ability to use transportation, (3) ability to shop for food and clothing, (4) ability to prepare meals, (5) ability to do housework, and (6) ability to take care of money and financial matters. Each item is rated using a three-point scale in which a score of 1 indicates that the individual can perform the activity with no assistance; 2, a need for some assistance; and 3, complete inability to perform the activity.

ENVIRONMENTAL ASSESSMENT

Environmental assessment finds its origin in the concept, long at the heart of social work, of a fit between the person and the environment. An environmental assessment ascertains whether surroundings contribute to or detract from the individual's independent functioning and well-being. The environment may be as narrowly defined as the home or institution in which clients live or as broadly defined as the community of which they are members. The assessment of the community may overlap some of the aspects covered in the social assessment as captured using the ecomap. Assessment of the environment involves the examination of the functional abilities of the individual and the demands of the environment narrowly and broadly defined, followed by an appraisal of the degree of congruence between the two.

Although considerable agreement exists on the importance of the environment for clients' optimal functioning, there is less agreement on how to assess it. Much of the literature focuses on institutional settings such as nursing homes (McCaffree & Harkins, 1976) or noninstitutional congregate living situations (Hulicka, Morganti, & Cataldo, 1975; Moos, Grauvian, Max, & Mehran, 1979). Less has been written about adults living in the community (Lawton, 1980).

One of the categories that researchers agree on is the adequacy and safety of the architectural environment, whether private residence or institution. For example, there are checklists that review fire safety, accessibility of kitchen appliances, and the absence of obstacles such as cords, scatter rugs, and poorly lit areas. In the community, one might consider whether the client can walk safely on streets or has easy access to transportation.

A second category captures more subjective and inclusive aspects of the "emotional environment" and "interpersonal opportunities." An assessment of the emotional environment in an institutional setting addresses such things as the courtesy of staff members, their attention to clients' social and health needs, and their respect for clients' privacy and freedom of choice. In a household, this would include an evaluation of the interaction between members that focuses on how it supports or interferes with clients' functioning. Assessment of interpersonal opportunities addresses the question of whether clients are able to have contact with friends and family members or play an active role in civic and voluntary groups.

The third category focuses specifically on instrumental activities. For instance, does the client's home have adequate cooking and refrigeration facilities to prepare and keep food? Does the client have easy access to a telephone or some other way of getting help in an emergency? An assessment also may address the issue of whether the size and structure of the home (for example, stairs) present a problem of upkeep or a barrier to moving around for a person with impairments. With reference to community, the focus is on whether the client has ready access to shopping, health and social services, and recreation and volunteer or civic opportunities, by walking or by using private or public transportation.

The environmental assessment should be adapted to the client's specific setting or community to evaluate the degree of fit between the person and the environment as well as to help identify possible areas of intervention and modification. One tool that addresses both the home and community, as well as issues of environmental adequacy and safety, is the Thomas (1985) environmental assessment inventory, which uses Maslow's concept of levels of well-being as a method for indexing and assessing the impact of the environment on an individual's functional well-being.

McKnight and Kretzmann (1992) discussed mapping community capacity by identifying strengths or assets in community resources. As a counterpoint to the usual problem-centered approach to needs assessments for both clients and communities, their approach coincides with the general approach taken throughout this book, namely that change comes through building on the capacities, skills, and assets of adults, their families, and communities. An inventory of the capacity and resources of communities, individuals, and families recognizes all of these parties, singly and together, as agents of change responsible for their own fates.

Additional Considerations for Assessments

Besides assessing individual functioning in the six dimensions already identified, social workers also should inventory clients' strengths, the services they are currently receiving, and their values and preferences about the interventions and services they wish to receive (Cowger, 1994). Questions relating to these considerations may be asked throughout the assessment process rather than covered independently.

CLIENTS' STRENGTHS

In public social services, it is often the practice to focus, at times almost exclusively, on clients' problems, risks, and pathologies. It is problems that bring clients to the agency for help. However, in keeping with the emphasis on empowering clients, social workers also should gather information on the client's and the family's strengths (Bricker-Jenkins, 1990; Saleebey, 1992), because these are often the client's best resource. The social worker who seeks to engage clients and their families fully in self-care must assess the resources and opportunities they bring to the problem-solving process. The assessment offers ample occasion for doing this. For example, assessment of social functioning through the compilation of a list of strengths and a list of problems can identify resources in the client's family network and larger social and community environment. Building questions about personal strengths into the assessment process helps reinforce a balanced and integrated approach to problem solving by pointing out to the client what resources are already available and suggesting better ways to make use of them.

CLIENTS' PREFERENCES

Assessing clients' preferences is of central importance to the assessment and especially to the subsequent process of planning services. Clients exhibit different degrees of willingness, hardiness, and capability to live with perceived hardships and problems, not all of which can always be completely addressed. Individuals also demonstrate different degrees of willingness to assume risk—perhaps the risk of falling because of infirmity or the risk of failing at a new challenge such as a new job or treatment program. Many of these differences arise from values the clients hold. For many, the value of remaining at home may outweigh any increase in safety and care associated with moving to a board-and-care home or nursing facility (Kane, 1985). The value of having family close by may influence a client not to leave an apparently abusive situation. In all these cases, the social worker must shape interventions that acknowledge and respect the value systems of clients, even when the social worker's own values are strongly challenged. Identifying clients' values and preferences as they relate to identified problems, strengths, service preferences, and ethical and moral considerations is a critical part of a thorough assessment (Gallo et al., 1988). Clients will not participate successfully in interventions that conflict with their values or do not meet their preferences, making all the social worker's efforts useless.

SERVICES RECEIVED

Kane (1985) made the point that, in addition to uncovering clients' unmet needs, assessments should identify services they are already receiving. In identifying such services, the assessment should distinguish between those provided formally by a public or private entity and those provided informally by families and friends. In either case, but particularly with informal providers, the social worker also should examine how stable the assistance is and its intensity for the provider. For example, does the client rely totally on one daughter for care or is there a small rotating network of family and friends who provide assistance and support? Knowledge of what help the client already receives and what needs are still unmet helps the adult services social worker assist the client better in constructing a well-designed and integrated service plan. Knowledge of all services involved also helps the worker and agency make judgments about possible duplication of services and overall service plan costs to make the most efficient use of scarce agency resources.

Multidisciplinary Teams

Assessment of adults requires social workers to be familiar with many different domains of functioning, but social workers are not equally expert or comfortable in all areas. Multidimensional assessments may at times require the participation of a multidisciplinary team. Depending on the client's presenting problem, team members can include mental health specialists, physicians, nurses, and allied health professionals. In certain instances, adult services social workers may have access to a nurse on the agency's staff, but gaining access to experts in other disciplines will require the worker to know whom to contact and how to contact them. Some agencies have already established teams to review challenging adult services cases, but in most instances workers will have to pull together a team themselves. Quality assessments and the quality of the intervention depends on having access to accurate and timely assessment information. In all, adult services social workers must know the strengths and limits of their own knowledge and when to seek expertise from others.

Summary

The comprehensive functional assessment provides the knowledge base on which clients, families, and social workers begin their work together. Functioning, rather than diagnosis, is the basis of the assessment because it is a more reliable indicator of an individual's resources for making change. A comprehensive assessment considers functioning in six domains: (1) social, (2) environmental, (3) mental health, (4) physical health, (5) ADLs (including personal care and instrumental), and (6) economic. Diminished functioning in any domain usually affects functioning in others, but conversely, strengths in some domains can often be used to compensate for impairments in others. A carefully made formal assessment provides a solid foundation for identifying problems and areas for change and for setting the stage for the development of goals and service plans.

Key Points

Excellent adult services social workers
- understand the distinction between functional assessment and diagnosis

- conduct a functional assessment in the social, economic, mental, physical, ADL and IADL, and environmental domains
- assess clients' strengths and problems
- assess the services the client currently receives as well as the client's values and preferences
- know the strengths and limits of their own knowledge and when to seek help from others.

Excellent adult services managers
- provide administrative support for comprehensive functional assessments of adult clients when developing workload plans
- provide administrative support for comprehensive functional assessments when developing training plans
- provide supervisory support to social workers in the implementation, refinement, and use of functional assessments
- encourage and support the use of multidisciplinary teams, both formally and informally.

Excellent leaders
- provide support to adult services managers and social workers for conducting functional assessments through policy, guidance, training, and other initiatives.

References

Antonucci, T. C. (1985). Personal characteristics, social support, and social behavior. In R. H. Binstock & E. Shanas (Eds.), *Handbook of aging and the social sciences* (pp. 94–128). New York: Van Nostrand Reinhold.

Beck, A. T., Ward, C. A., Mendelson, M., Mock, J., & Erbaugh, J. (1961). An inventory for measuring depression. *Archives of General Psychiatry, 4,* 53–63.

Bernstein, L. H. (1992, December). Functional Facts™: A public health approach to functional assessment. *CARING Magazine,* pp. 32–38.

Biegel, D. E., & Blum, A. (Eds.). (1990). *Aging and caregiving: Theory, research and policy.* Newbury Park, CA: Sage Publications.

Bricker-Jenkins, M. (1990, Spring). Another approach to practice and training. *Public Welfare,* pp. 11–16.

Campbell, L. A., & Thompson, B. L. (1990, August). Evaluating elderly patients: A critique of comprehensive functional assessment tools. *Nurse Practitioner,* pp. 11–18.

Cowger, C. D. (1994). Assessing client strengths: Clinical assessment for client empowerment. *Social Work, 39,* 262–268.

Donald, A. (1983). Social supports for the elderly. In R. J. Vogel & A. C. Palmer (Eds.), *Long-term care* (pp. 270–291). Washington, DC: Health Care Financing Administration.

Fillenbaum, G. G. (1984). Assessing the well-being of the elderly. *Advances in Research, 8,* 1–10.

Fillenbaum, G. G. (1985). Screening the elderly: A brief instrumental activities of daily living measure. *Journal of the American Geriatrics Society, 23*(10), 698–706.

Foley, W. J., Menar, M. S., & Schneider, D. R. (1980). A comparison of the level of care predictions of six long-term care patient assessment systems. *American Journal of Public Health, 70,* 1152–1161.

Folstein, M. F., Folstein, S., & McHugh, P. R. (1975). Mini-mental state: A practical method for grading the cognitive state of patients for the clinician. *Journal of Psychiatric Research, 12,* 189–198.

Gallo, J. J., Reichel, W., & Andersen, L. (1988). *Handbook of geriatric assessment.* Rockville, MD: Aspen Publishers.

Garvin, C. D., & Seabury, B. A. (1984). *Interpersonal practice in social work.* Englewood Cliffs, NJ: Prentice Hall.

Giannetti, V. J. (1983). Medication utilization problems among the elderly. *Health & Social Work, 8,* 262–270.

Gurland, B., Kuriansky, J., Sharpe, L., Simm, R., Stiller, P., & Birkett, P. (1977). The comprehensive assessment and referral evaluation (CARE). *International Journal of Aging and Human Development, 8,* 9–42.

Hinrichsen, G. A. (1990). *Mental health problems and older adults: Choices and challenges.* Santa Barbara, CA: ABC-CLIO.

Hulicka, J., Morganti, J., & Cataldo, J. (1975). Perceived latitude of choice of institutionalized and non-institutionalized elderly women. *Experimental Aging Research, 1,* 27–39.

Ivry, J. (1992). Teaching geriatric assessment. In M. J. Mellor & R. Solomon (Eds.), *Geriatric social work education* (pp. 3–22). New York: Haworth.

Kahn, R. L., Goldfarb, A. I., Pollack, M., & Peck, A. (1960). Brief objective measures for the determination of mental status in the aged. *American Journal of Psychiatry, 117,* 326–328.

Kane, R. A. (1985). Assessing the elderly client. In A. Monk (Ed.), *Handbook of gerontological services* (pp. 43–69). New York: Van Nostrand Reinhold.

Kane, R. A., & Kane, R. L. (1981). *Assessing the elderly: A practical guide to measurement.* Lexington, MA: Lexington Books.

Katz, S., Ford, A. B., Moskowitz, R. W., Jackson, B. A., & Jaffee, M. W. (1963). Studies of illness in the aged. The index of ADL: A standardized measure of biological and psychosocial function. *Journal of the American Medical Association, 185,* 914–919.

Katzman, R., Brown, T., Fuld, P., Peck, A., Schechter, R., & Schimmel, H. (1983, June). Validation of a short orientation-memory-concentration test of cognitive impairment. *American Journal of Psychiatry, 140,* 734–739.

Lawton, M. P. (1980). *Environment and aging.* Monterey, CA: Brooks/Cole.

Lawton, M. P., Moss, M., Fulcomer, M., & Kleban, M. A. (1982). A research and service oriented multilevel assessment instrument. *Journal of Gerontology, 37,* 91–99.

Libow, L., & Sherman, F. T. (1981). Interviewing and history taking. In L. Libow & F. T. Sherman (Eds.), *The core of geriatric medicine* (pp. 37–58). St. Louis: C. V. Mosby.

Maddox, G. L. (1962). Some correlates of differences in self-assessments of health status among the elderly. *Journal of Gerontology, 17,* 180–185.

Mattaini, M. A. (1993). Visual EcoScan for Clinical Practice (Version 1.0) [Computer software]. Washington, DC: NASW Press.

McCaffree, K. M., & Harkins, E. M. (1976). *Final report for evaluation of the outcomes of nursing home care.* Seattle: Battelle Human Affairs Research Center.

McKnight, J. L., & Kretzmann, J. (1992). *Mapping community capacity.* Evanston, IL: Center for Urban Affairs and Policy Research.

Moos, R. H., Grauvian, M., Max, S. W., & Mehran, B. (1979). Assessing the environments of sheltered care settings. *Gerontologist, 19,* 74–82.

Pfeiffer, E. (1975). A short portable mental status questionnaire for the assessment of organic brain deficit in elderly patients. *Journal of the American Geriatrics Society, 32,* 433–441.

Ryback, R. S. (1974). *The problem-oriented record in psychiatry and mental care.* New York: Grune & Stratton.

Saleebey, D. (Ed.). (1992). *The strengths perspective in social work practice.* New York: Longman.

Smilkstein, G., Ashworth, C., & Montano, D. (1982). Validity and reliability of the family APGAR as a test of family function. *Journal of Family Practice, 15,* 303–311.

Thomas, J. D. (1985). Assessing and adapting the home environment. In M. Hogstel (Ed.), *Home nursing care for the elderly* (pp. 107–130). Bowie, MD: Brady Communication.

Thornton, H. A. (1989). *A medical handbook for senior citizens and their families.* Dover, MA: Auburn House.

Turner, F. J. (1992). *Mental health and the elderly: A social work perspective.* New York: Free Press.

U.S. Department of Commerce, Bureau of the Census. (1990). *1990 Census of population. Social and economic characteristics* (CP-2-1). Washington, DC: U.S. Government Printing Office.

Williams, T. F., & Williams, M. (1982). Assessment of the elderly for long-term care. *Journal of the American Geriatrics Society, 30*(1), 71–75.

Yesavage, J. A., & Brink, T. L. (1983). Development and validation of a geriatric depression screening scale: A preliminary report. *Journal of Psychiatric Research, 17*(1), 37–49.

CHAPTER 6

Case Management

GARY M. NELSON

Adult services social work helps people overcome their problems and make positive changes by capitalizing on their strengths; accessing formal and informal resources; and, if needed, engaging them in a therapeutic, counseling relationship to overcome barriers to functioning. Case management and counseling are the two principal service intervention strategies provided directly by social workers as a result of the assessment conducted according to the family assessment and change method outlined in chapter 3. These intervention strategies represent more-narrowly defined interventions of the adult services practice method. In the context of a family-centered approach, they are both intended to promote the general goal of empowering adult clients to assume control of their circumstances successfully.

Case management, according to White (1987), "is a service function directed at coordinating existing resources to assure appropriate and continuous care for individuals on a case-by-case basis" (p. 92). The identification of case management as a professional component of adult services practice recognizes the needs of adult clients, honors their requests for concrete resources, and acknowledges the knowledge and skills necessary for social workers to address these needs and requests.

Brief History of Case Management

The history of case management is rooted in the early emergence of the field of social work. The efforts of interdenominational groups in the 1830s to provide mutual consultation and aid in helping poor people used some of the primary tenets of case management (Grisham, White, & Miller, 1983). Massachusetts established one of the earliest case management programs under the aegis of its Board of Charities in 1863 (Greene, 1987). The dual purpose of that early effort has a familiar ring even today: to coordinate public services and conserve public funds. Present-day Medicaid-waiver programs for community-based care share that objective. The contributions of early social reformers and social workers such as Mary Richmond, Jane Addams, and Joseph Tuckerman established a basis for many current case management standards. These workers stressed the importance of trained staff, encouraged working relationships with other disciplines, and underscored the importance of understanding the objectives and methods of other organizations engaged in helping people in need. They also recognized and supported comprehensive assessments and fostered the development of the case conference as a mechanism for bringing multidisciplinary specialists together in a common problem-solving and change-oriented forum. Rothman (1991) emphasized the importance of case management for empirically based, outcome-oriented practice.

The pioneer efforts in case management often were submerged in the general practices of casework, community work, and social work. In this book both case management and counseling are seen as specific interventions associated with a generalist, family-centered practice method. Discrete case management programs and positions that carried the title "case manager" began to emerge only in the late 1960s and early 1970s (Kaplan, 1990). The rapid growth during this period of categorical social programs (programs aimed at different populations and funded through separate legislation) was accompanied by a corresponding sense of fragmentation, resulting in calls for increased coordination and integration of services for clients.

In 1972 the federal government identified coordination and integration of social services as priority issues for ensuring the efficient use of resources and appropriate access to needed services. Case management became a central component of a number of federal initiatives: in 1972, the Services Integration Targets for Opportunity; in 1975, the Education for All Handicapped Children Act; in 1977, the revised Community Mental Health Legislation; and in 1988, the Special Education Act and the Family Support Act. Case management also has become a prominent feature of home and community care efforts for older adults (National Governors Association, 1988). Case management seemed so essential and successful that in 1985 Congress encouraged its inclusion as an optional service under Medicaid as part of the Consolidated Budget Reconciliation Act of 1988. Nationally, case management in adult services programs has been around since the early days of Title XX of the Social Security Act Amendments of 1974.

Case Management as an Intervention Strategy

The family assessment and change method focuses on factors that contribute to problems in the client's and family's functioning and on factors, strengths, and capacities that help either to overcome or to ameliorate these problems. Many functional problems have their origin with the client, perhaps as nonproductive beliefs or emotional difficulties, whereas others stem from external sources, perhaps as constraints in accessing needed material resources. Some problems may stem from a combination of internal and external barriers, and, regardless of the source, problems in one area will often create new problems in the other. Similarly, individual and family strengths and capacities may be found in a mixture of internal psychological assets and family traits and external individual and family social and community networks.

Case management involves a set of intervention skills that can be used, once the nature of the problem and strengths have been assessed, to access and coordinate both tangible and intangible resources to address instrumental and psychological issues. Case management can both marshal tangible resources to support individuals and families and teach more intangible problem-solving and change-oriented skills.

The family assessment and change method is used to assess whether case management or counseling or some combination of these two intervention strategies is most appropriate for a particular client or family. This is adult services social work practice at its best. There is, however, an important distinction to be made between the family assessment and change method, which underlies adult services social work practice, and its two central intervention strategies. Besides including many of the discrete steps frequently associated with "traditional" case management as described in the social work literature (see, for example, Applebaum & Austin, 1990; Rothman, 1991), the family assessment and change method also includes such clinical skills as crisis intervention and counseling, community development and advocacy skills, program-specific skills, and record-keeping skills. Case management is the service intervention strategy by which social workers marshal needed resources, link clients to informal and formal support networks, and monitor services. As such, the primary focus of this chapter is on the activities and roles of social workers.

Before case management as an intervention strategy begins, the social worker as case manager will have completed with the client the beginning steps of the family assessment and change method: functional assessment, identification of problems and strengths, compilation of a change list, and the setting of functional goals with the individual and family. Once the decision to provide services has been made and the goals and plan determined, the remaining steps of the method coincide with the principal activities of case management. Planning and linking clients to informal and formal service providers and monitoring the services once they are in place are the basis of resource coordination. The rest of this chapter addresses both of these activities.

Steps in Case Management

CORE KNOWLEDGE AND SKILLS FOR SERVICE PLANNING

The development of a service plan based on findings from the assessment requires that social workers know what goes into a service plan, which functional deficits might be remedied with which resources, what strengths can be built on and restored, and how to link clients with these resources. A service plan is an agenda for action by all involved parties—the client; the client's family, friends, and neighbors; the social worker; the adult services program; and all other involved service providers.

Characteristics of a Service Plan

The elements of a written service plan are elaborated in other chapters, including those on the family assessment and change method (chapter 3) and on record keeping (chapter 9). The service plan should be recorded on a standard agency form or using a standard format that captures the following six essential elements: (1) change list, (2) performance goals for the client and, when appropriate, goals for the family, (3) the tasks and resources for which the client is responsible, (4) the tasks and resources for which the members of the client's informal support network are responsible, (5) the resources to be obtained from the adult services program and other agencies, and (6) those events or developments that will trigger a reassessment of the client's progress or maintenance of functioning.

Functional Scope of a Service Plan

The goal of using the family assessment and change method, and through it, functional assessment, is to bring appropriate resources to bear on those tangible and intangible barriers that reduce the client's optimal functioning. Decisions about what resources to use as service interventions should flow directly from the assessment and the client's and family's desired change list and should focus on the client's and family's instrumental and affective needs.

Instrumental needs and the resources to address them include such matters as income, help with transportation, assistance with activities of daily living (ADLs), meals, and basic home maintenance. Affective needs are addressed through the use of resources that support psychosocial functioning. Although family and friends may be one of the better resources, the community may offer such complementary needed services as psychiatric day treatment programs, counseling, respite care, socialization through senior centers, or friendly visiting programs (Steinberg & Carter, 1983).

Regardless of the focus of any given service, social workers and clients also should try to identify additional benefits that the service may offer. For example, participation in a congregate meal program can address the client's need for improved nutrition and, as a secondary benefit, provide an outlet for socialization. The benefit of a comprehensive functional assessment is that it helps identify needs in all areas. Resources also should be assessed from the functional perspective, to see what possible help they can offer in areas that are not necessarily their primary focus. In a time of scarce resources, efficiently using those that are available is a primary consideration.

Planning services can—and should, whenever possible—go beyond merely putting a bandage on the problem to exploring strategies for enabling and empowering clients and families to build their capacities for self-care and problem prevention. This may include developing new attitudes about problems and the approach to living with them, because some problems cannot be entirely resolved. One goal for case managers is to put themselves out of a job, by modeling for clients and families how to identify resources (both internal and external), how to match them with needs, how to make a plan of action, how to implement it, and how to modify it when necessary. The goal is to demonstrate for clients and families how to be their own effective case managers and so return choice and control to them.

Linking with the Informal Social Support Network

The term "social support network" combines two interrelated concepts, social network and social support. *Social network* generally refers to a specific set of interrelated people. The social worker's assessment may identify the client's social network as being made up of family members, friends, and neighbors. *Social support* refers to a broader array of social relationships. It may include participation in voluntary associations and formal and informal relationships among family, friends, and colleagues (Specht, 1988). For this discussion, the social support network involves integrating both concepts in a manner that focuses on all the social ties and connections that can be tapped and enhanced to support the functioning of a client.

Based on an extensive review of research on social networks and social support, Ell (1984) held that

> not only do social ties increase individual well-being, but they also seem to enhance people's immunity to physical illness and psychological disorders, aid in problem-solving and coping, and increase the likelihood of positive outcomes. Supportive social ties help individuals maintain a balance between environmental demands and personal resources, thereby enhancing host resistance to pathogenic agents such as disease and stress. Support systems are more readily subject to intervention than life stresses, and social work has a rich tradition of experience in working toward enhancing support exchange within primary networks as well as in developing support systems for persons with special needs. (pp. 143–144)

Interpreting assessment data for possible social support interventions can result in a range of options for adult services clients. Social workers can enhance clients' capacity to address present and future problems in several ways. First, they can provide clients and their families with information about the problem (for example, what happened to other people with similar problems and what successful strategies they developed to cope). For some problems, the social worker can renew the client's or family's ability to manage by exploring with them how they dealt successfully with similar situations in the past. Then he or she can inform them about services and how they can be used to help. Finally the social worker's ability to model problem-solving and change skills provides an example that may enable the client and family to solve problems and create positive change more effectively.

In terms of prevention, social workers must learn how to imagine probable outcomes for clients and foresee the challenges that face them. For example, although diagnosis does not necessarily go hand in hand with functional disability, it is an indicator of risk. A client who has suffered a stroke or has been diagnosed with pulmonary disease or diabetes is at higher risk for predictable sorts of impairments, some of which may be preventable. A client with progressive dementia will experience functional impairment as the disease progresses, for which the client and his or her family can prepare to some extent. Social interventions that can support, alleviate, and possibly prevent problems include linking clients and families with respite services, helping them to arrange for relief through their own social networks to reduce the burden of caregiving, or connecting them to voluntary self-help associations and support groups (for people with Alzheimer's disease, strokes, diabetes, mental illness, or other conditions).

Helping clients to remain hopeful is important in motivating them to change. Although no two clients or situations are identical, many clients share common human experiences. It is part of the social worker's expertise to understand these common experiences and use them to help clients prepare for the future and take action to minimize problems.

This book emphasizes family-centered practice, giving a broad definition to the term "family." Not all adult services clients, however, have intact or functioning families or social support networks, which makes them particularly vulnerable in some regards. For example, an older person who lives alone and does not have access to family or friends who could assist with basic ADLs is at greater risk of being institutionalized if he or she experiences significant functional losses. Many people have no living family members, and because of the mobility of people in this country, many others have no family nearby. Others may be neglected by, abused by, or estranged from their families. In these cases social workers may aim to help clients construct a surrogate "family" network from different formal and informal sources of social support or help them reconnect with family members who are estranged.

Linking with Formal Resources: Working with Organizations

The social worker's responsibility for coordinating existing resources to ensure that clients receive appropriate care may embody some conflict in roles (Moore, 1992). On the one hand, the worker is responsible for following program guidelines that may restrict the availability of some services because of limits on eligibility or resources and on the other must advocate on behalf of the client for needed resources from the adult services program and from other organizations in the community. The professional judgment of the social worker about what the client needs may conflict with administrative guidelines that govern eligibility. This conflict, however, can be more positively reframed to acknowledge and support the social worker's exercise of a measure of professional and administrative discretion in helping clients obtain needed services, identifying and overcoming barriers in the service system, and helping to develop new services.

Many of the instrumental resources needed by clients are held by public or private organizations. In adult services, formal resources usually belong to agencies in the community. Accessing needed resources depends on the social worker's knowledge of the client's needs, derived from a professional assessment, and his or her knowledge of regulations and policy regarding eligibility. In this sense, the worker must be able to assess not only the individual's circumstances but the health and human services organizations in the community to make the best match. According to Specht (1988) the case management task in this area for adult services social workers is to see that clients are able to access "what they are entitled to—no more, no less" (p. 200).

The apparent "objectiveness" of determining what the client is entitled to, however, is never as cut-and-dried as it might seem. Decisions about the allocation of human services are often so complex that although they can be guided by policy and practice precepts, there is often a significant margin for administrative and professional discretion (Moore, 1992). When they marshal resources for their clients, adult services social workers exercise both administrative and professional discretion regarding clients' needs, prognoses, agency policy, law, and issues of cost and efficiency. For example, an adult services social worker who manages cases for the Medicaid home and community waiver program for adults with disabilities constantly makes professional and administrative judgments about the distribution of scarce resources to a high-risk population. Such a worker, responsible for a caseload of 50 clients whose monthly service costs come to $800 each, is administering a program whose annual budget is nearly half a million dollars.

In helping clients gain access to resources, the social worker is guided by agency policy and professional training. Both are important, because the complex nature of adult services cases not only allows but calls for considerable administrative and professional discretion with respect to allocating agency resources, identifying and overcoming barriers in the service system, and identifying new resources and services that must be developed in the community. Adult services social workers are entrusted with a great measure of authority, conferred by the agency and the community, to promote and secure the welfare of adults in need.

MONITORING SERVICES AND ASSURING QUALITY

Monitoring services is one of the principal steps in the family assessment and change method and is an important part of case management as a service intervention strategy. Monitoring is a mechanism for maintaining accountability and for providing necessary technical assistance. Its role in promoting accountability ensures that services are being implemented as planned and that the client's and family's goals are being achieved. Services include both formal public and private services and what the client and family have agreed to do for themselves. Technical assistance is included as a corrective mechanism to help keep the plan on course. The extent to which social workers can influence the delivery of planned services depends on whether they have direct control over the resources being applied. In the absence of this control, they must have particularly strong advocacy and organizational skills. However direct the social worker's influence, monitoring is an essential mechanism for assuring quality care.

Quality assurance in case management involves two specific types of monitoring: (1) for process and (2) for outcomes (Rothman, 1991). Monitoring the process means asking whether the activities included in the service plan have been implemented and are being carried out according to design and according to the program's standards of quality. Monitoring the outcomes means asking whether the service plan is producing the intended results for the client. Applebaum and Austin (1990) identified five central questions for quality assurance of both process and outcome that are applicable to adult services programs:

1. *How well does the agency implement program eligibility and targeting criteria?*
2. *Does the agency complete structured client assessments and formalized care plans in a timely fashion?*
3. *Are the service plans actually implemented as designed?*
4. *Are clients satisfied with the case-managed care received?*
5. *Do the service plans produce the intended outcomes with clients?* (p. 91)

How well the agency implements its criteria for eligibility and targeting depends on how clear and well-specified those criteria are. Although recipients of many adult services programs no longer have to pass a means test, many still do (for example, for those programs associated with Medicaid). Access to adult services programs may be restricted, if only by the capacity of the agency to provide needed personnel and services. One function of the mission statement for the adult services is to specify who the agency intends to serve and in what way. If services are not targeted to clients appropriately, projected outcomes cannot be achieved.

The timeliness with which assessments are performed and service plans are implemented also assumes that there are standards for various services. Measuring timeliness is part of process evaluation, because it focuses on the social worker's activity, rather than the result for the client, and is predicated on the assumption that good services are those that are provided in a timely manner. Some adult services programs already have standards for timeliness. Adult protective services require evaluations to be initiated within a specified time. Good practice also dictates that essential services such as APS, services for individuals at risk of institutionalization, and services for other high-risk populations be provided within a specified period. Recognizing that such standards contribute to quality services, a number of states are developing standards for timeliness in adult services program areas using various resource management methods.

Whether service plans are implemented as designed is also part of process evaluation, and ensuring that clients receive the specified services is a central function of case management. If services are not implemented as planned, they may no longer meet clients' goals. More important, in some instances, clients may be put at risk of further harm.

Clients' satisfaction with services is an important, although indirect, measure of whether the service plan is working. Efforts to obtain measures of clients' satisfaction are a necessary and critical acknowledgment of the importance of their participation in the design and implementation of any service plan. As such, determining clients' levels of satisfaction measures their opinions about the acceptability and effectiveness of services.

Finally, the bottom line for service plans, excellent case management, and the efficacy of the agency is whether interventions produce outcomes that match the client's and family's stated goals. To answer this question, the agency and the social worker or supervisor reviewing individual caseloads or the clientele of an adult services program must compare the array of goals for clients and possible service strategies with the plans that are actually implemented and the outcomes as seen by the clients. The agency, worker, and supervisor also must know what potential clients have not been served.

This sort of systematic program evaluation is a mark of excellence; however, it is rarely done. First, it is difficult to do, and second, it requires a change in organizational mind-set and a different mental and theoretical framework that emphasizes both process and client- and family-specific outcomes (Gowdy, Rapp, & Poertner, 1993; Monkman, 1991; Rothman, 1991). Nonetheless, it stands as a goal toward which agencies, programs, and individual practitioners should direct their efforts.

Case Management Roles

The social worker using case management as an intervention strategy can assume one or more of several roles, depending on which the comprehensive assessment suggests might be appropriate. The central role is that of service coordinator. When developing a service plan that brings together external resources, the social worker is faced with questions and choices about how to organize, mobilize, seek involvement, shape agreements, and keep the pieces of the plan together. Additional roles that support this central role include acting as educator, broker, advocate, mediator, facilitator, and developer of new resources.

As educators, social workers provide clients and their families with information about the resource network and the change process. As brokers, they serve as intermediaries to obtain or purchase necessary resources in the service plan. As advocates, they must use a number of different techniques and strategies for linking the client to the resource network—through persuasion, negotiation, or perhaps even aggressive confrontation with service providers (Rothman, 1991; Steinberg & Carter, 1983). As mediators, they clarify disagreements or conflicts between clients and providers of resources (for example, among in-home aides, agencies, or family members). As facilitators, they help clients and families draw on their strengths to improve their capacity to meet current circumstances and plan for the future. Finally, as developers of new resources, they identify gaps in resources for an individual or group client and act to spur the development of solutions.

Case Example

The various roles associated with case management as an intervention strategy can be illustrated with a case example.

> Mr. S is a 70-year-old man who is recovering from a recent stroke. His family contacts the public services social worker to ask about getting him assistance with personal care needs, activities, and transportation to medical services. The social worker visits Mr. S in his home to perform the comprehensive functional assessment, which suggests that he is experiencing significant depression resulting from the loss of positive self-image and functioning associated with the stroke.
>
> In working with the client and his family, the social worker provides them with information regarding the effects of the stroke, in particular, that it can cause depression. As a broker of services, the social worker may help them purchase or arrange for home health services that might help the client not only compensate for his ADL impairment but also regain through physical and speech therapy as much functioning as possible. If the client is willing, the social worker might also refer him to a mental health professional for treatment of depression. In securing transportation services for the client, the social worker may have to advocate on his behalf with a provider who does not believe Mr. S qualifies for the agency's services. The social worker also may encounter conflict within the family about Mr. S's perceived abilities, the likelihood of his regaining his independence, and the options available if he does not. The social worker may mediate this conflict by providing information, acting as a referee in discussions, and modeling appropriate listening and communication skills. As facilitator, the worker's practice should be an active demonstration of problem-solving skills and planning techniques that the client and family can use for themselves in the future. Finally, if the social worker discovers that a number of the other adult services clients and families could benefit from a stroke support group, he or she might join with others in the community to develop one.

Professional Status of Case Management Activities

The roles associated with the practice of case management by adult services social workers are complex and require considerable skill and professional training. The goal of case management is ambitious. These facts must be restated because many of the most evident activities of case management may seem at first glance to be mundane to the point of not requiring professional judgment to carry them out. For example, Grisham et al. (1983) reviewed how case managers in an in-home service program for adults with disabilities spent their time (Table 6-1).

One of the difficulties associated with the practice of case management is the perception that a number of its activities do not constitute professional social work practice. Many conceive of social work as limited to a therapeutic relationship between a worker and a client, such as occurs in a counseling relationship. In this view, the "resource" belongs to the professional in the form of expertise in offering a psychosocial intervention. In the exchange between worker and client, the social worker has a therapeutic function, and the organization is only a setting where the exchange takes place (Specht, 1988). The social worker experiences a greater sense of control over the process and often feels an immediate sense of appreciation for the benefits provided to the client through the counseling intervention. For case management, however, it may seem that the resource is possessed not by the social worker but by the social worker's agency or by other agencies and individuals in the community. The social worker serves as an intermediary for the therapeutic interactions of others and may feel deprived of an immediate sense of efficacy with respect to clients. Compared with counseling as an intervention strategy, case management may seem only to offer indirect therapeutic benefits to clients.

The perception that social workers using the case management strategy may spend twice as much time doing paperwork or contacting service providers and family members as they spend with clients is deceptive. If what clients are really asking for is action taken on their behalf, the case management activities testify that is exactly what social workers are doing. What is more important is the professional method behind all this activity and the multiple roles that social workers perform. Case management activities rely on conferring with clients and families, evaluating possibilities, suggesting strategies, and helping implement them.

CASE MANAGEMENT MODELS

The social worker's ability to do his or her job well rests to a large degree on support from the agency. In addition to the information they provide about case

Table 6-1 _____

BREAKDOWN OF TIME SPENT IN VARIOUS CASE MANAGEMENT ACTIVITIES

Activity	Percentage of Time
Contact with clients	22–24
Paperwork	22–24
Contact with family members, providers, physicians, and informal support	18–24
Meetings	15–21
Travel	6–10
Miscellaneous	6–10

Reprinted with permission from Grisham, M., White, M., & Miller, L. (1983). Case management as a problem solving strategy. *PRIDE Institute Journal of Long Term Home Health Care, 2*(4), 24.

management activities, Grisham et al. (1983) identified a number of models under which case management is practiced, according to the various degrees of authority they offer to command resources for clients and families. With some alteration of Grisham et al.'s original notion of a continuum, Figure 6-1 illustrates how the job increases in complexity as levels of command and responsibility increase. Examples of these models of practice can be found in adult services programs throughout the nation.

No Case Management

On the left of the continuum, individual providers claim only authority and responsibility for services they make directly available to clients. They take no responsibility for assessing and coordinating resources beyond what they themselves can provide. Examples of these individual providers include a job service office, a dentist, or an optometrist. The crucial distinction is that the provider does not assume responsibility for identifying through assessment all of the client's needs but only considers the needs it can meet directly.

Limited Case Management

Next on the continuum, there are agencies that provide information and referral services based on brief screening. These agencies assist clients in using resources by referring them to appropriate service providers, but they assume no responsibility for the care of these clients. Adult services programs that operate information and referral services with no or minimal follow-up are practicing limited case management.

Brokerage Case Management: Limited Service Access

In this model, the social worker as case manager has full responsibility for coordinating the care of clients but possesses limited authority to purchase services on their behalf. The case manager performs all the underlying essential steps of the process—intake, screening, and comprehensive assessment—but when it comes to developing and implementing a service plan, he or she must hustle, advocate, beg, borrow, and broker to obtain services to meet clients' essential needs. The limited authority to purchase services allows the social worker to put in place a minimum set of services over which the worker and the agency have some control. The social worker acting for an in-home services client may be able to provide agency support in the form of aide services, transportation, and home-delivered meals, depending on the agency's resources. However, other essential services (particularly those related to health care) may be more difficult to secure, although they might be critical elements of a high-quality service plan.

Centralized Case Management: Moderate Service Access

A more comprehensive model of case management involves both full responsibility for coordinating services for the client and centralized access to community-based services through the authority to purchase them. The Medicaid-waiver program for adults with disabilities is the best example of such a model. The regulations for this program give the designated case manager the authority to purchase services from community providers for clients with disabilities who meet the income requirements and who would otherwise require placement in a nursing home, providing the total cost of services does not exceed the cost of placement. Case management under this model serves a gatekeeping function, in that it can be used to limit access to nursing homes, but it responds to clients' common desires to remain at home as long as possible. The important distinction is that with this program the case manager has access to a number of health and medical services—including nursing and rehabilitative therapy—that are normally only indirectly available to adult services social workers. With this model, the case manager is able to combine elements of a more traditional social model of long-term care with the elements of a medical model of chronic care. Because authority to purchase does not ensure automatic access, the Medicaid home and community care case manager in most instances still has to advocate and negotiate to obtain needed services.

Centralized Case Management: Comprehensive Service Access

The most comprehensive, centralized version of case management can be found when the manager not only has authority to obtain community-based services but also serves as intermediary for determining appropriate access to nursing home and hospital care. In Oregon, for example, the case manager's authority includes making or deferring decisions on nursing home placement through preadmission screening programs and referring clients who would be good candidates for home and community care to alternative service arrangements (Oregon Association of Area Agencies on Aging, 1993). A New York program called Project Access gives case managers the authority to refer hospital-bound clients to nursing homes or to community care as a less expensive and more appropriate service alternative. Beyond these programs, there are social and health maintenance organizations that are more comprehensive still. These programs allocate a certain amount of money

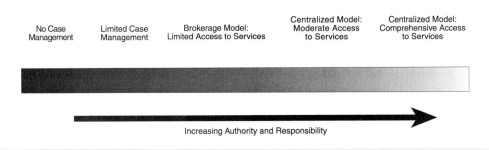

Figure 6-1

MODELS OF CASE MANAGEMENT

Adapted from Grisham, M., White, M., & Miller, L. (1983). Case management as a problem solving strategy. *PRIDE Institute Journal of Long Term Home Health Care, 2*(4), 22–23.

to be spent per client (often adjusted to take into consideration risk factors for categories of clients) for care over a designated period. The social and health maintenance organization assumes financial risk for all care and is profitable to the extent that it can manage clients' services, whether health or social, in a way that costs are less than revenues and that clients are satisfied with the quality of services they receive (Weiner & Illston, 1993).

Given that case management is one of the social worker's two principal intervention strategies, which of these models the adult services agency selects governs the work life and professional stature of the social worker. Although many would agree that adult services cannot opt for the no case management model and still use its resources wisely, there remains some room for choice among the other options. The brokerage model is probably the most common form in use, but it offers the most possibility for burning out the social workers who must work within it, because the constant competition for resources is wearing. Through interagency agreements, however, adult services programs can probably reduce the stress associated with this model. In defining its mission, the agency might consider whether "information and referral" is a valid choice for some services, whereas movement toward a centralized model with moderate access is the best choice for others. Although a centralized model with comprehensive access might be the most efficient in the best of all possible worlds, it would require fundamental changes in the way public human services are provided through state and county levels.

Summary

Case management is one of the two intervention strategies that adult services social workers use to help clients and families and to enable and empower them to help themselves. Excellent practice in using this strategy requires a high degree of professional competence in six areas, in that social workers must (1) make use of the family assessment and change method to identify problems, strengths, and desired changes; (2) understand the implications for clients of bringing about change; (3) have a detailed knowledge of available resources and the policies that govern their use; (4) match resources with clients; (5) creatively develop new resources where none exist or negotiate on behalf of clients when resources are scarce; and (6) model methods of problem solving and change with the goal of returning as many case management activities to clients and their families as possible. How can social workers become expert at all the aspects of case management? It can be done through the support of management at the level of the agency and the state, including continuing training, clear agency guidelines, value placed on necessary tasks that are not glamorous, and well-developed relationships with other service providers. Finally, the agency's choice of a model for case managers plays a critical part in empowering professional staff members and through them the clients they serve.

Key Points

Excellent adult services social workers

- understand case management as an intervention strategy for marshaling external resources on behalf of clients
- understand how the family assessment and change method fits with the activities of case management
- know and value the complexity of their responsibilities for using this intervention strategy.

Excellent adult services managers

- acknowledge and value case management as a key to quality social work practice through its potential for delivering services efficiently and its monitoring functions
- provide training support for this complex activity
- provide administrative support to the practice of case management through a clear mission statement for adult services
- understand the various models of case management and apply them thoughtfully to program areas.

Excellent leaders

- provide policy support for case management by incorporating its steps and skills in practice manuals, training, and development of program guidelines
- identify the tasks of case management and set reasonable workload standards in those services in which the case management strategy is used.

References

Applebaum, R., & Austin, C. (1990). *Long-term care case management: Design and evaluation.* New York: Springer.

Consolidated Budget Reconciliation Act of 1988. P.L. 99-272, 100 Stat. 82.

Education for All Handicapped Children Act of 1975. P.L. 94-142, 89 Stat. 773.

Ell, K. (1984). Social networks, social support, and health status: A review. *Social Service Review, 58*(1), 133–149.

Family Support Act of 1988. P.L. 100-485, 102 Stat. 2343.

Gowdy, E. A., Rapp, C. A., & Poertner, J. (1993). Management is performance: Strategies for client-centered practice in social service organizations. *Administration in Social Work, 17,* 3–22.

Greene, R. R. (1987). *Case management: Helping the homeless, mentally ill, and persons with AIDS and their families.* Silver Spring, MD: National Association of Social Workers.

Grisham, M., White, M., & Miller, L. (1983). Case management as a problem-solving strategy. *PRIDE Institute Journal of Long Term Home Health Care, 2*(4), 22–28.

Kaplan, K. O. (1990). Recent trends in case management. In L. Ginsberg et al. (Eds.), *Encyclopedia of social work* (18th ed., 1990 suppl., pp. 60–77). Silver Spring, MD: NASW Press.

Monkman, M. M. (1991). Outcome objectives in social work practice: Person and environment. *Social Work, 36,* 253–258.

Moore, S. T. (1992). Case management and the integration of services: How service delivery systems shape case management. *Social Work, 37,* 418–423.

National Governors Association. (1988). *State long term care reform.* Washington, DC: Author.

Oregon Association of Area Agencies on Aging. (1993). *Smart government: Oregon's long-term care system.* Salem: Author.

Rothman, J. (1991). A model of case management: Toward empirically based practice. *Social Work, 36,* 520–528.

Social Security Act Amendments of 1974. P.L. 93-647, 88 Stat. 2337.

Specht, A. (1988). *New directions in social work practice.* Englewood Cliffs, NJ: Prentice Hall.

Special Education Act of 1988. P.L. 99-457, 100 Stat. 1145.

Steinberg, R., & Carter, G. (1983). *Case management and the elderly.* Lexington, MA: Lexington Books.

Weiner, J. M., & Illston, L. H. (1993). Options for LTC financing reform: Public and private insurance strategies. *Journal of Long-Term Care Administration, 21*(3), 46–57.

White, M. (1987). Case management. In G. Maddox (Ed.-in-Chief), *Encyclopedia of aging* (pp. 92–96). New York: Springer.

CHAPTER 7

Counseling

VICKIE L. ATKINSON

Many of the challenges encountered by adult services clients are the result of a need for tangible resources: a better or safer place to live, help with personal care, or assistance with managing money. Case management is the intervention strategy social workers use to obtain and coordinate these external, tangible resources for clients. For some clients, however, the greatest need is to use intangible psychological resources so they can make use of tangible resources, achieve the necessary motivation to change behavior, cope with losses, regain morale, develop or sharpen skills, or improve interpersonal relations with family and others in their support system to bring about and sustain change. Counseling in adult services is the intervention strategy to help clients manage their internal, intangible psychological resources effectively. Although this book devotes separate chapters to counseling and case management (chapter 6), together these interventions constitute a holistic approach to interventions with individuals and families.

This chapter presents a brief history of counseling in social work, defines counseling for adult services, describes key counseling tools, and discusses at length the experience and practice of counseling. It underscores the importance of family-centered practice, counseling in the context of a hierarchy of needs, the influence of setting on counseling, and issues of empowerment as clients move from dependency and needing support to interdependence and self-support. The chapter also discusses communication and relationship-building skills, counseling in the context of the family assessment and change method, knowledge and effective counseling, and various theoretical approaches to counseling. The chapter concludes with a brief discussion of the type of professional support that adult services social workers need to perform their counseling role well.

Brief History of Counseling in Social Work

Counseling to help clients use their internal resources to maximize the fit between themselves and their environment has a long tradition in direct social work practice. Social casework, the method that has shaped social work during much of its history, is associated most with Mary Richmond's (1917) book *Social Diagnosis.* Social casework emphasizes direct practice with individuals and the need to understand their functioning in their environment. Perlman (1957) made a major contribution with her book *Casework: A Problem-Solving Process,* in which she identified and described a framework for problem solving that involves the person, place, problem, and process.

Other significant approaches to work with clients now in the social worker's repertoire are group interventions, developed in the 1930s (Glasser, Sundel, Sarri, & Vintner, 1985, provided a good review), and family-centered interventions, whose development began in the mid-1950s (Hartman & Laird, 1983). Specific methods of practice have since enriched social work and emphasized distinct aspects of the therapeutic interaction between social workers and individuals, families, and groups. Among these are crisis intervention; the cognitive approach; the behavioral approach (chapter 8); life review or reminiscing, specifically for older clients; group work; and family therapy, all of which are described later in this chapter.

Counseling in Adult Services

Counseling is purposeful communication and dialogue with clients and families about change. It is performed in the context of a respectful, genuine, and empathetic relationship. The medium by which this dialogue is initiated and maintained is through in-depth conversations about change between worker and client. The goal is to empower clients and families by helping them find ways to change thoughts, feelings, attitudes, and behaviors that interfere with their abilities to meet their goals or to use resources in ways that would enable them to function optimally.

The tasks of helping people, meeting tangible needs for resources, and addressing their interpersonal and psychological needs are frequently intertwined. For many people, accepting services involves a change in self-image and lifestyle. Services that affect an individual's daily routine and self-concept often stir up intense emotional feelings (Bumagin & Hirn, 1990). Change is difficult.

In adult services the task of dealing with tangible needs, through case management, and addressing interpersonal and psychological issues, through counseling, frequently fall to one worker. Only in larger, more-specialized adult services agencies are the functions explicitly separated, and even then the roles of case management and counseling interact. When clients require specialized, advanced treatment for severe and persistent mental disorders, they should be referred to specialists. However, even in these instances, social workers in adult services agencies have something to contribute as counselors, often in providing support for intensive treatment.

Counseling as part of the clinical skills that social workers bring to the family assessment and change method refers to the ongoing purposeful interactions among clients, families, and social workers that are intended to bring about changes in functioning. Counseling should be carefully distinguished from notions of psychotherapy or other mental health interventions aimed at alleviating some major mental illnesses. Nonetheless, counseling in the context of adult services practice is and should be therapeutic. Every interaction among client, family, and social worker is potentially an intervention, even though adult services counseling frequently occurs in informal situations over the phone, in a car on the way to an appointment, at the kitchen table, or on the front lawn. Although the interactions may seem casual, they are purposeful and professional. Their intent is to facilitate change and improved functioning for adult services clients through empathic listening and to help overcome resistance to change through reframing and sometimes through acceptance of only partial resolution of problems (Bumagin & Hirn, 1990).

For the most part, counseling in adult services is not focused on changing clients' personalities. Rather, its purpose is to collaborate with clients in the short term to make changes in specific attitudes, emotions, and actions that might interfere with their use of services, prevent them from obtaining support or interacting productively with others, or block their ability to function optimally. The following case example illustrates the scope of counseling in adult services.

CASE EXAMPLE

Mrs. P came to the adult services agency after an accident left her disabled enough to need assistance in preparing meals and keeping house. She has had three in-home aides in the past six months, all of whom she dismissed because she felt they were lazy, clumsy, and uncaring. No other client has complained about these aides, and the adult services social worker suspects that Mrs. P has attitudes and feelings that make it hard for her to accept help. One of the aides mentioned to the social worker that Mrs. P wanted to go live with her daughter after her accident. While ensuring that Mrs. P's personal care needs are being met through temporary arrangements, the social worker initiates short-term counseling to help Mrs. P resolve her dissatisfaction with her in-home care and help her accept and make better use of this assistance. Based on the aide's information and the social worker's assessment of the situation, the worker decides to focus attention on Mrs. P's feelings about her accident, her dependency on the aides, and her expectations of her daughter.

There are many situations and problems encountered by adult services social workers that indicate a need for counseling. Some clients may react to events in their lives with persistent emotional upset, yet they lack access to private or public counseling resources in the community. Others would benefit from support, information, or skills to reach their goals that case management alone cannot provide. Still others are unable to use resources and services that are available because their emotions, beliefs, or behaviors get in the way.

PRINCIPLES OF COUNSELING FOR ADULT SERVICES

Several principles guide counseling in adult services agencies: It is family-centered; it occurs in the context of a hierarchy of needs (Maslow, 1968); it is shaped by the agency and organizational context; it acknowledges the frequently painful limits of how much change can be effected; and it focuses on helping clients gain empowerment to the degree they are able.

Family-Centered Practice

If one of the principal goals of work with adult clients is to enhance their fit with their environment, family is often a paramount component of that environment. In many cases, families are the first place clients with needs turn for help, so the family as resource cannot be underrated. The family has always been important in shaping who the client is. Even for those who no longer have living family members, ways of interacting learned when those family members were alive shape the client's current ways of dealing with the world through cultural heritage, communication style, values, and in many other ways. Counseling with an adult client in a family-centered context should focus on the reciprocal interactions among client and family members.

Conflict in families or inattention to clients by their relatives may reflect a lack of agreement on goals or a lack of family involvement in setting goals. For example, the primary caregiver for an older parent may complain that her siblings do nothing to help. Her brothers and sisters, on the other hand, may feel shut out and unsure of what she wants them to do. The social worker plays a key role in identifying and helping to resolve these conflicts when they occur and by including the family with the client in any planning, especially when it has direct implications for family members. Adult clients deserve to be treated as individuals, yet their needs often impinge on family members. The success of many interventions may depend on the social worker's ability as mediator of the need for a client's autonomy and the need for collective action by the family.

Hierarchy of Needs

Maslow (1968) identified a "hierarchy of needs" for people that runs from basic requirements for survival and safety (food and shelter) to affiliation, self-actualization, and creativity. He proposed that individuals must first have their basic needs for survival met before they can turn to the "higher" needs. As counselors, adult services social workers assess where along this continuum clients fall in the course of their work together, attending first to clients' needs for shelter and safety, particularly in emergency situations, before turning to other needs.

However, by listening actively and assessing comprehensively, skilled workers may identify situations when the client's lack of avenues for affiliation and self-actualization may precipitate situations in which the client is not motivated to assume responsibility for meeting basic requirements. In these cases, helping the client to set goals to meet the "higher" needs first may provide the inspiration to meet basic needs more effectively. Paradoxically, demoralization that results from the loss of a job or the loss of social outlets for an older adult may be addressed best by meeting higher needs first or at least simultaneously with efforts to meet the basic needs for food and shelter. By listening actively and setting goals congruent with the individual's situation, adult services social workers may sometimes best serve the individual or family by resisting the urge to do something tangible.

Agency and Organizational Context

The adult services agency and organizational context shapes the nature of the counseling experience and counseling opportunities in profound ways. First, in contrast to counseling provided in mental health or family services agencies, counseling in adult services is more likely to take place in the client's home. This location provides both opportunities and challenges. Clients may be more receptive to counseling on their own territory and more comfortable sharing personal information. The social worker's understanding of clients is usually deepened by seeing them in their own environment. On the other hand, the worker has less control over those environments: The television may be too loud, family or friends may walk through the room, and the telephone may ring. To capitalize on the benefits of seeing clients in this setting, social workers must find ways to minimize distractions and ensure privacy.

A second consideration for counseling in adult services is that it usually accompanies the provision of some specific service, such as in-home aide assistance, representative payeeship, or locating a board-and-care home or nursing home. Unlike counseling in other settings, it is also likely to be short term and focused on facilitating change around specific issues, such as helping a client use placement services. In this example, counseling might focus on helping the client recognize and accept the need to move to a board-and-care home, mourn the loss of his or her original home, express feelings about moving, enable him or her to accept the new role of "resident," adjust to the limitations on personal privacy, and empower him or her to find ways to assert control over a new living situation.

A third consideration for counseling in adult services concerns its opportunistic nature. Although social workers will sometimes schedule specific appointments to counsel clients and families as part of a service plan, more often than not this intervention will consist of brief "conversations," for example, during home visits, during telephone calls, or when providing transportation. Because this service is so opportunistic, effective counselors make a special effort to keep in mind the issues to be addressed and the goals and changes to be achieved. Counseling in this manner is no less important because it happens on the fly, capturing openings for constructive dialogue and providing supportive assurances as the opportunities arise.

Finally, with respect to some of the unique attributes of adult services counseling, individuals served by social services or agencies for elderly people are frequently people who might not have or seek access to mental health services through formal mental health providers. Many adult services clients live in poverty. Many have limited education, so they lack information about mental health services. Many are wary about turning to mental health or other professionals for help with personal problems. Cultural influences may predispose clients to regard personal problems as signs of failure or weakness, and consequently they may not accept or use counseling through mental health services. Through the relationship adult services social workers develop with clients while providing concrete assistance, workers have an opportunity to provide clients with access to counseling in a way that may be more acceptable, enabling them to understand and benefit from this intervention.

Limits of Change

As many adult services workers know, many problems can be solved through the provision of tangible resources, but others can be only partially solved or cannot be solved at all in this manner. Many clients will remain poor, regardless of their best efforts and public income support; their loved ones will die or move away; others may contract chronic diseases; and still others may not find ideal living arrangements. Despite their best efforts, social workers may feel frustrated and helpless when they have assisted clients in garnering all the resources available and yet find that this assistance does not solve all of the client's problems. Nevertheless, good workers can still help clients feel capable and in control. The client, with help from the social worker, can identify better ways of managing or coping with problems that cannot be resolved fully. Clients can become more self-actualized despite real limitations. Counseling is often the starting point for this process. It is important for social workers to be aware of their limitations and be prepared to refer clients to other professionals.

Empowerment: From Support to Self-Reliance

The method described in this book holds as a central tenet that workers should support, enable, and help clients and families gain empowerment on a path to self-care and interdependence. Early in the relationship, support from the social worker—and dependence on the part of the client—is likely to predominate, although the worker must be sensitive to ways to enable greater self-reliance and opportunities for clients and families to exercise their own empowerment. Support is most associated with emergency intervention, case management, and getting external resources to clients in need. Any counseling that is done is primarily to help the client get through the crisis, to encourage acceptance of services, and to foster emotional equilibrium. Some dependency on the part of clients is appropriate during this phase. In fact, part of what the worker will be doing is encouraging the client to agree that accepting help is legitimate. The expectation is that once crisis needs are met, clients will be ready to use their resources (sometimes with the help of counseling) to move on to more-independent functioning.

Although the concept of "enabling" has negative connotations in the context of substance abuse, here we mean to focus on its positive aspects. Through teaching, modeling, provision of information, coaching, and providing moral support, social workers can enable clients to develop and use personal skills. When clients feel less anxious and more secure that basic needs are being met, they may be receptive to increasing their own control by learning additional skills, cultivating alternate resources, or looking at their situations from different perspectives. Strictly speaking, social workers cannot empower clients, because clients must feel empowered and act on that feeling themselves. Empowerment often must be a long-term goal, tackled only after short-term supportive and enabling interventions have been put in place to prevent further decline or suffering and clients identify and learn new ways of interacting with their environment. From the beginning, however, clients' self-reliance and reliance on their own resources should be nurtured as much as possible.

Some clients never move beyond the desire for emotional support. Through their lack of involvement in the counseling process or lack of progress over time, they signal that they do not want to participate in a process to increase their independence. Social workers must then step back and help clients reassess the need for change and counseling. As Rooney and Wanless (1985) noted, "Practitioners and clients who see each other over a period of years can lose a sense of what they are working on and why." Some clients, they suggested, "prefer to have a supportive rather than a change oriented relationship" and want "regular visits from a friendly, supportive person" (pp. 189–193). Workers must help these clients reassess whether they actually desire to become more self-reliant or whether their wish is for continued support. If the client only wants to continue to receive outside emotional support, because of the agency's mission and the constraints on the worker's time, the worker will likely need to find other ways to arrange for this support, through facilitating the client's relationships with family members, neighbors, friends, church groups, or volunteers. Although the client's need and desire for support are legitimate, it is a better use of professional resources for the social worker to arrange for someone else to provide it. As developer of new resources, the social worker might find the opportunity here to initiate programs for friendly visiting or peer counseling if nothing else is available.

Counseling that enhances skills and competence enables clients to assume more control of their lives. It means shifting the power differential that often develops during the support phase, when the worker appropriately encourages some dependency, to a situation in which clients are encouraged to assert their abilities. Counseling approaches during this phase focus on the strengths that clients have shown, on past successful coping strategies, and on other resources and people in clients' lives on which they may rely. During the enabling phase, workers are helping clients to make a transition from being dependent to becoming independent. Workers assess in greater depth with clients their internal strengths, resources, and deficits. Workers use these strengths and resources to help clients develop a sense of self-governance, identifying those areas of the clients' thoughts, feelings, and behaviors over which they have some measure of control and challenging them to strengthen that control.

For example, a middle-aged man who feels guilty and compelled to respond to every request of his widowed mother can be helped to see that he is behaving responsibly toward her by arranging in-home help, visiting once a week, and calling her frequently. He can diminish his guilty feelings by valuing what he does to help her, by recognizing the extent of what he can and cannot do, and by being enabled to accept those limitations without guilt. He must be able to say to himself, "It would be nice if my mother could be happy, but I cannot make that happen."

As a function of enabling and increasing clients' self-efficacy through counseling, workers help clients and families determine which abilities and choices are under their control. Workers also clarify the resources and limitations of the agency. With some clients, social workers must set limits on agency resources and on their own time. This must be done sensitively and fairly but in a matter-of-fact way. Workers should make sure that clients understand what the limits are and the consequences of violating them. Other family members or professionals may need to be involved in the limit-setting process to ensure that all are working together to enable the client to assume greater self-control. (See chapter 8 for more on setting limits as a way of modifying challenging behaviors.)

Empowerment is the culmination of support and enabling. It is motivation coupled with the belief that one has choice and is competent to achieve one's goals. To help clients gain empowerment is to transfer power from worker to client and reduce external support to only that which is necessary to complement what the client can provide. The function of counseling for empowerment is to identify what motivates individual clients and what blocks and enhances that motivation. Empowerment helps clients move beyond passive acceptance of life to the belief that they can change aspects of external reality or see their situations in ways that cause them to feel less victimized and more in control of their feelings.

COMMUNICATION AND RELATIONSHIP-BUILDING SKILLS

Exchanges among people are based in communication and result in some form of relationship, however tenuous. What is unique to the helping relationship between professionals and clients is a contract (either expressed or implied) that obligates workers to use themselves and their skills consciously to assist clients in making changes. Although effective communication and professional relationships are critical to case management and advocacy, they are the essence of counseling.

The type and quality of relationships between social workers and clients will depend largely on the communication skills, purpose, and values of the worker. Perlman (1979) stated that the professional helping relationship "is charged with enabling, facilitative powers toward both problem solving and goal attainment" (p. 2). Furthermore, she asserted that the social worker "is involved in the relationship with his client not out of kindliness or for his own gratification but because he knows how to be of help and is charged and authorized by his agency with giving help. Thus the idea that one 'gives a client a relationship' is fallacious; rather the relationship develops out of the professional business the case worker and client have to work on together" (p. 69). This type of relationship develops as a result of purposeful communication and commitment to change. The social worker does not set out to develop a relationship with the client. Instead, according to Perlman (1957), "a professional relationship is formed and maintained for a purpose recognized by both participants, and ends when that purpose has been achieved or is judged to be unachievable" (p. 69).

The purposive nature of the professional relationship is important. Workers, for example, who describe their roles as "the client's best friend" or "like being a member of the family" risk losing their objectivity, promoting inappropriate dependency in clients, and compromising the function of the agency.

The initial relationship between the adult services social worker and client is usually defined in terms of what problem the client brings to the agency. It is in the context of purposeful conversation that assessments are conducted, problems and strengths identified, a change list specified, goals formulated, and services planned. Once established, the relationship among clients, families, and workers becomes a tool to be used in helping accomplish goals. Workers can use their positive relationships with clients to motivate them to consider alternatives or attempt actions that they might not otherwise try. For example, a client who was initially reluctant to accept medical care might be willing to go for an examination when encouraged to do so by a worker he or she has come to trust.

Empathic listening is one of the most important interpersonal skills a social worker must demonstrate in counseling. Empathy involves hearing both the content and the feelings that clients communicate and reflecting that perception to clients so they feel they have been understood. For example, a client with diabetes might say, in a quavering voice, "This sugar's really got me down." The worker might respond, "You seem pretty worried about the sugar. Can you tell me more?" If done sensitively, using the client's words can be helpful in conveying understanding. The formula "I understand you feel _____, because _____" also may be helpful. Empathic listening is a way that workers can check their perceptions about what the client thinks and feels. Empathic listening alone can have a therapeutic value for clients, whose problems and circumstances often make them feel that no one hears them and, as a consequence, that they are powerless. Empathic listening can confirm to clients their unique worth as individuals and validate their desires for a better life.

Although social workers use their skills as empathic listeners in any exchange with the client and family, one of the times it is necessary is during the sequence of events that forms the bridge from the assessment to the identification of areas for change. At the end of the assessment, the social worker generally summarizes with the client and family the principal concerns and findings that the assessment has revealed. This provides the opportunity for the social worker to validate the concerns of the client and family—often therapeutic in itself—and to invite them to correct, modify, and add to the information they have provided. This process of summarization also allows the social worker to begin the process of reframing seemingly intractable problems into items for change, items whose improvement is possible and even likely. This process can provide the initial motivation for the hard work of change that is to follow.

RIGHTS TO PRIVACY

Clients' rights to privacy and confidentiality are significant aspects of counseling. The National Association of Social Workers (1994) *Code of Ethics* maintains that the social worker has an ethical responsibility to "respect the privacy of clients and hold in confidence all information obtained in the course of professional service" (p. 6). To engage successfully in counseling, clients must be able to talk about personal issues in surroundings where they cannot be overheard and trust that what they say will not be repeated. The agency can support social workers in keeping confidentiality by providing interviewing rooms or offices that allow privacy, by setting standards for what information must be recorded in case records and what can or should be omitted, and by raising the awareness of all staff members about this issue. Because adult services clients often are involved with other agencies, managers also should provide guidelines about obtaining signed releases when information is to be shared.

Counseling and the Family Assessment and Change Method

Like case management, counseling as a discrete service intervention begins with and incorporates the family assessment and change method outlined in chapter 3. Because counseling is also an adjunct to all of the steps in the method, it is necessary to comment on its role with respect to assessment, setting goals and planning services, monitoring, and terminating services.

ASSESSMENT

Central to assessment is the client's and social worker's joint commitment to identifying barriers to improved functioning and to bringing about change. However, before they can set goals or develop strategies for change, the client and the worker must perform a "perceptual" assessment (that is, determine how the client perceives any given problem and proposed change). For example, imagine two clients who receive representative payee services. One says that she sees this as a gross invasion of her personal rights. The other says he is relieved that he no longer has to worry about getting around to paying his bills, although he is saddened that he has "come to this." The difference in the ways these clients perceive having a payee makes a difference in how they feel about the service they are receiving and how they respond to the actions of the worker.

Recognition of these differing perceptions informs and guides the counseling the worker undertakes with these clients. With both, the worker focuses on their perceptions of the event and how they feel as a result. With the first client, who is angry because something she values has been taken away, the counseling targets thoughts like "I am entitled to do whatever I want with this money," and focuses on helping her understand that there are limits on what she can and cannot do and still retain control. The goal of counseling in this instance might be to help her identify ways to exercise more self-restraint that will enable her to take over the management of her affairs again. With the second client, who seems to have overgeneralized his loss of financial responsibility to be a sign of his total incompetence, the focus of counseling might be to help him identify and value his remaining abilities. With the first client, the counseling intervention focuses on her recognizing limits; with the second, it focuses on his realizing that limits do not remove all freedoms or responsibilities. In each of these cases, counseling enables the client to make use of a necessary service.

IDENTIFYING FUNCTIONAL PROBLEMS AND STRENGTHS

There is an almost infinite continuum along which problems may lie—from predominantly external (too little money, poor housing, or no significant others) to largely internal (poor judgment, inappropriate social skills, or limited motivation). Strengths, too, may predominate more in one area than another (economic resources and family support or a strong history of successful coping and a positive attitude). But often problems and strengths will be in both areas—external problems will affect the client's evaluation of the situation and internal problems will impair the client's ability to use resources. Social workers should be careful to record clients' functional strengths as well as their functional problems in both internal and external areas (Bricker-Jenkins, 1990). Problems in using internal resources will indicate a need for counseling, and internal strengths will be used as a resource (Gold, 1990).

SETTING GOALS AND PLANNING SERVICES

In identifying goals and related service interventions, social workers help clients and families visualize new options and possibilities. They help clients explore these options and identify the possible negative and positive consequences of each. The worker helps the client choose which goals to commit energy to achieving and assists in developing the service strategies to pursue them.

Although the counseling skills we have been describing throughout this chapter are integral to effective adult services practice, in some cases, counseling as a discrete service intervention will be recommended as part of the intervention package. The following case example illustrates a situation that could be addressed effectively by planning a short-term series of counseling visits in the client's home or in the worker's office. Using the steps of assessment and problem identification, goal development, and action around the presenting problems (Egan, 1986), the worker can engage the client in an effective change process.

CASE EXAMPLE

An older woman cares for her husband, who has dementia. She has become overwhelmed by the caregiving responsibilities. However, she feels very guilty about asking for outside help, believing that by doing so she is betraying her husband and shirking her responsibilities.

Although her husband will likely come to the agency's attention as the designated client, in this case, the wife, as a member of his family system, is the one who can be helped to identify goals for herself. These likely would address changing "the meaning and feeling" for her of asking for help and assisting her in recognizing the realistic limits of her abilities to provide care, as well as including strategies to decrease the emotional and physical burdens of caregiving.

Even when the agency provides services for the husband (for example, in-home services, day care, respite, or placement), counseling can help the wife sustain her involvement in her husband's care.

MONITORING

As case manager, the social worker will determine whether the services planned are being provided; as counselor, the social worker will determine whether they are acceptable to the client. If assessment and goal setting suggested that the client would need to make some change in thoughts, feelings, or behaviors, the monitoring process allows the worker and client to see whether counseling is facilitating the change and with what effect. The monitoring phase also requires that the social worker use empathic listening skills to the best of his or her ability to identify and address new problems.

TERMINATION OF SERVICES

Here, too, the social worker's skill as counselor plays a big part, because one possible goal of counseling in adult services is to prepare clients to resume independent responsibility for managing their affairs whenever possible. In effect, termination of services should be the mark of empowerment for clients when it occurs for reasons other than that the client has died or moved to a setting where adult services intervention is no longer appropriate. Even in these last two cases, a sensitive approach to termination of services on the part of the worker can help clients and their families accept the changes before them and make appropriate adjustments.

KNOWLEDGE FOR EFFECTIVE COUNSELING

The values that the social worker needs to provide effective counseling have been discussed at length, and they apply to opportunistic as well as formal counseling interventions. Personal skills, in the ability to communicate effectively, are also of critical importance. Although some workers are gifted in this regard, it is a skill that can be learned and perfected.

Beyond these specific counseling skills is the substantive knowledge that workers require about human development and what is common or expectable at various stages of the life cycle; how social roles and cultural beliefs and expectations influence individuals; and specific information on challenges facing adult services clients—violence, mental illness, death and dying, poverty, substance abuse, physical illnesses, and others. To provide good counseling, workers must constantly seek to improve their knowledge through training, reading professional books and journals, and seeking supervision of their work. Part of counseling is providing accurate information to clients about their conditions. To do this effectively, workers must have substantive knowledge of the circumstances and issues facing their clients and families.

The guiding value in counseling adult services clients is helping them to regain a sense of control and self-efficacy—a reasonable belief that they can be successful in some aspects of their lives. According to Egan (1986), clients' "expectations of themselves have everything to do with their willingness to put forth effort to cope with difficulties, the amount of effort they will expend, and their persistence in the face of obstacles" (p. 15). The following case example illustrates how social workers' knowledge of human development, family violence, and chronic illness can mesh with effective counseling skills to nurture clients' innate ability to improve and change their circumstances.

CASE EXAMPLE

Mrs. L provided complete care for her husband, who had severe dementia. Her husband's adult son lived with them and worked at a nursing home. He helped some with his father, but he abused his stepmother verbally and sometimes physically. The adult services social worker became aware of the family's problems through a concerned neighbor. The worker offered Mrs. L help in resolving the situation, and Mrs. L accepted.

In reviewing what had gone on, Mrs. L was able to explore her current situation and recall that she had effectively managed her husband's condition before her stepson moved in. The social worker helped her explore the options she had in dealing with the problem: telling her stepson she wanted him to stop hitting her, involving other family members, asking him to move out, or pressing charges against him. Mrs. L decided that she would like for her stepson to stay, but she wanted the abuse to stop. The worker and the client explored what Mrs. L could say and do to prevent him from abusing her further.

After deciding to confront him verbally, Mrs. L practiced with the social worker what she could say and how she might respond to his words or actions. As Mrs. L began to feel that she did have options and that she could better manage her situation, she became more willing to take action.

Counseling Interventions

Many counseling interventions may be appropriate in an adult services setting, but space in this book does not allow for an exhaustive consideration of them. This section, however, outlines some of the most likely and appropriate methodological and theoretical approaches to counseling.

CRISIS INTERVENTION

Crisis intervention must be differentiated from providing emergency services. Providing emergency interventions is the approach the social worker takes to secure immediate resources for clients or families who are in danger of serious harm or death. For example, the social worker might call an ambulance for a client who seems gravely ill, negotiate with the power company to keep a destitute client's power from being shut off in extremely hot or cold weather, or help find short-term placement for an adult with disabilities whose caregiver falls suddenly ill. Emergencies require immediate action.

Crises are situations in which clients' usual problem-solving approaches, skills, and resources are inadequate, and they have difficulty responding effectively to their situation. Emergencies may or may not provoke crises for clients, depending on clients' abilities to respond to whatever threatens their well-being. Although crises produce extreme emotional discomfort for clients, they are not generally life-threatening in and of themselves. Clients experience acute distress that could ultimately jeopardize their health or security, but they are not in imminent danger of serious harm or death. Individuals usually turn to adult services agencies for help with crises only when their usual methods of coping (self-help, support from family, friends, or other informal systems) have been inadequate. Crises are often time-limited, and although they require prompt action, they are generally not so pressing as emergencies and respond better to more deliberate problem solving.

Crises for individuals and families may trigger anxiety for social workers. One of the principal ways of averting or minimizing this anxiety is adequate agency guidelines about how to distinguish between emergencies and crises and what actions to take. Beyond this, supervisors can and should support workers in dealing with emergencies by helping them identify appropriate resources quickly and by helping them keep a healthy perspective on who "owns" the emergency or crisis. Additionally, supervisors must enable and empower social workers by helping them prepare to act independently. This is part of the teaching function of supervision—to help social workers refine their skills and judgment and to support them in exercising professional discretion.

Because crises can be handled with more deliberation than emergencies, crisis intervention is a short-term variation on the family assessment and change method. Golan (1987), in his entry "Crisis Intervention" in the 18th edition of the *Encyclopedia of Social Work*, suggested that "the goals in crisis intervention are primarily to cushion the impact of the stressful event by offering immediate emotional first aid and by strengthening the client's coping and integrative struggles through on-the-spot therapeutic clarification and guidance" (p. 366).

Crises result from acute situational disturbances (the death of a loved one or loss of a job), developmental or maturational life events (birth of a child or retirement), or human-made or natural disasters (riots or floods). Crisis situations are characterized by five stages: (1) hazardous events, (2) vulnerable states, (3) precipitating factors, (4) active crisis, and (5) reintegration. Periods of increased stress in the lives of individuals, groups, and families are initiated by hazardous events that change the client's status quo into a vulnerable state. Individuals may perceive the events that led to the crisis as a threat, a loss, or a challenge. The change is accompanied by increased anxiety. Hazardous events might include moving into a board-and-care home or the accumulated stress of living with a chronic illness, in that these events change what seems "normal" for people and make them more vulnerable. Precipitating factors (a rude remark by a staff member at the board-and-care home or an acute episode of illness) push people into active crisis—a state of confusion, disequilibrium, disorganization, and immobility. Reintegration, which takes place whether there is an outside intervention or not, occurs as the person regains equilibrium.

Crises provide opportunities for growth because people suffering intense anxiety and discomfort are more motivated to change and open to intervention so as to reduce the problem. Rapoport (1970) specified the first four goals of crisis intervention as follows:

    1. relief of symptoms
    2. restoration to the precrisis level of functioning

3. *understanding of the relevant precipitating event that led up to the state of disequilibrium*
4. *identification of remedial measures that the client or family can take or that are available through community resources.*

Rapoport suggested that, when possible, given the characteristics of clients and their situations, two additional goals may be sought:

5. *recognition of the connection between the current stress and past life experiences and conflicts*
6. *initiation of new models of perceiving, thinking, and feeling and the development of new adaptive and coping responses that can be useful beyond the immediate crisis situation.* (pp. 298–299)

Crisis intervention occurs in three phases. The beginning phase encompasses providing clients with emotional support and allowing them to ventilate feelings; assessment of the crisis situation; development of the problem and change list; agreement on the most important priorities for action; formulation of goals; and specification of tasks and working plan.

The middle phase focuses on implementing the plan and helping clients carry out and master tasks. Case management activities that link people with external resources (money, information, and services) are extremely important during the middle phase. Social workers are usually active during the early part of the middle phase but diminish their activity as clients carry out tasks and experience increased control over their actions and emotions.

Termination is the focus of the ending phase—reviewing progress and anticipating future activity and improvement in the client's circumstances. Termination also may include referring clients for a complete functional assessment and additional formal services to prevent new crises.

COGNITIVE APPROACHES

An effective counseling skill that adult services social workers can use with some clients, particularly with those who seem interested in talking about their feelings or willing to reflect on their situations, is a cognitive approach. This perspective helps clients and workers see that it is not necessarily the situations that clients face that cause them to be depressed, angry, demoralized, frustrated, or anxious, but their thoughts and beliefs about those situations. In the *Encyclopedia of Social Work,* Sherman (1987) noted that cognitive approaches are being incorporated into many forms of helping and counseling, including social work, because they are based on common sense, they are easy to understand, and they are effective. In the 19th edition of the *Encyclopedia of Social Work,* Granvold (1995) confirmed that cognitive interventions, demonstrated by empirical research to be effective during the past several years, "have been widely accepted by social workers and other mental health practitioners" (p. 525).

The central principle of cognitive approaches is that "most human emotions and behaviors, whether rational or irrational, functional or dysfunctional, are largely the result of what people think, imagine, or believe. . . . Therefore, it is not simply the specific events, interactions, or circumstances people encounter that lead to emotional and behavioral problems; rather, it is what people think or believe about these events, interactions, or circumstances that leads to such problems" (Sherman, 1987, p. 288). For example, one might imagine two sisters, living together, who one day receive a letter from a brother who has not been in touch with them for more than five years. One sister might weep for joy because she is so pleased to know that her brother is alive. The other sister reads the same letter and is furious that her brother has put her through the worry of the past five years. Although the event was the same for both women, their differing emotional reactions reflect the meaning of the letter to each. If clients can change their thoughts or perceptions, often they can change their feelings. Listed below are some common cognitive distortions or negative thinking patterns that inhibit people's ability to cope with difficult situations (Burns, 1980). All are traps that may prevent clients from functioning well, and as such, any may be the focus of a counseling intervention.

- All-or-nothing thinking: "If I can't stay in my home with this disability, I might as well die, because I couldn't be happy anywhere else."
- Overgeneralization: "Because I can't manage my money now, I am completely helpless to take care of myself."
- Disqualifying the positive: "Sure, my daughter calls me every day, but my son never visits."
- Jumping to conclusions: "I can't imagine my sister will go along with this plan. She never listens to what I say."
- Should statements: "I should take better care of my mother. If I were really a good daughter, I would move my mother into my home now that she's disabled, even though I can't afford it."
- Labeling and mislabeling: "Well, daddy's old. Of course he's senile."
- Personalization: "If I don't take care of all the details, he'll get hurt, and then it will be all my fault."

Cognitive approaches deal with the client's reality and with conscious thoughts and motivations. Social workers often realize that clients' negative feelings get in the way of using help, adapting to changes, coping with losses, and involving themselves in positive interpersonal relationships. Using a cognitive approach to help clients confront their feelings and identify dysfunctional thinking gives workers the framework and tools to help clients solve and manage problems.

Beyond its usefulness for clients, the cognitive approach can be especially valuable to workers in dealing with their own personal beliefs about clients' abilities to have a better quality of life. For example, a social worker might believe that because one of her clients is old, sick, and lives alone, he also is depressed. However, this worker will not be effective in helping the client envision another possibility because the worker believes that the situation is the cause of his feelings and the worker does not see how the situation can be altered. But if the worker understands that the client is depressed (at least in part) because of the way he sees his situation, the social worker will believe that other interpretations are possible and that with help the client may be able to see his situation differently and feel somewhat better. Once the social worker acknowledges to himself or herself that not every client in this situation is depressed, other perceptions are possible and therefore the interactions with the client reflect hopefulness.

Ellis (1974) suggested that the steps in a cognitive intervention can be summarized alphabetically—ABCDE, for activating event, belief, consequence, disputation, and evaluation. First is the activating event (for example, a client has a stroke and suffers temporary immobility). Second is the belief he or she holds about that event, which can be rational or irrational. Third is the consequence, which will be rational or dysfunctional feelings, depending on the client's belief. If the client's beliefs are irrational, she may believe that the stroke was unfair, that she is doomed to have another, and that she can never do any of the things she did before. The client will feel angry, frightened, anxious, and depressed. With these feelings, the client may make work difficult for the in-home aide and may drive away family members. If the client's beliefs are more rational—that the stroke was frightening but a warning to take better care of herself and that with physical therapy she will regain her mobility—she will feel hopeful and motivated to use help. The fourth element, disputation, occurs when social workers help clients with their irrational thoughts or beliefs (that is, to recognize, question, and challenge any beliefs that display cognitive distortion). Counseling helps clients explore other interpretations of events. The client and worker then evaluate whether these alternate interpretations are helping the client change negative feelings and function better.

CASE EXAMPLE

Mr. J falls and breaks his hip (activating event). Because he lives alone and has no family close by to assist him, his doctor recommends that he go to a nursing home. Mr. J is devastated. He imagines that he is now an invalid, believes that he will never go home again, and is sure that all nursing homes are horrible places (beliefs). He feels depressed, hopeless, and helpless (consequences). The adult services placement worker involved with him listens with empathy and conveys her understanding of his feelings. The worker knows that Mr. J is reacting to a traumatic event and recognizes the distortions in his thinking that are contributing to his distress. The worker points out to him that many people have a similar reaction to such an event, which helps to normalize the experience, and then she begins to help him explore his beliefs about nursing homes (for example, asking him what he has heard and seen about them) and provides him with more-accurate information. She also asks him what he believes an "invalid" is.

Mr. J answers that an invalid is someone who cannot do anything for himself. The social worker then helps Mr. J identify all the things he can do for himself. Using his definition, Mr. J and the worker refute that he has become an invalid (disputation). Through exploration and questioning of distorted thoughts, Mr. J can modify his feelings and have a more balanced outlook. He and the worker talk about whether the specific disputations are working and whether reframing ("I'm going into the nursing home for rehabilitation, not for life") is having a positive effect for him (evaluation). Although he still does not look forward to spending time in a nursing home, he comes to realize that not all nursing homes are "horrible," that he is not an "invalid," and that if he applies himself to rehabilitation he may go home again.

Other ways to help clients reframe their situations are to ask them what they might suggest to a friend who was in a similar situation, to suggest they look at the evidence for their beliefs, to point out shades of gray as a challenge to all-or-nothing thinking, and to suggest that they substitute less-loaded language for things they are telling themselves. As an example, a woman caring for her mother might berate herself for not anticipating all her mother's needs: "I should be able to care for my mother better." If she can substitute the statement, "I want to be able to care for my mother better," she may be able to change the guilty feeling to a more hopeful, positive one. Hearing this woman make the first statement, the social worker could point out that saying "should" often makes people feel guilty. The worker might ask the daughter if saying "I want to care for my mother better" would feel better to her. If she agrees, the worker can help the daughter identify similar statements and rephrase them in ways that are more helpful (Burns, 1989). There are many techniques that can be learned and used successfully, but the central approach is to help clients become aware that they contribute to their distress by the meaning they attach to events and that they can change that meaning and thereby change their feelings.

Cognitive approaches at their best are empowering for clients because they give them the tools to have more control over their perceptions and feelings. These approaches are empowering for workers because they are tools to use with clients in modifying internal beliefs when external problems cannot be changed or can only be partially improved.

LIFE REVIEW OR REMINISCENCE THERAPY

Life review, or the somewhat structured process of organizing memories, seems to be an activity that many older people normally engage in and enjoy. Although a focus on the past was once thought to be a symptom of senility, reminiscing allows older people to reflect on their lives, celebrate their achievements, reexperience emotions associated with significant people and events, and organize their memories in ways that allow them to see their lives as meaningful and to derive peace from that meaning.

Encouraging reminiscence may be useful for social workers who are just beginning to develop a relationship with the client. Although this technique may be useful with people in the last stages of life, reminiscence is also a way to help clients identify times in their lives when they have been successful or happy and to draw on the lessons of those times for coping strategies in the present. It can also point to dysfunctional perceptual patterns that contribute to present problems.

The social worker facilitates reminiscing, individually or in group settings, for several purposes. Among older clients, it provides an opportunity for sharing times in their lives when they were successful and vital, and it may minimize the differences in power and status between client and worker or between client and family members by reminding everyone that the client, too, was once young and accomplished many things. Sharing not only memories, but the feelings they evoke, can strengthen the bond between the client and worker or between the client and family members.

Many older people are inclined to reminisce and need only be given the opportunity to do so, whereas others may need prompting—looking at old pictures, hearing familiar music, or being questioned about their lives. Reminiscing may be especially beneficial for clients with dementia because it allows them to take pleasure in their remaining abilities to remember past experiences and times when they could function better. Topics for reminiscing include the following:

- What do you remember about your first day at school?
- Tell me about your first date.
- Where did you grow up?
- Can you describe the house you spent most of your time in?
- What do you remember most about World War II (or World War I or the Great Depression)?
- How did your mother do spring cleaning?
- Tell me about your first job.

Another possibility might be to make a genogram (see Figure 5-1 for an example), because it provides a structure for the life review process. Clients are able to see themselves graphically represented in the continuity of their family tree. Constructing a genogram offers a springboard to reassessing family themes, relationships, and memories, and it can help clients clarify time sequences and the relationships between important people. Clients may find the genogram to be one aid to coming to terms with their lives and to completing unfinished business, thus helping them to achieve integrity in the final phases of life (Hartman & Laird, 1983).

Some clients, however, do not benefit by reminiscence—they become fixated on difficult circumstances in their past, feel overwhelmed with negative emotions, and feel helpless to change things. When this occurs, it is best to refocus the interview on positive topics, distract the client, or use another form of counseling, such as a cognitive approach, to deal with the unresolved issues from the past.

GROUP WORK

The previous discussion of reminiscence suggests that it could be the focus of group work for some clients. Group approaches provide adult services social workers with additional opportunities. Besides the obvious value of serving more clients with the same resources, there are benefits to group approaches that cannot be obtained from other forms of intervention. Groups offer opportunities for socialization, which may be beneficial for isolated clients. Groups provide peer support and validation of feelings from those who have experienced some of the same difficulties or life events, and this can fill some clients' needs for affiliation. Groups also can provide the context for working on problems in interpersonal communication. Members see patterns in each other that contribute to difficulties with relationships outside the group. By pointing these out, they provide feedback on how to get their needs met effectively.

Groups are organized and operated differently depending on their purpose. Adult services social workers are most likely to be involved in facilitating support groups (such as a caregiver support group) or special-purpose groups that address specific needs—such as an assertiveness training group or an in-home aide training group.

Support groups are usually open and open-ended, that is, people come in or leave the groups as their needs dictate and the groups go on with no specified ending point. These groups are excellent vehicles for sharing practical and emotional support. Support groups for the families of people with Alzheimer's disease are a good example—members learn about recent research developments and share creative strategies they have used in managing difficult behaviors and caring for family members.

Special-purpose groups, such as resocialization groups, are established for a distinct purpose and end when that purpose is accomplished. These groups are usually closed—members begin and end together, and new members are generally not added during the group cycle. For example, a social worker whose caseload includes several isolated older men living in the same apartment building or neighborhood might establish a group to bring them together to strengthen their interpersonal relationships so that they function more effectively. Such a group might not run more than six or eight sessions.

Groups are not appropriate for all clients, however. Social workers involved in establishing a group must screen potential members carefully to determine which are likely to benefit and to exclude those whose behavior is likely to disrupt or distract from the group experience. Some factors that require careful consideration and often indicate inappropriateness for groups are severe hearing impairment (unless the group is specifically designed for such participants and assistive devices or personnel are available), personality disorders that seriously impair ability to relate to others, disruptive behavior, paranoia, and psychosis. Among the purely practical challenges for adult services workers engaged in developing a group are finding a suitable location or room for meeting, at the agency or elsewhere, and arranging transportation for potential members. For caregiver support groups, the social worker also may need to identify a source of respite.

FAMILY COUNSELING

We have defined counseling as helping clients change thoughts, feelings, attitudes, and behaviors that interfere with their abilities to meet their goals or to use resources in ways that would enable them to function optimally. Thoughts, feelings, and behaviors are powerfully affected by beliefs, communication, and interaction between people. Not surprisingly, interactions among family members are an important influence because of the emotional and long-lasting impact of these relationships (Herr & Weakland, 1979). Because of the great effect that family members have on one another, family counseling can often be vital to the success of any interventions to assist an individual client or the family as a whole. As with other types of counseling in adult services agencies, the social worker does not try to address remote causes of problems or to change personalities; rather, the goal is to help the family address those concerns that will help them meet their current goals or use resources effectively.

Particularly for families adjusting to their older member's impairment and increased dependency, there are developmental tasks that may be effectively supported by family counseling. Cohn and Jay (1988) described these tasks as grieving for losses in the older individual's independence and functioning, maintaining family integrity and identity in the face of vast changes, coping with the physical and emotional demands of caregiving while caring for the needs of family members without impairments, managing fixed or diminishing resources, supporting the growth and development of all family members, and providing sufficient emotional and physical support for all members. These are major family issues that cannot be resolved by one member alone. It takes cooperation and work among all members for these developmental tasks to be mastered successfully. The needs of the family system must be met in such a way that the autonomy of the older adult with impairment is respected and preserved as much as possible. At the same time, other family members, particularly children and grandchildren, must be able to accept that some dependency on the part of the older person is appropriate and to take responsibility according to the situation.

The family's beliefs and assumptions about changing parent–child and other roles must be identified and sometimes challenged. Gradual or sudden impairment in a family member may change the family's rules or the ways power is exercised. If the family member with impairment has typically taken responsibility for making family decisions, the family may experience disorientation when that member no longer can act as before. A family member with impairment may use illness or dependency as a key to exercising more power through demands on the family, or conversely, family members may take power over the member with impairment by taking charge of his or her care.

Herr and Weakland (1979) proposed a seven-step process of problem solving with older adults and their families that includes approaching the family system, identifying the problem, determining attempted solutions, determining goals, comprehending the family system, mobilizing it to respond to the challenge, and terminating the intervention. These steps parallel those of the family assessment and change method and fit well with the cognitive approach to counseling described in this chapter.

The first step, approaching the family system, involves being available and extending permission to family members to discuss feelings and problems. It is a willingness to go beyond merely helping to solve the presenting problem to hearing the underlying associated feelings.

The second step, determining the problem, involves encouraging each family member to describe his or her view of the problem. Often one family member—in many cases, the frail older adult—is identified as having the problem, and it is the social worker's task to help reframe the family's perception so that the members see it as a problem shared by all. For example, when one family member requires a lot of care, the entire family is affected because of the impact on time, resources, roles, and responsibilities of all members. As all members present their viewpoints, they can see their individual issues in the context of the whole family's needs. Focusing on the multigenerational nature of difficulties also puts the problem in a broader context, spreading responsibility over more potential helpers and expanding the options and resources available to address it. Collecting information from as many people as possible also enlarges the client's view of the situation (Brown, 1991).

The third step in the process is determining which solutions have already been tried. Each member of the family participates in this. By examining what has already been done and what the results have been, the social worker avoids recommending strategies that have already been tried and have failed, discovers potential solutions that are working for one or more family members, and finds out whether the strategies being tried are more problematic than the problem itself (for example, if the frail older client is moved to an unfamiliar place and consequently becomes disoriented, the solution has produced a new, more serious problem).

The fourth step, determining goals, is done as a collaborative process with the family members, all of whose viewpoints are important. Even when all members are not present or when the social worker is working only with the designated client, it is important to acknowledge interactions and potentially differing goals within the family.

The fifth step involves taking time to think about the information that has been gathered and giving everyone relief from taking immediate action. During this time, the social worker thinks about whether the family still needs counseling to meet its goals and considers such things as the extent of the family system, the family's rules, and which members exercise power. The social worker attempts to determine whether there are family members who have been overlooked, especially people who may have no blood relationship but whose views influence family decision making. These might include friends, the family physician, a minister or rabbi, or other helping professionals.

The sixth step, mobilizing the family system, incorporates both planning the interventions and implementing them. The social worker's involvement in this process may vary according to how readily the family takes on this task, but the goal for the social worker is to help the family arrive at step seven, terminating his or her involvement, when the family takes credit for what it has accomplished and anticipates and prepares for the future.

Family counseling may not be appropriate in all situations encountered by adult services social workers. However, it is a good tool to use in situations in which a problem affects a number of family members. Family counseling involves empowering family members to make choices by "providing information, teaching decision-making skills, and clarifying family rules (common beliefs) about the process of making good decisions" (Qualls, 1988, pp. 235–236).

Family counseling may be of value when the adult client cannot communicate or engage in problem solving. In such situations, the social worker may need to engage the rest of the family in counseling to resolve issues of caregiving and decision making. Family counseling also is useful when there are significant disagreements among family members about care of an adult with impairments. As with the other counseling methods presented here, if the social worker does not feel capable of providing family therapy, arranging for family therapy from another provider can be an important part of case management activities on behalf of the client.

Summary

Counseling is an essential component of adult services. To be effective in using this intervention strategy, social workers must have the necessary values, skills, and time. Returning to the notion that much of the counseling performed in adult services is opportunistic, a thorough knowledge of necessary values and skills is even more essential. The investment is worth the agency's effort. If clients are unable to use the agency's material resources well because of problems in emotional functioning, those resources are wasted.

When social workers are expected to provide formal counseling, their workloads must reflect the time needed to provide it. Beyond this, some adult services programs may decide to develop clinical social work positions within their agencies to serve clients with serious emotional difficulties. This service would provide clients with greater access to specialized counseling. Although this is not an option for most adult services programs, it is something each agency should consider when developing its mission for adult services. A decision on developing clinical services will be based on an assessment of unmet needs in the community; the availability of resources, including qualified staff; and agreements with other service providers, including the local mental health agency. Social workers in adult services are not and should not be the principal providers of mental health services in the community. However, they can offer a valuable source of support to clients whose desire for change is complicated by emotional and psychological issues.

Key Points

Excellent adult services social workers

- understand that empathic communication and professional relationships that reflect respect and genuineness are essential for effective practice
- use counseling to help clients mobilize their internal resources to solve problems and cope with problems that cannot be solved
- use the family assessment and change method to keep focused on their purpose in providing counseling
- value clients' self-determination and empowerment and act to support them.

Excellent adult services managers

- understand that workloads must reflect the time needed to provide counseling and do what is within their power to support social workers providing counseling services
- realize that providing clients with supportive relationships may not be the most effective use of social workers' time and encourage workers to arrange support from family members and other sources whenever possible
- understand the importance of specialized education, training, and supervision in counseling as an intervention strategy that social workers use in support of the family assessment and change method.

Excellent leaders

- support job designs that recognize the value of counseling as an intervention strategy for adult services clients and provide the time necessary for this task
- arrange specialized training to prepare workers to provide effective counseling.

References

Bricker-Jenkins, M. (1990, Spring). Another approach to practice and training: Clients must be considered the primary experts. *Public Welfare*, pp. 11–16.

Brown, F. H. (Ed.). (1991). *Reweaving the family tapestry.* New York: W. W. Norton.

Bumagin, V. E., & Hirn, K. F. (1990). *Helping the aging family: A guide for professionals.* Glenview, IL: Scott, Foresman.

Burns, D. D. (1980). *Feeling good: The new mood therapy.* New York: New American Library.

Burns, D. D. (1989). *The feeling good handbook.* New York: William Morrow.

Cohn, M. D., & Jay, G. M. (1988). Families in long-term-care settings. In M. A. Smyer, M. D. Cohn, & D. Brannon (Eds.), *Mental health consultation in nursing homes* (pp. 142–168). New York: New York University Press.

Egan, G. (1986). *The skilled helper: A systematic approach to effective helping* (3rd ed.). Pacific Grove, CA: Brooks/Cole.

Ellis, A. (1974). *Humanistic psychotherapy: The rational–emotive approach.* New York: McGraw-Hill.

Glasser, P., Sundel, M., Sarri, R., & Vintner, R. (Eds.). (1985). *Individual change through small groups* (2nd ed.). New York: Free Press.

Golan, N. (1987). Crisis intervention. In A. Minahan (Ed.-in-Chief), *Encyclopedia of social work* (18th ed., Vol.1, pp. 360–372). Silver Spring, MD: National Association of Social Workers.

Gold, N. (1990). Motivation: The crucial but unexplored component of social work practice. *Social Work, 35,* 49–56.

Granvold, D. (1995). Cognitive treatment. In R. L. Edwards (Ed.-in-Chief), *Encyclopedia of social work* (19th ed., Vol. 1, pp. 525–538). Washington, DC: NASW Press.

Hartman, A., & Laird, J. (1983). *Family-centered social work practice.* New York: Free Press.

Herr, J. J., & Weakland, J. H. (1979). *Counseling elders and their families: Practical guidelines for applied gerontology* (Vol. 2). New York: Springer.

Maslow, A. H. (1968). *Toward a psychology of being* (2nd ed.). Princeton, NJ: Van Nostrand.

National Association of Social Workers. (1994). *NASW code of ethics.* Washington, DC: Author.

Perlman, H. H. (1957). *Casework: A problem-solving process.* Chicago: University of Chicago Press.

Perlman, H. H. (1979). *Relationship: The heart of helping people.* Chicago: University of Chicago Press.

Qualls, S. H. (1988). Problems in families of older adults. In N. Epstein, S. E. Schlesinger, & W. Dryden (Eds.), *Cognitive–behavioral therapy with families* (pp. 215–253). New York: Brunner/Mazel.

Rapoport, L. (1970). Crisis intervention as a model of brief treatment. In R. W. Roberts & R. H. Nee (Eds.), *Theories of social casework* (pp. 267–311). Chicago: University of Chicago Press.

Richmond, M. (1917). *Social diagnosis.* New York: Russell Sage.

Rooney, R. H., & Wanless, M. (1985). A model for caseload management based on task-centered practice. In A. E. Fortune (Ed.), *Task-centered practice with families and groups* (pp. 187–199). New York: Springer.

Sherman, E. (1987). Cognitive therapy. In A. Minahan (Ed.-in-Chief), *Encyclopedia of social work* (18th ed., Vol. 1, pp. 288–291). Silver Spring, MD: National Association of Social Workers.

CHAPTER 8

Creative Responses to Challenging Situations

VICKIE L. ATKINSON

In adult services social work, some clients have behaviors that present substantial challenges to the social worker and agency. This chapter focuses on creative approaches that social workers and their agencies can use to respond to clients' expectations of the agency and to clients' difficult behaviors. The first section examines the agency's part in supporting and empowering workers in their dealings with clients whose expectations of the agency and problematic behaviors create difficulties for agency and staff. The second section focuses on specific interventions that social workers use with individual clients—methods of setting limits to help clients make better use of agency resources and principles of interaction to minimize discord. The chapter concludes with a discussion of special considerations, including workers' safety and circumstances that present challenges to practice in adult services. The agency's role comes first in this chapter because any worker's success in interacting with "difficult" clients depends in great measure on the agency's support for setting limits, including guidelines about what sorts of consequences inappropriate behavior can entail and on well-developed strategies to prevent disruptive behavior.

To set limits on clients' behaviors may initially seem at odds with the notion of empowering them, and from one perspective it is, because it suggests that clients must fit some set of norms to receive benefits from the agency. However, limitations on behavior can offer the disruptive client some insight into self-control and some training in how to get needs met in general. Attempts by clients to exert control in the worker–client relationship are not themselves problematic. Disruptive and manipulative behavior that results in the client steering the relationship in harmful directions, including unduly influencing methods and issues of who is included as the client, can be dysfunctional (Bumagin & Hirn, 1990; Hepworth, 1993). Guidance of the helping relationship is an inherent responsibility of the adult services social worker.

Understanding how to gain access to resources and participate effectively in a case management or counseling relationship can be empowering for a client. By steering the helping relationship, the social worker acts as a role model for how to assert direction and control in relationships without being manipulative or authoritarian. Effective responses to clients' difficult behaviors helps clients, social workers, and the agency. It helps preserve other clients' access to the agency's resources, specifically the social worker's time.

For various reasons, adult services programs will not be able to meet all the needs and desires of all their clients. Sometimes resources are limited, and sometimes clients need or want services for which they are ineligible. Confronted with these barriers, clients may express frustration in ways that cause difficulties for the staff and for other clients. In addition, some clients have conditions such as mental illness or developmental disabilities that can contribute to disruptive behaviors. Personal circumstances—for example, the frustration of being referred from one agency to another with no immediate prospect of getting assistance—also may contribute to disruptive behavior. Agencies and individual social workers must find creative ways to diffuse difficult situations to help clients get the services they need.

Social workers can find themselves the target of profane, abusive, or threatening language. Clients can be aggressive in demanding time and attention on the telephone or in the office. When social workers act as payee, clients frequently may demand money. Occasionally, workers are confronted with physical or sexual threats. The agency and the social worker have the responsibility for uncovering the causes of these behaviors, looking for the opportunities that even difficult situations present, and finding solutions.

Agency's Role in Addressing Difficult Situations
IMPORTANCE OF A WELL-ARTICULATED MISSION
Adult services programs characteristically are charged with many complex responsibilities in the community. Because of the important role adult services play in addressing the needs of vulnerable citizens, it is not surprising that the community turns to the adult services program for help in solving many community problems that are going unaddressed. The adult services agency often is seen as the safety net for vulnerable people. Unfortunately, even with the most bounteous resources, no agency can meet all the needs of impoverished people or of those with serious disabilities.

The best approaches on the part of the agency are those that anticipate difficulties. One useful tool and source of strength for an adult services program is a clear statement of mission. Such a mission statement defines the scope and limitations of the adult services program. It should be made with the consultation and cooperation of the program's community board and local elected officials. It should reflect a process of negotiation and consensus building. The statement should be well publicized with the general public, community leaders and elected officials, and related public and private agencies. It should clarify the program's primary target populations and its role in serving those populations. As the agency defines itself publicly over time, the number of inappropriate expectations and requests for help from citizens and community agencies should diminish. Clarifying the scope and limitations of the agency's services for the community is a first step in preventing or reducing the many difficult situations that can result from inappropriate expectations on the part of clients and families.

"HONORING THE CLIENT" AS A MEANS OF PREVENTION

A great deal can be done to avert and reduce difficult situations and behaviors by cultivating an attitude of respect within the agency for individuals. If the agency holds and rewards the philosophy that its staff exists to support, enable, and empower adult services clients, this philosophy will be translated into actions that demonstrate these values.

One of the simplest signs of this philosophy in action is routine courtesy. Staff members should greet clients in a courteous and professional manner, see them promptly, explain and apologize for delays, listen carefully and empathically to clients' perspectives on their problems, acknowledge their strengths and resources, respect their values, and work alongside them to find solutions. This attitude of respect should permeate the agency from receptionist through director.

ASSESSING AND ADDRESSING PROBLEM BEHAVIORS
ACROSS THE AGENCY

Defining the scope and limitations of the agency mission and roles and cultivating an attitude of respect and appreciation for its clientele will go far in reducing the incidence of difficult situations. These approaches will not, however, alleviate all problems. The agency's next step is to perform an assessment of all the difficult situations that arise between the agency and its clientele.

One useful tool in conducting this assessment is the "ABC" approach to identifying the causes of disruptive situations and determining possible solutions. The ABC approach (for antecedent, behavior, and consequence), is based on psychological research into the causes of difficulties and ways to overcome them (Egan, 1986). Individual and group behavior is the reaction to a stimulus—the antecedent. For example, a harried receptionist might speak abruptly to a client. The client in turn responds with curses and threats—the behavior. Inappropriate behavior can be reinforced or diminished by the consequences that follow it. If the client who curses the receptionist and makes a great deal of noise gets to see the social worker more quickly—the consequence—he or she may do the same thing again. Even negative attention can serve as a reward. On the other hand, ignoring unwanted behavior that is neither dangerous nor destructive can diminish it, because it goes unrewarded.

An important initial step in the agency's assessment is to identify problematic situations or problem behaviors. One way might be to ask all personnel who have contact with clients to keep a list of difficult situations and behaviors that occur during a designated period (perhaps one or two months) or perhaps do a quarterly review as an ongoing process. The agency or unit might then appoint a task force composed of receptionists, clerical workers, aides, social workers, and managers to review these situations and determine which are the most disruptive, dangerous, or time-consuming and need response. Some unpleasant situations or behaviors may not be sufficiently problematic to require a response. Among the situations and behaviors selected, the group should establish priorities and select a few specific behaviors or situations to try to change. Some relevant questions for selecting behaviors might be: "Can this be fixed easily?" "What is the danger in not fixing this?" "Does this problem take up a lot of staff time?"

The task force's next step would be to describe the targeted situations and behaviors in as much detail as possible. This description should include what the clients' and workers' actions were, what the antecedents of behavior were, and what the clients' and workers' personal characteristics were, particularly those that might contribute to the behavior. Other factors to be considered include the nature of the clients' presenting problems (for example, mental illness or substance abuse), the services involved (such as representative payeeship or in-home services), which staff members were involved and how they handled the situation, issues involving racial and cultural clashes, and any other relevant information (for example, whether the clients had been waiting for a long time).

After making a careful assessment, the task force can set priorities among situations and behaviors to change and develop measurable goals for charting progress. Then the task force would examine the agency's resources and develop a plan of action. Some strategies may focus on the agency's physical characteristics: Can the waiting room be made more pleasant and comfortable? Some strategies may concern the way the agency does business: Can waiting times be diminished? Is caseload composition (for example, all representative payee cases assigned to a few social workers) contributing to problem behaviors? Are clients' and workers' personal characteristics assessed before case assignments are made to avoid potential problems? Do the agency's procedures reward disruptive behavior in some way? Other strategies may focus on training: Can staff members be made more aware of the impact of their behavior on clients? Do they need training in how to recognize signs of conflict and minimize it? Finally, in light of the agency's mission for adult services, are there some clients or categories of clients who could be served better by some other agency?

The ability of a social worker, supervisor, or program manager to set limits with clients successfully depends almost entirely on the backing of the agency and community. Guidelines for responding to difficult situations and behaviors and enforcing consequences must be spelled out clearly. Policies must be developed in such a way as not to deny clients services to which they are entitled yet ensure that problematic situations and behaviors are diminished. The agency's responses might include limiting such clients' time with workers, restricting their access to certain parts of the building, asking them to leave the premises or having them removed by law enforcement officials when warranted, barring them from the agency except at specified times, and encouraging workers to press charges when they are threatened or assaulted. It is important that consequences be enforceable and used consistently.

Clients who consistently exhibit difficult behaviors in the adult services agency also may be clients of other agencies. When this is true, agencies may need to coordinate responses. (More will be said later in this chapter about how social workers can do this for individual clients.) For example, the adult services program might develop an agreement with the local mental health authority on case staffings for clients seen by both agencies whose behavior causes problems. Such an agreement should address five items: (1) which characteristics or behaviors indicate a need for joint staffing, (2) who will be involved from each agency, (3) what roles each agency's staff members will take in initiating and coordinating staffings, (4) what follow-up responsibilities each agency will have, and (5) who will assume the monitoring function to ensure that agreed-on actions are implemented. Written agreements among those involved would summarize responsibilities, reinforce commitment, and lessen the possibility of misunderstanding.

Not all difficult situations occur at the agency—sometimes they take place in clients' homes, in board-and-care homes, or in other settings. If the agency's assessment of behaviors reveals that staff members are concerned about a pattern of difficult behaviors they encounter in contacts with clients outside the agency (for example, during protective services evaluations or when providing in-home services), then the agency should develop strategies for those situations as well. These might include guidelines on when social workers should visit clients accompanied by a supervisor or another worker and when involving law enforcement agents would be appropriate. Chapter 14, on in-home services, discusses some of the problems aides and social workers may encounter and suggests some solutions. It is important that staff members feel safe in carrying out their duties and that they know the agency supports them.

Some clients are already aware of their right—and if not, they should be informed—to seek other avenues of response if they feel they are not being treated appropriately by the worker or agency. They may contact local elected officials, state or federal legislators, state agencies, hot lines, or the news media. When clients resort to these actions, the agency may find it useful to have a policy for requesting clients to sign a release of information, emphasizing to clients that only by doing so will the agency be able to talk freely about their concerns in any public forum. Other positive approaches include having an agency policy that identifies who speaks to the press, that promotes openness in dealing with reporters, and that supports sharing information about general situations even when communication about a specific case is protected by confidentiality rules and laws. It is also useful to have guidelines about which incidents or complaints should be brought to the attention of management so that, whenever possible, management is prepared to respond.

The involvement of other parties can frustrate or intimidate social workers who have been trying to work constructively with clients, but sometimes the involvement of a third party can be helpful to social workers in getting a different perspective of the client's problem or in gaining support for their actions. It also provides an opportunity to educate the public, media, or elected representatives about some of the special problems of adult services clients and the agency. Involvement of other parties also can empower clients to let them know that the agency has heard from the people or organizations they have contacted.

Finally, from a broader perspective, involvement in threatening or uncomfortable situations produces emotional wear and tear for both individual workers and the agency. Careful planning to prevent these situations and development of clear agency policies and guidelines can reduce stress, particularly if staff members have major involvement in designing them. Training and practice in conflict management can give staff members the confidence and skills necessary to cope with difficulties. Beyond this, supportive supervision or peer support—debriefing, time for ventilation, support of feelings, constructive problem solving—can help social workers manage the discomfort that confrontation with a client or other parties may trigger.

Social Worker's Response to Challenging Behaviors

The practices and philosophy of the agency greatly determine what response individual social workers can make to their clients. In turn, social workers have a responsibility to contribute to the agency's recognition of problems and to developing solutions. They also have an obligation to know and follow agency policies about limits and consequences. Beyond that, there are many things that social workers can do as professionals to avert or reduce conflict. Chapter 7 discusses the social worker's role as counselor and ways to develop successful relationships, and those relationships are the foundation for working with clients whose behaviors present difficulties. In addition, there are individual strategies for managing conflict and difficult situations.

The difficult situations that adult services workers encounter may be produced by clients who loudly insist on seeing workers, are verbally abusive, come daily to ask for money when the agency serves as representative payee, are under the influence of substances, disturb other clients or personnel and refuse to leave the agency, deny they have problems, overtly or covertly threaten workers or make sexual advances, call repeatedly, demand money or services, or threaten to call local or state officials or the newspaper. Staff members who must deal with this sort of conflict find it emotionally draining. However, understanding some of the factors that lead to and diminish conflict and having a plan to manage conflict when it does occur help increase workers' competence and confidence in being able to resolve these situations.

As a resource in this area, Hepworth (1993) provided a useful discussion of effective responses to manipulative behavior in the helping relationship. Hepworth and Larsen (1993) similarly outlined useful tips for enhancing motivation with involuntary and ambivalent clients. Aronson, Bennett, and Gurland (1983) and Brink (1987) also provided models and practice strategies for addressing difficult situations and behaviors involving older adult clients. The following discussion of responses to difficult situations and client behaviors draws on these and other references, as well as the practice experience of the author.

SELF-AWARENESS

Social workers and other staff members who have contact with clients must be aware of their own values, tolerances, and intolerances. They must know their "buttons" and what pushes them. Some people react strongly to profanity, whereas others do not find it especially offensive. Some staff members are sensitive to clients' criticism of their work, whereas others take it in stride. Increasing self-awareness allows workers to identify their own automatic responses and prepare more-appropriate ways of acting.

For example, if cursing is especially offensive to a social worker, he or she can choose an assertive response and say "I find it hard to listen carefully when you are cursing," instead of becoming angry with the client. If the social worker does not recognize and deal with personal negative feelings, they may come out in unintended ways—not acting as quickly on clients' requests, not taking complete action, or not advocating as strongly for these clients. Self-awareness also helps social workers set reasonable, rather than punitive, limits with clients. Examining these issues in the course of supervision helps workers discover the effects specific behaviors have on them.

Well-developed skills in empathic listening in conjunction with cognitive approaches also can help the social worker alter her or his response to clients. If the worker can identify the client's point of view, he or she may be able to reframe the problem behavior and respond differently. If the worker can say (and feel) that "Mr. Jones is very persistent about getting his needs met and anxious to change his situation" rather than "Mr. Jones is manipulative and is driving me wild with his frequent phone calls," he or she may be able to respond to the client's anxiety and defuse it some, so that they can work more productively together.

RELATIONSHIP AND COUNSELING SKILLS

The importance of the quality of the relationship the social worker develops with the client, the communication and counseling skills used, and the attitudes toward the client cannot be overemphasized. Chapter 7 discusses the techniques and uses of counseling to help clients make good use of internal and external resources. Some clients are more challenging than others for social workers to help in meeting this objective.

The guiding principles for social workers seeking to prevent difficult behaviors are (1) give clients choices and (2) help them save face. Using a change-oriented approach to remedying difficult behaviors with individuals provides the framework for acting on these principles. Just as the change process for the agency begins with an assessment, so does the social worker's interaction with individual clients. Like the agency, the social worker must describe the problem behaviors, identify their antecedents (When and where are they occurring? Is there some event or circumstance that precedes them?), and consider their consequences (Is the behavior getting the client something he or she wants—speedier service or more attention?).

For example, consider a social worker who makes home visits to a client and always spends more time with her than she can afford. As the worker gets ready to leave, the client begins to cry and finds yet another "urgent" problem for the social worker. In this case, the worker must assess whether she is contributing to the problem through what she does before the client begins to act this way, whether the discussion before the client's crying spells focuses on any particular subject, and what kind of attention the client receives as a result of her behavior.

After identifying the problem behaviors and assessing their antecedents and consequences, the social worker determines, in consultation with the supervisor and others who might be involved, which behaviors can be tolerated and which must be changed. The social worker then looks at the resources available to assist in rewarding appropriate behaviors and sanctioning inappropriate ones. One significant resource is the worker's time and attention and the way in which it can be made available or limited. Agency policy also can offer guidelines about the frequency or duration of visits, on procedures for asking clients to leave the premises and enforcing their removal, and for involving other staff members in interviews.

If the social worker decides to set limits with a client, he or she must consider how the intervention can reflect an attitude of empowerment rather than control. Empowerment here is characterized by responsibility for problematic behaviors and commitment to change. A combination of limits and alternate choices through which clients can express their needs for control can be an effective strategy for reducing inappropriate behaviors.

For example, for clients receiving representative payee services, is the social worker making sure to involve them in all possible decision making or do they feel that the worker is controlling not only the money but also them? Is there a plan to help rehabilitate or teach clients the skills needed to help them regain all or partial control of their money—enabling them to feel some control and hope? Are clients involved in deciding when and where they will get their money? Does the social worker encourage these clients to be involved in deciding how to spend the money or how their money is allocated?

Limits and choices also may include how often the social worker sees a client, where the worker sees the client, how long visits last, how often the worker accepts phone calls, and what is discussed during contacts. This sort of limit is often more for the social worker's benefit than for the client's, and social workers should be frank about their needs to control their time and work. Nonetheless, workers should vigorously seek to involve clients in these agreements, because clients are more likely to abide by limits when they help develop them—once again, giving clients choice—and when they see that the social worker is willing to negotiate. Honoring agreements about limits is an exercise that increases self-control for some clients, and for them, success can be enabling and empowering.

When the client agrees to limits he or she does not entirely like, the social worker should look for ways to reward the client for honoring them. There also are ways to frame the limits to minimize the negative connotations for the client. For example, if the social worker only sees the client once a week at a specified time, this means the client will have all of the worker's attention during that time. The client might be given a choice about how that time is spent. Most of the challenging behavior described so far in this chapter has included some measure of threat or conflict. Social workers may be even more uncomfortable in setting limits with clients with difficulties and handicapping conditions, but whose neediness is more of a nuisance than a threat. Social workers are sometimes hesitant to be yet another person who says no. However, workers have limited time and energy, and agencies have limited resources. The following case example suggests strategies for working with clients to help them get their needs met while recognizing that the social worker alone may not be able to meet those needs. Here, too, the emphasis is on giving the client a choice, even if that choice is restricted.

CASE EXAMPLE

Mr. S calls his social worker almost every day to talk about minor complaints and problems. Once Mr. S has the worker on the telephone, he usually keeps her occupied for 20 to 30 minutes. In the context of his situation and her busy caseload, she decides that two phone calls a week is all she can accept from him. Mr. S does not agree that limiting his contact to two phone calls is adequate. She tells him that she understands that he would like to talk more frequently, but because of her responsibilities to other clients, and except in an emergency, she simply cannot spend so much time on the telephone with him. However, she asks him to choose which days and at what time he would like to call, and because he comes to the agency once a month, she offers to set aside half an hour to speak with him on those days, during which time she is careful to listen attentively and with empathy.

During one of his visits to the agency, she helps him develop strategies for meeting his need for contact and puts him in touch with a telephone reassurance program. During the first week of the new plan, Mr. S calls on Tuesday and Thursday, as he agreed, but he also calls on Friday to test the new limits. The worker reminds him of the new plan and tells him that in the future she will hang up if he calls for other than an emergency. The next week, when he calls on Monday, she finds out briefly the reason for his call (not an emergency) and says, "I cannot talk with you now, Mr. S. There is no emergency. I will talk with you on Tuesday. Good-bye," and hangs up.

Social workers must plan appropriate consequences for clients who push beyond the limits. Sometimes limit setting with individual clients will involve the cooperation of several people—the receptionist, the supervisor, other staff members, and perhaps representatives from other agencies. Case conferences may be necessary to involve all interested people in identifying and understanding difficult behaviors, developing strategies to respond to them, and developing a consensus on what the consequences of the client's response to limits will be. To the extent possible, clients should be involved in this process.

An example that occurs fairly frequently in the home setting involves the client who makes excessive or inappropriate demands of the in-home aide ("favors" that are not in the service plan) to compensate for loss of control of the home environment. A case conference among the client, aide, and social worker can help establish areas of flexibility and compliance. Both the aide and the client can agree to call the social worker if limits are not maintained. Through counseling skills, the social worker also may assist the client in finding legitimate outlets for the need for control (for example, determining the aide's arrival time, specifying how certain tasks are to be completed, or identifying other areas of the client's life in which he or she can increase control).

This suggests a method workers can use to manage challenging behaviors or to prevent conflict. To clarify responsibilities, social workers, clients, and any concerned others can draw up a contract that specifies the extent and limitations of involvement. Informal written agreements, with copies given to clients, reinforce commitment and prevent misunderstanding (Hepworth & Larsen, 1993). These contracts include such things as what the worker will do, what the client will do, and the frequency and length of interviews and phone calls. The social worker assigned to work with this client must be prepared to confront individuals who are not upholding their part of the contract. For example, another professional or a family member might need to be reminded of his or her agreement to refer the client to the adult services program rather than to respond personally to an inappropriate request.

RECOGNIZING AND DEALING WITH CONFLICT

The first principle, to give clients a choice, is important in managing conflict. Perhaps more important is the second, to help the client save face. Conflicts arise between clients and social workers, and conflict in itself is not necessarily negative. It focuses attention on issues that have not been adequately addressed, it highlights differences in perceptions among people, and it leads to opportunities for growth and change. Conflict that is not recognized or handled well, however, can escalate and become problematic for both worker and client.

Social workers must know how to deal with situations that are escalating into conflict. Recognizing behavioral reactions that signal increased tension, both in oneself and in the client, is important. These may include markedly increased or decreased eye contact, rapid shallow breathing, increased body tension—clenched fists or jaws, changes in skin coloring—and changes in loudness, pitch, or tremulousness of the voice. The client's changes toward an emotional outburst will likely provoke similar changes in the worker, who finds himself or herself in a normal "fight or flight" reaction. The worker may feel his or her adrenaline level rise and feel the urge to lash out or become defensive. Alternately, the worker may want to run away from the confrontation. Because of the nature of the job and the need to maintain a relationship with the client, the social worker does not often have the option of running away, which leaves the worker with the alternative of becoming defensive and counterattacking. Neither flight nor fight, however, is likely to be productive, because worker and client perceive that they are in a win–lose position and neither wants to lose. The first step in defusing the situation is for the social worker to be aware of his or her own reactions and to do what he or she can to relax and regain control of his or her behavior. A slow, quiet, deep breath can help the worker relax and focus attention on what must be done.

Burns (1989) suggested an approach that can produce a win–win situation for the social worker and client—the "disarming" approach. This can often forestall a nonproductive confrontation (for example, when a client accuses the social worker of not doing something he or she wants done). It is effective, but it takes some practice, because it is the opposite of what one might normally do when attacked. To use the disarming approach, the worker finds something in what the client says to agree with. For example, if the client says, "I'm still living in that rat hole and you haven't done anything to find me another place," rather than point out all the work he or she has done (a defensive maneuver), the worker acknowledges the client's perspective by saying, "You wanted me to find some possible places for you to live before your check came in and I haven't done that." The key to disarming is agreement rather than arguing or defensiveness.

The worker also may show empathy by recognizing the feeling the client is expressing and acknowledging that feeling with the client: "I understand that you're really angry with me." The worker continues to listen carefully to the content of and the feelings behind what the client is saying and agrees with something at each stage until the client feels understood and ceases to be as angry. Then the worker may take a further step and say how he or she feels: "I feel sorry I let you down" or "I'm sorry I wasn't able to do what you expected, and I know you're disappointed. I feel upset, though, when you shout at me."

Disarming and empathizing also can work with people who complain a great deal but are not ready to change or engage in problem solving. These clients often need someone to listen to them before they are able to consider their circumstances. The client who constantly complains that "no one ever helps me with anything" is likely to respond much better to a worker's acknowledgment of his or her perspective—"You don't get the help you want"—than to a logical listing of all the services he or she receives. Sometimes empathic listening—someone to understand their viewpoint—is all clients really want. Also, sometimes when people feel that they have been understood they are willing to explore new options.

Special Considerations

WORK ENVIRONMENT

The way social workers arrange their offices promotes professional, helpful, and safe interactions with clients. If office furniture is arranged so that workers and clients face each other at eye level, it eliminates subtle cues about power differentials that one person looking up or down at the other can convey. Arranging seating so that worker and client can face each other without barriers can contribute to open communication. However, to prevent the possibility of being cut off from the outside, the worker can place his or her chair closer to the door than the client's.

Social workers—and anyone who works in an office and has contact with the public—should be sensitive to the meaning and unintended function of pictures and objects in their offices. An office that reflects the social worker's personality provides him or her with a comfortable setting in which to work. Nonetheless, workers must be especially sensitive to pictures or other objects that might be offensive or provocative. For example, posters that display religious symbols may be offensive to some clients. Although violent clients are rare, social workers should consider that sharp or heavy objects in their office can become weapons. Social workers' offices should be inviting and professional, designed with careful consideration of the potential benefits and consequences of the arrangement for clients while reflecting their own comfort and self-expression.

As the agency performs its assessment of problem behaviors, the task force may discover that certain common areas of the building figure frequently in incidents. Some of this may be because most clients use these areas. Nonetheless, it is worth examining what features of waiting rooms and other common areas contribute to disruptive behaviors. Too much noise, activity, or visual stimulation often have a bad effect on clients with mental impairments, and overstimulation often contributes to the stress levels of clients generally. Although there may be substantial restrictions on what sort of remodeling or rearrangement can be done, just setting up the chairs in the waiting room to divide clients into smaller groups or restructuring the way clients and personnel walk through the area can alter the level of activity.

Because clients are entitled to confidentiality in dealing with the agency, private, quiet rooms for interviewing, especially for clients who are distraught or angry, are necessary. Arranging for privacy and quiet in a client's home may be more difficult, but the worker can ask to have a noisy television turned off or for a quieter room in which to talk. In a board-and-care home, the worker can arrange with a staff member for a private place to talk with clients.

CONSIDERATIONS FOR CLIENTS

It is extremely important to consider the characteristics, special needs, and circumstances of clients in assessing and managing behaviors. It is unreasonable to have the same level of expectation for someone who has a serious mental illness, dementia, or developmental disabilities as for people without these problems. The worker and the client (sometimes in consultation with other professionals or family members) must determine what expectations are reasonable and work to see that they are met.

Some behaviors are caused by illness or medication (for example, pacing and restlessness). Clients with schizophrenia may have difficulty sitting in noisy waiting rooms (Anderson, Reiss, & Hogarty, 1986); people with developmental disabilities or cognitive impairments may need simple, concrete directions or statements of fact. For example, the receptionist might say to an agitated client who seems to have some impairment, "I'll show you to Ms. Jones's office today so that you can find your way next time," rather than "Go down the corridor and turn left through the third doorway, go on until you get to the next corridor and turn right, and she'll be in the office at the end of the hall." Complicated explanations and attempts to reason with these clients are likely to be counterproductive. The following list provides tips for dealing with clients with mental disabilities:

- Use clients' names to make sure you have their attention.
- Speak slowly and clearly.
- Use short, simple statements and directions.
- Speak concretely—avoid abstractions.
- Avoid or minimize explanations.
- Avoid agreeing with or contradicting clients without dementia who are delusional or hallucinating; respond to their feelings or change the subject.
- Accept what clients with dementia say or distract them—don't contradict or try to reason. For example, don't insist that an 85-year-old woman's mother is not coming to visit; rather say "I know your mother means a lot to you. Maybe this sofa would be a comfortable place to wait—here's a magazine to look at."
- Simplify the environment; minimize distractions.
- Convey respect and attention through speech, eye contact, and nonverbal communication.

The best predictor of future behavior is past behavior. The agency and the social worker must assess serious disruptive or dangerous behaviors carefully and put plans in place to minimize further occurrences. For example, if a client with alcoholism verbally abuses a worker any time she comes to the agency under the influence, it might be advisable to include another worker in the interview or station a security guard near the room. Alternatively, the client could be directed to leave the agency and return when she has not been drinking. When social workers or in-home aides arrive at clients' homes and agreed-on limits are being violated, they should leave.

Assaultive behavior is rare, but excellent workers have a plan to deal with it if it occurs. The following steps should be taken face-to-face with the client; note that the agency should have plans to guard the security of employees (Epstein, 1985):

- Try to calm the client with a diversion.
- Stop the action, if you can.
- Do not make interpretive remarks that could be understood as criticism.
- Stand up and move close to the door or leave the room.
- Get another staff person to participate.
- If you cannot calm the client, activate as quickly as possible the security system that the agency uses.
- Do not rush matters; these incidents take time to resolve.
- Do not argue with the client.
- If the client is armed, get the police.
- Keep onlookers away; the fewer people present, the less likely somebody will inadvertently escalate the situation or get hurt.

Assaultive behavior also occurs in the home or community setting. Epstein (1985) offered some good advice about this situation:

> Don't make home visits alone in neighborhoods that are known to be dangerous or at hours that are dangerous; the police can provide information about this. Do not be afraid of your intuition. If you start to fantasy getting assaulted, if your breath almost stops, or if your mind goes blank with fear—don't ignore it. You are getting a message and you should obey it. You may on occasion make a fool of yourself by being scared of nothing. It doesn't matter; better to be embarrassed than in the hospital. (p. 269)

If someone in a home where aides or social workers are visiting is violent or threatens to become so, staff members should remove themselves from the situation as quickly and calmly as possible and seek help from the agency or law enforcement office immediately. Excellence in social work practice requires live, healthy social workers.

Summary

Most difficult behaviors can be prevented by cultivating a climate in which clients receive appropriate, individualized responses from staff members who show them respect and who focus on empowering them by providing choices even when they must be limited. To empower personnel generally, the agency itself must determine who its clientele will be, set limits on what behaviors it will tolerate, develop strategies for dealing with problematic situations, train employees in methods of conflict management, and support employees in using their best professional judgment to maintain the agency's most valuable resource—themselves.

Social workers and other employees who have direct contact with clients must understand how to recognize the signs of potential conflict to prevent it and know how to use disarming techniques and empathic listening to reduce it if it occurs. The two most important principles are to give clients choices and to help them save face.

Key Points

Excellent adult services social workers

- recognize their responsibility to evaluate the climate of the agency, to contribute to agencywide solutions for problem behaviors, and to know and follow agency policies concerning limit setting and enforcing consequences
- prevent and minimize conflict and difficult behaviors through their relationships with clients, their communication and counseling skills, and their attitudes
- share relevant information with other staff members who might be involved in dealing with difficult behaviors
- give clients choices and help them save face
- use interventions that empower clients to gain or regain control of their behaviors rather than trying to control those behaviors
- contract with clients about the extent and limitations of the worker's interventions with them
- forestall confrontation with the disarming approach; that is, find some point of agreement with the client's point of view and work from there
- use empathic communication—which reflects understanding of the client's feelings—and allow clients to ventilate their emotions to prevent conflict
- use case conferences to involve all interested individuals in identifying and understanding problem behaviors, developing strategies to manage them, and developing consensus on limits
- follow their instincts and err on the side of caution when confronted with a potentially dangerous situation
- furnish and arrange their offices in such a way as to promote professional, helpful, and safe interactions with clients.

Excellent adult services managers

- define the scope and limitations of the adult services program to inform the public and to support agency personnel
- prevent problem situations and behaviors by cultivating an agencywide attitude of respect for the consumers of adult services
- assess problem behaviors for the agency, examine their antecedents and consequences, determine which will be tolerated and which will be targeted for change, and implement strategies to manage problems
- set limits and determine consequences in consultation with boards, county commissioners, law enforcement agencies, attorneys, and other relevant individuals and entities

- provide support and training for social workers who must confront and manage difficult behaviors.

Excellent leaders
- develop policies that support setting limits on difficult behaviors
- consult with agencies on plans for managing these behaviors
- provide training in preventing and dealing with conflict and in managing disruption.

References

Anderson, C. M., Reiss, D. J., & Hogarty, G. E. (1986). *Schizophrenia and the family: A practitioner's guide to psychoeducation and management.* New York: Guilford Press.

Aronson, M. K., Bennett, R., & Gurland, B. J. (1983). *The acting-out elderly.* New York: Haworth.

Brink, T. L. (Ed.). (1987). *The elderly uncooperative patient.* New York: Haworth.

Bumagin, V. E., & Hirn, K. F. (1990). *Helping the aging family: A guide for professionals.* Glenview, IL: Scott, Foresman.

Burns, D. D. (1989). *The feeling good handbook: Using the new mood therapy in everyday life.* New York: William Morrow.

Egan, G. (1986). *The skilled helper* (3rd ed.). New York: Brooks/Dale.

Epstein, L. (1985). *Talking and listening: A guide to the helping interview.* St. Louis: Times Mirror/Mosby.

Hepworth, D. H. (1993). Managing manipulative behavior in the helping relationship. *Social Work, 38,* 674–682.

Hepworth, D. H., & Larsen, J. A. (1993). *Direct social work practice: Theory and skills* (4th ed.). Pacific Grove, CA: Brooks/Cole.

CHAPTER 9

Record Keeping

MARGARET L. MORSE

What are the purposes of case records and what constitutes good record keeping about clients? Supervisors and administrators in adult services programs seem to feel the shorter case records are, the better; workers are unhappy about the time they spend keeping records, yet some do not wish to give up the less tangible, qualitative aspect of their practice that "dictation" and other discursive notes capture. Most adult services social workers and managers would agree that their practice should be accountable and that this accountability is primarily reflected in clients' records. The phrase "not written, not done," heard from adult services supervisors, underscores the importance of the written word for documenting interventions, capturing clients' and social workers' successes, and identifying areas for additional work.

Although most social workers and supervisors concur that good record keeping is essential, there is little in basic social work texts that models how to keep records effectively. For example, Sheafor, Horejsi, and Horejsi (1991) devoted seven pages of a 521-page text to the subject, whereas Hepworth and Larsen (1993) discussed record keeping mostly in the context of confidentiality (in two of 668 pages). Compton and Galaway (1994) provided three pages on maintaining case records. These books do provide narrative case examples throughout that demonstrate a type of record keeping about clients (the summary report), but there is no direct examination of why and how these examples might work as good case records. Gambrill (1983) is an exception: She provided 12 pages of commentary on what to record specifically and an appendix of forms to use in doing so.

Kagle's (1991) *Social Work Records* is the only recent book devoted exclusively to this topic. It reviews the trends in methods of record keeping, proposes what good records should contain, and describes and provides examples of several methods of recording casework, along with brief discussions of practice issues, confidentiality, and computerization.

Much of the literature on record keeping for social work describes methods designed for settings that provide psychosocial rehabilitation. These methods often capture the process of the interaction among designated client, family, and social worker, and they measure outcomes in terms of changes in target behaviors. The job of public services social workers, however, is substantially unlike that of social workers who practice in settings principally oriented to helping clients modify psychosocial problems. Most of the reasons that clients come to adult services agencies is that they are experiencing some difficulty in interacting with their environment that is often exacerbated by the lack of financial means to resolve the problem independently. Their needs may produce emotional discomfort or a total inability to cope with the problems that beset them, but the principal goals of interventions will first be to improve clients' functioning by helping them find ways to meet material needs, and second, to modify behaviors.

For this reason, some of the articles with the best suggestions for assessment and identification of problems come from nurses, physicians, or members of allied health professions, whose therapeutic interventions are frequently aimed at restoring or improving functioning after an illness (see, for example, Bernstein, 1992; Rubenstein, 1989). These suggestions fall short of the needs of public services social workers, because although they focus on functional status rather than identifying and modifying problem behaviors, they do not accommodate the client's potential need for counseling, case management, or advocacy for new community resources. One might think that consulting articles on effective assessment might provide clues to how the process is recorded and synthesized, but they too are silent on how to record findings effectively.

For the most part, then, record keeping would seem to be a skill taught orally at the agencies that serve adult clients, and the style of recording seems to depend on the agency's need and preference for documentation. Certainly records must be suited to the place where they are used, but it is surprising to find so little emphasis on training social workers on the more general aspects of how to document professional activities.

Public services social workers act as gatekeepers for many of the assistance programs funded locally or by the state or federal government. Record keeping in public agencies has been seen foremost as a matter of documenting the execution of a public trust, often involving the disbursement of substantial sums of money. It is neither surprising nor misguided that these workers must demonstrate accountable practice. However, one may wonder what record keeping's contribution should be to social work practice with clients. Is it (should it be) an important component of the practice method, or is it just part of the "housekeeping" that goes with most jobs?

McKane (1975) remarked that "the paradox is that social work thrives on the power of words—as long as they are spoken. A worker persuades, cajoles, reveals and emphasizes through the spoken word. She (or he) continually develops techniques of talking and inciting talk. Workers brag of and compete for prowess in the oral arena, but when it comes to writing they cower" (p. 593). This attitude is mirrored in the lack of attention to record keeping in contemporary textbooks on social work practice relative to a more exhaustive treatment of methods of interacting verbally with clients. This leaves unanswered such questions as:

- How do social workers learn to keep records?
- What is the relationship between the spoken process of social work and the written record?
- What is the role of record keeping in effective practice with clients?
- For whose purposes are records kept? Can they address multiple needs?

McKane (1975) was silent on the first two questions, but she went on to propose focusing on the needs of the reader of the record. In her article on current record-keeping practices, Kagle (1993) expanded on who this reader might be:

> During the past 20 years, records have assumed an increasingly important role in the oversight of social services organizations. Social workers now prepare their records for a wider audience that includes not just the supervisor and other colleagues, but also third-party payers, clients, their families, and the courts. This new audience, which includes nonprofessionals and professionals from other disciplines, seeks information that differs in form and content from the traditional case record. This audience is primarily interested in monitoring service delivery. It looks to the record to find a rationale for professional decisions and actions and an accounting of service activities and their results. (p. 193)

One trainer–practitioner suggested that social work lies in the verbal interactions among worker, client, and family and that record keeping is "where you hang it all up at the end of the day." Does some element of social work practice lie in record keeping itself? Kagle's (1993) various audiences include the client and family, but her description of record keeping as "rationale" and "accounting" addresses more directly the needs of administrators and auditors. Do records assist social workers in their practice with clients and families? If so, how? More important, do records assist clients and families in achieving their goals?

This chapter considers how record keeping might benefit the client, family, and social worker by supporting the practice method. It gives a brief description of a project to develop standard record-keeping tools for North Carolina's county departments of social services that might be generalized to other states and settings. It also looks at the administrative uses of records and, in that context, automation and computerization of the record-keeping process, because most public agencies will likely confront this issue in the future, if they have not already.

Record Keeping to Support Excellent Practice

What part might record keeping have as a component of a method of practice? There are two reasons for writing case records. First, preparing to write and actually writing both can play an important part in the learning process, for both the social worker and the client. For social workers, a principal use of records should be as a tool for problem solving—a structure that prompts creative thinking. In the same way that carrying a camera can heighten awareness of the visible world (making one look for just the right camera angle or quality of light), using a good record-keeping format can prompt workers to gather information in a more holistic, directed manner; listen more carefully to what clients tell them; and reflect as they write up their notes on what the information means.

Second, it provides a concise way to communicate with others who may be involved in the case or with colleagues who may need to assist the client when the principal social worker is not available. Good records provide the social worker, the client and family, the supervisor, and others with a concise, usable account and documentation of why the client came to the agency; what the presenting problem was; what goals were developed; what interventions were planned and implemented; how the interventions worked for the client; and what, if any, aftercare was provided (Kane, 1974).

Wolf and Kolb's (1984) learning cycle is presented in chapter 20 as a process by which people learn new things. Although Wolf and Kolb said that people proceed through the four phases of this cycle—(1) concrete experience, (2) observation and reflection (including "publication"), (3) formation of abstract concepts and generalizations, and (4) active experimentation—to learn something, they suggested that everyone has a preference for where to begin the process and where to concentrate their energies. Wolf and Kolb also stated that people tend to select activities, whether hobbies or professions, that give precedence to their preferred steps in the cycle. For example, social workers as a group generally prefer concrete experience and active experimentation to observation and reflection or abstract conceptualization.

Social work activities belong to several parts of the cycle. Conducting the assessment and all subsequent interactions rely heavily on the social worker's concrete experience of the client and family. Writing case records, however, depends first on reflection and observation and then on abstract conceptualization. For most social workers, the two steps involved in writing records are likely to be their least favorite ways to learn. However, summarizing the assessment aloud with the client and family and testing hypotheses about why things are as they are and what can be done about them brings the worker back to what may be a more congenial part of the learning process—active experimentation. The actual writing of the case records entails "publishing" findings. For many, it is easier to discuss the assessment with the client and family and with a supervisor or a colleague than to write about it, as suggested by McKane (1975).

Designing a Record-Keeping System

The history of this book and the collaboration among the Center for Aging Research and Educational Services (CARES), the Adult Services Branch of North Carolina's Division of Social Services, and representatives from county departments of social services was described in the introduction. As a second step in the process of implementing the practice method outlined in this book, the collaborators felt that a set of tools for record keeping that supported each phase of the family assessment and change method would help social workers and provide a consistent framework for recording their work with clients and families.

After two years of development and field-testing, the state division has made eight tools available: (1) an intake–information sheet, (2) a face sheet, (3) a comprehensive functional assessment, (4) an adult and family services plan, (5) a contact–activity log, (6) a quarterly review, (7) a comprehensive functional reassessment, and (8) a closing–transfer summary. Figure 9-1 shows how these fit with the steps of the process.

The goals that guided development of these tools focused on the needs of both social workers and supervisors. For social workers we believed the tools should

- support the steps of the family assessment and change method
- prompt social workers to gather information in a holistic manner
- demonstrate social workers' reflective thinking and professional judgment
- capture important information and decisions clearly in as little space as possible and with a minimum of burden to client, family, and social worker
- provide case continuity and a historical context for chronic problems.

For supervisors the tools should provide a basis for

- supervising appropriate practice steps and interventions
- identifying skills and competencies needed by social workers
- giving consultation at critical decision points
- evaluating the effectiveness of adult services practice (including quality and timeliness) and programs.

The recording documents are called tools, rather than forms, to emphasize the freedom with which the developers hope social workers will use them to record their interventions with clients and families. "Forms" seemed to emphasize compliance with rules set up for regulatory purposes, and although documenting compliance is important, it should not be given more weight than good practice. Furthermore, good practice will almost inevitably meet standards for compliance. We intended the recording instruments to be "tools"—that is, a resource to social workers acting in their professional capacities that would support their work with clients rather than dictate it.

One can see problem-oriented recording (Weed, 1968, 1969) in the parentage of the tools we developed. As Ryback (1974) and others have noted, methods that focus on problems provide a way of thinking about how problems can be approached and treated. Record-keeping formats that embody such methods can help

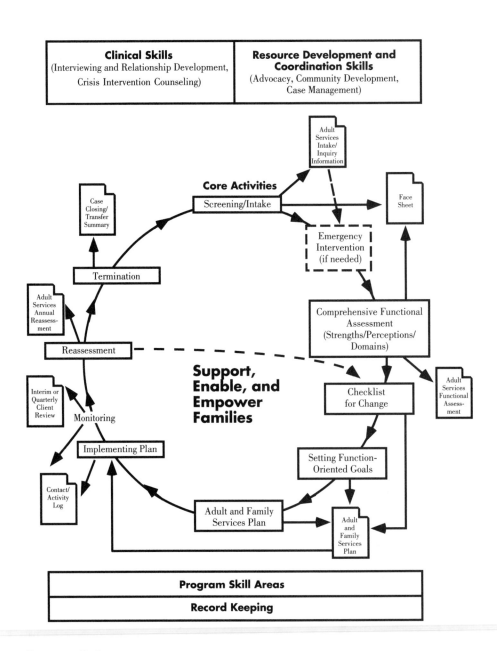

| Clinical Skills (Interviewing and Relationship Development, Crisis Intervention Counseling) | Resource Development and Coordination Skills (Advocacy, Community Development, Case Management) |

Adult Services Intake/ Inquiry Information

Core Activities

Case Closing/ Transfer Summary

Screening/Intake

Face Sheet

Termination

Emergency Intervention (if needed)

Adult Services Annual Reassessment

Comprehensive Functional Assessment (Strengths/Perceptions/ Domains)

Reassessment

Support, Enable, and Empower Families

Checklist for Change

Adult Services Functional Assessment

Interim or Quarterly Client Review

Monitoring

Implementing Plan

Setting Function-Oriented Goals

Contact/ Activity Log

Adult and Family Services Plan

Adult and Family Services Plan

| Program Skill Areas |
| Record Keeping |

Figure 9-1 _____

RECORD-KEEPING TOOLS THAT SUPPORT THE FAMILY ASSESSMENT AND CHANGE PROCESS.

Reprinted with permission of Family Forum, School of Social Work, University of North Carolina–Chapel Hill.

direct, organize, reflect, and record a systematic approach to services. However, we did not use the SOAP (subjective, objective, assessment, plan) format Weed proposed. The SOAP format has been the topic of some debate in social work literature, because some authors (see Beinecke, 1984, for a summary) felt that its categories did not meet the record-keeping needs of human services professionals outside the medical setting. Others have criticized the use of "subjective" to describe the client's complaint and "objective" for the professional's view of that complaint, because some feel the terms imply that the "objective" view is somehow more real or valid than the "subjective." In a medical setting, where a hematocrit or liver function value provides independent evidence about a condition, the term is perhaps more useful. In the tools we designed, information that might previously have been recorded as "subjective" or "objective" instead appears together in the relevant domain of the functional assessment (for example, as an open-ended question such as "How does the client view his financial situation?" and a brief budget sheet for recording income and expenses).

Weed wanted the problem-oriented record to contain a database (found primarily in our face sheet, intake–inquiry tool, and functional assessment). The summary of the functional assessment tool should contain a synthesis of the information gathered, as well as a description about how the client's functional problems and strengths interact with one another. This is what Weed more narrowly defined as "assessment," the A in SOAP. One of the troublesome issues of problem-oriented recording is whether to lump problems together or split them to take action. The assessment summary invites the social worker to consider the client's problems holistically to begin with and then to negotiate with the client ways to produce change in one or more areas, whenever possible using strategies that ameliorate functioning in several domains at once.

Weed also proposed a numbered list of problems with associated plans. We have, however, turned away from the emphasis on problems that "problem-oriented" recording requires. Instead, we have sought to emphasize change as the desired focus of social work practice, and so the tools contain a "checklist for change" rather than a "problem list." Although it is true that clients come to adult services agencies because they are experiencing problems, what they are seeking is help in making positive changes. As Weed proposed, though, the items for change are numbered and keyed to the services and activities meant to address them (corresponding to his plan). Intervening between these two lists, however, is a place to write time-limited, functional goals for each problem, to emphasize the importance of establishing a concrete way to measure progress. Here is a brief description of the eight tools and a rationale for their development.

INTAKE–INQUIRY INFORMATION
This tool is designed to capture information that helps the intake worker make an initial brief assessment and screening of the client's and family's needs, to refer the case properly within the agency, or redirect the inquiry to another source of

assistance. It captures a minimum of identifying information about the client, the type of contact with the agency (for example, telephone call or office visit), the person making the referral (client, family member, or other professional), the client's level of involvement in the contact, the presenting problem and its history, the expectation of the person contacting the agency and urgency of the need, a preliminary review of the client's functioning in the six functional domains (social, environmental, mental health, physical health, activities of daily living [ADL], and economic), what action was taken at the end of this first contact, a place to note potential hazards to a social worker making a home visit, and space for additional comments. The emphasis on functional abilities reflects the basic tenet of the family assessment and change method that functioning is a better indicator than anything else of the client's ability to act independently and that helping the client regain or compensate for impaired functioning underlies the social worker's professional activities.

FACE SHEET

This document (often filled out in conjunction with the inquiry tool) contains the following demographic information about the client: name, sex, race, date of birth, marital status, education, social security number, address, telephone number, directions to house, emergency contacts, household composition (with some demographic information), significant others outside the household, professional contacts, information on Medicare or Medicaid, veteran status, insurance information, guardian–payee–power of attorney, a history of services previously requested or received from the agency, and space for additional comments.

The face sheet is intended to come first in the case record file and offers a ready reference that can be updated easily as the client's circumstances change. Because it is the principal place the names and particulars of the client's family and social contacts are recorded, the face sheet begins the work of recording the evaluation of the client's social context.

FUNCTIONAL ASSESSMENT

This tool contains questions, prompts, and checklists for recording information from the initial comprehensive functional assessment. Again, because of the emphasis of the family assessment and change method on functioning, rather than diagnosis, the assessment tool is organized into sections for each functional domain—social, environmental, mental health, physical health, ADL or instrumental activities of daily living (IADL), and economic. The handbook for social workers that accompanies the tools emphasizes that the assessment document is not an interviewing tool and does not suggest a fixed order in which information should be gathered or recorded. Rather, because the order given above is common in the literature on aging, we also chose that order. In interviewing clients, as in recording the information later, social workers are encouraged to start in the most logical place, usually with the client's and family's areas of greatest concern, and gather or record information in other functional domains as they are relevant.

The questions in each domain of the assessment tool begin with the client's and family's perception of how the client functions in that domain. (This example suggests why the guide cautions social workers not to use the tool as an interviewing format. "Functional domain," "perception," and "functioning" belong to the professional language of social workers, but not usually to clients.)

In the interest of speeding up the recording process, some domains contain checklists with spaces for comments: environment has a list of potential hazards in the home; mental–emotional health provides a list of diagnoses and symptoms; physical health also includes such a list as well as one for durable medical equipment; ADL–IADL provides a grid asking whether clients need help for an array of activities, and if so, whether they receive it. Economic functioning has a space for making a brief review of the client's budget. There is a grid for listing formal services and entitlements currently received. Finally, there is space for information from collateral contacts, additional notes (information that does not fit elsewhere), and a summary of findings.

ADULT AND FAMILY SERVICES PLAN

This tool offers space to record items for change, goals associated with those items, target dates for accomplishing the goals, the activities and services used to meet them, the person or agency responsible for carrying out the activity or providing the service, and a place to note when the goal is met. The tool has a place for the client, family members, and social worker to sign, so it serves as an informal contract among all the parties to activities on the plan.

CONTACT–ACTIVITY LOG

This tool is a formal version of what most social workers already use for day-to-day work with clients. It is a grid with space for the date, a notation of the type of contact or activity, and results. We recommend that contact logs generally not be included in the permanent record. Important information from them is summarized and entered on the client's quarterly review, and then they are discarded. (However, if litigation may arise, we suggest that workers keep these logs.) Of the tools we provided, this and the interim or quarterly client review (described next) were the most popular among the social workers using them.

INTERIM OR QUARTERLY CLIENT REVIEW

This tool provides checklists to indicate where the review took place; sources of information during the review (which often were noted on the contact log); a place to note significant changes in the client's status since the last review; areas for summarizing new problems, worsening conditions, improvements, and new resources and accomplishments in each of the domains; and a section for recording progress on the goals noted on the adult and family service plan, with a checklist for indicating the disposition—discontinue, pursue ongoing goal, continue work, try new strategy, revise goal, and make other plan.

FUNCTIONAL REASSESSMENT

Every fourth quarter—or more often if the client's situation changes radically— the review of the client's progress is more detailed than the quarterly reviews. There are two goals for reassessment. First, the client's functioning since the previous assessment or reassessment is examined to see how the interventions have affected it. As with the quarterly reviews, this offers a set time for evaluating how well goals are being met in the short run and also compares the client's current status with the status when the work began. Second, the reassessment provides the opportunity to look again at the client's and family's situation as if for the first time. When social workers have seen clients over the course of a year or more, it is possible for them to develop a fixed view of clients and their various problems. Stepping back to view the case with detachment may make it possible to see issues and strengths that have not yet been identified or to reevaluate the situation in new and constructive ways. This also allows the social worker, client, and family to review whether the agency's services still match the client's needs. The reassessment tool mirrors the original assessment in the comprehensiveness of its review of the domains, but it focuses on change. If the client is to continue receiving services at the end of the reassessment process, we recommend that social workers develop with clients a new checklist for change, set of goals, and plan for activities and services, as they did at the end of the initial assessment.

CASE CLOSING–TRANSFER SUMMARY

This short tool provides space to mark the disposition of the case—closed or transferred—as well as the reason for this action. It provides space to indicate changes since the most recent review or reassessment, pending activities, unresolved concerns, and the client's and family's response to closing or transfer. It can be used as a way to communicate with new workers taking over the case if the case is transferred, or of tying up loose ends if it is closed.

Capturing and Supporting the Helping Process through Recording

In developing a method of record keeping to parallel the family assessment and change method, we hoped to support the social worker by improving the link between engaging in the helping process and recording its activities efficiently. For this reason, the documents themselves mirror the steps of the method and provide prompts to help the social worker gather relevant information and synthesize it with the client and family, record important contacts and activities as easily as possible, and focus on the outcomes of the intervention.

This chapter has taken issue with the authors of basic social work texts for not explaining in detail what a good case record looks like, and unfortunately, this chapter is open to the same criticism, because there is no room here to show how the record might mirror the helping process. We can offer some suggestions, though.

Although the assessment and reassessment tools provide the database on which social workers and clients rely for their work, the summary is the most important part of each tool. It should capture the social worker's synthesis of the assessment data. It is based on the worker's summary made aloud with the client and family, reflecting their feelings and concerns, and pointing out connections they have not made. It is the place where social workers record how they, the client, and family have made sense of what they have learned together. On the tool, as in summarizing aloud, the social worker identifies not only how the client functions in each domain but how functioning in the domains interact with one another. The worker helps the client and family identify areas in which they have strengths and begins to plan with them how to use strengths to support change in areas in which there are problems. The worker helps them make a preliminary identification of areas in which they most want to see change and set priorities for beginning to work on them.

On the tool itself, social workers can note when their evaluation of the situation differs from that of the client. For example, the social worker may identify a situation that the client does not perceive to be a problem but that has potential for causing trouble. It is usually futile to set goals and develop interventions for areas in which the client does not seek change (and doing so works counter to helping the client gain empowerment), but social workers can use their skills to make clients more aware of the present and potential effects of these unclaimed problems and can record their own professional judgment in the summary.

In some ways, the adult and family services plan has been the tool with which we have most tried to reshape current practice. In most of the case records reviewed before developing the tools, social workers recorded thorough functional assessments. Less frequently, however, does one find a clear written statement of the problems identified in the course of the assessment and, more rarely still, the client's goals for the intervention framed in measurable, functional terms. In many cases, the process seems to go from the presenting problem to services, and one result is that interventions are not always tailored to the needs of the client but applied only according to what formal services the agency has available. Another result is that social workers, clients, and families do not have a clear idea of what the intervention is intended to do, how to measure whether it is working, and how to know when to discontinue it.

As mentioned in chapter 5, social workers may overlook important resources for clients if they think that the only interventions at their disposal are the material services that "belong" to their agency. Most clients bring intangible, easily overlooked resources with them, and the social worker's professional skills, whether through counseling or case management, are the real wealth of the agency. Because these resources are less tangible than "10 hours per week of in-home aide services" or "transport to and from medical appointment," social workers tend to underestimate their value.

Using a tool that asks the social worker to record the client's and family's goals shifts the emphasis and responsibility for the intervention back toward the client. It also makes it easy to see the range of possible ways to promote change in the client's life—often but not exclusively through the use of the agency's material services. Goals developed with the client at the end of the assessment (or reassessment) process are keyed to the activities and services designed to meet them. These goals are carried forward to the monitoring process of each quarterly review. At each point, the social worker reviews them with the client to see how well they are being met and whether the activities and services should be continued, revised, or ended.

In designing a set of tools for North Carolina's adult services social workers, we hoped to support practice by providing a format that would echo the process social workers use with clients, provide space to record the most relevant details of that process, and prompt them to gather a minimum set of relevant information. These tools became available to county social workers just before this book went to press, and initial comments are favorable. It remains to be seen what the long-term effect for social workers and clients will be. Nonetheless, we hope that providing social workers with a method of recording that parallels practice will enable them to work more efficiently and with greater clarity of thought. The effect of record keeping for clients is indirect, but if the new tools meet these two goals, clients should profit by it.

Confidentiality of Case Records

Confidentiality is of central importance to record keeping. Social workers, supervisors, and administrators should share a clear understanding about applicable rules and policies for confidentiality of client-specific information. This includes when and during what circumstances client case records can be shared with others inside and outside the agency. Clients' rights to see their own records, except as restricted by state laws, should be part of this understanding.

Whether case records are a form of "privileged communication," sheltered from scrutiny in the same way that medical records and interactions between lawyer and client are, is fiercely debated in certain types of cases. Social workers who are involved in adult protective services cases or other cases with significant implications for the legal rights of individuals and their families will want to consult agency legal standards on the issue of privileged communication and client confidentiality.

Because clients, and potentially the legal system, have access to case records, anything a social worker writes (or says) about clients should reflect respect for and sensitivity to them. Similarly, any statement about a client's condition should include the basis on which it is made. Because materials included in the record usually may not later be removed, social workers should take care not to include extraneous items.

Records and Administrative Practice

How should program managers and supervisors use records? Supervisors use records to provide clinical supervision to social workers (that is, to train and help them improve their performance). Administrators and supervisors use records to document compliance with the regulations of funding sources, demonstrate accountability to community oversight bodies, evaluate programs, and plan for the future. Records also document the quality, quantity, and timeliness of services provided. The data compiled in the case record can serve as an important part of the agency's information system and accordingly may contribute to an analysis of workloads and costs. Because the empowerment of adult services clients in part turns on the empowerment of social workers, supervisors, and program administrators, information on agency performance and accountability must be linked to client outcomes. To the degree possible, agencies should avoid developing separate information systems, one for social work practice and another for agency compliance, evaluation, and planning.

TEACHING AND SUPERVISION

Kadushin (1985) gave substantial attention to the teaching function of supervisors. Adult services supervisors provide practice supervision and teaching to social workers in support of the family assessment and change method. Use of a function-oriented record that mirrors the steps of the practice method can enable the supervisor to review the social worker's knowledge and problem-solving skills with respect to assessment, prioritizing areas for change, goal setting, service planning, implementation, and writing progress notes associated with monitoring and reassessment. The supervisor can use this information to assess the quality and completeness with which assessments are done; establish whether necessary linkages exist between assessed findings; identify areas for change, strengths, and goals; and review progress notes and reassessments for both form and substance.

The primary function of supervision in a model that seeks to empower social workers, and through them clients, is to use the teaching opportunity that case records afford to improve practice. Accordingly, when the supervisor reviews records, he or she may point to areas that need strengthening and identify different methods for sharpening work skills in those areas, including the use of supervision and training.

PROGRAM EVALUATION

Monitoring agency services and social work practice is important in the lives of all managers and supervisors, because compliance with regulations from funding agencies is the primary evidence of accountability to the public that supports social services. Although there are only indirect measures of quality, the manner in which forms are filled out and evidence of whether proper documentation is timely are important. In a practical sense, whatever is not documented did not happen, and this can have legal repercussions that may affect the supervisor, the worker, and ultimately the client.

In terms of program evaluation discussed in chapter 19 and here, measures of compliance can document the quality, quantity, and timeliness of effort, and when paired with client outcomes they can address program effectiveness. One of the challenges for adult services programs is to link the assessment of the agency's effort and compliance with regulations to measures of performance (that is, client-centered outcomes). For this to happen, agencies must integrate and automate their record- and information-keeping processes and track service inputs and outcomes for clients.

A standardized record-keeping method can be a useful tool to evaluate program effectiveness. It allows the reviewer to compare the client's progress with findings made at assessment or reassessment in light of the service goals and plans. What is more, such a record-keeping method, particularly if it is automated, can put information about clients as a group in the hands of the social worker, who can use it to help empower clients and improve their well-being. A record-keeping method that gathers usable, outcome-oriented data in a simple and understandable format enables the social worker to assess and, if necessary, revise practice.

In addition to enabling social workers to evaluate their practice with respect to either one particular case or even a caseload, an automated standardized record-keeping system can provide program administrators and supervisors with the tools and information for evaluating service effectiveness in specific areas, as well as overall effectiveness in adult services. In addition, to the degree that the record-keeping format assesses clients' functioning and identifies problems for which there are either no or insufficient services, it serves as a database for planning and program development.

Records are only as good as the information they contain. The information is only as good and as useful as the model that directs what information is gathered and how it is analyzed. Good records derive from a well-formulated mission statement for the adult services program that focuses on client- and family-centered performance and empowerment. Records that focus on documenting outcomes for clients reflect a commitment to their well-being. Developing a record-keeping system that puts such information in the hands of social workers and that allows and calls for them to evaluate their practice empowers those workers to develop service interventions tailored to their clients' needs.

Automation, Databases, and Record Keeping

Developing automated record-keeping systems that integrate information on outcomes for clients with information on social workers' activities empowers supervisors and administrators to evaluate agency effectiveness and plan for the future. However, the agency that plans to automate its information management systems has a difficult but potentially valuable task. In "Computerization and the Dehumanization of Social Services," Murphy and Pardeck (1992) provided a stark indication of the reaction of many social work practitioners to the idea of automated record keeping and suggested some of the resistance to change agencies may encounter. Another barrier to automation may be that computerized systems are often called management information systems, rather than something that suggests their utility to the line practitioner or the client. Both of these point to potential sources of resistance to automation in social work settings in two ways: (1) the fear that the use of computers dehumanizes what has been a preeminently human and humane activity and (2) the issue of management of professionals and how monitoring is balanced with autonomy.

Both issues provoke worries about the deprofessionalization of social work practice, the first from the concern that computer programs (particularly "expert systems") might replace the judgment of the trained professional, leaving social work in the hands of anyone who can use a keyboard. It also creates some fears that public social work might become more narrowly defined as assessment for eligibility for benefits with no place for the helping process.

Use of management information systems contributes to fears about supervision and oversight: Can one measure social work outcomes for the clientele of individual practitioners in the same way one might measure the accuracy, speed, and productivity of a typist? Neither of these fears is justified, yet neither is completely chimerical, and managers who propose to automate record keeping in their agencies must confront both.

Frans (1993) concluded that computerization can lead to empowerment by studying empowerment and the diffusion of computer technology among 520 social workers who responded to a survey sent to a sample of members of the National Association of Social Workers. Those members in settings that made greater use of computers and those members with high computer use where decision making was more decentralized rated themselves as more empowered. How, then, can one get the benefits of automation while avoiding the pitfalls? In this as in so many other aspects of adult services, a clear mission for the agency and its programs is the necessary starting point.

GATHERING DATA

To be effective, databases in a management information system must contain data that are primarily categorical, because this is the type of information that computers can handle with relative ease. Computers can quickly count the number of records that match a given set of criteria: How many men are in the total client population? How many women are under age 24 and have more than three living children? How many clients over age 65 live alone and have one, two, or three impairments in ADLs or IADLs? Much of this information is invaluable to those who plan programs and assess the need for services. It also can be directly useful to the line practitioner who uses summary reports about clientele to measure individual progress or effectiveness of certain interventions for clients with similar needs.

Individuals and families are unique up to a point, just as they are similar up to a point. Categorical data-gathering risks capturing only the broadest of similarities and missing the attributes that make clients unique. Because one of the goals of social work practice is to assist clients in achieving a better fit with their environment, either by changing the environment or by helping the client to change, what is unique about the client in practice may be what is most important in the therapeutic relationship. Although computerized data-gathering may be helpful to people who plan programs and work to develop needed services, for the practitioner working with individuals, it can miss their unique qualities and take valuable time to record, and so may be of little direct use.

This brings up the problem of who is served by the data-gathering process, computerized or not. The activities of gathering the type of data most useful for management information systems may not be identical to those most useful for working with clients. Kagle (1993) noted in her study of record-keeping practices that "in general, workers preferred outlines that called for brief narrative entries as opposed to checklists or standardized forms [the best format for gathering categorical data], which they found confining and associated with nonprofessional practice. As one worker said, "I would not take a job where record keeping meant filling out forms" (p. 194). This suggests potential resistance on the part of social workers to using record-keeping formats that make categorical data gathering easier. Whether this sort of data gathering should be part of the direct practitioner's job needs careful consideration in light of the agency's mission, and if the answer is yes, careful planning to make the gathering process for the social worker as transparent and uncomplicated as possible. However, as computer software evolves to be able to identify and tabulate equivalent phrases, this may become easier to do.

FORMULATING THE QUESTIONS FOR PROGRAM EVALUATION

Kirwin (1994) pointed out that many of the concepts regularly discussed in the research literature on geriatric social work were not consistently defined. In her review of four publications that list ADLs, she noted that one named 13 ADLs; one, eight; one, seven; and one, six. Beyond this lack of consistency of definition, Kirwin contended that the measurement of such concepts is often poorly put into practice in any given study and inconsistent across studies. Her concern was that terms such as "at risk," "well-being," "needs assistance," and "caregiver burden" become "well ensconced in state and federal statutes and operational regulations and are used in making major decisions about the lives of older people and their families. Most funding, planning, and evaluating decisions are based on these quantitatively expressed measures as if they were precise, agreed upon, functional indexes" (p. 467).

This suggests one of the salient problems facing program managers who wish to develop systems for program evaluation—the definition of what is to be measured and how to go about measuring it. Once again, a carefully developed mission statement provides guidance about what important outcomes the adult services program should produce. From there, technical consultation with experts in research design and data gathering can help managers focus on obtaining what is necessary to do effective evaluation.

TAMING THE TECHNOLOGICAL TIGER

One possible key to successful use of computers in social work practice may be to step back from their use as a way to gather information about a client population to consider how social workers can use them to make other tasks easier. One possible approach was discussed by Clark (1988), a private practitioner in Arizona, who described how the use of a computer has helped him in his daily activities. The equipment available in 1988 has been replaced by more powerful equipment, but the functions he used it to perform are similar to what one could easily do today: word processing for recording the flow and major points of therapy sessions, keeping a file of clients' records, and preparing letters and reports; a spread sheet for billing and accounting and preliminary collection and analysis of data about clients; and electronic mail to contact colleagues, receive referrals, and consult the local university library's catalog. Current software supports all of these functions. Successful automation of records may, and perhaps should, be a secondary benefit of social workers using computers to help carry out their daily practice.

Summary

In many ways this chapter demonstrates some of the shortcomings of the social work texts referred to in that it does not demonstrate specifically how social work as documented in the case record relates to the lively vocal process among social worker, client, and family. Indeed, more must be done. One self-instructional guide to practice says in its guidelines for effective recording, "Select pertinent information to record" (Austin, 1986, p. 468) but gives no indication of what is pertinent in the context of a record. However, knowing what is pertinent and recording it can demonstrate the quality of professional judgment, so good record keeping can serve as a touchstone of excellent practice. Just as social workers learn to hear their clients effectively, the reflection about clients' situations necessary to good recording can sharpen professional skills. One first step in making this process easier can be accomplished by designing tools that fit the social worker's practice method. Supervision or peer review based on the records can provide an ongoing way for social workers to improve their practice.

Automated record keeping and data gathering can be a powerful tool in the hands of the direct practitioner and the agency's managers. Nonetheless, for the greatest likelihood of success and acceptance, plans to introduce computers into the workplace must first focus on direct benefits to clients and practitioners in their day-to-day interactions and then on their potential for gathering data for program evaluation and development.

Key Points

Excellent adult services social workers

- use a function-oriented record-keeping method as a way to ensure careful examination and improvement of practice
- remember that records are open to the client and so should reflect respect for and sensitivity to the individual; similarly, any statement about the client's condition should include the basis on which it was made
- consider that other workers and managers may need to consult the record to assist clients or for supervisory purposes and state clearly what has been done for the client, why that plan was chosen, and what the results have been
- remember that records document performance of a public trust.

Excellent adult services managers

- acknowledge the value of good record keeping for helping clients change and its associated cost in time and effort
- recognize that good record keeping is a skill that must be learned and support appropriate training for workers, whether through one-to-one supervision, in-house training, or training from some other source
- understand the link between record keeping for evaluating program effort and compliance as well as outcomes
- understand not only the value of automation as an important support for adult services but also the possible sources of resistance to it.

Excellent leaders

- support the use of standardized record-keeping methods that mirror social work practice
- advise agencies on how to gather data efficiently for program evaluation and planning.

References

Austin, M. J. (1986). *Delivering human services*. White Plains, NY: Longman.

Beinecke, R. H. (1984). PORK, SOAP, STRAP, and SAP. *Social Casework, 65*(9), 554–558.

Bernstein, L. H. (1992, December). Functional Facts™: A public health approach to functional assessment. *Caring*, pp. 32–38.

Clark, C. F. (1988). Computer applications in social work. *Social Work Research & Abstracts, 24*(1), 15–19.

Compton, B. R., & Galaway, B. (1994). *Social work processes*. Belmont, CA: Brooks/Cole.

Frans, D. J. (1993). Computer diffusion and worker empowerment. *Computers in Human Services, 10*(1), 15–34.

Gambrill, E. (1983). *Casework: A competency-based approach.* Englewood Cliffs, NJ: Prentice Hall.

Hepworth, D. H., & Larsen, J. A. (1993). *Direct social work practice: Theory and skills* (4th ed.). Pacific Grove, CA: Brooks/Cole.

Kadushin, A. (1985). *Supervision in social work* (2nd ed.). New York: Columbia University Press.

Kagle, J. D. (1991). *Social work records* (2nd ed.). Belmont, CA: Wadsworth.

Kagle, J. D. (1993). Record keeping: Directions for the 1990s. *Social Work, 38,* 190–196.

Kane, R. A. (1974). Look to the record. *Social Work, 19,* 412–419.

Kirwin, P. M. (1994). The search for universal meaning: Issues in measurement. *Social Work, 39,* 466–468.

McKane, M. (1975). Case-record writing with reader empathy. *Child Welfare, 54*(8), 353–397.

Murphy, J. W., & Pardeck, J. T. (1992). Computerization and the dehumanization of social services. *Administration in Social Work, 16*(2), 61–72.

Rubenstein, L. V. (1989, March 30). Functional evaluation of the elderly. *Hospital Practice,* pp. 101–106.

Ryback, R. S. (1974). *The problem oriented record in psychiatry and mental health care.* New York: Grune & Stratton.

Sheafor, B. W., Horejsi, C. R., & Horejsi, G. A. (1991). *Techniques and guidelines for social work practice* (2nd ed.). Boston: Allyn & Bacon.

Weed, L. L. (1968). Medical records that guide and teach. *New England Journal of Medicine, 8,* 593–600, 652–657.

Weed, L. L. (1969). *Medical records, medical education, and patient care.* Cleveland: Case Western Reserve University Press.

Wolf, D. M., & Kolb, D. A. (1984). Career development, personal growth, and expertise learning. In D. A. Kolb, I. M. Rubin, & J. M. McIntyre (Eds.), *Organizational psychology: Readings on human behavior in organizations* (4th ed., pp. 124–152). Englewood Cliffs, NJ: Prentice Hall.

The reader is also referred to Kagle, J. D. (1995). Recording. In R. L. Edwards (Ed.-in-Chief), *Encyclopedia of social work* (19th ed., pp. 2027–2033). Washington, DC: NASW Press.

CHAPTER 10

Skills in Working with Special Needs Populations

MARY ANNE P. SALMON

Older adults are heavily represented in the caseloads of most adult services social workers. However, a growing number of adult services consumers are comparatively young people with special needs resulting from a disability. There are four major categories of disabilities that bring clients into the social services system: (1) sensory impairments (blindness–visual impairment, deafness–hearing impairment); (2) developmental disabilities (for example, mental retardation, cerebral palsy, autism); (3) neuromuscular conditions or injuries that occur in adulthood (for example, multiple sclerosis [MS], amyotrophic lateral sclerosis [ALS, or Lou Gehrig's disease], muscular dystrophy, head and spinal cord injuries); and (4) acquired immune deficiency syndrome (AIDS). Each condition of each category requires specialized knowledge and brings unique challenges to providing counseling and support services, yet there are commonalities among these diverse populations and the skills that social workers need to address them.

This chapter addresses the knowledge, skills, and attitudes important to effective practice with adult services clients who have special needs. Stigma, countertransference, unrealistic expectations, and cultural competency as it applies to people with disabilities are discussed in terms of their impact on practice. Challenges to providing services, such as management of stigma, dealing with family dynamics, issues of parenting and sexuality, stress management, housing, responding to talk of suicide, and the need for legal services, also are addressed.

Knowledge and Attitudinal Issues for Social Workers

Every helping relationship the social worker builds brings with it some personal and emotional challenges. This is not unique to work with clients with special needs. However, some issues that may be likely to arise in this area of adult services include dealing with stigma, countertransference, and unrealistic expectations and developing cultural competency for working with these populations. In many cases, social workers will have to help clients and their families work through the same or closely related issues, and to do so, they must first have resolved these concerns satisfactorily for themselves. This section discusses these four attitudinal issues, which may affect social work practice with clients in special populations, the consequences of such attitudes, and some ideas about addressing them.

REACTING TO CLIENTS' DISABILITIES AS STIGMA

Goffman (1963) described stigma as an "attribute that is deeply discrediting" (p. 3) to one's social identity. In other words, stigma results from some observable or unobservable characteristic that causes a negative response in many or most other people in the culture. The person perceiving another as stigmatized may be angry, repelled, fearful, or some combination of these traits. Typically, there is a fear that the stigma is "catching" in some way, and there is some research to indicate that stigma attaches to those who work, live, or otherwise associate with members of a stigmatized group (Mehta & Farina, 1988).

A condition that is stigmatized in one setting or culture may be an asset in another, and a culture may change over time. Nevertheless, there are three types of traits that tend to be stigmatizing in most societies. These are

1. physical abnormalities (for example, observable disabilities, or unusual appearance even when it is not disabling, such as a scarred or asymmetrical face)
2. blemishes of character inferred from a record of some disapproved behavior (for example, history of mental illness, drug or alcohol abuse, unemployment, homosexuality, or political activism)
3. tribal stigma representing hereditary membership in a stigmatized group (for example, race, religion, nationality, or social class).

Although social work, as a profession, has been one of many forces trying to reframe and destigmatize all three of these categories in contemporary Western society, much of the problem of stigma remains. As the above criteria make clear, stigma is not limited to special populations. For example, Monk (1981) asserted that old age is a stigmatized condition that contaminates those who work with older adults. Nevertheless, the level of stigma associated with visible disabilities may be quantitatively or even qualitatively different from that attached to older adults or to people who are perceived as unattractive. Hollins (1989) gave a good overview of this literature in his chapter, "Attitudes and Emotional Reactions to Blindness."

Snyder, Kleck, Strenta, and Mentzer (1979) conducted a series of experiments to measure college students' reactions to a person with a visible disability.

In one of these experiments, subjects were asked to view and evaluate a film. They were given a choice of two films based on a brief paragraph describing each. A videotape of the film would be shown on a television monitor. Furniture was arranged so that there were two chairs for each monitor and a partition divided the two monitors from one another, making a sort of viewing booth. When the subject entered the area, he or she could see that each booth already had another "subject" seated, waiting to begin viewing. Both of these were confederates of the researcher, one of whom was wearing a leg brace and had metal crutches propped on the table. The other showed no signs of any disability. The confederates took turns wearing the brace to control for any differences in their personal attractiveness to the subjects. A substantial majority of the subjects chose to sit by the confederate who was not wearing the brace. In a similar experiment in which the subject was told one of the video players was broken, so the same film would be shown on both monitors, people were slightly more likely to sit by the person with the brace. In a replication of this study, when students were interviewed after the experiment, most reported that their choice had nothing to do with the other person in the booth but was strictly a matter of preference for the film. A few of the people who sat by the person with the brace mentioned choosing to do so because they did not want the "handicapped" person to feel that he or she was being avoided, but none of the people who chose to sit by the "normal" person made any mention of the brace or the assumed disability in reporting why they chose their seat.

Despite the compassionate feelings that lead people to become adult services social workers and the professional training and experience that help them channel these feelings into appropriate attitudes for working with a variety of people effectively, social workers are still products of the larger society. Levy (1993) pointed out that a person meeting someone with a stigmatized trait will tend to feel ambivalence brought on by conflicts between his self-perceptions as caring, compassionate, friendly, and helpful and his perceptions of himself as "judicious in his evaluations and treatment of others" (p. 228). Thus, many social workers will have some internal feelings of fear or aversion to a person with a noticeable impairment, yet because of these personal and professional values, they are likely to be ashamed or otherwise uncomfortable about having such feelings.

Although Snyder et al.'s experiment dealt with a physical disability, mental retardation and other developmental disabilities that affect intellectual functioning may be as stigmatizing as or more stigmatizing than physical handicaps (for example, Schneider & Anderson, 1980). Visual and hearing impairments are sometimes less obvious to the casual observer, and thus people who have these impairments might be expected to suffer less public reaction, a double-edged sword that may lead to a lack of appropriate accommodation. Unpublished research by Siller and Chipman (1967) reported that of all people with disabilities, the public has the most favorable reaction to those who are deaf or blind. However, Hollins (1989) reported that this population experiences problems of stigma that are not different from those of other people with disabilities. Helen Keller wrote on this problem:

"Not blindness, but the attitude of the seeing to the blind is the hardest burden to bear" (quoted in Hollins, 1989, p. 89). For a more comprehensive view of how stigma affects a variety of special populations, see Levy's (1993) list of recent research.

Social workers may face the greatest problems of stigma in working with clients who have AIDS or have tested positive for human immunodeficiency virus (HIV). This can be true for a variety of reasons. First, as discussed above, stigma is based in part on the irrational fear that we might "catch" the stigmatized condition. In the case of AIDS, the fear is not totally irrational, because the HIV virus is transmitted from person to person. Although social work activities do not typically expose the social worker to the clients' body fluids, accidental exposure is a possibility. Even though the probability of this exposure is small, the serious consequences (as this book goes to press, HIV-positive status is a death sentence) make it difficult for many people to work with this population.

A second type of stigma that may be attached to clients with AIDS is related to the personal moral values social workers may hold about one or more of the behaviors that increase the risk of this illness. Gay men are still the largest segment of the AIDS patient population in the United States, although this is expected to change because other segments are growing more quickly. People who are or have been intravenous drug users are a large and increasing segment. Although most social workers will have internalized the professional norms of acceptance, they may still, overtly or subtly, disapprove of one or both of these lifestyles. It can be difficult to separate health, moral, or religious disagreement about these high-risk behaviors from stigmatizing feelings about people who have engaged in these behaviors. Conversely, it is easy to fall into the trap of emotionally separating the "deserving" or "innocent" client who contracted AIDS through a blood transfusion and the "undeserving" client who "brought it on himself" through drug use or sexual contact.

AIDS is not the only condition that may trigger feelings that the client "deserves" his or her fate. Working with an obese person who loses a limb because of poorly controlled, adult-onset diabetes, a person with a respiratory condition who continues to smoke, or even a client with mental retardation whose poor social skills lead to the loss of one job after another may lead an overworked social worker to wonder whether these clients are worth the trouble. Referring specifically to this judgment with HIV-positive clients, Stein (1992) wrote, "Defining clients as being either deserving or undeserving is of particular significance when resources are limited and budget cutbacks require decisions about who gets served and how" (p. 108).

ISSUES RELATING TO CULTURAL COMPETENCY

Although cultural sensitivity is a requisite skill for any effective social work (see chapter 11), some special populations call for a broadened awareness of potential cultural differences. For example, both African American and Hispanic people are, in most parts of the country, overrepresented among clients who acquired AIDS through intravenous drug use. However, the social worker who was sensitive only to cultural issues of ethnicity or even the interface of ethnicity and social class in working with this population would be missing the real cultural components of intravenous drug use.

Similarly, although young adults with sickle cell anemia are nearly all African American, there may be a superimposed culture of "people with sickle cell anemia," especially in areas where children with that condition grow up in frequent contact with each other through support groups, camps, and ongoing treatment. By contrast to clients with sickle cell, those with hearing impairments may be of any ethnic group, but those who choose to communicate with American Sign Language, regardless of the severity or timing of their hearing loss, have their own culture. Some of the more militant proponents of the rights of individuals with hearing impairment have demanded that deafness be considered a cultural variation rather than a disability. People with similar levels of impairment who use lip reading and oral communication, by contrast, usually prefer to be called "hard of hearing" and usually associate more with hearing people, disassociating themselves from the deaf culture.

In addition to cultures built on specific lifestyle choices (for example, drug use or sexual preference) or underlying condition (for example, sickle cell anemia or deafness), there are cultural approaches and attitudes that have grown out of the movement to secure rights for people with disabilities. United in their advocacy and activism, people coping with a variety of illnesses and functional impairments have created a culture and a political force.

Although social workers need to be aware of the cultural richness and complexity among these special populations, they also must be aware that they cannot assume that any given client is a member of the cultures associated with his or her lifestyle or condition. For example, a man with AIDS contracted through a homosexual experience may be a part of the gay community or culture or he may be totally isolated from it (separate from but clearly related to how he may feel about his own homosexuality). African American and Hispanic men who have sex with other men are, for cultural reasons, less likely than white men to identify with the gay community or even to consider themselves homosexual or bisexual (Harragin, 1992; Taylor-Brown, 1993, made the same statement about Hispanic and Mediterranean men). However, this does not mean that there are no African American or Hispanic members of the gay culture. Similarly, as just described, people with moderate to complete hearing loss may not consider themselves to be members of the deaf community and may not be considered deaf by that community.

COUNTERTRANSFERENCE ISSUES

Sometimes social workers have emotional problems in dealing with clients from one or more of these special populations for personal reasons that go beyond culture or stigma. These may grow out of countertransference (a projection of personal emotions or issues onto the person with whom the helping relationship is formed). Although the term is used more commonly to describe a hazard to those providing psychosocial counseling, the same process can occur in a broader social work context. For example, when adult services social workers feel frustrated by the real or perceived inadequacy of the services and counseling they can provide in the face of a client's enormous, complex, and painful problems, they may reframe their feelings of inadequacy by seeing the client as demanding, unrealistic, or manipulative. This form of countertransference may be a particular danger to social workers whose clients have ALS, AIDS, or any other conditions or diseases that are both degenerative and fatal.

Similar feelings may occur in working with people suffering from MS, whose symptoms and functional capacity vary unpredictably from day to day. If an adult services social worker has, consciously or unconsciously, taken credit for an improvement in the client's functional capacity that stemmed, at least in part, from a temporary abatement of symptoms, he or she will find it hard not to feel disappointment when a return or worsening of the symptoms causes the functional capacity to deteriorate. It is easy to project this disappointment onto the client by believing he or she is undermotivated or noncompliant.

Issues with clients' sexual, substance use, or other lifestyle choices that appear to be based on differing cultural values or stigma also may reflect countertransference. An especially strong reaction to clients with substance abuse problems from a social worker who is accepting of a wide range of other behaviors may grow out of painful previous experience with similar clients or out of an unresolved personal relationship with a person who abused the same substance.

UNREALISTIC EXPECTATIONS

Like the general public, social workers may err in one of two directions in their expectations about people with special needs. Perhaps the most common error is to generalize the one real limitation to a variety of other limitations. For example, blind people frequently report that new acquaintances speak louder to them than to other people, suggesting a conscious or unconscious assumption that, because they cannot see, they also have difficulty hearing. Similarly, people may express surprise when a person with speech problems, stemming from hearing impairment or from damage to some part of the vocal apparatus, exhibits normal or above average intelligence, mistakenly assuming that because articulate people tend to be intelligent, then inarticulate people must have low intelligence.

A related problem is an exaggerated focus on the limitations imposed by the disability. For example, the social worker may assume that a client is condemned by the disability to an isolated life or may assume that the most appropriate services are those in which someone else performs the tasks needed for the personal care or household management of the person with a disability. A more realistic focus will lead to developing strategies for independent coping and for enriching social opportunities if isolation is a problem.

The opposite error occurs when adult services social workers mistakenly underestimate the problems faced by a client with a disability. In the most extreme cases, they may ascribe a variety of spiritual or even supernatural qualities to people with a chronic illness or disabling condition. The idea that blind people have a "sixth sense," that deaf people have especially keen vision, or that people with disabilities are refined by their suffering to a special kind of nobility or sweetness is akin to believing that all African American people can dance and play basketball.

A subtler danger is underestimating the degree of impairment of a client who tries to appear as "normal" as possible. For example, the adult services social worker who meets a new deaf client may assume that the hearing aid provides near normal hearing, which is seldom the case. If the deaf client is a lip reader and the social worker uses some basic skills, such as taking a position directly opposite the client, speaking slowly, and making sure that his or her mouth is not obscured, the worker may not realize that the client will still only be able to understand about half of what is said, because 40 percent to 60 percent of words look alike. The quick fatigue level of clients with a variety of neuromuscular conditions also may be easily overlooked by adult services social workers who may believe that these clients are not trying hard enough.

CONSEQUENCES OF SOCIAL WORKERS' ATTITUDES
Avoidance–Detachment
The first obstacle to effective adult services social work imposed by stigma or countertransference is a desire to avoid the client. In the most extreme cases, this may result in outright refusal to take on clients with specific disabilities or conditions, which solves the problem for the specific social worker at the expense of the agency and its other staff members. In other cases the avoidance may be more covert, in that the social worker knowingly or unknowingly spends as little time as possible with clients whom they perceive as stigmatized. This neglect may be more or less subtle, but it almost inevitably results in less-than-optimal services and relationship building.

Another social worker with the same feelings may be physically "there" for the client but withholds empathy and other appropriate emotional involvement. This is detachment—not the therapeutically necessary detachment that draws important boundaries around the professional relationship, but an undermining and destructive detachment.

Inability to Build a Helping Relationship
Goffman (1963) pointed out that social interaction between a person with a stigmatized condition and one who is "normal" is characterized by one or more of several uncomfortable responses—guarded references to the condition, fear of using everyday expressions (such as saying "I see what you mean" to a blind person), being noticeably careful not to look at the visible stigma (the wheelchair or the missing limb), being artificially cheerful or joking, nervously talking too much, or being unnecessarily serious. Although these behaviors will lessen as the client and

social worker become more accustomed to each other, they will, nevertheless, present a barrier to forming the kind of professional relationship necessary to effective social work.

Burnout

Social workers who are aware of a conflict between their feelings and the demands of their professional role may exert themselves to give the best of their time and skills to clients with whom they are uncomfortable. This may work effectively for a while, although it may be difficult for them to appear genuine to the client. However, over time, the stress created by these unresolved feelings may take its toll in disaffection, low morale, or burnout.

Unreasonable expectations also may hasten burnout. The social worker helping clients with AIDS, for example, must be able to celebrate the successes found in helping the client have a better quality of life, resolve wills and other legal matters, and get palliative services in place. Those with covert expectations of helping the client live longer, rather than better, will be constantly struck with "failure" and the resultant destruction of morale that goes beyond the sadness of seeing a client die.

Lost Credibility

Among some groups within our culture, the profession of social work is stigmatized. Social workers are seen by these groups as ineffectual do-gooders who invade people's privacy and provide little benefit in exchange. The chance that clients will perceive the adult services social worker as stigmatized in these terms will be enhanced if the social worker appears "ignorant" about the client's condition, either through misconceptions about the condition, unrealistic expectations (in either direction), or the kind of uncomfortable behavior that characterizes the first encounter with a stigmatized person.

Making Matters Worse

Although some clients will perceive that the social worker is stigmatizing them and will discredit the social worker, others will respond by further discrediting themselves. Like social workers, clients with disabilities are products of their society and have internalized the same norms. Self-deprecation may be based on stigma itself (for example, feeling disgusted when they look in the mirror), on the degree of dependence they feel on others (for example, fear or disgust at "being a burden on the family"), or on their tacit acceptance of stigmatization from others (for example, "taking all the B.S. people dump on me").

Sometimes family members or professionals have encouraged children with hearing, visual, or mild intellectual impairments to hide their disability from people they encounter in daily life. Although this can be a successful stigma management technique when deliberately chosen by an adult (see the subsection "Stigma Management" in this chapter), the child may learn that his or her disability is something shameful to be hidden and carry this emotional content into adulthood.

Even if clients have successfully resolved their own issues about stigma, it is unfair to expect them to manage the negative feelings of social workers and other providers. Harangody and Peterson (1992) wrote on this topic for health care workers serving patients with AIDS, "A gay client who may have experienced a lifetime of isolation and oppression as a result of society's homophobia should not be forced to deal with homophobic health care workers" (p. 53).

DEALING WITH ONE'S OWN ATTITUDINAL BARRIERS

To serve effectively, social workers must first honestly face their feelings in each of these areas, working them through with a supervisor or peer group before going into the field. If stigma or countertransference is particularly strong, it may be necessary to seek professional help to deal with it.

Social workers also should have a safe, constructive outlet for the feelings of stigma, hopelessness, and fear that arise in the course of their work. Staffing cases may provide just such an outlet for feelings and for sharing the emotional burden and the problem-solving challenges of a difficult case. However, leaders of case staffing must handle emotionally difficult cases with great sensitivity. It is temptingly easy for the team to develop an "us" and "them" attitude about the clients and to reinforce one another's tendencies to project frustrations onto the client rather than counteracting them. Harangody and Peterson (1992) wrote

> Sometimes a client's behavior may be considered manipulative and angry by care team members when such behavior is in fact a legitimate response to inadequate care. Team meetings may degenerate into criticizing the client to avoid examining failures in service provision. Case managers must take the lead in such situations by remaining objective and advocating for the client. (p. 57)

Special Challenges in Providing Services

Although many of the services social workers will arrange or provide for clients in these special populations are similar to the ones that they will provide for other clients, there are some service needs and challenges that are specific to people with certain conditions or groups of conditions.

STIGMA MANAGEMENT

Clients from special populations must deal with their feelings of being discredited, based on their internalization of the larger societal expectations about social identity, as well as with the stigmatizing reactions of the people they meet. For those for whom stigma is a difficult problem, counseling in stigma management, as a specialized service, may be desirable if available.

In the absence of such services, Levy (1993) reported several strategies that the social worker may help clients explore. For those clients whose conditions are not immediately observable, such as those with visual or hearing impairments or mild cognitive or intellectual impairments, some strategies may center around the disclosure of information. First, the social worker and client review all of the possible consequences of disclosure and nondisclosure to relevant individuals and groups and make careful, informed decisions about who should be told. For example, is the client obliged to report this information on a job application? Does the client have an obligation to tell his or her employer or supervisor after he or she is hired? What will be the likely relative consequences of self-disclosure compared with accidental disclosure from another source? If this process leads to a decision that some people must be told, strategies for framing this disclosure are developed. To use one of Levy's examples, a person with bipolar disorder may describe it as a severe and persistent mental illness or as a physiological imbalance of the central nervous system that, once controlled by medication, will allow a high level of functioning. Both are accurate descriptions, but the latter is more likely to receive a sympathetic, nonstigmatized response.

A third decision the social worker may help the client make, which Levy characterized as part of information control, is the degree to which the client will choose to associate with people who have similar conditions or with people who do not. Individual clients will differ substantially in the degree to which this "differential association" is possible or desirable. For some clients, being with people who have similar experiences is supporting and nurturing. For others, it is a relief from constantly having to brace for, receive, and handle the curiosity, ignorance, and hostility of others. For others still, it feels isolating and depressing. For example, in working with adults with MS, Welch (1987) reported that participants in volunteer groups found sharing information with others helpful. However, Selder and Breunig (1991) found that clients who were not part of a support group said they were not interested because they did not want to hear morbid stories about what had happened to others. Nonetheless, some clients in that same study, although uninterested in support groups, said they liked being in a room with other people with MS because they did not have to explain things.

Brooks (1991), on the other hand, focused on societal rather than individual reasons for encouraging some differential association. She wrote that stigmatized people who have been, to one degree or another, dependent on others, need to start in a safe environment of people with the same conditions to begin developing the fundamental political process skills—creating alliances, building coalitions, overcoming organizational barriers, and engaging in political action that will enable them to change their position effectively.

For those clients who choose to disclose their conditions or whose disabilities are immediately observable, Levy described another pair of strategies, which he classified as "other-oriented." These are *dissonance induction* and *confrontation*. Dissonance induction is based on helping the client find direct or indirect ways to take advantage of the ambivalence most people feel about stigma. These strategies involve legitimating the helpful, friendly, and compassionate part of the observer's feelings, thus weakening the power of the judiciously discriminating part. This may include pointing up common feelings and concerns or demonstrating competencies and achievements. Confrontation is based on challenging behaviors rather than perceptions. It involves making the stigmatizing person aware of the inappropriateness of the behavior and the possible consequences of continuing. For example, a person in a wheelchair might say to a sales clerk, "I am the one who is going to be wearing this shirt. Please don't talk to my aide as if I were not here." For the client who feels comfortable using this technique, it can be very empowering. Some clients report that even when the confrontation does not bring about the desired change in behavior, the process has given them a renewed sense of self-respect. However, this strategy is not for everyone. Inappropriately used, it may add another emotional burden for a client whose coping resources are already stretched thin. Appropriately used, it can help redefine disability to mean "inadequate societal response to differences" rather than "individual shortcomings."

FAMILY-CENTERED SERVICES

Steinglass (1992) identified four characteristics that can be found in most families coping with the ongoing stress of severe chronic illness:

1. *Everyday family needs are typically subordinated to needs and requirements of the illness. [Steinglass suggested that this is adaptive in the acute or emergency phase but maladaptive in long-term chronic care.]*

2. *Within-family emotional alliances and exclusions often develop in response to, or are exacerbated by the illness. . . . This bond may conspicuously exclude and isolate other family members and lead to divisive and destructive family interactions.*

3. *These patterns of family responses are adhered to rigidly. The family finds it difficult, if not impossible, to change the ways it handles the illness, even if the current coping strategies are not working effectively.*

4. *The rigidity of family coping style is sustained, at least in part, by the isolation experienced by the family as they cope with the demands of the chronic medical condition.* (p. 88)

These findings suggest two strong implications for social work practice: (1) Social workers need to initiate preventive work with families, and (2) they should help legitimate the family's pursuit of goals that are not related to the client's condition.

The emphasis on preventive social work with families of clients with special needs is important, because traditionally family counseling has been recommended only when significant dysfunction is evident. The predictable result is that family members perceive a recommendation for family counseling as an accusation of failure. However, when the social worker suggests a combination of education, information sharing, and dealing with small problems as they arise as a means of preventing dysfunction, the family is not further stigmatized and there is a better chance of preventing destructive family dynamics before they become entrenched (Steinglass, 1992).

The particular problems that family members face will vary with the client's condition and history as well as the specific family member's role. For example, parents of adults who develop a chronic illness or sustain a disabling injury may feel strongly driven to return to an earlier stage of parenting, with the undesirable results of infantilizing the adult client and greatly increasing their own caregiving burden (Burks, 1992). Similarly, parents whose children have congenital or childhood-onset disabilities may have trouble letting them grow up and experience levels of independence appropriate to their age and capacities. Both parents and spouses may have extreme guilt that their loved one is suffering (or dying) while they remain unscathed (Burks, 1992; Mayer, 1991). This guilt not only adds an additional burden to their coping challenges but may effectively keep them from setting legitimate boundaries with the client.

Children of adults with disabilities are often expected to take on levels of caregiving responsibility that are too heavy for their age. This is particularly, although not exclusively, a problem when the parent who has no disability abandons the family. The child's feelings of burden may be discounted by the parent whose emotional need to assert independence causes him or her to minimize how much care the child is actually providing (Miller, 1992). Under similar circumstances the children of deaf parents may have the additional burden of being called on to translate in interactions with doctors, creditors, and other adults who convey information that the child may find disturbing, confusing, or embarrassing. Ludders (1987) mentioned this problem specifically in the context of communication with physicians, but it may easily be extrapolated to other types of interactions in which adults do not generally involve their children.

For the client with AIDS, the family may be dealing with all of the issues just outlined in addition to adjustments to new revelations about the client's lifestyle. Even if the family is able to react nonjudgmentally to the information that one of their members is homosexual or is or has been an intravenous drug user, there may be anger over the client's "hiding" this information from the family. For the spouse or romantic partner, a diagnosis of AIDS may be the moment of revelation of sexual infidelity with all of the feelings about "betrayal" that accompany such a discovery, added to the fear of exposure to the disease. The family member who is newly disabled may also feel special challenges within the family roles of spouse–partner and parent.

PARENTING

Although there are some overlapping concerns, the issue of parenting is different for the parent who develops a disabling disease or condition, and the adult with disabilities who must decide whether or not to become a parent. Let us first think about the case of the parent who becomes disabled.

Like other parents, parents with disabilities will differ in how central the parenting role is to their life and their sense of self. However, social workers should be aware of the practical and emotional centrality of this issue to many of their clients who are newly disabled. They also must guard against the assumption that regaining function in this part of their life is key for women but less important to men, just as they must guard against the converse assumption about the importance of career.

Parents who become disabled may need practical advice and training in learning to adapt ways of performing standard parenting tasks such as lifting or changing a baby. They may need informed advice and empathic listening to help them set realistic goals about which parts of their parenting role they can maintain or regain and which tasks or aspects of parenting they may have to discontinue. This sort of planning is more difficult for parents with MS, who must cope with the unpredictability of the disease, so that contingency plans and flexibility are especially important. Facilitating communication between parent and child also may be an important role for the social worker. Children need to be able to ask questions, to get good age-appropriate information about the condition, and to express their feelings, as well as to express their interests and plans completely unrelated to the parent's condition. This is usually an important part of their relationship with the parent. However, it may be useful for them to have another "safe" source of meeting these needs, including an age-appropriate support group or individual time with the social worker or counselor. If the disabling condition is fatal (such as ALS), the parent may need help in deciding how to talk to children about his or her impending death, and the child may need additional help in dealing with this information. Furthermore, the parent may need to plan for and reassure the child about who will provide care when the illness progresses further or when the parent dies.

Although there may be predictable dangers for the children of parents with disabilities, as discussed in the family dynamics section, many people with disabilities are excellent parents. However, in disputes involving custody of children, courts may automatically assume that the burden of child rearing is too great for a person with disabilities or that he or she is automatically unfit—especially for the single-parent role. In such cases, social workers may have to assume roles as educators and advocates on behalf of their clients.

Although single parents—in particular single mothers—are overrepresented in the public services system, many service programs do not take into consideration their specific needs. Social workers who serve clients whose disabilities are caused by, exacerbated by, or contribute to substance abuse problems are quick to point out this inadequacy. Although it is widely held that an initial intensive residential detoxification and recovery program is more likely to be successful than lower-intensity outpatient programs, there are few residential programs that provide on-site care for the children of recovering addicts. Many educational and vocational programs for people with disabilities also remain unresponsive to the needs of the parent who is the sole caregiver of young children.

For most people, the decision to have a child brings with it a host of difficult and emotionally loaded issues that may be made even more complex by a number of different disabling conditions. For a couple in which one or both partners have a stable, nonhereditary disability such as blindness, the decision may closely mirror that of any other prospective parents. "What are the current demands on our time? What are our resources? Why do we want a child? What will change in our lives if we have a child? How will our relationship change? Is having a child worth undergoing these changes? What does it take to be good parents? Do we agree about our respective roles as parents? Do we have what it takes to be good parents?" For a variety of other conditions, there are additional questions.

For the woman with MS, for example, there is the question of the hereditary component of the condition and the question of what her condition will be during and after her pregnancy. Into the 1950s, it was widely held that women with MS should not have children because pregnancy and delivery would exacerbate the condition (Birk & Kalb, 1992; Matthews, 1985). Birk and Kalb (1992) reported a fairly large body of accumulated evidence since that time that women are at little or no greater risk of worsening symptoms during pregnancy compared with any other nine-month period. However, their review of studies attempting to establish whether MS becomes more severe in the months following childbirth have had more-mixed, less-convincing results. The nearly unanimous advice against having children is no longer applicable, but the amount of risk (if any) associated with this choice is still not fully known. Even if there is no change to the mother's MS symptoms related to giving birth, she still faces the daily uncertainty that is part of that condition. For example, she may be able to lift her baby on Monday but be unable to do so on Tuesday.

HIV-positive women often receive their diagnosis when they are pregnant. For them, the question is not whether to become pregnant but whether or not to terminate the pregnancy. Within the first 15 to 18 weeks after conception, all fetuses are seropositive. However, after that time, without drug therapy, 60 percent to 70 percent will spontaneously "convert" to HIV-negative. After three years of clinical trials at 59 sites, giving AZT (zidovudine) to HIV-positive pregnant women has been shown to reduce the number of HIV-positive infants to 8 percent (Connor et al., 1994). When the Centers for Disease Control figures suggested in 1985 that the probability of the child being HIV-positive was 50 percent to 65 percent, health care providers routinely advised women to terminate their pregnancy and found it difficult to understand personal and cultural factors that led many women to choose to give birth in the face of this information (Macks, 1988).

Although medical progress has increased the probability of giving birth to a healthy baby, many problems remain for any woman who decides to give birth while suffering a fatal disease or condition, including not being able to watch the child grow up, guilt for leaving her children motherless, planning for the care of the child when her functioning is more limited, and the challenges of planning custody.

Prospective parents whose disabling conditions are hereditary or who have some genetic risk factor must not only deal with the "odds" of having a child with disabilities but must directly confront their feelings about whether it is better to live with this disability or to "have never been born." They may need help from the social worker in finding their personal answers to this question as well as coping with the "advice" they receive from family and friends.

This difficult and personal decision-making process is complicated additionally when the prospective parent has diminished capacity to make decisions owing to mental retardation or some types of cognitive impairment. Although such laws are increasingly challenged, some states continue to prohibit or restrict the marriage of people with mental retardation and some specifically require sterilization as a condition of marriage (Edmonson, 1988). Social workers helping adults with mental retardation who wish to marry and have children will need to have good legal advice in addition to good social work judgment and skills. As the independent living movement seeks to redefine and uphold perceptions of universal human rights, social workers may become activists in this area.

Historically, most parents and caregivers of people with moderate and severe retardation have believed that such people should not undertake parenthood, but because some people with mild retardation have been good parents, the question is more controversial for them. Some argue that because alcoholics, people who have never liked children, and others who have risk factors for bad parenting are not routinely prevented from becoming parents, those with mild retardation should not be prevented from being parents if they choose. Issues of the client's ability to understand the consequences versus the rights of adults to make these choices when competent to do so may be hard to resolve in many individual cases. For clients who are competent to make this decision, social workers help them think about the availability of social support and other coping resources and to anticipate the changes that will have to be made.

Equally hard decisions about the rights of adults versus the need to protect those with diminished capacity to consent arise around issues of contraception, sterilization, and termination of accidental pregnancies that result from exploitation, rape, or unprotected sex. For clients with diminished cognitive capacity, the distinction between exploitation and consensual sex may be difficult to draw, and interpretation may be subject to powerful biases on the part of the family or helping professional.

SEXUALITY

Some investigators have reported that social workers and other service providers fail to address the need for information and counseling about issues of sexuality among clients with disabilities. Workers may feel uncomfortable or incompetent to talk about these issues or they may, consciously or unconsciously, believe that sexuality is irrelevant or inappropriate for these special populations (Boyle, 1993; Edmonson, 1988; Sigler & Mackelprang, 1993). This belief also may extend to clients in the older age groups, whether or not they have disabilities. Nevertheless, clients with disabilities have the same range of interests and concerns with sexuality as other adults, and they may have some rather specialized concerns as well. As with parenting, the issues surrounding sexuality are somewhat different for the person who confronts a disability as an adult, after a pattern of relationships and sexual preferences has been established, than for the person who experiences physical and emotional maturation while learning to manage a disability.

For the person who experiences a change in functioning from injury or an adult-onset illness or condition, the primary concern may be the challenge to self-image and fears about others' perceptions—"Am I still the man I used to be?" "Does my husband still see me as a desirable partner or does he see me as a responsibility?" However, there also are specific questions of coping with the disability. "What are the chances that MS (or some other neuromuscular disorder) will impair my ability to sustain an erection?" "What do I do about my in-dwelling catheter when I have intercourse?" "How can I continue to have a meaningful sexual relationship when pain and fatigue are frequent in my daily experience?" For the client with AIDS, questions about maintaining intimacy while minimizing the partner's risk are the most salient.

For the client who grew up with a disability, the most pressing problem may be forming potentially intimate relationships. Because of stigma, a pervasive societal myth that people with disabilities are asexual, and a tendency for families with children who have a disability to isolate themselves, the person with disabilities often does not have the number and richness of social contacts growing up and, especially, the chance to meet with age peers away from parental supervision. Social situations away from parents provide the setting for much of our informal learning about flirting, picking up and responding to nonverbal cues, building romantic relationships, and making sexual overtures appropriately. Therefore, the absence of these opportunities may leave a gap in social skills.

Some disabilities bring their own potential barriers to full participation in the preliminaries of an intimate relationship. For example, blind teens and young adults must learn to express and encourage interest through tone of voice or appropriately casual touch, rather than the sidelong glance or fluttering eyelashes. More seriously, people with cognitive impairments and mental retardation may find it difficult to read subtle social cues, which may in turn lead them to behave inappropriately so that they experience difficulties in forming friendships as well as more intimate relationships. Deaf couples may have good communication with each other (some have a separate system of signing for intimate communication), but communication problems may make relationships with hearing partners difficult—the divorce rate is higher among couples with one deaf member than among deaf couples. Deficits in language skills for those who are prelingually deaf (onset before age three) may make verbal communication difficult.

For the person with disabilities who does not have a regular partner, sexual questions become complicated further by a variety of religious, social, and political beliefs about sexual expression. Masturbation and the use of sexual surrogates may provide reasonable outlets for some people (although it is difficult for women to find surrogates of either sex), whereas others would find these outlets guilt-provoking or damaging to self-esteem. Reliance on prostitutes (again an alternative more available to men than to women) raises the same issues of the client's values and self-esteem, as well as exposing the client to a variety of dangers including legal prosecution, sexually transmitted diseases, and street crime. (See in particular Comfort, 1978; Mackelprang & Valentine, 1993; and Monat-Haller, 1992.)

In addition to concerns about not getting wanted sex, many people with disabilities have to cope with issues of receiving unwanted sexual attention or attention about which they are ambivalent. Some evidence suggests that people with disabilities are more likely than others to be the victims of sexual abuse or sexual exploitation (Edmonson, 1988; Sigler & Mackelprang, 1993). This may range from the more overt exploitation to which people with mental retardation are subjected (Edmonson, 1988; Sigler & Mackelprang, 1993) to the sometimes subtler pressure a woman with a disability may feel that she should be appropriately "grateful" for any attention given her and that she has no right to refuse anyone.

What is the social worker's role in dealing with clients' issues around sexuality? One promising model, developed for work with a general population and suggested for work with clients with disabilities, by Boyle (1993) has the unwieldy acronym PLISSIT. This is a four-stage model representing successively greater levels of information and counseling skills:

P = permission
LI = limited information
SS = specific suggestions
IT = intensive therapy.

With this model, it is not expected that every social worker will be able to work at all four levels. Rather, it is expected that all social workers with adult clients will be able to work at the permission level, at a minimum. Beyond that, social workers perform at their own level of competence and comfort and are able to refer clients who need a higher order of services to appropriate providers.

The permission stage requires only that the social worker validate the client's interest and concern about sexual issues. This is accomplished through empathic listening, modeling the social worker's own comfort and sense of appropriateness of the topic, and using permission-giving statements. Boyle's (1993) examples of such statements included

> *"You may have questions about how your disability will affect you sexually. If so, I will be happy to discuss them with you."*
> *"That's interesting—tell me more."*
> *"Many women have similar concerns. Let's talk about it."*
> *"I'm glad you brought that up. I can see that it's really important to you."*
> *"Many men are worried about the same thing. Tell me more about what your particular worries are."* (p. 56)

Once clients have been able to discuss their concerns and clarify their questions or problems, their social workers have a basis for assessing whether they can provide the additional information or services needed or whether they should refer clients for additional help.

The limited information stage involves being able and willing to provide basic education on human sexuality, such as answering questions about the human reproductive system or even about the etiquette and social norms of courtship ("How do I know if she is interested?"). This simple information may be needed by clients who have reached adulthood living with their parents in relative social isolation. Even parents who have tried not to be overprotective may not have thought sexuality a legitimate concern for a person with disabilities, or they may have been too uncomfortable with the topic to discuss it. (Even the most enlightened among us may have some difficulty thinking of our children as legitimately sexual beings.)

The specific suggestions stage requires some taking of the client's sexual history, a fair degree of knowledge about the specific condition of the client (cerebral palsy, MS, spinal cord injury, ALS), and a rich understanding of sexual practice and emotional intimacy. In this stage, the social worker helps the client plan strategies for enjoying sexual intimacy by working around barriers imposed by the condition. Examples include planning the medication schedule so that private time with a partner routinely occurs about an hour after pain medication is taken, finding positions that do not put stress on arthritic joints, using mechanical interventions to correct for neuromuscular problems with male potency, or if necessary, developing a style of sexual expression that is not based on conventional genital contact or achieving orgasm.

The intensive therapy stage is for people whose sexual adjustment requires more than a general comfort with the topic and specific problem solving. It might include a diverse range of issues. For example, a man may need to work through feelings that his confinement to a wheelchair emasculates him. A person with a spinal cord injury may need extensive work on impulse control to improve his social and sexual functioning. This type of ongoing work on sexual–intimacy issues will fall outside the expertise of most adult services social workers; thus, it will usually require a referral.

STRESS MANAGEMENT

There are few clients (or social workers) who could not benefit from improved stress management. However, some disabling conditions are demonstrably exacerbated by stress. For clients with these problems, it is important that the social worker either be able to teach and reinforce stress management techniques or be able to make referrals for this service.

Stress may work directly to exacerbate the symptoms of an illness, as it does in MS and some other neuromuscular problems. In other instances, people whose disabilities produce high levels of stress for them may respond in destructive ways (for example, they may attempt self-medication to reduce stress through the abuse of alcohol, drugs, or other substances). It is not clear that people with disabilities are more or less subject to substance abuse than the general population, but the literature of several specific disabilities mentions the use of alcohol or other drugs as self-medication for stress, isolation, or despair related to the underlying problem. This includes but is not limited to people with mental retardation, deafness, severe and persistent mental illness, chronic pain, and HIV-positive status.

When substance abuse compounds another diagnosis, it is important to treat the substance abuse directly, as well as helping to deal with the underlying stress, but it may be difficult to find adequate treatment for people with multiple problems. For example, it is difficult to find detoxification facilities with translation available to the deaf, and some facilities are not well adapted for use by people who are in wheelchairs even if they technically meet access requirements. Group therapy and support groups (in outpatient or residential settings) also may present problems for clients with disabilities. Those with sensory impairments may have communication problems that interfere with group dynamics, and people with any kind of disability face the same risk of stigma in a therapy group that they do in any other new social setting, often undermining their contribution to the group and the benefits they can receive.

Of course, the adult services social worker will want to help reduce stress and help the client find less-destructive ways to cope with it before a problem such as substance abuse arises. This may involve one or more of a variety of strategies. Counseling with the client around such issues as acceptance may be an important step for reducing stress in the client who is newly disabled or newly diagnosed. For example, Krausz (1980) wrote about the denial of adults who experience sudden loss of sight, "There was a magical quality to this denial. It seemed to imply the patient's belief that 'if I accept rehabilitation, I will really be blind; however, if I do not learn how to be blind (rehabilitate), I will remain sighted'" (p. 38). The emergence in popular culture of the hero or heroine who overcomes a fatal disease or disabling condition by sheer strength of will and by disregarding all medical advice may serve to reinforce such defensive denial. Individual counseling or group counseling with people who share the same disability can help foster needed acceptance. Work with stigma management also may be appropriate to reduces stress and isolation.

For those who have adapted to their specific disability and found satisfactory ways of coping with the reaction of those who do not share it, traditional stress reduction approaches may be useful. These include a variety of meditation techniques, breath control, and physical exercise consistent with the client's abilities.

EMPLOYMENT

Employment issues vary with both the condition of the clients and the job skills or potentials they bring. For the person with a congenital or childhood-onset disability, the social worker may become involved in supporting a continuation of the educational or training efforts begun in childhood. This may mean anything from helping a student who is sensorially or physically handicapped get a scholarship to a college or university to finding a community college placement for a student with mild retardation to supporting a worker with moderate retardation being trained in a sheltered workshop.

For the client who develops a disabling condition later in life, it may mean extensive job retraining (for example, if a commercial airline pilot becomes blind), moderate adaptations of the workplace (for example, if a secretary needs to be in a wheelchair), or anything in between. For example, a computer programmer who becomes blind can still do his or her job, but the adaptive equipment is expensive and will require training to use. Retraining also may be important when the nature of the workforce changes. For example, deaf people were once employed in a number of industrial settings where the noise of the machinery disturbed workers with normal hearing. As many of these jobs were automated out of existence or moved to other countries, retraining has been necessary for a large number of deaf workers.

For people with mental retardation and certain types of cognitive impairment, training in social skills may be as important as specific career or academic training. Poor social skills combined with some of the limitations posed by these conditions may result in impulsive or unusual behavior on the job. (For example, an insufficiently socialized employee with mental retardation may initiate the same conversation over and over again, or a person with a spinal cord injury resulting in poor impulse control and missed cues may carry a practical joke to an uncomfortable extreme without comprehending that his or her behavior is inappropriate.) Such behaviors make employers, coworkers, or customers uncomfortable, leading to a substantial amount of job turnover that can be a problem for this group of clients (Lagomarcino & Rusch, 1988; Sigler & Mackelprang, 1993).

When people with disabilities have good job training or education and good social skills, social workers may still need to use their networking skills and contacts to help clients find appropriate employment. In many cases, it is difficult to protect and advocate for the rights of the worker and also show some sensitivity to the needs of the employer. Is it reasonable to ask a small business to invest large amounts of money in adapting its office to accommodate the one blind secretary in its pool of applicants? Is it discrimination or reasonable self-interest not to promote a talented deaf employee to a supervisory position if most of the people the employee would be supervising are unable to understand his or her speech? Although adult services social workers need to have some sensitivity to the needs of employers to work with them harmoniously and effectively, they also may have to take a role in advocacy and referral to legal services when clients experience overt discrimination in hiring or promotion or encounter work settings that do not conform to their needs.

HOUSING

Appropriate housing is a challenge for many special populations. Clients with AIDS often lose their homes as they become too ill to work and are unable to keep up rent or mortgage payments. Finding new housing is typically made difficult by decreased financial resources, fear of AIDS among potential landlords and neighbors, and the need for adaptations to anticipated declines in the client's functioning.

For the young adult with a congenital or childhood-onset disability, "a place of my own" is important to independent adult status. Finding a place that is adapted or adaptable to the clients' special needs (for example, accessible to a wheelchair accepting of guide dogs or other animals trained to provide services), economically feasible, and reassuring to parents who may have emotional issues with the transition can be extremely difficult for the client and social worker alike.

Clients whose physical, cognitive, or intellectual disabilities are too severe to permit completely unassisted independent living are often capable of considerable independence within a range of assisted-living facilities. Unfortunately, the number and variety of such settings is severely limited in most parts of the country, despite the efforts of the independent living movement and other advocates for people with disabilities. Until such facilities are more available, clients with these problems are often forced to choose between continuing to live with their family of origin, contending with problems of social isolation and negotiating independence from concerned and protective parents, or placement in an institution that may be poorly designed to meet the needs of younger adult clients.

For the roughly 10 percent of clients with AIDS who develop AIDS-related dementia, the problem of placement can be especially difficult. Facilities designed primarily for the care of physically frail older adults are not prepared to contend with people with fatal, transmittable disease who may still be physically strong and active while severely cognitively impaired. Symptoms of AIDS-related dementia can include combativeness and sexual aggression, which add substance to the fear that the disease may be transmitted to other residents or staff members.

Although the placement of younger adults with mental retardation and other disabilities in nursing homes does not present problems as dramatic as those seen for clients with AIDS-related dementia, there is often a poor fit between the services and activities provided for the older nursing home resident and the needs of the younger client.

There is, however, one misconception about the lack of fit that is common in both the literature and the conversation of some social workers. This is the idea that conditions found in some nursing homes such as lack of privacy, lack of resident autonomy, and activities aimed at killing time rather than stimulating the mental, physical, and creative capacities of residents are acceptable for older adults but inadequate for younger clients. The need for privacy, reasonable autonomy, and stimulation is essential to adults of all ages. If the presence of more vocal and better organized young residents challenges the infantilizing practices of some facilities, then this should be a benefit to all residents, no matter what age or condition.

DEALING WITH TALK OF SUICIDE

In most cases the social worker encounters talk of suicide among clients suffering from depression. This also may be the case among clients with a terminal illness or with a newly diagnosed disabling condition. That is, depression about their condition may be the source of suicidal ideation and should be treated by one or more of the approaches used with depression from other sources. However, there is a growing awareness that thoughts and talk of suicide among people coming to terms with their own imminent death can be an expression of a need to maintain some control over their lives. This assertion of control may be a healthy part of the coping process. It may require substantial social work skill and experience to differentiate between these two manifestations of the same behavior and, thus, to know how to respond appropriately. There is indeed a third position, that a person with a painful, irreversible, terminal illness has the right not only to voice this control over the end of his or her life but also to exercise it. This view, which implies a laissez-faire response to talk of suicide, may be inconsistent with the social worker's personal or professional ethics. Like many ethical questions in social work, it requires the practitioner to find the balance between competing obligations—to protect the interest of the client and to acknowledge the rights of adults to make decisions even when they do not conform to the social worker's own beliefs.

LEGAL SERVICES

Although a range of legal issues may be relevant to the needs of special populations, there are two broad types of need that are frequently encountered: (1) advice on fighting discrimination and (2) planning for the end of life.

People with disabilities working in the independent living movement and other sociopolitical groups have been effective in winning acknowledgment and protection of their rights. It is appropriate, and empowering, that they have taken the lead in their own liberation, and many cases of discrimination can be referred directly to local advocacy groups. Nevertheless, when these avenues and the social worker's own advocacy efforts fail, legal services may be needed to address discrimination in housing, child custody, hiring and employment issues, school admissions, and public accommodation.

For people with terminal illnesses or conditions such as ALS and AIDS, legal plans for the event of their death may be comforting, even though some social workers report that it is difficult for them to talk to younger people about their death (Lew-Napoleone, 1992). Plans for the care and custody of children during the final stages of illness and after death are vital to the peace of mind of many terminally ill clients, as well as to the lives of the children themselves. Similarly, preparing a will is important when the client has substantial assets. Among gay and lesbian couples, where the state does not recognize the rights of the partner, a will may be important even when the monetary value of property is negligible. This is especially true when the client's family of origin does not accept the surviving partner and cannot be relied on to recognize his or her ownership of assets they have collected as a couple. Finally, young clients with short life expectancies, like older adult clients, may want to make a living will, durable power of attorney, or other arrangement to ensure that their final treatment is consistent with their wishes if they become unable to give or withhold consent.

Summary

All clients are special, and all clients are individual. However, we learn and build our experience from grasping the common threads while still treasuring the unique qualities of each client. This chapter has explored some of the things that adults with a wide variety of conditions and disabilities may experience. They are no substitute for a thorough grounding in information about the specific conditions of clients. However, they do point up some major areas of awareness that the public social worker must cultivate to work effectively with any of these special populations.

Key Points

Excellent adult services social workers

- find that the basic model of empowerment and the steps of the family assessment and change model apply equally well to clients with special needs as to any other group of clients
- combat attitudes such as stigma, lack of cultural competency, countertransference, and unrealistic expectations that may inhibit effective work with special populations
- learn to address service challenges in working with special populations, such as stigma management, family dynamics, parenting, sexuality, stress management, housing, dealing with talk of suicide, and the need for legal services
- find that counseling on how to manage stigma can be a valuable service to individual clients; however, part of the social worker's role as advocate and educator is to help destigmatize disabilities on a societal level
- know that families that include a person with special needs often become "hostage" to the illness or condition and are in danger of forming destructive intrafamily coalitions and at risk of suffering unnecessary guilt and subordination of their individual needs; social workers use proactive intervention to prevent or ameliorate some of these risks
- recognize that adults of both sexes have concerns about parenting—whether or not to become parents or how to continue parenting responsibilities in the face of a new disability or worsening condition
- are sensitive to and accept issues of sexuality and intimacy that arise for many adults with disabilities; some use the PLISSIT model, which empowers them to provide support up to their level of competence and make referrals for services beyond their skills
- know that because stress may directly or indirectly exacerbate many illnesses and disabilities, stress management is an important service element for special populations
- provide or refer for employment services needed by these groups, including education, job training or retraining, social skills training, help in finding jobs, and advocacy–legal action in the face of discrimination

- help find appropriate housing for clients with disabilities, whether the client's needs and preferences include total independence, assisted living, or institutional care
- understand that talk of suicide among terminally ill people may represent depression, a coping mechanism reflecting maintaining control over destiny, or (some people believe) a rational choice to avoid pain when recovery is not an option; social workers may need to consult mental health professionals experienced in this situation to distinguish among meanings of suicidal ideation in this population
- are prepared to refer appropriately for two major legal needs of special populations: (1) handling discrimination in a variety of settings and (2) making plans for the end of life, including wills, custody of children, health power of attorney, and advance directives
- recognize that all clients are part of some special population and that all clients, whatever their challenges, are unique; nevertheless, there are important social work lessons to learn from the shared experiences of people with a wide variety of physical, sensory, and cognitive problems.

Excellent adult services managers
- recognize that adult services social workers may need help in dealing with their emotions about disabling conditions and are able to provide direct help or referral to support their social workers
- model comfort and competence in interactions with clients and social workers who have disabilities
- use case staffings to diffuse countertransference and client-blaming, making sure not to reinforce it
- recognize that no individual social worker can learn everything needed to ensure maximum effectiveness with a variety of disabilities; the agency may be able to hire or develop experts in different disabilities and the competencies needed for work with that specific population
- make sure that the agency's physical and social environment is welcoming to special populations.

Excellent leaders
- cooperate with and work to advance civil rights for people with disabilities
- put competent people with disabilities in visible public positions.

References

Birk, K. A., & Kalb, R. C. (1992). MS and planning a family: Fertility, pregnancy, childbirth, and parenting roles. In R. C. Kalb & L. C. Scheinberg (Eds.), *Multiple sclerosis and the family* (pp. 51–62). New York: Demos.

Boyle, P. S. (1993). Training in sexuality and disability: Preparing social workers to provide services to individuals with disabilities. *Journal of Social Work and Human Sexuality, 8*, 45–62.

Brooks, N. A. (1991). Self-empowerment among adults with severe physical disability: A case study. *Journal of Sociology and Social Welfare, 18,* 105–120.

Burks, J. (1992). A dynamic model for understanding the physician's relationship with patients and their families. In R. C. Kalb & L. C. Scheinberg (Eds.), *Multiple sclerosis and the family* (pp. 25–34). New York: Demos.

Comfort, A. (Ed.). (1978). *Sexual consequences of disability.* Philadelphia: George F. Stickley.

Connor, E. M., Sperling, R. S., Gelder, R., Kiselev, P., Scott, G., O'Sullivan, M. J., VanDyke, R., Bey, M., Shearer, W., Jacobson, R. L., Jimenez, E., O'Neill, E., Bazin, B., Delfraissy, J. F., Culnane, M., Coombs, R., Elkins, M., Moye, J., Stratton, P., & Balsley, J. (1994). Reduction of maternal–infant transmission of human immunodeficiency virus type 1 with zidovudine treatment. *New England Journal of Medicine, 331,* 1173–1180.

Edmonson, B. (1988). Disability and sexual adjustment. In V. B. Van Hasselt, P. S. Strain, & M. Hersen (Eds.), *Handbook of developmental and physical disabilities* (pp. 91–106). New York: Pergamon Press.

Goffman, E. (1963). *Stigma: Notes on the management of spoiled identity.* Englewood Cliffs, NJ: Prentice Hall.

Harangody, G., & Peterson, R. (1992). A model for AIDS home care. In H. Land (Ed.), *AIDS: A complete guide to psychosocial intervention* (pp. 51–64). Milwaukee: Family Service America.

Harragin, V. (1992). AIDS and the homeless: HIV prevention and care. In H. Land (Ed.), *AIDS: A complete guide to psychosocial intervention* (pp. 187–197). Milwaukee: Family Service America.

Hollins, M. (1989). *Understanding blindness.* Hillsdale, NJ: Lawrence Erlbaum.

Krausz, S. L. (1980). Group psychotherapy with legally blind patients. *Clinical Social Work Journal, 8*(1), 37–49.

Lagomarcino, T. R., & Rusch, F. R. (1988). Competitive employment: Overview and analysis of research focus. In V. B. Van Hasselt, P. S. Strain, & M. Hersen (Eds.), *Handbook of developmental and physical disabilities* (pp. 150–158). New York: Pergamon Press.

Levy, A. J. (1993). Stigma management: A new clinical service. *Families in Society: The Journal of Contemporary Human Services, 74,* 225–231.

Lew-Napoleone, S. (1992). Hospice service and AIDS. In H. Land (Ed.), *AIDS: A complete guide to psychosocial intervention* (pp. 65–77). Milwaukee: Family Service America.

Ludders, B. B. (1987). Communication between health care professionals and deaf patients. *Health & Social Work, 12,* 303–310.

Mackelprang, R. W., & Valentine, D. (Eds.). (1993). *Sexuality and disabilities: A guide for human services practitioners.* Binghampton, NY: Haworth Press.

Macks, J. (1988). Women and AIDS: Countertransference issues. *Social Casework, 69*(6), 340–347.

Matthews, B. (1985). *Multiple sclerosis: The facts* (2nd ed.). Oxford, England: Oxford University Press.

Mayer, R. F. (1991). Living with amyotrophic lateral sclerosis. In L. I. Charash, R. E. Lovelace, C. F. Leach, A. H. Kutscher, J. Goldberg, & D. P. Roye, Jr. (Eds.), *Muscular dystrophy and other neuromuscular diseases: Psychosocial issues* (pp. 23–30). New York: Haworth.

Mehta, S. I., & Farina, A. (1988). Associative stigma: Perceptions of the difficulties of college-aged children of stigmatized fathers. *Journal of Social and Clinical Psychology, 7*(2/3), 192–202.

Miller, D. (1992). Some effects of MS on parenting and children. In R. C. Kalb & L. C. Scheinberg (Eds.), *Multiple sclerosis and the family* (pp. 9–24). New York: Demos.

Monat-Heller, R. K. (1992). *Understanding and expressing sexuality: Responsible choices for individuals with developmental disabilities.* Baltimore: Paul H. Brookes.

Monk, A. (1981). Social work with the aged: Principles of practice. *Social Work, 26*, 61–68.

Schneider, C. R., & Anderson, W. (1980). Attitudes toward the stigmatized: Some insights from recent research. *Rehabilitation Counseling Bulletin, 23*(2), 299–312.

Selder, F. E., & Breunig, K. (1991). Living with multiple sclerosis: The gradual transition. In L. I. Charash, R. E. Lovelace, C. F. Leach, A. H. Kutscher, J. Goldberg, & D. P. Roye, Jr. (Eds.), *Muscular dystrophy and other neuromuscular diseases: Psychosocial issues* (pp. 89–98). New York: Haworth.

Sigler, G., & Mackelprang, R. W. (1993). Cognitive impairments: Psychosocial and sexual implications and strategies for social work intervention. *Journal of Social Work and Human Sexuality, 8*(2), 89–106.

Snyder, M. L., Kleck, R. E., Strenta, A., & Mentzer, S. J. (1979). Avoidance of the handicapped: An attributional ambiguity analysis. *Journal of Personality and Social Psychology, 37*(12), 2297–2306.

Stein, J. B. (1992). HIV disease and substance abuse: Twin epidemics, multiple needs. In H. Land (Ed.), *AIDS: A complete guide to psychosocial intervention* (pp. 107–115). Milwaukee: Family Service America.

Steinglass, P. (1992). Multifamily group therapy. In R. C. Kolb & L. C. Steinberg (Eds.), *Multiple sclerosis and the family* (pp. 83–96). New York: Demos.

Taylor-Brown, S. (1993). HIV positive women: Finding a voice in the AIDS pandemic. In V. J. Lynch, G. A. Lloyd, & M. F. Fimbres (Eds.), *The changing face of AIDS: Implications for social work practice* (pp. 123–151). Westport, CT: Auburn House.

Welch, G. J. (1987). Social work intervention with a multiple sclerosis population. *British Journal of Social Work, 17*, 45–59.

Additional Readings

Cadwell, S. (1993). Gay men and HIV: The band plays on. In V. J. Lynch, G. A. Lloyd, & M. F. Fimbres (Eds.), *The changing face of AIDS: Implications for social work practice* (pp. 153–173). Westport, CT: Auburn House.

Catanzaro, M., Fish, D. G., Jones, M. V., & Saideman, E. M. (1992). The financial and legal implications of MS for the family. In R. C. Kalb & L. C. Scheinberg (Eds.), *Multiple sclerosis and the family* (pp. 35–49). New York: Demos.

Chachkes, E. (1993). AIDS: Future directions for education and practice. In V. J. Lynch, G. A. Lloyd, & M. F. Fimbres (Eds.), *The changing face of AIDS: Implications for social work practice* (pp. 3–18). Westport, CT: Auburn House.

Dick, J. E. (1989). Serving hearing-impaired alcoholics. *Social Work, 34*, 555–556.

Foley, F. W., & Iverson, J. (1992). Sexuality and MS. In R. C. Kalb & L. C. Scheinberg (Eds.), *Multiple sclerosis and the family* (pp. 63–82). New York: Demos.

Frankel, D. (1984). Long-term care issues in multiple sclerosis. *Rehabilitation Literature, 45*(9–10), 282–285.

Kerlin, B. A. (1985). Social work education and services for the handicapped: Unfulfilled responsibilities—unrealized opportunities. *Journal of Social Work Education, 21*(1), 48–55.

Lloyd, G. A. (1992). Contextual and clinical issues in providing services to gay men. In H. Land (Ed.), *AIDS: A complete guide to psychosocial intervention* (pp. 91–105). Milwaukee: Family Service America.

Piette, J. D., Thompson, B. J., Fleishman, J. A., & Mor, V. (1993). The organization and delivery of AIDS case management. In V. J. Lynch, G. A. Lloyd, & M. F. Fimbres (Eds.), *The changing face of AIDS: Implications for social work practice* (pp. 39–62). Westport, CT: Auburn House.

Reamer, F. G. (1991). AIDS, social work, and the "duty to protect." *Social Work, 36*, 56–60.

Schwartz, L. B., Devine, P. A., Schechter, C. B., & Bender, A. N. (1991). Impact of illness on lifestyle. In L. I. Charash, R. E. Lovelace, C. F. Leach, A. H. Kutscher, J. Goldberg, & D. P. Roye, Jr. (Eds.), *Muscular dystrophy and other neuromuscular diseases: Psychosocial issues* (pp. 3–21). New York: Haworth.

Siller, J., & Chapman, A. (1967). *Attitudes of the non-disabled toward the physically handicapped* (Final Reports, Grant No. RE 707). Washington, DC: Vocational Rehabilitation Administration, Department of Health, Education, and Welfare.

Soderberg, J. (1992). MS and the family system. In R. C. Kalb & L. C. Scheinberg (Eds.), *Multiple sclerosis and the family* (pp. 1–7). New York: Demos.

Spear, J. H. (1984). On the road again: A mental health map to the mainstreamed hearing impaired. *Volta Review, 86*(5), 3–15.

Stein, J. B., & Hodge, R. H. (1993). Substance abuse and HIV disease: A multidimensional challenge to caregivers. In V. J. Lynch, G. A. Lloyd, & M. F. Fimbres (Eds.), *The changing face of AIDS: Implications for social work practice* (pp. 199–212). Westport, CT: Auburn House.

Underwood, M. M., Kahn, K., Johnson, T., & Godin, S. (1993). Addressing HIV disease issues with the seriously and persistently mentally ill. In V. J. Lynch, G. A. Lloyd, & M. F. Fimbres (Eds.), *The changing face of AIDS: Implications for social work practice* (pp. 175–197). Westport, CT: Auburn House.

Vernon, M., & Andrews, J. F. (1990). *The psychology of deafness: Understanding deaf and hard-of-hearing people.* New York: Longman.

Wilson, P. A. (1993). HIV disease: Toward comprehensive services for families. In V. J. Lynch, G. A. Lloyd, & M. F. Fimbres (Eds.), *The changing face of AIDS: Implications for social work practice* (pp. 79–103). Westport, CT: Auburn House.

Zola, I. K. (1992). MS and the family—On the necessity of a larger context. In R. C. Kalb & L. C. Scheinberg (Eds.), *Multiple sclerosis and the family* (pp. 97–107). New York: Demos.

CHAPTER 11

Cultural Diversity

GARY M. NELSON

MARY ANNE P. SALMON

ROBERT LEIBSON HAWKINS

ANNA SCHEYETT

As the general population becomes more diverse, both in racioethnic makeup and age, so too will the population of adult services programs become more diverse. In 1992, 12.4 percent of the U.S. population was African American, 3.3 percent was Asian, and less than 1 percent was Native American. In addition, 9.4 percent, from all racial groups, was of Hispanic origin. By 2050, 15.1 percent will be African American, 9.3 percent will be Asian, 1.3 percent will be Native American, and 18.4 percent will be of Hispanic origin (U.S. Bureau of the Census, 1993). It is estimated that by 2020, 40 percent of the population in the service delivery system will be people of color (Cross, Bazron, Dennis, & Issacs, 1989). Just as the population is changing its racioethnic composition and becoming racially more diverse, it is also aging. In colonial times half of the population was under age 16; currently, fewer than one in four are in that age group. The fastest growing population group are people age 85 and older (Bass, Kutza, & Torres-Gil, 1990).

Like the general population, the older population is becoming more racially diverse. In 1990, 8.3 percent of the older population was African American, but by the year 2020 that number will increase to 10.7 percent. The growth in the Hispanic older population is even more dramatic. In 1990, 3.6 percent of the older population was Hispanic, and by the year 2020 that figure will more than double to 7.4 percent (Taueber, 1990). Because of survival rates, the aging phenomenon that we see occurring is also a gender-based phenomenon; women continue to outlive men. Currently, older women outnumber men by greater than three to two, but as recently as 1930, the number of older women was equal to the number of older men (Taueber, 1990).

What do these changes mean for adult services? They have at least two important implications:

1. We must develop cultural competence in our work with clients and families. This competence will increase our credibility and give us the sensitivity needed to help families make the life changes they need without compromising their cultural values and identities.

2. We must learn to work together with colleagues whose professional social work culture overlays a worldview that may be different from our own. When we have achieved this, we can benefit from the enrichment of other perspectives without letting our differences undermine our common goals.

This chapter explores the meaning and implications of cultural diversity for practice in adult services; defines culture, diversity, and cultural competence within the context of practice in adult services; discusses the implications of cultural competence or culture clash in working with adult clients and their families; and explores the advantages and challenges of a multicultural workforce and how agencies approach diversity within organizational boundaries. The chapter concludes with a discussion of the value base that underlies culturally competent practice and concepts, as well as techniques and tools for enhancing the cultural competence of adult services personnel.

Diversity encompasses differences that grow from race or ethnicity, gender, social class, religion, sexual orientation, language, and region. People with disabilities also contribute to diversity. Much of the material on stigma presented in chapter 10 is equally applicable to ethnic minorities and other groups who face discrimination. Similarly, much of the discussion in this chapter on diversity is directly relevant to clients and professionals with disabilities. However, whereas chapter 10 drew its examples from people with disabilities, this chapter will draw its examples primarily from other areas of diversity.

Cultural Diversity and Cultural Conflict

Cox (1994) defined a *cultural group* as "an affiliation of people who collectively share certain norms, values, or traditions that are different from those of other groups" (pp. 5–6). Culture defines how people see themselves and the world. Each person develops a worldview based on that culture, which includes values—the standards by which actions can be judged "right" or "wrong." These values are so ingrained that people frequently believe that only their culture has the "right" values and represents the "right" way to think and behave and that someone from a different culture, with different values and behavior, is wrong (Kogod, 1992). When people from different cultures who believe their own is "right" meet one another as coworkers or as worker and client, there is little chance that they will understand or appreciate each other's worldviews.

This is an oversimplified but useful basic description of the challenge at the heart of diversity. Why do people often experience negative emotions such as fear, discomfort, or anger when they interact with people of different cultures? Although there is a wealth of psychological literature on the subject, the question has not been satisfactorily answered. Davis and Proctor (1989) suggested that the best-documented and most satisfactory explanation is that of "perceived differences." According to this view, we generalize observable differences such as skin color into a variety of assumptions about differences in viewpoints, values, and status. They went on to reason that we seek the company of people like ourselves, based on "Byrne's Law of Attraction," which holds that perceived similarity between individuals or groups has a positive emotional effect because it is reinforcing, and conversely, that perceived differences imply rejection or challenge (Byrne, 1971).

Whatever the psychological basis of discomfort among people of diverse races or cultures, this discomfort is overlaid by both the global and the personal history of experiences with people of other groups. For example, members of groups that have been oppressed may have developed survival mechanisms such as concealment and suspicion that may be functional in some situations but make it difficult to form open relationships with people of other groups. People of advantaged groups may have feelings of guilt over their group's history. This guilt can lead in some cases to blaming the victim (that is, continued discrimination because "they must somehow have brought it on themselves") and in other cases to denial of the salience of race or culture in any of their relationships ("I treat everyone exactly the same. I don't even notice a person's race"), which also raises barriers against open relationships (Davis & Proctor, 1989)

Working with Clients and Their Families

Cultural differences and the social worker's cultural competence (the ability to recognize and respect cultural differences without overlooking essential human similarities) have serious implications for working with clients and their families, including barriers to service delivery, barriers to building an effective helping relationship, and failure to reflect cultural priorities when helping the client set goals and plan activities.

BARRIERS TO SERVICE DELIVERY

Different culturally diverse populations have the weight of the law to ensure a fair hearing in both adult services programs and in the courts. National legislation has outlawed discrimination on the basis of sex, color, race, religion, pregnancy, national origin, age, or physical disability. The Civil Rights Act of 1964 (as amended in 1972), the Pregnancy Discrimination Act of 1978, the Age Discrimination Act of 1967, and more recently the Americans with Disabilities Act of 1990 have added protections and assurances that have benefited the well-being of many individuals traditionally served by adult services programs around the country. Nevertheless, while de jure discrimination has been largely eliminated for many people, de facto discrimination as a function of persistent discriminatory patterns, values, and attitudes remains.

A major area where cultural or racial discrimination patterns are believed to exist concerns access to health and human services. Research on differential access to adult services is sparse and focuses primarily on issues of minority access, much of it presuming a disadvantage for people of color in accessing social services (Bass et al., 1990; Carlton-LaNey, 1991; Cunningham, 1991). This presumption is made against an understanding of disproportionate need within the minority community. It is not generally thought that members of cultural minorities are overtly denied services but rather that insufficient effort is made to remove barriers for or actively extend services to these groups.

One of the few studies that systematically examined the use of social services by older people of color in a national sample found the levels of service provision to them to be inconsistent across counties (Holmes, Holmes, Steinbach, Hausner, & Rocheleau, 1979). The authors also found, not surprisingly, that agencies that did make special efforts at outreach, recruitment of diverse staff, and location of services in communities where racial and ethnic groups reside were more effective at reaching proportionally greater numbers of older group members of the specific population (Holmes et al., 1979).

Other studies have examined possible barriers to serving older people of color (Bastida, 1989; Wood, 1989; Yeatts, Crow, & Folts, 1992). In examining the use of services by older Hispanic and African Americans, Bastida (1989) found a strong relationship between the group's participation in agency decision making and receipt of services by older group members. She also found that the presence of younger group advocates in the community increased the resources available to older minority group members. In an extensive review of the literature on minority access to services, Yeatts et al. (1992) pointed to several commonsense, but no less important, strategies for overcoming service barriers. These included involving racial and ethnic group members on agency boards to ensure that services are attractive and useful to them, offering services in settings familiar to community members, and engaging a culturally diverse workforce delivering services. Such strategies have relevance to all adult services programs targeted to culturally diverse groups.

BARRIERS TO THE HELPING RELATIONSHIP

There are two potential sources of cultural barriers to forming an effective helping relationship among the adult services social worker, the client, and the family. The first is the perception that the client and family have about the social worker, which may be based, at least in part, on social class, race, or membership in the social work profession. The second is the perception that the social worker has about the family, which may be based, at least in part, on social class, race, or having the kinds of problems that lead one to seek help at a human services agency.

The Client's Perceptions of the Social Worker

Although research into the question of whether clients prefer a social worker of the same ethnic group is somewhat mixed in both quality and result, Davis and Proctor (1989) concluded that the social worker's race is a salient characteristic in a client's preference for a worker but not necessarily the most salient one. For example, clients might prefer social workers with social styles similar to their own rather than workers of the same ethnic background with unfamiliar social styles. Whatever the extent of such feelings in the general population, every adult services social worker of every conceivable cultural perspective will sometimes be assigned clients who are suspicious, angry, or contemptuous of them because of their cultural identity. Learning to manage the anger and indignation that such behavior can arouse and finding ways to help the client and themselves move beyond this barrier is one of the challenges of cultural competency.

Social Workers' Perceptions of the Client and Family

Clients are not the only ones who bring their preconceptions, based on ethnic or cultural factors, to the first meeting between client and social worker. Health and human services professionals are also prone to some unwarranted assumptions (Gregory, Wells, & Leake, 1987; Johnson, Kurtz, Tomlinson, & Howe, 1986). Gregory and colleagues at the University of California–Los Angeles School of Medicine conducted an experiment that is suggestive of this point. They showed first-year medical students a series of eight slides of potential patients who were matched by type of clothing (middle class), age (early 20s), and facial expression (a slight smile) but who differed in gender and ethnicity—African American, Hispanic, Asian, and white subjects, with a man and a woman from each ethnicity. Students were asked to answer questions indicating their expectations about the interaction with this "patient." Students expected to be least comfortable interviewing the African American patients, and they felt that the African American man and woman and the Latino man would be the least likely to comply with the doctor's recommendation. African American and Latino medical students reported more comfort and higher expectations of compliance from these patients than white and Asian students did but still rated them less likely to comply with the doctor's instructions than the other patients.

Such an experiment has its limits. For example, people forced to make judgments from slides will be making their decisions entirely on appearances, whereas in real life they may or may not put more faith in other indicators. Furthermore, because the experiment used only one slide representing each ethnic group, it is difficult to know whether students responded to an individual picture based on the person's race or some other characteristic of their appearance. (The Hispanic woman was overwhelmingly thought the most comfortable "patient" to interview, which was interpreted by the authors as reflecting her maternal appearance rather than her status as a Latina.) Still, the recurrence of similar findings in a variety of experimental designs reinforces what many social workers admit, that their early expectations of a client may be influenced by that client's race, religion, sexual orientation, level of education, and other cultural factors.

Robins (1994) provided a developmental perspective on the concept of cultural competence. In this perspective, cultural competence is a continuum that ranges from cultural destructiveness, exemplified by hate groups and their beliefs, to cultural proficiency, in which there is a systematic approach to working with, socializing with, and readily adapting to people in many cross-cultural situations. In between these two states, people may experience cultural incapacity—that is, fear, denial of positive differences, or lower expectations of people from varying cultural backgrounds. They may also experience cultural blindness, believing that only the dominant culture is correct, illustrated by such attitudes as "if only blacks (Hispanics, gays, women) just tried to get along, everything would be all right." Holding such views can undermine the social worker's effectiveness. An adult services social worker who works with an older lesbian client and who feels repelled by the lesbian lifestyle or by any acknowledgment of sexuality among older adults will find it virtually impossible to bring forth the empathy that is essential to working effectively. By contrast the worker who minimizes or trivializes the client's lesbian identity may find it difficult to understand the family and community dynamics to which this client and her partner have to adapt. Either response will weaken the social worker's credibility with the client ("If she thinks that about me because I am a lesbian, what else doesn't she understand?").

RECOGNIZING CULTURAL VALUES

For those working in adult services, many of the challenging issues faced when working with clients and their families as a client system are directly related to working with the culture of that system. These issues can include what constitutes a family and how its members behave, social supports, beliefs, religion, and spirituality, among many other things. Many of the failures of the helping professions stem from miscommunication among worker, client, and family because they often do not "speak the same language," even when they share a common mother tongue.

Culturally competent adult services social workers are those who can understand an individual and family within the cultural context that has meaning for them. Informed by that understanding, the workers serve and advocate for that family (Williams & Weil, 1994). They possess the ability to engage diverse client systems and go beyond the presumption of cultural similarity to actually "hear and feel" what the client and family are saying and meaning in the context of their culture. This allows them to provide responses that enable individuals and their families to gain control, shape their own circumstances, and maximize their well-being.

Bennett (1984) noted that cultural competence begins when cultural differences are acknowledged, explored, and accepted, and Kogod (1992) gave seven basic tips for achieving this:

1. *understand and recognize that differences exist*
2. *acknowledge personal stereotypes and assumptions*

3. *develop consciousness and acceptance of one's own cultural background and its values and beliefs*
4. *learn about other cultures*
5. *provide employees who are different with what they need to succeed: access to information and the opportunity for relationships with people in power*
6. *treat people equitably but not necessarily uniformly*
7. *encourage positive and constructive discussion about all differences.* (pp. 246–247)

A more active stage of cultural competence is typified by the adaptive adult services program or worker who can use knowledge of the differences in cultures to help in problem solving and bringing about change. A fully culturally competent program and worker are able to adapt flexibly to many cultural situations and foster a climate of cultural diversity that taps the strengths of various cultures for effective change and problem solving.

Cultural Diversity and Organizational Effectiveness

Developing a diverse workforce that matches the composition of the service population is an agency response that also can help overcome cultural barriers in communication and problem solving with clients. It is generally presumed that a culturally diverse and sensitive organizational environment will contribute to more-effective outcomes for both minority and nonminority employees (Bass et al., 1990; Cox, 1994; Davis & Proctor, 1989). Writing on cultural diversity in organizations, Cox presented an interactional model that encompasses individual career outcomes and organizational effectiveness. The model holds that the climate of diversity in the organization establishes a pattern for either negative or positive career outcomes for minority group members in the organizations. (Anyone can be a minority group member.) These patterns in turn govern the effectiveness of the organization, including treatment of minority group consumers. The degree of personal and intergroup conflict or consensus and the organizational culture collectively define the climate of diversity of an organization.

Again, research in this area is slim with respect to the human services and absent for adult services in particular. The connection between the climate of diversity within adult services programs, career paths for adult services workers, and outcomes for adult services clients is unknown. One of the few studies of an adult services workforce that does exist (for North Carolina in 1989 and for only one possible cultural group) indicates that 21 percent of line workers, 19 percent of supervisors, and 9 percent of top administrators were African American. Although the proportion of line workers who were African American matches the general makeup of the state's population, it does not match the composition of the service population, which is disproportionately African American (Center for Aging Research and Educational Services [CARES], 1990). The proportion of African American people in this adult services workforce decreases as one moves up the career ladder. Such a pattern is probably not atypical from what might be found in other state adult services programs or in the private business sector (Cox, 1994).

POTENTIAL BENEFITS OF DIVERSITY

Palmer (1989) commented that organizations have historically used three different approaches to dealing with diversity in the workplace. The first she calls the "golden rule" approach, which holds that all people should be treated the same, no matter how they differ. An issue with this approach, however, is that people from different cultures find that they must adapt to the culture of the organization, which generally reflects the dominant culture of the society. Sacrificing one's culture can produce one of two reactions: anger or withdrawal and isolation. This appears to represent the organizational equivalent of minimizing the cultural differences of a client.

The second possible approach is the "right the wrongs" strategy, which recognizes the legitimate anger or isolation of people put at a disadvantage for not belonging to the dominant culture. In this approach the disadvantaged group is offered special advantages to compensate for the barriers they face, and the dominant culture is educated and sensitized to the unique concerns of the disadvantaged group. In Palmer's opinion, this approach often results in a "we/they" situation, which may increase the anger among members of the disadvantaged group and cause defensiveness or avoidance among the dominant group.

The third approach Palmer identifies, to "value all differences," is perhaps the newest strategy, and organizations are still learning how to operate in this way. In this approach, the organization celebrates difference and encourages consciousness of and responsiveness to diversity in such things as ethnic background, gender, class, physical ability, and sexual orientation. The desired result is that rapport develops among individuals that supports a team spirit. Diversity training in organizations helps staff members know how the issues of diversity relate to them personally and how they can adjust to diversity.

This concept, also referred to as "value in diversity," asserts that diversity in the workplace has positive effects on communication, creativity, and problem solving (Cox, 1994; Cox, Lobel, & McLeod, 1991; Mandell & Kohler-Gray, 1990). These writers and others argue that properly managed, diverse organizations and groups have performance advantages over homogeneous ones (Cox, 1994). There are four primary advantages attributed to diverse organizations. Based on the discussion of Cox and Blake (1991), each of these is highlighted briefly below.

1. Positively managed organizations that offer career opportunities for members of racial and ethnic groups and women are thought to be more effective at recruiting top talent.
2. Individuals who are rewarded in a nondiscriminatory fashion are believed to exhibit greater job satisfaction, organizational identification, and job involvement. Such factors are seen as contributing to increased worker productivity and decreased turnover and absenteeism.

3. A diverse workforce that mirrors the makeup of the consumer or client population seems to improve the effective marketing of the organization's product. In the language of human services, one might say that it improves access to needed services on the part of diverse cultural groups.

4. Advocates of the philosophy of value in diversity argue further that the diversity and heterogeneity of work groups and work teams increases creativity, innovation, and problem-solving abilities. Multiple perspectives on organizational problems or on possible ways of understanding the needs of clients and families can contribute to a more holistic picture of what is going on. This results in multiple and more-effective strategies for change.

POTENTIAL PROBLEMS OF DIVERSITY

Cox (1994) also noted that culturally diverse workplaces are not devoid of problems. Two related areas in which problems may arise are group cohesiveness and communication. Given the propensity to associate with individuals and groups with similar attributes, an underlying factor in cultural conflict, diverse groups may experience greater problems at achieving cohesiveness. Cohesiveness is an important prerequisite for channeling individual talents and abilities into meeting group goals. This bond can be found in diverse groups, but it typically takes more work to achieve.

The road to such cohesiveness is paved with clear and effective communication among organizational members. Such communication among people of mixed racial, ethnic, age, gender, and other cultural backgrounds is a challenge. All the possible misattributions of abilities and disabilities, values and attitudes that exist among different cultural groups in the larger community must be worked out in the organizational environment. This almost inevitably leads to more-frequent disagreement and misunderstanding at first, but if everyone from the director down to the newest social worker tries to keep communication open and honest, this challenge can be met and the benefits of diversity appreciated.

Enhancing Cultural Competence

Creating a positive climate of diversity within adult services or in any organization involves (1) a commitment to improved self-knowledge of one's own culture, (2) a belief in multicultural values, and (3) an ongoing dialogue between diverse individuals and groups. Fortunately, there are techniques available to help pursue these three objectives.

SELF-KNOWLEDGE

The most effective route to understanding another's culture is to first understand one's own culture and how it shapes one's worldview and interaction with others. Our beliefs and values are so deeply rooted and taken for granted that we do not even think of them as cultural beliefs. Most of the time we are not aware of our belief systems because we are with others who share our "understanding." Our cultural belief system may become evident only when it is challenged (North Carolina Family and Children's Resource Program [NCFCRP], 1994).

Enhancing self-knowledge can be both an individual and a group process. There are a number of activities and exercises that can help meet this goal. However, human services professionals wanting to use such group exercises in their agencies are advised to arrange for a trained facilitator to lead the process and help encourage open and honest dialogue.

A skilled facilitator can keep the group process from being pulled into a discussion where various participants engage in a contest. Bohm (1965) characterized it as a Ping-Pong game in which the contestants strive to persuade one another of the essential "rightness" of their own cultural values. By suspending assumptions and facilitating the presentation of different worldviews, the facilitator can foster a more fluid, less competitive process that allows for change.

One possible activity to increase self-knowledge is called "cultural introduction." In this activity a group of participants, led by the facilitator, focus on themselves as members of variant cultures. Participants complete a cultural identification card, which lists their name, race, gender, education, social class identification, ethnic background, and other items that might be culturally relevant. They are then asked to draw up a list of words that describe their cultural orientation. Using this card and these phrases, participants are asked to introduce themselves culturally to the group. For example, "I am a Hispanic American, female, a Westerner, a college graduate, middle class, a Catholic, and partially deaf." By asking a number of questions (for example, what category was the easiest or the most difficult to describe, what category or response did you most identify with, what surprised you about the shared information?), the facilitator moves the individual participants to reflect on the diversity of the group. This encourages discussion among group members about each other and allows for self-reflection. Remember that the key to enhancing cultural competency is letting people who are different communicate with each other, discovering not only differences but similarities.

A similar exercise uses cultural self-identity questions (Table 11-1) developed by Pinderhughes (1989) and adapted by NCFCRP (1994). These questions help group members reflect on their own background and culture while also thinking about others. Although the questions presented here focus on issues of racioethnic identity, they could be modified to include other cultural dimensions such as gender, class, and disability.

The facilitator should lead the group in a discussion about their responses to the questions and focus on which questions were hardest or easiest to answer. The facilitator also could ask the group how they think their answers would affect their work as adult services providers.

Table 11-1

CULTURAL SELF-IDENTITY QUESTIONS

1. What is your ethnic background?
   - What do you like about your ethnic group?
   - What do you dislike?
2. Where did you grow up and what other ethnic groups resided there?
3. What are the values of your ethnic group?
4. What was your first experience with feeling different?
5. What are your earliest images of race and color?
   Whites: How do you think people of color feel about their color identity?
   People of color: How do you think whites feel about their color identity?

Reprinted with permission from Pinderhughes, E. (1989). *Understanding race, ethnicity, and power.* New York: Free Press.

DIALOGUE ON DIVERSITY

The measure of effective communication that leads to a respectful work and service environment can be found in the distinction between the concepts of discussion and dialogue. As noted above, discussions of diversity often are framed in competing win–lose terms. Dialogues about diversity, in contrast, can yield a win–win understanding and change. Dialogue serves to uncover inconsistencies between our personal and professional beliefs and our actions. The creative tension that arises when we clearly state a vision of the type of organization or worker that we want to be and telling the truth about where we currently are—our "current reality"—provides the necessary tension and energy for change (Senge, 1990b).

The process of change—reconstruction or reformation of already formed beliefs and values—involves mutual participation or a discourse between people holding different worldviews. Cultural competence should emphasize communication that encourages honesty and openness through dialogue. In a dialogue, individuals explore the meaning of words, actions, and culture through many different vantage points. Dialogue helps to reveal the incoherence between our beliefs, thoughts, and actions.

The most powerful outcome of such dialogue is to reveal our hidden stereotypes. Senge (1990a) argued that prejudice depends on our ability to hide these assumptions from ourselves:

> *Once a person begins to accept a stereotype of a particular group, that "thought" becomes an active agent, "participating" in shaping how he or she interacts with another person who falls into that stereotyped class. In turn, the tone of their interaction influences the other person's behavior. The prejudiced person can't see how his prejudice shapes what he "sees" and*

how he acts. In some sense, if he did, he would no longer be prejudiced. To operate, the "thought" of prejudice must remain hidden to its holder. (p. 241)

Thus, to become culturally competent, members of the agency must work to bring their covert thoughts and feelings out into the open, even though this may feel threatening. Argyris and Schön (1978) evolved a technique for illustrating the difference between what we think (the "left-hand column") and what we say (the "right-hand column"). Regardless of what appears in the right-hand column, it is the left-hand column that serves as the basis for our actions. Argyris and Schön (1978) and later Senge (1990b) referred to these contrasting positions as the difference between our theory in use (left-hand column) and our espoused theory (right-hand column). In some cases we may claim to be more culturally sensitive and diverse than we actually are.

Figure 11-1 demonstrates some of the underlying problems in communication that can take place between individuals and groups with different worldviews of the same event, in this case a suggestion that they participate in cultural competency training. This example points to the absence of honest dialogue. The participant minimizes the fears and discomfort he or she feels when invited to participate in cultural competency training, yet these are the feelings that will limit his or her ability to grow from such an event. Members of the staff may be encouraged to write their own "left column" examples to bring their fears and unspoken assumptions to the surface. Acknowledging these feelings creates a natural tension that can serve as the basis for dialogue and change.

DIALOGUE

Senge (1990a) noted that Bohm (1965) has identified three conditions as necessary for real dialogue and change. They are
1. *all participants must "suspend" their assumptions, literally to hold them "as if suspended before us"*
2. *all participants must regard one another as colleagues*
3. *there must be a "facilitator" who "holds the context" of dialogue.* (p. 243)

Both the participant and the facilitator in cultural competence training must be willing to hold their assumptions out for view, making them accessible to questioning and observation (Senge, 1990a). Actual lists of contrasting assumptions and viewpoints may be drawn up. Assumptions must be seen as contrasting cultural viewpoints rather than inconvertible facts. Bringing these assumptions to the surface is not the same thing as defending opinions. It is not a discussion in which the parties try to persuade each other of the rightness of their viewpoints.

Change can only occur if participants see each other as colleagues who are committed to a common quest for deeper understanding and coherence. Participants must trust and respect each other's motives. There must be a willingness to enter into a dialogue whereby different views of the same event can be aired and considered. Honest dialogue is not possible when the agency hierarchy has already decided on the "proper" worldview and uses training as a means for in-

Figure 11-1

THE ABSENCE OF HONEST DIALOGUE

forming workers and converting them. Empowered and democratic organizations allow and foster dialogues on differing worldviews. This does not mean that the organization will not strive for a consensus on which beliefs and values it will use to guide its actions. Rather, the process of achieving that consensus should be open and democratic and subject to continual challenge, change, and learning.

MULTICULTURAL VALUES

Although changes in attitudes cannot occur overnight, what begins to emerge from group discussions about culture is a better appreciation of diversity. Increased knowledge of one's cultural values, uncovering hidden thoughts and feelings, and beginning a dialogue with others also can identify common values for culturally diverse programs.

Although multicultural values mean nurturing a growing appreciation of "many worlds and worldviews," it also should be recognized that within a defined cultural community there is additional diversity. Those individuals who look or sound the same do not always share the same beliefs, habits, or values. The growing appreciation and power of multiculturalism in adult services and human services in general demands flexibility and openness on the part of workers, supervisors, and administrators. Perhaps the greatest challenge that accompanies diversity is balancing respect for differences among individuals and groups and an understanding of those values and beliefs that are universal to all groups. Such universal values in adult services include but are not limited to an individual's right to a life free of abuse, neglect, and exploitation. Additional universal rights and values should include the right to culturally sensitive services.

Adult services workers and adult services organizations see opportunity for change in the creative tension that exists between where the person or organization would like to go and where they are. Leadership in cultural diversity demands a grand vision and respect for the value and contribution of difference. Although it is tempting to avoid the tension and conflicts that can arise when practice falls short of vision, responsibly used, such tension can create positive change. In his letter from the Birmingham jail, Martin Luther King, Jr., said, "Just as Socrates felt that it was necessary to create a tension in the mind, so that individuals could rise from the bondage of myths and half truths . . . so must we . . . create the kind of tension in society that will help men rise from the dark depths of prejudice and racism" (1987, p. 187).

Key Points

Excellent adult services social workers, managers, and leaders

- learn to acknowledge their own cultural heritage, values, and beliefs
- come to see how personal cultural views can shape perceptions and actions toward people of other cultures

- provide learning opportunities that enhance cultural understanding and support the value of diversity within the organization and community
- value the contributions that a culturally diverse work environment can bring to the family assessment and change process
- empower culturally diverse individuals and groups to take responsibility for and direct their own change process.

References

Age Discrimination Act of 1967. P.L. 90-202, 81 Stat. 602.

Americans with Disabilities Act of 1990. P.L. 101-336, 42 USCS 12101.

Argyris, C., & Schön, D. (1978). *Organizational learning: A theory-in-action perspective.* Reading, MA: Addison-Wesley.

Bass, S. A., Kutza, E. A., & Torres-Gil, F. M. (1990). *Diversity in aging.* Glenview, IL: Scott, Foresman.

Bastida, E. (1989). The increasing significance of the social context in the utilization of aging services by Mexican American and Black elderly. *California Sociologist, 12*(1), 22–44.

Bohm, D. (1965). *The special theory of relativity.* New York: W. A. Benjamin.

Byrne, D. (1971). *The attraction paradigm.* New York: Academic Press.

Carlton-LaNey, I. (1991). Some considerations of the rural elderly Black's underuse of social services. *Journal of Gerontological Social Work, 16*(1/2), 3–17.

Center for Aging Research and Educational Services. (1990). *Manpower in county departments of social services. Executive summary and full report* (Prepared for the Adult and Family Services Branch of the North Carolina Division of Social Services). Chapel Hill, NC: Author.

Cox, T. H. (1994). *Cultural diversity in organizations.* San Francisco: Berrett-Koehler.

Cox, T. H., & Blake, S. (1991). Managing cultural diversity: Implications for organizational competitiveness. *Executive, 5*(3), 45–56.

Cox, T. H., Lobel, S., & McLeod, P. (1991). Effects of ethnic group cultural difference on cooperative versus competitive behavior in a group task. *Academy of Management Journal, 34*, 827–847.

Cross, T. L., Bazron, B. J., Dennis, K. W., & Isaacs, M. R. (1989). *Towards a culturally competent system of care.* Washington, DC: CASSP Technical Assistance Center.

Cunningham, C. V. (1991). Reaching minority communities: Factors impacting on success. *Journal of Gerontological Social Work, 17*(3/4), 125–135.

Davis, L. E., & Proctor, E. K. (1989). *Race, gender and class.* Englewood Cliffs, NJ: Prentice Hall.

Equal Employment Opportunity Act of 1972. P.L. 92-261, 80 Stat. 662.

Gregory, K., Wells, K. B., & Leake, B. (1987). Medical students' expectations for encounters with minority and nonminority patients. *Journal of the National Medical Association, 79*(4), 403–408.

Holmes, D., Holmes, M., Steinbach, L., Hausner, T., & Rocheleau, B. (1979). The use of community-based services in long-term care by older minority persons. *Gerontologist, 19*(4), 389–397.

Johnson, S., Kurtz, M., Tomlinson, T., & Howe, K. R. (1986). Students' stereotypes of patients as barriers to clinical decision-making. *Journal of Medical Education, 61*, 727–735.

King, M. L., Jr. (1987). Letter from a Birmingham jail. In J. Williams (Ed.), *Eyes on the prize: America's civil rights years, 1954–1965* (pp. 187–189). New York: Viking.

Kogod, S. K. (1992). Managing diversity in the workplace. In J. W. Pfeiffer (Ed.), *The 1992 annual: Developing human resources.* San Diego: Pfeiffer.

Mandell, B., & Kohler-Gray, S. (1990). Management development that values diversity. *Personnel, 67*, 41–47.

North Carolina Family and Children's Resource Program (1994). *Family-centered services curriculum.* Chapel Hill, NC: Author.

Palmer, J. (1989). Three paradigms for diversity change leaders. *OD Practitioner, 21*(1), 15–18.

Pinderhughes, E. (1989). *Understanding race, ethnicity and power.* New York: Free Press.

Pregnancy Discrimination Act of 1978. P.L. 95-555, 92 Stat. 2076.

Robins, K. (1994). The cultural competence continuum. In M. O'Malley & T. Davis (Eds.), *Dealing with differences* (pp. 361–365). Carrboro, NC: Center for Peace Education.

Senge, P. M. (1990a). *The fifth discipline: The art and practice of the learning organization.* New York: Doubleday/Currency.

Senge, P. M. (1990b, Fall). The leader's new work: Building learning organizations. *Sloan Management Review,* pp. 7–23.

Taueber, C. (1990). Diversity: The dramatic reality. In S. A. Bass, E. A. Kutza, & F. M. Torres-Gil (Eds.), *Diversity in aging* (pp. 1–45). Glenview, IL: Scott, Foresman.

U.S. Bureau of the Census. (1993). *Statistical abstract of the United States* (113th ed.). Washington, DC: U.S. Government Printing Office.

Williams, E., & Weil, M. (1994). Cultural diversity and cultural competence. In I. N. Zipper & M. Weil (Eds.), *Case management for children's mental health: A training curriculum for child-serving agencies.* Raleigh, NC: North Carolina Division of Mental Health, Developmental Disabilities, and Substance Abuse Services, Child and Family Services Branch.

Wood, J. (1989). Communicating with older adults in health care settings: Cultural and ethnic considerations. *Educational Gerontology, 15*, 351–362.

Yeatts, D., Crow, T., & Folts, E. (1992). Service use among low-income minority elderly: Strategies for overcoming barriers. *Gerontologist, 32*(1), 24–32.

PART 3

Specialized Fields of Practice

CHAPTER 12

Adult Protective Services

VICKIE L. ATKINSON

GARY M. NELSON

This chapter focuses on protective services for adults with disabilities. Adult protective services (APS) represent the central service intervention used by virtually all adult services programs for adults with disabilities and older adults who experience risk of abuse or neglect. For many, APS and its commitment to advocate for the needs of abused or neglected adults is synonymous with the field of adult services (Johnson, 1991; Tatara, 1993).

This chapter frames the discussion in terms of the adult services family assessment and change method and places APS in the broader context and continuum of adult services programs and interventions. To do this, the chapter reviews definitions and estimates of need for APS, identifies factors contributing to abuse or neglect, presents a series of general APS practice issues, and applies the family assessment and change method to the service intervention. The chapter concludes with a case example; a general discussion of the delicate balance between empowerment and protection; and the overall community responsibility to prevent, detect, and respond to the abuse and neglect of adults with disabilities.

Characteristics of Abuse, Neglect, and Exploitation

DEFINITIONS AND ESTIMATES OF NEED

A number of organizations and researchers have attempted over the past two decades to estimate the extent of elder abuse and neglect in this country. As early as 1981, the U.S. House Select Committee on Aging estimated that 4 percent of the nation's older population, or about 1 million people, were abused each year (U.S.

House of Representatives, 1981). Somewhat later Pillemer and Finkelhor (1989) in Boston and Podnieks, Pillemer, Nicholson, Shillington, and Frizzel (1990) in Canada estimated, through random sample surveys, that 3.2 and 4 percent, respectively, of the older population experienced mistreatment.

Using data collected from a national survey of state APS programs and aging agencies, Tatara (1993) went further in providing national estimates and data on reports of elder abuse. Working with data collected by the National Aging Resource Center on Elder Abuse (NARCEA), he provided estimates of the number of elder abuse reports, the rates of substantiation, descriptions of those who most commonly report abuse or neglect to APS agencies, types and frequencies of maltreatment, relationship of abusers to victims, and gender and age profiles for older adults who neglect themselves.

Definitions of adult maltreatment vary from state to state and community to community. Definitions used in the NARCEA study included physical abuse, sexual abuse, emotional or psychological abuse, neglect, financial or material exploitation, self-abuse or neglect, and all other types of mistreatment identified by the states but not included in the previous definitions (Tatara, 1993).

In 1990 an estimated 211,000 reports of domestic elder abuse were made nationally (Tatara, 1993). The figure increased to 227,000 in 1991, up nearly 8 percent. Substantiation rates for the states reporting stood at nearly 55 percent in both 1990 and 1991. Most substantiated cases of older adult maltreatment were for self-neglect (nearly 58 percent of all substantiated cases in 1990 and 51 percent in 1991). Abuse by others accounted for nearly 39 percent of all substantiated cases in 1990 and 45 percent in 1991. Physical abuse is the most frequent type reported, followed by financial and material exploitation and psychological and emotional abuse. Although sexual abuse is devastating when it occurs, it is uncommon.

Most abusers are male; most victims are female. Abusers are usually family members, most frequently a spouse. Friends and neighbors accounted for only 7.5 percent of abusers in substantiated reports in 1991; service providers accounted for 6.3 percent (Tatara, 1993).

Although the etiology of abuse is complex, neglect and self-neglect are no less so. In most communities across the nation, APS responds to both types of neglect. Self-neglect, as opposed to neglect by others, makes up the largest share of APS caseloads (Rathbone-McCuan & Fabian, 1992). Tatara (1993) noted that most self-neglecting older adults were female and that most were of advanced years (age 79 on average in 1991).

FACTORS CONTRIBUTING TO ABUSE AND NEGLECT

In instances of abuse and neglect by friends, neighbors, and service providers, a common denominator is the victim's physical, emotional, or physiological dependence, often accompanied by impairments in judgment. However, only a minority of abusive situations involve "relative strangers"—about 80 percent of cases involve family caregivers (Tatara, 1993).

Bendik (1992) and Vinton (1992) provided a thorough examination of factors contributing to abuse or neglect by family caregivers. The emotional, financial, and physical burdens that accompany caring for people with severe impairments push some family caregivers to the breaking point. Depression, anger, and a lost sense of control over one's life can trigger abuse and neglect. Stressful situations can be further complicated by drug or alcohol abuse. Nearly a quarter of family caregivers and 34 percent of nonfamily caregivers were reported to be experiencing alcohol problems in Vinton's study (1992). Bendik (1992) pointed to the importance of social support and problem-solving skills on the part of caregivers as a way to avoid anger and loss of control. Social outlets and respite for the caregiver, an understanding of what the adult with impairments is going through, and an understanding of the care recipient's chronic illness or disability can make stressful situations manageable.

During the past several decades, sensitivity to the rights of adults with disabilities, including the right not be abused or neglected by others, has increased. At the same time, there has been acknowledgment of the right of adults to make what society perceives as poor choices and to live in situations that may be offensive to the mores of the general community (Regan, 1978). The difficulty in handling cases of self-neglect reflects the tension inherent in balancing society's responsibility to protect adults with disabilities with the individual's right to self-determination. Laws governing protective services attempt to safeguard those people who are unable to look after themselves while upholding the rights of individuals who have the capacity to make decisions, however "inappropriate" or unpopular.

REPORTING AND RESPONDING TO
ABUSE, NEGLECT, AND EXPLOITATION

The definitions and legal responses to instances of abuse and neglect vary from state to state (NARCEA, 1990; Tatara, 1993). Most states have laws covering mandatory or voluntary report of adult abuse or neglect, although some states limit reporting to older adults or members of other specified populations. One of the first laws in the nation in this area was enacted in North Carolina in 1973. The initial law applied only to adults age 65 or older, but the law was changed in 1975 to extend protection to all adults with disabilities. As in many other states, North Carolina's law makes it mandatory that "any person having reasonable cause to believe that a disabled adult is in need of protective services shall report such information" (North Carolina General Statute 108A-102). The law provides protection for adults of any age with disabilities, in any living arrangement, with or without caregivers, and includes self-neglect as well abuse or neglect by others.

Because abuse or neglect of older adults is increasingly recognized as a crime and because both professionals and the general public are considered to have a responsibility to report instances of maltreatment, it is interesting to note who actually reports such cases to APS. Tatara (1993) found that nearly half of all reports came from service providers—in-home and personal care service providers or physicians and other health care professionals. A minority of reports came from family members, and an even smaller number came from friends and neighbors.

In a study of public perceptions of and responses to elder mistreatment in a midwestern community, Blakely and Morris (1992) observed that the public had limited knowledge about what should be reported and to whom it should be reported. Few had knowledge of the existence or role of APS. The 1992 amendments to the Older Americans Act that call for increased advocacy by aging network programs to prevent abuse represent an increased recognition of the need for the broader community to become involved in responding to the growing problem of abuse and neglect of adults with disabilities and older adults.

General Issues in APS

There are certainly a host of issues to complicate and make APS a challenge even to the most senior workers. Among these are working with involuntary clients, working with caregivers who are abusers, self-neglect, and informed consent.

INVOLUNTARY CLIENTS

One of the challenges to protective services occurs because clients are almost always involuntary. Clients seldom come to adult services programs requesting protective services for themselves. Instead, these services are most often requested, unbeknownst to the potential client, by a community service provider, physician, friend, or neighbor. Sometimes those who make the request do not want their identity revealed, which may make it difficult for the worker to approach the client who wants to know the source of the referral.

The worker is often faced with the challenge of gaining entry, assessing the client's situation, assessing the need for services, and then offering assistance the client has not requested and may not want. Workers must frequently try to work with people who are angry or hostile, refuse to provide information, and resent the uninvited intrusion in their lives.

The dual mandate of making sure the client is safe and maintaining freedom of choice calls for a complex mixture of strategies that include the effective use of relationship, persuasion, positive inducements in the form of concrete services, and the sensitive wielding of power associated with the threat of legal action and removal of the individual from the home (Abramson, 1991). The moral issues and uncertainty associated with leaving an individual in an unsafe environment or enmeshed in a process of self-neglect must be counterbalanced with the moral issues associated with the use of power and the right to self-determination.

WORKING WITH CAREGIVERS WHO HAVE
BEEN ABUSIVE OR NEGLECTFUL

A particularly difficult challenge for the APS worker is working with caregivers who have been abusive, neglectful, or exploitive. APS workers are faced with playing two seemingly contradictory roles. First, they must determine whether mistreatment is occurring or did occur and if protective services are needed, during which time the caregiver, and even the alleged victim, may see them as adversaries (Blunt, 1993). If it is found that protective services are warranted, and if the victim consents to becoming a client, workers then must become the ally of both victim and caregiver to provide counseling and services that will prevent further mistreatment.

Vinton (1992) found that in situations where family caregivers had committed the abuse, two unfortunate things transpired. First, the victims were more likely to be placed in a board-and-care home or nursing facility. Part of the reason may be that victims of family caregivers are generally frailer than victims of nonfamily caregivers. Although placement is not always inappropriate, it does suggest that when the person committing the abuse is a family member, interventions that include help from other family members or community-based services may be overlooked in the rush to protect the victim. Community-based services, home care, crisis, and intake services were offered less frequently than would have appeared warranted.

Second, when a family caregiver has committed the abuse, treatment and services that address the needs of the caregiver often are overlooked. Again, Vinton found that 25 percent of the abusive family caregivers and 34 percent of the abusive nonfamily caregivers were reported to have alcohol problems, but only 3 percent in both cases were referred for alcohol or drug treatment.

SELF-NEGLECT

Neglect by others and self-neglect represent conceptually different domains in APS cases, but in the real world they coexist. Self-neglect makes up the largest category of protective services investigations and substantiated cases. Effective practice must, through the process of screening and assessment, distinguish between the two (Quinn & Tomita, 1986). The etiology of neglect by others can be traced to delinquent or uninformed caregivers, whereas the etiology of self-neglect is rooted in the individual (Rathbone-McCuan & Fabian, 1992).

Self-neglect is closely linked to issues of adaptation to loss and capacity for self-care. It can also be linked to depression and cognitive impairment in old age. In some instances, impaired capacity for self-care has persisted for years, whereas in others, frailty that results from normal aging or from illness, the loss of caregivers, or other life events may trigger a crisis in self-care. In other situations, past coping and adaptation strategies fail. When this happens, the social worker's task may be to help clients refurbish their self-concepts, motivation, and coping skills to regain control over their own care and remain independent. In other cases the worker's task may be to help clients move to a new supportive living environment (for example, a nursing home or assisted-living facility) to compensate for irreversible losses in self-care abilities. It is also part of the worker's task to help these clients adapt to changes in living environment and maintain as much control and independence as the new setting will allow.

INFORMED CONSENT

In many APS cases, particularly those involving neglect and self-neglect, there may be some question of the client's ability to consent to services. A thorough physical and mental health assessment helps the worker ascertain whether the client seems capable of informed consent and if not whether to seek a legal determination of the client's capacity to refuse services.

Clear-cut cases of dementia or acute or chronic mental illness resulting in impaired judgment are often the exception. Workers frequently find themselves having to watch a client refuse services that they believe to be in the client's best interest. When this happens, workers will have to take time to reassess how much their own values and attitudes influence their perception of the client's actions. The right to self-determination, including the right to make seemingly unwise or unsafe decisions, is important. Clients have the right to assume risks in how they live their lives. In many such cases, the worker's professional obligation is to provide information to clients or their families about potential risks and to help identify alternatives to the present course of action and behavior. However, once the client has been informed, the client will have to decide.

Protective Services and the Family Assessment and Change Process

Adults frequently come to the attention of protective services workers as a result of a crisis in which caregivers reach a breaking point and mistreat the adult with disabilities (Bendik, 1992) or when the adult can no longer care for himself or herself (Rathbone-McCuan & Fabian, 1992). There are many events that can overwhelm the individual's personal problem-solving capacity and ability to change. The triggering event may stem from gradual or sudden disability on the part of the client or caregiver (a stroke, dementia, an exacerbation of mental illness); a breakdown in supportive resources in the client's environment (a homeless client discharged from a psychiatric hospital; gradual or suddenly increased stress on the primary caregiver). Whatever the cause of the breakdown in usual methods of coping, the result is that someone identifies the client as an adult with disabilities who is in need of protective services.

The family assessment and change method in APS emphasizes the importance of a systematic approach to working with clients and their families. Effective social work intervention with older adults in need of protection often benefits from a family systems perspective (Greene & Soniat, 1991; Sheafor, Horejsi, & Horejsi, 1988).

Although each state's system for reporting and managing adult abuse or neglect is different and involves a complex array of mandated reporters and community services, APS can benefit from the guidance offered by the family assessment and change method applied here and throughout this book. Steps associated with this method and discussed here include screening, assessment of problems and strengths, identification of items for change, setting goals, planning services, and termination. However, because protective services cases are by definition causes for concern—most states require that they be investigated within a short time, and when abuse is substantiated, measures be taken immediately to abate the danger to the client—the process is done quickly. Once the immediate danger is reduced, the client or family may be referred to social workers elsewhere in the agency for additional assessment and planning (Tomita, 1982).

SCREENING

APS is rarely initiated as a voluntary service and, as a result, it differs from most other adult services. The screening–intake step of the family assessment and change method as it applies to protective services requires special attention. Because of the intrusiveness of the evaluation, a proper reporting or screening of the allegations is imperative to be sure that evaluations are not initiated for individuals who do not need APS.

Screening or reporting of suspected cases of abuse or neglect may be initiated by a number of mandated community reporters, depending on state law and agency regulations. The reporter may be a family physician or an adult services home care worker who has come on a suspicious situation in which mistreatment is suspected. The decision tree developed by Braun, Lenzer, Schumacher-Mukai, and Snyder (1993) in Hawaii to aid people from the community and from agencies in reporting their suspicions of abuse or neglect has proved to be useful in the screening process. Their decision tree helps address the confusion that arises around issues of when and how to refer a client to protective services and what to do if abuse is not substantiated. The decision tree provides responses for situations in which emergency services are required, including for people in a nursing home or board-and-care home, for those who appear legally incompetent, for those who are competent but refuse services, and for those who have a guardian suspected of abuse. The authors report that most community agencies experimenting with this screening tool have found it useful in deciding whether to refer individuals for protective services and are using it to choose appropriate interventions.

ASSESSMENT: PROBLEMS, STRENGTHS, AND PERCEPTIONS

The various elements of a comprehensive assessment outlined in chapter 3 apply to assessments in protective services. However, beyond making a good functional assessment, detecting the client's and family's strengths and identifying the perceptions of the client, family, and worker about what is going on are even more important in protective services cases where the stakes are much higher and complexity and confusion about what is happening and how to change it is much greater.

It is crucial that APS workers focus on client's strengths as well as problems in their assessment of client and family functioning. For example, a client with a progressive dementia who is beginning to neglect himself or herself may not have a primary caregiver, but he or she may have a network of extended kin that can provide the essential services needed to live safely in the community for some period of time. Few communities have all the resources APS clients need, and it is easy for social workers to be overwhelmed trying to meet clients' needs. This situation is compounded because most people for whom the need for protective services is not substantiated still need community services to alleviate their difficult circumstances (Sharon, 1991).

For these and other reasons, it is important for the APS worker to look for and rely on clients' strengths to resolve problems. When social workers look for the positive aspects of clients' situations, they may find many more areas for which they can help clients achieve some success, and an associated benefit will be that workers will feel better about their role as an agent of change. As a result they will be more likely to find the work stimulating and challenging rather than burdensome and overwhelming.

Creative workers who are able to reframe "difficult" situations, clients, or family members as "challenging" may be successful in developing productive relationships with those clients and families and realizing possibilities for change. The worker might recognize the client as being "able to obtain what is needed" rather than as "manipulative," acknowledge an abusive caregiver as a person trying to cope with a great deal of stress, or understand a client's self-neglect in the context of his or her struggle to remain independent and not become a burden. Reframing in this way helps the worker build on the actual and potential strengths clients possess.

Protective service workers also should assess clients' and families' perceptions of their situations. This assessment provides essential information about whether clients and family members see situations as abuse, neglect, or exploitation, whether they perceive a need for help, in what ways they want or might accept help, and how they might benefit from information and counseling. These perceptions may be different from objective information obtained about functional disabilities or from the worker's professional perceptions.

For example, management of uncorrectable incontinence may be perceived by one caregiver as a terrible burden causing severe stress and bringing that person to the breaking point. Another caregiver may view the same incontinence as just a part of the illness to be managed and not have any serious problems coping with it. The difference in perceptions and attitudes of the caregivers toward incontinence may cause behaviors that result in the need for APS in the first situation, and in the second, lead to constructive problem-solving about how best to treat or cope with incontinence.

An assessment of perception also is needed when looking at strengths and support systems. Different clients may have the same number of supportive individuals in their lives yet perceive the availability of help differently. For example, a client with mental illness (but not a danger to self or others) may have several family members interested in helping, but the client is unwilling to accept their help. In this situation, the priority for APS intervention is to obtain treatment for the client and to find sources of assistance the client will accept. It is not necessary to expand the resources of the family but to try to support the members' continued interest in the client. Another client who has physical disabilities and an addiction to alcohol believes he has all the help he needs through his two sons. The sons, on the other hand, refuse to care for their father and feel no responsibility toward him because he abandoned them as children. If the worker finds no flexibility in the sons' view of their father or willingness to be involved, then he or she must help the client confront and adapt to this reality. Clients' and families' perceptions of the availability and acceptability of support are essential information for assessing appropriate interventions.

SERVICE PLANNING

On the basis of specific problems identified and their priority of resolution and of identified strengths and perceptions, the client, family, and worker determine what changes and goals they wish to achieve. The worker and client identify the resources currently and potentially available to assist the client in achieving these changes and goals. A combination of internal psychological resources and external support resources are pulled together in a service plan.

Protective services workers draw on the internal, intangible resources of the client and family, including such things as attitudes, motivation to change, problem-solving skills, and coping abilities. Workers also orchestrate external supportive resources as the informal social support available to the individual in the form of family, friends, neighbors, and others. External resources also include formal resources such as home-delivered meals, psychosocial rehabilitation clubhouses, or shelters for abused or homeless people. Social workers must not only identify formal resources needed by the client and where they may obtain them but also be prepared to help the client and family accept and use these resources appropriately.

A service plan that supports, enables, and empowers adults is an integral part of the provision of protective services. The service plan grows out of the evaluation and assessment, the identified problems and strengths, and the jointly formulated change list and service goals. It builds on the strengths, resources, and motivation that can be engendered by the worker in the affected client and family system. Service plans should always be guided by the principle of client self-determination and the preference for services in the least restrictive environment.

The principles of self-determination and provision of services in the least restrictive environment present an ongoing challenge for protective services workers. The difficulty of achieving the state interest of protecting the client while honoring the client's and family's right to self-determination is like walking a tightrope. The stakes are high, and the balance is frequently precarious. Because court-ordered protective services represent an intrusion on the person's and family's right to self-determination and privacy, they must be structured to enable client and family to retain as many choices and freedom of action and movement as possible.

The two core principles outlined in chapter 8 about working with challenging clients can be restated here: (1) Give clients a choice and (2) help them save face. Protective services mandates circumscribe how much choice social workers can offer clients, but inasmuch as clients are allowed to choose, they should be given the chance to do so. This provides the client and family some measure of control in a situation in which their control is substantially restricted. Because protective services cases may involve intrusion into the family system and may produce shame or guilt among all those involved, helping clients and family members save face whenever possible can help social workers avert some of the anger that arises from this intervention.

To give one example of providing choice among restricted alternatives, in a case in which the victim of abuse can be protected only by placement in a board-and-care or nursing home, the social worker can take into consideration the client's preferences in type and location of the facility. The values of the client and family should be carefully considered, and their collaboration in developing the goals and service plan is paramount. When clients are unable to make their values and wishes known, the worker should take steps to find out what those values are likely to be by exploring with family and friends what decisions clients made or expressed previously in related areas. (This is the concept of "substituted judgment," which will be discussed in more detail in chapter 13.)

Setting goals and planning services also must focus on the caregivers (if there are any) and the understanding that they are important to the successful resolution of APS cases. Even though the adult in need of protection is the client, goals and intervention strategies often must focus on the caregiver to eliminate the abuse or neglect. Research indicates that personality problems and mental health problems of caregivers frequently contribute to the abuse or neglect of adults (Bendik, 1992; Pillemer & Finkelhor, 1989). APS workers also should be aware of the stresses of caregiving.

Workers should help caregivers identify the consequences of their actions, assume responsibility for them, and encourage them to make use of available resources (Alcoholics Anonymous, mental health professionals, or other counselors). Workers should provide specific information about these resources (times, places, contact people) and follow up to ensure that caregivers are benefiting from these interventions. Workers will need to reassess service plans periodically to see whether they are meeting the goals of clients or their families. If not, they will need to modify the plans.

TERMINATION OF APS

Formal closure of APS may come more quickly than with most other adult services interventions. Social workers intervene with the goal of ending the current abuse, neglect, or exploitation and doing whatever is possible to prevent recurrence. When this mandated goal is met (that is, that the client's safety is reestablished), the case is closed to protective services. However, in developing goals to support the elimination of abuse, other services may have been put into place. In such instances, the case may be transferred to another program in the adult services agency and so involve transfer to a new adult services social worker. Transfer of work with the client should involve joint visits by both social workers whenever possible. It should be done openly and positively, acknowledging the changes that have occurred and building on the progress that the client and family have made in reaching the point at which APS is no longer needed.

General Issues of Empowerment in APS

The philosophy of supporting, enabling, and empowering adult clients steers and shapes the family assessment and change method used with APS clients. Empowerment recognizes that the impulse and motivation, as well as the ownership and commitment to change, must come from within the client and family system. No amount of court orders or externally directed service interventions can protect and improve the well-being of clients and families unless they are fully engaged and empowered in the process itself.

Goals and a service plan that are designed to empower help clients to identify as many options as possible for change, because choice is empowering. Boyajian (1991) stated "A caseworker usually cannot change the realities of another's life, but by providing needed information and offering choices, the caseworker empowers the client, whether the client accepts the choices or uses the information or not. Sometimes empowerment means learning only this: that one has the power to say no" (pp. 5–6).

Empowerment comes with assuming responsibilities for those choices. Responsibility is empowering. APS clients frequently have impaired abilities and compromised circumstances that severely limit information about what choices they may have. Workers should strive to make such choices evident and involve clients in making decisions with respect to those choices, and yet empowering clients also means allowing them what McLaughlin (1988) called "the dignity of risk" (p. 30). The APS worker must not only be concerned about clients' awareness of all options but also cognizant of their right to make and assume responsibility for those choices. Part of the price of freedom and self-determination is the right and responsibility for one's choices in life, including the various risks associated with those choices. As McLaughlin said, "a human life without some element of risk is in fact no life at all" (p. 31).

Empowerment goes beyond the mere exercise of choice to understanding the consequences of one's actions for oneself, as well as for others. For example, a client may value her family's well-being and also staying in her own home. She may not, however, recognize that her severe functional problems are taking her family beyond their capacity to care for her. While respecting her final right to choose her living arrangement, the social worker helps her look at all the options available and at the consequences of her choices, both for her own health and safety and for the welfare of her family. Just as the client is empowered through knowing her options and their consequences, the family is likewise empowered and may choose not to continue to offer the same kind of support as they have in the past.

Case Example

An adult services agency received a complaint that a bedridden, older woman was being neglected by her great-granddaughter, with whom she lived. The report alleged that the client was left for long periods in soiled clothing, that she was hungry and cold, and that her great-granddaughter did not properly care for her. As a part of completing a thorough assessment and evaluation, the worker individually and privately interviewed the client, her caregiver, and collateral contacts.

After substantiating that the woman with disabilities was being neglected and was in need of protective services, the worker involved the client in setting goals for herself. The worker was careful to support the caregiver at the same time that she discussed ways that the caregiver might be more attentive to the client's needs.

In an effort to enable the client and caregiver to cope with their situation better, the worker involved the great-grandson (who also lived in the house) in caring for the client. The worker coordinated services with the local home health agency and was able to have the nurse and in-home aide help educate the family members on proper care and nutrition for the client.

By way of empowering the client, the worker encouraged her to be more verbal in making her needs known to her family members. The worker continued to arrange to speak privately to the client, and she also helped the client have more choices by talking with her about additional in-home services and placement options.

In terminating the protective services case, the worker was able to cite improvement in the situation and growth on the part of the client and her family members and that the goals and objectives in the service plan had

been met. The client stated that she was not being neglected. The caregivers
had learned the skills needed to care for their relative better and had
learned to share responsibilities among themselves and call on community
resources. The client had been empowered to be more assertive in making
her needs known. She also knew that she had other options available to her
if she chose.

APS: A Community Responsibility

Successful treatment and prevention of adult abuse or neglect depends on a communitywide commitment to change. Blakely and Morris (1992) noted tremendous gaps in the public's understanding and responses to elder mistreatment. In writing about elder abuse and its recognition—or lack of recognition—among health professionals, Lucas (1991) addressed the need to change professional perceptions and responses to the mistreatment of adults. Harshbarger (1993), an attorney general for Massachusetts, noted the need for a unified approach in which state and local agencies, advocacy groups, and the community join forces to tackle elder mistreatment.

There are many promising efforts across the nation to make the commitment to change more a community affair. In the late 1980s, North Carolina effectively demonstrated an integrated approach to the treatment and prevention of elder mistreatment under the leadership of its state and local adult services programs (North Carolina Department of Human Resources, 1989). Through its model APS efforts, North Carolina has enhanced the capacity of local adult services programs to combat this difficult problem. Some of its strategies included self-assessments by local agencies, formation of multidicisplinary teams, campaigns to increase public awareness, and training for human services professionals. Local agency and community self-assessments address agency communication and collaboration around APS cases, issues of staffing, best-practice models and training in APS, and issues involving legal counseling and documentation (Salmon & Atkinson, 1992). In response to these self-assessments and in tandem with public awareness campaigns, state and local agencies have taken steps to improve the quality and effectiveness in APS.

Many communities have successfully experimented with the use of multiagency and multidisciplinary assessment teams to improve practice in APS cases. The San Francisco Consortium for the Prevention of Elder Abuse developed a community assessment team that drew its membership from a broad cross-section of community agencies, including APS, mental health, law enforcement, civil law, geriatric medicine, financial management, and family counseling (Wolf & Pillemer, 1994). Reasons cited for referring cases to the team were to "(a) clarify the individual agency roles, (b) receive help in handling a non-typical case, (c) seek solutions to cases that defied resolution, (d) resolve disagreements with other agencies regarding aspects of the case, and (e) obtain legal and medical consultation not readily available to them through other means" (p. 127).

Still other communities across the country are engaging advocacy, self-help, and volunteer groups on behalf of abused or neglected adults (Filinson, 1993; Wolf & Pillemer, 1994) for the empowerment of victims. Whether it is advocating for new laws, informing the public about issues of abuse or neglect, or forming victim support groups, such efforts are an important avenue to increased community awareness and action.

Finally, there are many important new efforts across the country to improve the skills of APS workers through improved training and practice models. Unlike the field of child welfare, no earmarked federal funding exists for training adult services or APS workers or for research and demonstration in adult services. Money that is available often comes from state and local funds for services, such as the Social Services Block Grant (the Social Security Act Amendment of 1974) or state and local general revenues.

Despite these funding issues, some states and universities have developed partnerships to train adult services workers. Through its Department of Human Services and the University of Hawaii School of Social Work, Hawaii has developed a special student training unit dedicated to preparing master's-level social workers for practice in adult services (Wolf & Pillemer, 1994). Other states, including North Carolina, Virginia, and West Virginia, have seen collaborative ties develop between their state universities and the adult services practice community, resulting in increased training for line practitioners. Nationally, NARCEA has provided welcome and much-needed leadership in this area.

Key Points

Excellent APS social workers
- use the family assessment and change method as a framework to support, enable, and empower adult clients and caregivers through the provision of APS
- are sensitive to the cultural diversity of clients
- are sensitive to issues of client and family self-determination and choice.

Excellent adult services managers
- consider the use of a community-based approach to prevention and remediation of abuse, neglect, and exploitation through (1) self-assessment by local agencies and communities, (2) formation of community multidisciplinary teams, (3) campaigns to increase public awareness, (4) improved training for APS and adult services professionals, and (5) increased consumer advocacy and volunteer support and self-help groups
- develop an awareness among staff members of cultural diversity that contributes to more-sensitive and appropriate APS and evokes greater support from the community.

Excellent leaders

- provide training and specialized information about APS for workers and supervisors
- seek increased funding for adequate staffing and supportive services in local communities.

References

Abramson, M. (1991). Ethical assessment of the use of influence in adult protective services. *Journal of Gerontological Social Work, 16*(1/2), 125–135.

Bendik, J. F. (1992). Reaching the breaking point: Dangers of mistreatment in elder caregiving situations. *Journal of Elder Abuse & Neglect, 4*(3), 39–59.

Blakely, B. E., & Morris, D. C. (1992). Public perceptions of and responses to elder mistreatment in Middletown. *Journal of Elder Abuse & Neglect, 4*(3), 19–37.

Blunt, A. P. (1993). Financial exploitation of the incapacitated: Investigation and remedies. *Journal of Elder Abuse & Neglect, (5)*1, 19–32.

Boyajian, J. A. (1991). Issues in patient and client rights. In J. A. Boyajian (Ed.), *Minnesota Adult Protection Guide* (pp. 2-1–2-8). St. Paul: Minnesota Department of Human Services.

Braun, K., Lenzer, A., Schumacher-Mukai, C., & Snyder, P. (1993). A decision tree for managing elder abuse and neglect. *Journal of Elder Abuse & Neglect, 5*(3), 89–103.

Filinson, R. (1993). An evaluation of a program of volunteer advocates for elder abuse victims. *Journal of Elder Abuse & Neglect, 5*(1), 77–93.

Greene, R. R., & Soniat, B. (1991). Clinical interventions with older adults in need of protection: A family systems perspective. *Journal of Family Psychotherapy, 2*(1), 1–15.

Harshbarger, S. (1993). From protection to prevention: A proactive approach. *Journal of Elder Abuse & Neglect, 5*(1), 41–55.

Johnson, T. F. (1991). *Elder mistreatment: Deciding who is at risk.* Westport, CT: Greenwood Press.

Lucas, E. T. (1991). *Elder abuse and its recognition among health service professionals.* New York: Garland.

McLaughlin, C. (1988, Spring). Doing good: A worker's perspective. *Public Welfare*, pp. 29–32.

National Aging Resource Center on Elder Abuse. (1990). *Elder abuse: A decade of shame and inaction* (Report for the Subcommittee on Health and Long-Term Care of the Select Committee on Aging of the U.S. House of Representatives). Washington, DC: U.S. Government Printing Office.

North Carolina Department of Human Resources, Division of Social Services. Adult and Family Services Branch. (1989). *Model for prevention and remediation of elder abuse: An integrated community services approach.* Raleigh: Author.

Older Americans Act Amendments of 1992. P.L. 102-375, 106 Stat. 1195.

Pillemer, K., & Finkelhor, D. (1989). Causes of elder abuse: Caregiver stress versus problem relatives. *American Journal of Orthopsychiatry, 59*(2), 178–187.

Podnieks, E., Pillemer, K., Nicholson, J. P., Shillington, T., & Frizzel, A. (1990). *National Survey on Abuse of the Elderly in Canada.* Toronto: Ryerson Polytechnical Institute.

Quinn, J. J., & Tomita, S. T. (1986). Elder abuse and neglect: Written protocol for identification and assessment. In M. J. Quinn & S. T. Tomita (Eds.), *Elder abuse and neglect* (pp. 267–274). New York: Springer.

Rathbone-McCuan, E., & Fabian, D. R. (1992). *Self-neglecting elders: A clinical dilemma.* Westport, CT: Auburn House.

Regan, J. J. (1978). Intervention through adult protective services programs. *Gerontologist, 18*(3), 250–254.

Salmon, M.A.P., & Atkinson, V. L. (1992). Characteristics of adult protective services social workers. *Journal of Elder Abuse & Neglect, 4*(3), 101–120.

Sharon, N. (1991). Elder abuse and neglect substantiations: What they tell us about the problem. *Journal of Elder Abuse & Neglect, 3*(3), 19–43.

Sheafor, B. W., Horejsi, C. R., & Horejsi, G. A. (1988). *Techniques and guidelines for social work practice.* Newton, MA: Allyn & Bacon.

Social Security Act Amendment of 1974. P.L. 93-647, 88 Stat. 2337.

Tatara, T. (1993). Understanding the nature and scope of domestic elder abuse with the use of state aggregate data: Summaries of the key findings of a national survey of state APS and aging agencies. *Journal of Elder Abuse & Neglect, 5*(4), 35–57.

Tomita, S. K. (1982). Detection and treatment of elder abuse and neglect: A protocol for health care professionals. *Physical and Occupational Therapy in Geriatrics, 2,* 37–51.

U.S. House of Representatives. Select Committee on Aging. (1981). *Elder abuse: An examination of a hidden problem* (Publication No. 97-277). Washington, DC: U.S. Government Printing Office.

Vinton, L. (1992). Services planned in abusive elder care situations. *Journal of Elder Abuse & Neglect, 4*(3), 85–99.

Wolf, R. S., & Pillemer, K. (1994). What's new in elder abuse programming? Four bright ideas. *Gerontologist, 34*(1), 126–129.

CHAPTER 13

Guardianship

VICKIE L. ATKINSON

GARY M. NELSON

This chapter discusses adult services and guardianship in protecting adults with impaired judgment. When appropriately used as an intervention strategy, guardianship can benefit the ward, who is the subject of the guardianship process, and the family. Guardianship can maximize the ward's self-reliance and independence and minimize the potential for abuse of power by the guardian. When improperly applied, it can result in an unwarranted deprivation of liberty and abuse of the adult with impairments.

We begin with a brief discussion of the need for guardianship, including a description of current deficiencies in the system. We then explore the role of adult services in diverting adults with impairments from inappropriate uses of guardianship and examines the role of adult services agencies as public guardians. This chapter includes an examination of both community and agency issues concerning the effective use of public agencies as guardians that is followed by an application of the family assessment and change method to public agency guardianship.

We conclude with a look at alternatives to guardianship administered by public agencies, including the use of family members, volunteers, and specialized nonprofit organizations. In outlining alternatives to guardianship as well as the development of quality guardianship programs, we drew heavily on *Protecting Judgment-Impaired Adults* (Dejowski, 1990) and recommendations on standards and ethics developed by the National Guardianship Association (NGA, 1991) and the Michigan Center for Social Gerontology.

Need for Guardianship

Historically, public welfare departments have accepted appointments as guardians for adults judged incompetent when no family, friends, other individuals, or organizations were available. With the growth in the numbers and types of people with impaired judgment, the types of agencies, individuals, and organizations serving as guardians have diversified, and the range of alternatives to traditional guardianship has expanded.

Older adults are among those most likely to be the subjects of guardianship petitions, because they are more likely to be victims of incapacitating illnesses or disability. Old age itself often is inappropriately equated with incompetence (Wang, Burns, & Hommel, 1990). Older adults with impaired judgment, however, are not the only ones in need of protection. Dementia associated with advanced acquired immune deficiency syndrome (AIDS), improved techniques to save the lives of people who have suffered head trauma and spinal cord injuries, extended life spans for people with developmental disabilities, and improved medications for people with chronic mental illness have increased the number of younger people who are likely to become part of the guardianship system (Iris, 1991). The nation's growing nursing home population also has shown an increased need for guardianship services (Hightower, Heckert, & Schmidt, 1990).

The growth in demand for guardianship services has been accompanied by efforts to reform shortcomings in the system, clarify the roles and responsibilities of guardians, improve safeguards associated with guardianship, and increase the range of alternatives to full guardianship. Even though guardianship is sometimes appropriate to protect the interests of the ward, the serious consequences for the individual call for caution in its application.

With traditional guardianship, individuals commonly lose such basic rights as the right to own property, vote, marry, and agree to or refuse medical treatment. Generally, there is no legal provision requiring the guardian to take into account the expressed desires of the ward. These traditional powers accorded guardians carry with them the danger of misuse (Wang et al., 1990). Reform measures have sought to expand the range of alternatives to guardianship, including a preference for limited guardianship, have focused definitions of incapacity on functional rather than diagnostic or age-related criteria, and have strengthened the procedural safeguards of the process. Highlights of a number of these reforms will be addressed in greater detail below.

Diversion of Guardianship

State and local public social services agencies and their adult services programs frequently assume the role of disinterested public guardian for those wards for whom no family or other appropriate disinterested parties can be identified. This role is discussed at length in this chapter. Less clear and less well articulated is the role of adult services programs in guardianship diversion and the identification of alternatives short of guardianship of adults with impaired judgment.

Some advocates for older adults, like Alexander (1990), are long-term opponents of guardianship. Alexander advanced the use of durable power of attorney and living wills as approaches to maximizing the autonomy of adults while also protecting their interest. Iris (1990) took a more moderate approach by suggesting that although guardianship is appropriate for some individuals, for others it is not always the most effective means for safeguarding their interests.

The best safeguard against an inappropriate guardianship petition is the comprehensive functional assessment outlined in chapter 3. A high-quality functional assessment can both help identify those individuals for whom guardianship is appropriate and divert others for whom such an intervention is unwarranted and too intrusive. The elimination of vague, normative standards to judge the individual's behavior will help eliminate arbitrary decisions regarding capacity. For example, separate assessments of physical and mental capacity will help to eliminate unwarranted judgments of incapacity based on age, appearance, or physical disability. New definitions based on functional assessments of mental capacity for making decisions and self-care will lead to more-appropriate determinations of overall capacity and recommendations for protection. Much of the criticism of the guardianship process has as much to do with shortcomings in the quality of human services assessments as it does with any shortcoming on the part of the court (Hull, Holmes, & Karst, 1990).

In diverting individuals to less-intrusive interventions, whether through such supportive services as treatment for depression, personal care assistance, money management, power of attorney, or some form of limited guardianship, adult services workers need to always keep in mind alternatives to guardianship. Iris (1990) presented a number of guidelines to help workers identify when alternatives to guardianship are warranted:

1. *Incapacity or incompetence is not always clear. Decisional capacity may vary, relative to a number of factors. These include but are not limited to: (1) the effects of medication, (2) time of day, (3) nutritional status, (4) orientation to a new environment, (5) loss of orientation in a restricted environment such as a hospital, (6) confusion and depression caused by illness, and (7) depression and withdrawal caused by loss. Because guardianships are almost impossible to overturn, one should seek other alternatives if any of these factors might be affecting the decision-making ability of an individual.*

2. *When a guardianship is sought to achieve a single purpose, such as discharge to a nursing home, some other alternative, less restrictive in its implications, ought to be considered. If no such alternative exists, legislation or statutory changes ought to be considered and pursued.*

3. *If the guardianship will have no long-term benefit to the ward, some other alternatives must be sought, because a guardianship "is forever."*

4. *If the goal is to preserve personal autonomy, some mechanism other than guardianship should be sought to provide the needed safeguards and protections. Guardianship rarely serves this function and should not be considered as a means to this end.*

5. *Guardianship should not be sought when a disabling condition is considered to be curable, reversible, or transitory.*

6. *Guardianships should not be used to resolve conflicts regarding estate management or custody and care of an impaired person. Guardianship alternative projects should include a component for referral to mediation and dispute resolution services to aid in such cases.*

7. *Individuals who are victims of abuse and neglect must be carefully assessed to determine whether or not decision-making incapacity is a real factor in the abuse situation. Guardianships should not be sought solely as a means for removing the victim from an abusive situation, especially when the abuse occurs within the home of the victim. Alternatives such as orders for protection and involuntary commitments for the abuser must be considered even though they may be more difficult to obtain.*

8. *Everyone, regardless of age, has the right to live with risk. The inability to make decisions should not be confused with bad decision making, nor should unitary standards of behavior be imposed. Incapacity should not be confused with eccentricity or bad choices. In addition, personal history and values plays an important role in assessing an individual's capacity. Finally, ethnic, cultural and social class differences must be evaluated before determining that real incapacity exists.* (pp. 69–70)

PUBLIC AGENCY GUARDIANSHIP

Survey research and published information on guardianship indicate a national movement away from using such public agencies as adult social services, mental health, and public health as guardians because of conflicts of interest in having an agency provide services to a ward for whom it is guardian (Hurme, 1990–1991; Iris, 1991). However many public agencies still play an important role as guardian when and if other options have been exhausted. This section addresses a range of issues that pertain to public agency guardianship on the part of adult services programs.

Adult services programs may become involved in guardianship when the service is needed by a client already served by the agency (for example, through adult protective services or when a request for a service such as placement requires the use of guardianship proceedings to facilitate provision of the service). The court also may designate the agency as guardian, after making an adjudication of incompetence.

In all cases the legal adjudication of incompetence that accompanies the designation of a guardian should reflect both the agency's and the court's best judgment that the individual is unable to make or communicate decisions because of some mental incapacity. At its best, guardianship is a means to enable and empower clients who cannot express their choices by using others who can make the decisions that the client would have made had he or she been able. As NGA (1991) stated, "Decision making is the fundamental responsibility of a guardian" (p. 14).

Case management, although used to implement the decisions of the guardian and monitor the provision of services requested by the guardian, is not the central function of guardianship. Guardians in adult services programs may procure case management services for the ward from their agency or from another agency (for example, mental health). The purpose of guardianship is to provide substitute decision makers who will exercise the rights of clients who have been judged incompetent and who are unable to exercise those rights for themselves.

Even when guardianship is an appropriate option, the agency and social worker should consider the powers of the guardian at appointment and plan to restore to the ward as many powers as the situation permits. Although wards may be unable to understand complicated medical, legal, or financial issues, they still may be able to express preferences regarding their social contacts, activities, and living arrangements. Toward this end, adult services programs that provide guardianship services should continue to emphasize the importance of limited guardianships with clerks of court and to involve wards in decision making to the extent possible.

Effective public agency guardianship involves both agency and community issues. The manner in which guardianship is handled within the agency and the community's role in guardianship are both instrumental in determining the quality of the service. States, as well as communities within states, vary considerably on the role, function, and quality of guardianship (Johnson, 1990).

ISSUES FOR THE COMMUNITY

As potential and actual "disinterested public agent guardians," adult social services directors, along with directors from mental health, public health, aging, and other public agencies, need to explore the growing needs and problems in guardianship. The current and projected demand for guardianship should be assessed, along with problems and opportunities in providing such services and the outlook of prospective providers. On the basis of the problems identified, the priorities of those involved, and the resources available, administrators can then develop goals for improving the delivery of services at the local level.

Any community seeking to improve its provision of guardianship services needs to resolve a number of issues, including (1) developing agreements as to who are potential guardians, (2) deciding which public agent guardians are most appropriate for wards with which types of problems, (3) implementing consultation and review agreements that minimize conflicts of interest, and (4) making sure that clerks of court or other appropriate legal entities understand and support the agreements.

In North Carolina, disinterested public agents, such as county departments of social services, become guardians only when there are no individuals, family members, or corporations more appropriate for appointment. Before becoming guardians themselves, county departments of social services try to help hesitant family members assume this responsibility by providing general information about the role and assistance with the procedure.

For example, family members may lack information or have faulty assumptions about the responsibilities associated with guardianship. They may believe that being appointed guardian means that they become responsible for the financial needs of their relative. Whether guardianship of the person and the estate are combined depends on state law and practice. The extent of the guardian's responsibilities need to be fully described and understood by potential nonagency guardians.

Families may need assistance with petitioning the court and dealing with public agencies involved in the life of the ward. When family members are not available to serve as guardians, there may be other appropriate choices, such as friends or neighbors. In addition to public guardians, some communities may offer private alternatives. Private nonprofit groups may include the Corporation for Public Guardianship and the LIFEguardianship Program of the Association for Retarded Citizens.

CASE EXAMPLE

Ms. D was referred to adult services for a protective services evaluation. She was extremely confused, needed protection, and had no one to assist her. She agreed to see a doctor, and the social worker made her an appointment at a geriatric assessment clinic. The clinic team ruled out reversible causes of confusion and diagnosed her condition as dementia of the Alzheimer's type. Because this diagnosis suggests that Ms. D's condition would continue to deteriorate, the clinic team recommended guardianship for her to assist with arrangements for her continuing care.

The APS worker questioned Ms. D's neighbors and was able to locate her nephew. He lived in a distant part of the state and visited infrequently, but he seemed to have some interest in his aunt. The worker told him of his aunt's situation and explained the services available to Ms. D from the adult services agency. The worker also explained the guardianship process, the responsibilities of the guardian, and the support the agency could offer during and after the process. The worker told the nephew that he was the most likely person to be able to make decisions based on his knowledge of his aunt's preferences. The nephew agreed to serve as guardian for his aunt with the understanding that the adult services program would be available to assist with support services, case management, and placement when needed.

As case manager, the adult services social worker maintained close contact with the nephew, providing him with information about his aunt. She also relied on his knowledge of his aunt's preferences to implement and monitor services whenever Ms. D could not provide information herself. The interventions of the adult services worker supported and enabled Ms. D's nephew to assume the responsibility of guardianship, thus best empowering the client to keep her values and preferences.

ISSUES FOR THE AGENCY

There are issues agencies must address to ensure the effective provision of guardianship services. One involves sensitivity and responsiveness to cultural diversity. Others include a full understanding of laws and regulations, how one conducts surrogate decision making, and an awareness of the potential for conflict of interest.

Whenever guardianship is provided by an adult services program, best practice requires that special efforts be made to acknowledge any differences in culture and lifestyle between guardian and ward. Although always an important dimension of practice, cultural sensitivity and awareness of preferences are critical in guardianship, because guardians are in the position of making decisions that wards can no longer make for themselves. It is imperative that those decisions reflect the cultural preferences of the ward when possible.

An adult services program committed to providing high-quality guardianship services begins with a thorough assessment of the agency's strengths and weaknesses in this area. Assessment begins with agency staff members' knowledge of state law and policies on guardianship. However, best practice in guardianship extends beyond knowledge of law and policy to familiarity with the complicated issues associated with guardianship and with recommendations for enhancing the decision-making process and improving the quality of guardianship programs.

Because decision making is the essence of guardianship, the agency should know about common standards for surrogate decision making. The two most widely used are *best interest* and *substituted judgment*. With best interest, the guardian acts as an objective representative of society and endeavors to decide what is in the best interest of the ward. With substituted judgment, the guardian tries to ascertain what decision the ward would have made in these circumstances if the ward ever had the ability to form an opinion on the matter.

The use of substituted judgment is based on the values of the individual rather than the society, and so it can meet better the goal of empowerment for clients. This view is taken by NGA (1991), which recommended that substituted judgment be used whenever the ward's presumed wishes can be obtained, because this standard best promotes self-determination. The NGA recommended use of the best-interest standard only when the preferences of the ward cannot be established or when "the guardian is reasonably certain that substantial harm will result if a decision is made in accordance with the preference of the ward" (p. 16).

Recently published standards for decision making and for the performance of guardianship duties (NGA, 1991) augment law and policy. The standards address models of decision making, including a model for wards with intermittent incompetence. The ethical code requires, among other things, that guardians "exhibit the highest degree of trust, loyalty, and fidelity in relation to the ward," that they "ensure the ward resides in the least restrictive environment available," and that the guardian provide informed consent when necessary, often for medical procedures (NGA, 1991).

Assessment of the agency's strengths and weaknesses addresses the capacity to provide guardianship services to a wide range of clients and the extent of the resources the agency can draw on for additional expertise when needed (for example, attorneys, physicians, or accountants). The agency should assess its capacity to serve as guardian of the estate, and if it does so, determine the size of estates it can reasonably manage. Excellence in providing guardianship services includes informing the court of the agency's limitations in this area. The assessment of the agency's capacity also includes determining the potential for conflicts of interest and identifying avenues the agency has available for minimizing conflicts.

For example, as disinterested public agent guardians, local adult services programs seeking guardianship for a client must ask the court to designate some other agency to review the status of the case at regular intervals. This requirement provides the opportunity to enhance the quality of services and minimize conflict of interest if the designated agency has some special expertise to offer. The adult services guardian may ask for a particular agency to be designated to receive status reports based on the expertise of that agency and the potential need of adult services for consultation.

For example, for a ward with medical problems, the adult services guardian might ask that a public health agency be designated. In other situations in which adult services is providing discrete services to a ward for whom the agency is guardian, adult services may ask for the designation of an agency that provides similar services. Because of its expertise but lack of direct involvement with the ward, the reviewing agency is in a position to identify conflicts of interest and provide objective opinions when needed.

Maryland, where local departments of social services provide guardianship, demonstrates another way of minimizing conflicts of interest. It has developed a Guardianship Review Board composed of community representatives who routinely review the actions of public agency guardians and make recommendations.

Assessment also addresses the agency's relationship with the court and resolves such problematic issues as when and how adult services is notified of appointments. Other areas of misunderstanding or misinformation between the courts and adult service agencies, such as who sends notices and handles paperwork and when they must do so, should be identified.

Because the adult services director or some other program administrator is often the named legal guardian while a social worker carries out the day-to-day case management activities, the agency's assessment of its capacity for guardianship should examine the communication between administrator and social worker regarding wards. The agency should develop guidelines that specify what responsibilities will be delegated to social workers and what types of situations require the personal involvement of the guardian.

Because the department of social services or the adult services program often is made guardian of the ward's person but not always the guardian of the ward's estate, the assessment also should clarify communication between the two sorts of guardians. Social workers acting on behalf of guardians of the person have responsibility for making decisions about the personal affairs of wards and so must communicate with guardians of the estate to obtain the resources to carry out these affairs. The adult services guardian should develop a written agreement with the guardian of the estate that guides communication and disbursement of funds necessary for attending to personal affairs.

On the basis of the assessment of the agency's strengths and weaknesses in delivering guardianship services and the problems that are identified in the process, the agency identifies goals for service delivery and develops strategies for enhancing services. Among the goals agencies may seek are improved communication between guardians and social workers through the development of protocols on decision making. Another goal might be to develop a more proactive stance in working with family members or friends who have the potential to become guardians—developing information packets and approaches to assisting them in filing to become guardians and then assuming their responsibilities. Another goal might be to develop procedures that facilitate transactions with guardians of the estate. Finally, it also may be helpful to develop procedures and policies for working with facilities when wards are placed in institutional settings. The Department of Social Services in Mecklenburg County, North Carolina, has developed a policy for some guardianship decisions involving wards who are placed in facilities, a copy of which is given to the facility (Figure 13-1).

RECOMMENDATIONS FOR NATIONAL STANDARDS

A national investigation of guardianship conducted by the Associated Press in 1987 (Ahearn, 1987) focused attention on problems in the delivery of guardianship services. Many organizations, including the American Bar Association, American Association of Retired Persons, and Michigan's Center for Social Gerontology, have studied various aspects of guardianship and have made recommendations for providing quality services.

NGA, a nonprofit membership organization, was formed in 1988 "to strengthen guardianship and related services through networking, education, and tracking and commenting on legislation" (NGA, 1995). According to its application for membership, the association is "dedicated to improving the quality of life for people in need of guardianship and alternative protective services."

Model service delivery standards for guardianship programs were developed by the Center for Social Gerontology in Michigan and published by the U.S. House of Representatives. Agencies pursuing excellence would be well guided by comparing themselves to the principles and standards in *Model Standards to Ensure Quality Guardianship and Representative Payeeship Services* (Hommel & Lisi, 1988). The standards address such issues as initial steps, personal contact and ongoing responsibilities, securing medical services and authorizing medical treatment, review of cases, and review of program.

Figure 13-1

MECKLENBURG'S GUARDIANSHIP POLICY FOR WARDS IN PLACEMENT

1. A "no code" order for a ward cannot be issued by a physician, family member, or anyone else without permission from [guardian's name], who requires the following information to make that decision:
   a. the ward's presenting condition
   b. whether the condition is terminal, incurable, and irreversible, according to the attending physician
   c. the second opinion of another physician
   d. what extraordinary means are requested to be withheld or withdrawn
   e. the wishes of the family member, if known
   f. the existence of a living will.
2. Wards cannot be transferred to another facility without the guardian's permission.
3. Facilities must notify DSS when our ward is involved in an accident that could result in injury, is involved in an adult protective services investigation, or when out-of-the facility visitation is requested.
4. DSS will not authorize pictures or videotapes of our wards that are made for publicity purposes. No newspaper or magazine articles or pictures will be allowed without prior consent.
5. Facilities must notify DSS immediately upon death of a ward. Within 30 days of the ward's death, their personal money and cost of care refunds should be sent by the facility to [address of the Clerk of Court].
6. The following burial plans have been made for this ward: [funeral home, cemetery, contact person].

In establishing criteria for making medical decisions requiring a second opinion, the standards are thorough. The guardian, except in an emergency, shall not grant or deny medical authorization without "two substantiating medical opinions from physicians who have examined the ward, at least one of whom is not affiliated with a health care institution in which the ward is placed" (Hommel & Lisi, 1988, p. 36) for the following:

1. *medical interventions requiring general or major anesthesia or involving a moderate to significant risk to the ward*
2. *administration of potentially damaging drugs, regimen, or therapy*
3. *extensive use of x-rays*
4. *interventions which drastically affect the appearance or functioning of the ward, such as surgery, amputation, eye surgery and cosmetic surgery*
5. *any treatments which require restraints, whether chemical or mechanical, or any adversive behavior modification. Before these treatments shall be*

> authorized the guardian shall explore and exhaust all less restrictive alternative interventions
> 6. interventions which pose a significant risk to the ward, due to the ward's condition or unique vulnerabilities
> 7. administration of anti-psychotic or psychotropic drugs
> 8. after-death donations of organs
> 9. prescription of contraceptives if deemed medically necessary
> 10. any other treatment or intervention which would cause a reasonable person to seek a second medical opinion. (pp. 36–37)

As agencies implement new approaches to solving the problems identified in guardianship services, the staff needs to evaluate the strategies for effectiveness in reaching the goals that were set. Ongoing evaluation leads to the identification of new opportunities for improving service delivery.

Guardianship and the Family Assessment and Change Method

Throughout this discussion of the need for guardianship, issues of its diversion, and the public agency's role, the general practice and philosophy of the family assessment and change method has been applied. What follows is a more specific discussion and application of the stages of the central process of working with clients who require guardianship services.

SCREENING AND INTAKE

The intake and screening of clients needing guardianship frequently differ from other services. Often clients are brought to the attention of adult services through appointment as guardian by the court. The adult services agency may not have had any contact with the client before the appointment. At other times the client may already be receiving other adult services (most often, protective services), and the agency may be seeking appropriate persons to petition and serve as guardian, may be the petitioner, or may serve as guardian. In addition to usual intake protocols, the worker should gather as much information as possible regarding the client's family and friends, because they are likely alternative candidates for guardians.

ASSESSMENT

The use of the family assessment and change method can help ensure that each ward receives only the amount of support necessary, is enabled to live a fuller life as a result of guardianship, and is empowered by having the guardian act on his or her wishes (as expressed now or in the past) whenever possible. A thorough functional assessment should be the starting point for planning guardianship activities, either before the petitioning process or after appointment. Sometimes a great deal of information may be available about the abilities and limitations of the ward, if the adjudication process involved evaluation by a multidisciplinary team (medical, psychological, and social work). Although the state laws often authorize or call for the completion of multidisciplinary evaluations, they are often not completed. Whenever adult services is involved in guardianship proceedings before adjudication, a multidisciplinary evaluation should be requested, received, and reviewed by the clerk of court before any final determination of competence. This information should be incorporated into the worker's functional assessment of the ward and govern subsequent recommendations.

Assessment may be complicated by the living arrangements of the ward. For example, if the ward lives in a state institution many miles away, the guardian or designated social worker must ensure that necessary information is obtained from the treatment facility. The guardian may want to contact the relevant adult services program in that county or region of the state for assistance in completing the assessment.

As with other clients, assessment should include as much direct information from the ward as possible, as well as information from other sources. With guardianship cases, however, much information will need to come from people who know or have known the ward. Some information will come from other professionals and paraprofessionals who have been involved. Family members, friends, former colleagues, and neighbors who can share information about past actions and conversations of the ward may be helpful in piecing together a picture of the perceptions, values, and preferences expressed by the person earlier in life.

The focus of these interviews is on finding out what prior decisions or strongly held opinions the ward has had about health care, living arrangements, and other matters of significance. The values history form, developed by the Center for Health Law and Ethics (Gibson, 1990), may be useful in gathering information for use in decision making. This form surveys written legal documents; expressed wishes concerning medical procedures; and attitudes toward health, control, independence, and other aspects of personal preference. Assessing the strengths and whatever remaining ability wards have to be involved in decisions about their activities, living arrangements, and general welfare also is important. For example, a ward may be unable to decide which facility is most appropriate for her care, but she may still be able to convey her dissatisfaction with her roommate or her interest in the activities of the facility.

FUNCTION-ORIENTED LIST OF PROBLEMS AND STRENGTHS

On the basis of the assessment information and in the normal course of events, the social worker would negotiate with the client and family a checklist for change. However, when the client has limited capacity to take part in this process and there is no family directly involved, the social worker may find it more helpful to develop a list of problems and strengths that identifies the needs and strengths of wards, such family as they have, and the general community support network. Among the problems identified will be some level of need for substituted decision making. A review of strengths will, however, help identify specific areas in which wards can still exercise their own judgment and decision making.

Because the guardian usually has far-reaching responsibilities for the ward, the list of problems and strengths must be especially thorough and anticipatory.

Inclusion of strengths helps to protect areas of remaining autonomy. The Center for Social Gerontology suggests careful consideration of a range of factors in making decisions and recommendations, including appropriateness of the current living situation; the ward's physical, psychological, and emotional state; repair, cleanliness, and safety of the living situation; adequacy of personal possessions; the ward's wishes with respect to the living situation; the quality of life offered by the facility; the availability of support and rehabilitative services; and the appropriateness of the peer group. Functional problems and strengths identified in the assessment provide guidance to identifying needed changes and setting goals.

SETTING GOALS

In setting goals for wards, social workers should take care to promote the greatest degree of self-determination possible in the least restrictive environment. Social workers must use clients' input and preferences and information from family members and friends in developing goals, using the standard of substituted judgment whenever possible.

The social worker and agency should work toward terminating, limiting, or transferring guardianship to other appropriate individuals or corporations whenever possible. Sometimes, with assistance from the adult services program, hesitant family members or friends may be helped to assume guardianship, although they were not initially willing to do so. For example, a brother might not be emotionally capable of initiating a petition for fear of jeopardizing his relationship with his sister. Once the petition has been initiated, however, and given a careful understanding of his responsibilities, the brother may be willing to serve as her guardian.

PLANNING AND IMPLEMENTING SERVICES

Case management is usually the primary method for implementing and monitoring services. A feature unique to case management in guardianship is the special need for communication between the case manager, who is often a social worker, and the guardian, who may be the agency director or some other member of the community. In other adult services, the capacity of clients to say what they want or need is assumed; this is not the case with guardianship. The social worker providing case management must communicate with the guardian about areas in which the client is incompetent to give consent.

Excellent guardianship services support, enable, and empower adult clients. Support is provided through professional relationships with wards and through case management activities to ensure that needed services are in place. Additional support through counseling is sometimes needed to help clients adjust to the emotional reaction (anger, devastation, confusion, sadness) of having guardianship imposed on them. Or counseling can be helpful in supporting family members or friends in their involvement with the client. Sometimes that involvement might lead to the assumption of guardianship responsibilities, but at other times it will supplement the professional relationship of the social worker and the ward with the special relationship of friends and family. That relationship may be especially important in later stages of decision making.

A social worker in an adult services program in North Carolina has provided an example of excellent practice in involving a ward's support system. In her role as case manager, the social worker developed and maintained an ongoing relationship with the ward's friends and family and continued to assess whether they might be willing to assume guardianship. They were not, but they did visit him, take him for outings, and purchase things for him.

The social worker's efforts in involving his support system were rewarded when the guardian was forced to make decisions about what medical interventions would be used near the time of the client's death. The client was hospitalized with pneumonia and incurable cancer. His doctors recommended that no extreme measures be taken to resuscitate him, but the county attorney advised the guardian, for reasons of liability, against consenting to these orders unless the family agreed. The previous efforts by the worker to involve friends and family and the relationships the worker had developed with them enabled the social worker to obtain their support for this decision and thus to prevent the client's unnecessary suffering in the face of an incurable illness.

For guardianship to be enabling and empowering, the provision of services must be grounded in the value of promoting self-determination for the client. To be empowering, the decisions should be the ones the ward would be making if he or she were still capable of making them. Guardianship should not be used as a way to substitute "good" decisions for "poor" ones if they contradict the client's value system. Empowerment can be operationalized through the use of the standard of substituted judgment whenever that approach is possible. As discussed with assessment, special care should be taken to learn the values and preferences of wards. This is done through interviews with people who knew them while they were competent so that this information is available to the guardian for decision making.

REASSESSMENT AND TERMINATION OF SERVICES

Reassessment in guardianship includes ongoing communication between guardian and case manager about the appropriateness, adequacy, and quality of the discrete services being provided for the ward. Reassessment always should include consideration of whether the ward continues to need guardianship or whether guardianship might appropriately be assumed by someone else.

Alternatives to Public Guardianship Programs

In many states and communities there is frequently a shortage of both qualified private and public guardians. Problems arise when no suitable family member is available to assume the responsibility. Even in those states where there are public guardianship programs, there may not be enough guardians available, owing to restrictions on the types of cases to which they can be appointed. In response to these issues and shortages, a number of states and communities have developed volunteer or quasi-volunteer guardianship programs.

In a discussion on legal problems of elderly people, Hurme (1990–1991) described a number of such programs around the country. These programs vary in the organizational auspices under which they are governed and also in the degree to which they are staffed by volunteers. All seek to ensure proper assessment of capacity and maintenance of maximum self-determination.

The Ebenezer Society in Minneapolis is a nonprofit organization that offers services to older people. It developed a panel of individuals who will serve as guardians or conservators for a fee or a county stipend. The society focuses on providing services to avoid conservatorship, but for clients who need them, it provides trained and competent conservators.

In San Mateo County, California, a court investigator recruited people from area businesses to serve as conservators for individuals who had no family or other options. The Friends of the Court are paid an hourly rate for managing the ward's estate; they work closely with the court and receive on-the-job training. Such individuals are used in time-consuming cases before the court and cases for which there are resources to pay for their services.

In Virginia, a number of volunteer guardian programs have been developed in partnerships with local aging network programs, adult services programs, and legal services. Clients judged incompetent who have complex problems are provided with a committee to manage their affairs, whereas people who are less incapacitated receive single guardians. Volunteers play a major role in all programs. In all of these efforts to ensure quality guardianship services for adults, public agencies that provide adult services will continue to play roles directly as public guardians or indirectly as organizers and supporters of community efforts to establish and govern volunteer guardianship programs.

Summary

Challenging issues face those states and communities still engaged in providing public agency guardianship in adult services, not the least of which is whether the agency should pursue guardianships in general, given the potential for conflict of interest. Having assumed such responsibilities, these agencies should perform a careful assessment of their capacity to do the job as well as possible. This assessment includes setting limits about the types of cases and involvement they can handle, ensuring training and adequate time for the social workers providing case management and necessary counseling services, and facilitating good communication between the case manager and the guardian. Good supervision and the development of agency protocols around decision making can help resolve difficult issues in guardianship cases.

Key Points

Excellent adult services social workers

- conduct thorough functional assessments as the starting point for planning guardianship activities either before the petitioning process or after the appointment

- take care to promote the greatest degree of self-determination possible for the client in the least restrictive environment and to involve family and friends appropriately
- communicate with the guardian about any areas in which the ward is incompetent to give consent
- provide counseling to help wards adjust to the emotional reactions (anger, devastation, confusion, sadness) of having guardianship imposed on them
- take special care to learn the values and preferences of wards through interviews with them and with people who knew them while they were competent, so that information is available for decision making.

Excellent adult services managers
- conduct agency self-assessments for excellence in guardianship
- take a proactive role in the community by contacting the court and human services agencies to solve problems in the delivery of guardianship services
- understand the central decision-making responsibilities of guardianship and use the standard of substituted judgment rather than best interest whenever possible, because substituted judgment best promotes self-determination
- consider the cultural and lifestyle differences between themselves and their wards, and ensure that decision making reflects cultural sensitivity and awareness of preferences of wards
- terminate, limit, or transfer guardianship to other appropriate individuals or corporations whenever possible.

Excellent leaders
- provide training in carrying out the responsibilities of guardianship
- offer leadership in solving the problems associated with providing guardianship.

Resources

Adult services agencies can join the National Guardianship Association by writing to NGA, c/o Office of Conferences and Institutes, Western Michigan University, Kalamazoo, MI 49008, calling (616) 387-4174, or faxing a request for information to (616) 387-4189. Membership brings with it an informative quarterly newsletter, a directory of other members, and notice of the annual national conference. Their publication *NGA Ethics and Standards for Guardians* is as an excellent reference. It is available free with membership or can be purchased from NGA at the above address.

The Values History Form, produced by the National Values History Project, appears in Gibson (1990). It may be freely reproduced or adapted for individual use. An important resource for guardians is the Model Standards to Ensure Quality Guardianship and Representative Payeeship Services, produced by Michigan's Center for Social Gerontology for the U.S. Congress, which is out of print. Because it is a government document (Committee Publication 101-729), it may be available through libraries that maintain collections of government documents.

References

Ahearn, W. (1987). *Guardians of the elderly: An ailing system.* New York: Associated Press.

Alexander, G. J. (1990). Avoiding guardianship. In E. F. Dejowski (Ed.), *Protecting judgment-impaired adults: Issues, interventions and policies* (pp. 163–175). New York: Haworth Press.

Dejowski, E. F. (Ed.). (1990). *Protecting judgment-impaired adults: Issues, interventions and policies.* New York: Haworth Press.

Dudovitz, N. S. (1985). The least restrictive alternative. *Generations, 10*(1), 39–41.

Gibson, J. M. (1990). National values history project. *Generations, 15*(suppl), 51–64.

Hightower, D., Heckert, A., & Schmidt, W. (1990). Elderly nursing home residents' need for public guardianship services in Tennessee. In E. F. Dejowski (Ed.), *Protecting judgment-impaired adults: Issues, interventions and policies* (pp. 105–122). New York: Haworth Press.

Hommel, P., & Lisi, L. (1988). *Proposed model standards for programs providing guardianship and representative payeeship services to adults.* Ann Arbor, MI: Center for Social Gerontology.

Hull, L., Holmes, G. E., & Karst, R. H. (1990). Managing guardianships of the elderly: Protection and advocacy as public policy. In E. F. Dejowski (Ed.), *Protecting judgment-impaired adults: Issues, interventions and policies* (pp. 155–162). New York: Haworth Press.

Hurme, S. B. (1990–1991). Programs address need for qualified guardians. *Bifocal: Bar Associations in Focus on Aging and the Law, 11*(4), 1–4.

Iris, M. A. (1990). Uses of guardianship as a protective intervention for frail, older adults. In E. F. Dejowski (Ed.), *Protecting judgment-impaired adults: Issues, interventions and policies* (pp. 57–71). New York: Haworth Press.

Iris, N. A. (1991). Editorial: New directions for guardianship research. *Gerontologist, 31*(2), 148–149.

Johnson, T. F. (1990). Guardianship in the South: Strategies for preserving the rights of older persons. *Journal of Aging and Social Policy, 2*(1), 33–50.

National Guardianship Association. (1991). *Ethics and standards for guardians.* Elmhurst, IL: Author.

National Guardianship Association. (1995). *Membership brochure.* Kalamazoo, MI: Author.

Wang, L., Burns, A. M., & Hommel, P. A. (1990, October). Trends in guardianship reform: Roles and responsibilities of legal advocates. *Clearinghouse Review,* pp. 561–568.

CHAPTER 14

In-Home Services

MARY ANNE P. SALMON

This chapter examines the family assessment and change method for social workers in in-home services. It first discusses the purpose of in-home services, providing a brief overview of the history and examining the question of who the client is. It then reviews each step of the family assessment and change method, with an eye to the strengths, weaknesses, and concerns of social workers in this area. It highlights some general issues that are relevant to in-home services social workers—coordination with other adult services functions, working with other professionals and agencies, and working with paraprofessionals. Finally, the chapter identifies barriers to excellence and summarizes findings.

Excellent social workers in in-home services use the family assessment and change method's steps to assess, plan, implement, monitor, and evaluate services such as personal care and homemaking provided in the client's home. These workers use the process, the services themselves, and their professional helping relationship to support, enable, and empower adult clients. In serving this population, which usually has multiple, interactive, and chronic impairments, the social worker's goal is always to help clients achieve as full and as satisfying lives as possible within the scope of their abilities and their preferences. Haslanger (1990) pointed out that even those people with severe cognitive impairments need some element of control over their lives when she wrote, "Good home care is about maximizing the client's ability to exercise those choices [for example, when and what to eat, who to see], to gain control on a daily basis" (p. 32).

Who Is the Client?

In-home services social workers balance two seemingly opposite and sometimes overtly conflicting ideas—the goal of supporting, enabling, and empowering the individual client and the need to recognize and support the entire family system. This balance is particularly complicated when the client is extremely frail, cognitively impaired, or severely mentally ill and when most of the social worker's dealings are with a specific family caregiver.

Supporting the entire family system may include arranging services in such a way that caregivers get respite, helping them find ways of dealing with the physical and emotional demands of caregiving, counseling to support their abilities to set limits, and other task and relationship activities. It may be necessary to learn about the client's lifelong preferences and values by talking with family members and friends when that client is no longer fully able to communicate. However, it is not appropriate to simply substitute the caregiver's report of a client's desires for the client's own expressed desires when he or she has any ability to communicate. Eliciting opinions from a client with limited cognitive ability or difficulty communicating may take extra time and effort, but it is essential to excellent social work.

At the same time that social workers have goals to support and empower their clients, they must be careful not to support them in gaining empowerment by enslaving family members and friends. There are common societal values about honoring parents and "caring for our own," which are likely to be held by social workers and family caregivers alike. Still, social workers need to temper these values with a realistic sense of how much people vary in their personal beliefs, their physical and emotional endurance, and their other role expectations beyond caregiving for the client. Just as the client is free to accept or refuse services, the family is free to decide what amount and type of support and care they can give, including refusing to give care altogether. In working with the family as well as with the client, and through building a trusting relationship with realistic mutual expectations, social workers can usually help families and clients avoid such confrontational, all-or-nothing choices.

Brief History of In-Home Services

Moore (1988) gave a brief history of the rise of one kind of in-home services in the United States—homemaker services. She pointed out that in the first part of this century, doctors, nurses, and public welfare social workers routinely made house calls, so the home was a setting in which people expected to receive services. At that time, large extended families were common, and there were few women in the labor force, so there was little need for the services we usually associate now with in-home aides. She explained that around 1920, paraprofessionals called homemakers were first used as substitute mothers when the mother in a family was temporarily absent or incapacitated by illness. Moore did not say when these services were first extended to older adults in this country, but she asserted that the rise of paraprofessional in-home services for older adults was facilitated by the passage of Medicare and Medicaid laws in the 1960s.

Moore argued that the real proliferation of aide services occurred in the 1970s with the rise of for-profit agencies, including national chains. However, the availability of Title XX funds under the Social Security Act Amendments of 1974, the precursor to today's Social Services Block Grant (SSBG), may have served as an impetus to public and private agencies alike. In the 1990s, Medicaid, along with SSBG, Older Americans Act resources, and state general revenues, are the primary funding sources for publicly supported in-home services (Benjamin, 1993).

Using the Family Assessment and Change Method

In-home services is perhaps the area of adult services where the social worker's role fits the family assessment and change method for task performance best. At the same time, in-home services calls for a deft handling of the relationship component of social work (described in chapter 7). The steps are the same as those detailed in chapter 3. This chapter is not meant to duplicate chapter 3 but to revisit some aspects of these steps that have particular relevance to in-home services social workers.

INTAKE–SCREENING

With in-home services cases, the person who calls or appears at the local adult services agency with a need for assistance is often not the client but a caregiver or relative. Useful screening information can generally be obtained from these informal caregivers. Sometimes there are options that can be ruled out at this step (for example, the caregiver has inquired about Medicaid waiver or personal care services, but it is clear that the client would not qualify for Medicaid), but a decision about ongoing services (as opposed to emergency interventions) is premature until several additional steps have been completed.

If the person who makes the initial contact is the potential client, an informal caregiver, family member, or friend, this is the stage at which relationship building begins. There is a need to share information about adult services and other community services (types of services, waiting lists, fees) and to explain necessary procedures, but the worker also may need to help make the potential client or family member comfortable with getting help (in general or specifically from adult services). The social worker may begin to explore the family member's feelings about the potential client and about other family members while he or she gathers information about who is providing care now.

EMERGENCY INTERVENTION

The two most common uses of emergency in-home services are for adult protective services clients and for clients needing immediate placement. If agencies have clear-cut procedures for identifying emergencies and providing short-term emergency services, it should be easier for social workers to take the necessary time to follow the remaining steps in the method—assessing; identifying problems and setting goals; and planning and providing long-term services, whether in-home, in the community, or in institutions. Excellent social workers learn to distinguish between true emergencies (when clients will suffer grave harm if they do not receive services immediately) and clients' and families' ordinary desire to receive service as quickly as possible.

ASSESSMENT

Most states have developed standardized assessment tools to aide in-home services social workers. In using these standardized protocols, social workers need to remember that all forms are just tools to aid practice, and they have both strengths and limitations. For example, some assessment forms do not ask about over-the-counter medications as well as prescription medications. An excellent social worker is aware that drug interactions can occur between prescription and nonprescription drugs, so he or she will ask about both kinds. To the degree that the assessment form provides a checklist to jog the memories of busy social workers and offers a structure for documentation, it can be a valuable tool and contribute to quality social work. If, on the other hand, the social worker sees the form as "another bureaucratic requirement" or a substitute for informed judgment, even a perfect in-home assessment tool is nearly useless. Accuracy, thoroughness, and informed use of assessment data in the remaining steps are measures of the assessment's value.

Although the adequacy, accessibility, and safety of the clients' physical environment is a part of every full assessment, it is especially important for in-home services and provides a good example of how to approach assessment of an individual's home environment. Clients' homes are the "facilities" where they will receive all or most of the services their social workers arrange or deliver. Their homes are also the workplace for paraprofessionals and skilled service providers. The qualities that make in-home care desirable to clients and foster their autonomy, such as privacy and the chance to exhibit personal style, may create challenges for the social worker and other care providers. Privacy means limited supervision of both the aide's performance and the client's compliance with health or medical regimens. Personal style may involve health and safety hazards ranging from throw rugs to an abundance of pets. The social worker is challenged to respect clients' rights to make their own decisions while making clear the possible consequences of some choices and helping to find satisfying but safer options.

Because the home environment is so important to in-home services, the social worker needs to be especially thorough about assessing the physical characteristics of the home and how they interact with the social environment and the client's functional limitations. An effective social worker will observe the client (and sometimes the primary caregiver) moving through the home and using kitchen and bathroom appliances and facilities. He or she will note the presence or absence of heat, light, and water and how that affects the client's functioning. The worker will ask the client what he or she likes about the home, as well as how things could be better. He or she will involve the client or family in using a home safety checklist or another safety tool.

In-home social workers think about the environmental implications of other parts of their assessment in deciding which parts of the environment may need more-careful evaluation. For example, if a client who moves slowly bathes herself, it is important to verify the safety of the water heater setting and document the presence or absence of handrails in the tub or shower. If, on the other hand, a client receives bed baths from a third party, the social worker may only want to document whether hot water is available at the tap or must be heated on the stove. Other health and safety hazards may be identified by in-home aides or by the social worker during quarterly reviews or other visits. If this occurs, additions should be made to the assessment and appropriate modifications made in the checklist for change, goals, and service plans.

For many clients the outdoor parts of the home are as important as the indoor. The social worker talks with each client and gauges how important it is to be outside or see the outside during each day and identifies barriers. In addition to the client's activities of daily living (ADL) or instrumental activities of daily living (IADL) functioning, does the outdoor environment present problems, such as cracked and broken pavement or danger of crime (real or perceived)?

The client's social functioning and his or her immediate social environment also may be key to the ability of the social worker and other agency and community personnel to provide in-home services and should thus be assessed carefully. When either the physical or the social environment is severely impaired, social workers face complications above and beyond addressing their clients' social and housing needs. It is not uncommon for home health agencies to refuse to provide services in an environment where they believe that the health or safety of the client or their workers is compromised or where they cannot give what they consider to be adequate care. Until such time as the housing problems can be addressed, the social worker must struggle with the ethical dilemma of leaving the client unserved or arranging services where the aides may be at risk. In addition to the ethical dilemma, there may be legal liability if the aide or client is injured during such circumstances and a legal liability to the client or family if the agency does not deliver services for which the client qualifies. In most cases, in-home services social workers will not try to deal with these problems alone. Adult services administrators, supervisors, and social workers may be involved in "staffing" such cases, often with input from the county's legal counsel. Some examples of problems and the types of solutions agencies might consider are given in Table 14-1, but such examples are no substitute for real brainstorming among social work professionals who know the case, the community, and their own resources.

Table 14-1

FACTORS THAT MAY PREVENT PROVISION OF SERVICES IN THE HOME

Situation	Possible Responses by Social Worker/Agency
Home Environment	
Client's home is heated by a woodstove with inadequate ventilation, causing danger from carbon monoxide and occasional sparks.	Investigate the client's feelings about alternate housing; pursue affordable, safe housing if feasible and if the client accepts.
There are rotting steps and floorboards in the client's home. The aide is concerned that she or the client may fall through the floor or that vermin may get in.	Investigate the client's feelings about changes to the house (for example, ask about symbolic or emotional ties to the woodstove, the spring, or the stacks of old newspapers and magazines) and work with the client to reach goals that are acceptable to her.
The only source of water is a spring or well some distance from the client's house, and the client needs bed baths as well as drinking water.	Determine whether the client can receive services elsewhere (for example, the home of a relative) for a short while during the time needed to address environmental deficits.
The client, who can take a few slow steps with her walker, lives in a third-floor apartment crammed with stacks and stacks of old newspapers, magazines, and other combustible debris.	Determine what costs, supplies, or labor family and friends might be willing to contribute to address deficits (for example, replacing the stove, replacing the stovepipe, adding plumbing, repairing rotting boards, or removing and recycling newspapers).
	Identify volunteer civic or religious groups that might help. (For example, would Boy Scouts remove papers if they could keep the money for recycling them? Would the school library be happy for the client's generous donation of 35 years worth of *Life* magazine or *National Geographic?* Would a local men's group give a Saturday of work mending the steps or soft places in the floor?)
	Identify agencies and funding sources to cover costs of fixing deficits. (For example, are there Older Americans Act, SSBG, state, or local funds for housing and home repair available?)

(continued)

Table 14-1 (continued) ━━━━━━━━━━━━━━━━━━━━

Situation	Possible Responses by Social Worker/Agency

Neighborhood

The client lives in a neighborhood where the crime rate is high and groups of unemployed young men spend much of the day on the street corner.

Although many cases involving dangerous environments must be resolved on a case-by-case basis, the agency will probably want to arrive at a set of safety guidelines and practices for both social workers and in-home aides when providing services in dangerous neighborhoods.

Client's or Family's Behavior in the Home

A client who must use oxygen at home continues to smoke cigarettes, even when the oxygen is in use.

A diabetic client is careless about how she disposes of her insulin needles.

Several members of the client's family are using crack and have been known to become threatening or abusive to aides, nurses, and social workers when under the influence.

A client with fairly severe ADL impairments is never satisfied with her aide. She constantly demands a new aide, disrupting the continuity of services to other clients. The social worker fears that if this behavior continues, the client will eventually try and reject every aide in the agency.

If the client is willing, talk with her to try to understand her feelings about the behavior and give information about possible options. (For example, does the smoker have an interest in quitting if help to quit is available, or does she consider cigarettes her last pleasure in life? Is the woman with diabetes dealing inappropriately with feelings about the unfairness of the disease? Is the client with the crack-smoking relatives close to these particular family members, or would she be happier living with someone else or asking them to move out? Is the complaining client looking for something she can control?)

If the client or relevant family member is willing, arrange for appropriate services to help deal with the feelings and change the behavior (for example, a self-help smoking cessation guide, nicotine patch, or gum; drug treatment; group or private counseling to help the woman with diabetes deal with her feelings; identification of appropriate responsibilities and avenues of choice for the complainer).

Set limits with the client or family. Let the client and family know that dangerous

(continued)

Table 14-1 (continued)

Table 14-1 (continued)

Situation	Possible Responses by Social Worker/Agency
Client's or Family's Behavior in the Home (continued)	behaviors will make it impossible for the social worker or aide to deliver services. For example, one social worker in North Carolina faced a situation in which a client with severe physical impairments but unimpaired judgment had his wife, who drank alcohol to excess, as sole caregiver. The caregiver would dismiss or physically threaten aides when she was intoxicated. She would also try to induce aides to drive her to buy beer, leaving the bed-bound client alone. After many attempts to talk with the caregiver, and a number of APS referrals (with services refused by the mentally competent client), the social worker drew up a contract with the caregiver. The contract specified conditions during which services could continue (for example, the wife was not to drink while the aide was in the home or be intoxicated when she arrived and the wife was not to change the aide's days and hours without notifying specified contacts at the Department of Social Services and the agency from which the aide's services were contracted). It also made clear, in writing, that the consequence of noncompliance was loss of the service. Similar kinds of limits could be negotiated with the complaining client (for example, a limit to the frequency with which she can request a new aide and rules about the treatment of the aide). If necessary, investigate the enforcement of public health and criminal laws in cases where there is general public danger.

MAKING A CHECKLIST FOR CHANGE AND SETTING GOALS

Based on a review of "best case records" in preparation for this book, identifying the problems and strengths of the client and family and using them as the basis for a checklist for change and for setting goals with client and family does not come easily for in-home social workers or for social workers generally. Most agencies have a limited number of formal service options, and they often fail to appreciate fully social workers' potential activities as counselors or as case managers for services found outside the agency. Clients often need services quickly, and consequently social workers feel they must "hit the ground running" with some elements of a service plan in their heads as they conduct the assessment. Although speed is often essential in finding services for frail clients, social workers who move directly from assessment to service plan without these intermediate steps may be sacrificing true efficiency. Helping the client and family identify areas for change and set goals leads to a service plan that fits the needs and tastes of the client; ensures the client's and family's cooperation and participation; models a way of dealing with future problems; and empowers both client and family. The quick fix may provide an appropriate service but in a way that may not be most suited to meet the client's unspoken goals, may meet resistance from the client or family, often overlooks resources outside the agency, and does little to help the client and family meet challenges. The time needed to adjust the plan and encourage acceptance by the family, as well as working with them on new problems that arise, may be much greater than any time saved initially by omitting these steps.

The goal of in-home services is that the client will be able to live safely at home and avoid inappropriate placement. Although this goal is an important motivator for in-home social workers as they serve all their clients, it is not useful as a client-specific goal. Rather, goals such as "Mr. Jones will be able to use his walker to move from his chair (the green one in the living room) to the refrigerator and back by the next quarterly assessment" or "Mrs. Brown will be able to dress herself completely except for her shoes within six months" will show Mr. Jones and Mrs. Brown that they are making progress. Even when the client is so frail that maintenance is the only realistic hope, goals can be written in a way that will allow the client to feel successful. Goals for these clients might be "Mrs. Smith will get outside in her wheelchair three times a week through the summer months" or "Mr. Brown will plan the three meals a week prepared by the aide." If Mr. Brown is very impaired, it might read "Mr. Brown will make at least one choice about each noontime meal prepared by the in-home aide—for example, pudding or ice cream, rice or potatoes."

Some clients with severe disabilities may be very limited in the degree to which they can participate in the goal-setting process or in working toward achieving their goals. In such cases the social worker may find it difficult to respect and respond to the needs and desires of the family while still giving highest priority to the client's preferences. Here, too, is a place where counseling and relationship-building skills are vital. The social worker will want to work toward establishing what the client would have wanted (substituted judgment) as a basis for making decisions on the client's behalf and will need to gain information from the family and enlist their support to do this.

PLANNING SERVICES

Social workers frequently have a more structured planning process for in-home services than for most other programs, although the extent of this planning is uneven across the range of possible services. For example, in addition to the broadly defined service plan for each client, there is often a written plan for the in-home aide that spells out the nature and frequency of the aide's tasks as well as his or her schedule of visits to the client. This sort of a plan is important for preventing misunderstandings between families, social workers, and in-home aides. This can be accomplished by reviewing the in-home aide service plan with everyone involved, making certain that the client, the aide, and the family all have the same understanding of what the aide is and is not expected to do. This recommendation was seconded by Chichin (1991), who found that 40 percent of in-home aides responding to her survey of New York City workers reported that they had been in situations where they "were expected (by the client and/or family) to do things not a part of the job," and most of them said it happened many times.

In North Carolina, if the client is receiving Medicaid-waiver in-home services, the social worker is required to plan his or her own hours of case management and the specific tasks that the family agrees to perform, as well as the services provided by other agencies. If the client is receiving services through the agency other than those covered by the Medicaid waiver, the social worker is often tempted to make specific plans only for the in-home aide service or for a few other community services (for example, one home-delivered meal per day, Monday through Friday) but to think of his or her own counseling and administrative time and the family's caregiving as being provided "as needed."

Just as an explicit plan for the in-home aide's services helps prevent misunderstandings about the paraprofessional's obligations and duties, a structured plan of the family's care and the social worker's scheduled visits recorded in the client's service plan can prevent similar misunderstandings about the family's and social worker's roles. These plans also help social workers and families schedule their time, allow easier identification of inadequate or impractical service plans, and prevent unrealistic expectations. Experienced social workers know that unplanned situations will still arise and that plans will have to be modified to meet changing needs, but this does not negate the importance of planning. It only suggests that anticipating problems should be part of the process.

IMPLEMENTING THE PLAN

All the things the social worker does for the client and family personally or arranges for the client fall into this step of the model. Implementation includes delivering formal services, helping clients and their families build on their own resources, and counseling clients and their families to help them gain empowerment.

It also may include introducing the client to the various people who will be coming into the home to provide services, such as an in-home aide or nurse. If the social worker cannot make these introductions personally, he or she informs the client and family about the specific people who will be coming and their reason for being there.

In the review of current practice in North Carolina's counties conducted for this book, we found that some of the most creative social work demonstrated by workers was not limited to arranging for in-home aide services but was apparent in their demonstration of practical problem solving. For example, one worker whose client had difficulty bending or reaching showed him and his family how to re-arrange the kitchen and other areas of the home so that most of the things he needed every day were within reach. As that worker pointed out, this type of adap-tation can make a client's life easier without using scarce service resources (al-though the worker was not counting her own time). This strategy also helped to empower the client, who was able to be more self-reliant. In parallel situations, the social worker may arrange for someone else to provide the hands-on assistance, but time spent with clients and families in such tasks also may be used profitably to build the professional caring relationship.

This example also points out the value of developing a list of problems, strengths, and goals that are related to functioning. If the time-limited, function-oriented goal specifies what the client's functional performance will be as a result of the intervention, the client, family, and social worker may be able to devise a number of strategies to achieve the same effect and choose the most promising. In the course of the assessment, the client and social worker also will identify values that influence the client's satisfaction with his or her performance. For example, for a client who is having difficulty with bathing, the service strategy may be differ-ent depending on whether the emphasis is on the client's being able to bathe him-self safely and effectively or on his desire to maintain a particular level of personal hygiene. In the first case, strategies might include rearranging the bathing facili-ties and helping the client obtain rehabilitative services; in the second, finding some-one suitable to bathe the client on a regular schedule may be more appropriate.

MONITORING

Monitoring to ensure the quality of services provided to clients is perhaps the most difficult and least understood task associated with the provision of in-home ser-vices (Kramer, Shaughnessy, Bauman, & Crisler, 1990). Although there is agree-ment that quality assurance is vital to the provision of services in the home be-cause the isolation of the home setting makes clients vulnerable to every danger of poor quality care (Applebaum & Phillips, 1990; Haslanger, 1990; U.S. Depart-ment of Health, Education, & Welfare, 1976), most of those who point out this vulnerability also mention the weakness of any existing method for assuring qual-ity. As Haslanger (1990) suggested, many of the most rigorous popular approaches, such as competency-based training and testing of aides and monitoring of agency policy, measure only the ability to give good service, not the quality of the service actually received.

Interviewing the client about service qualities may seem consistent with the general focus of empowering clients, but there is both research (Applebaum & Phillips, 1990; Eustis & Fisher, 1991) and the wisdom of some experienced social workers to suggest that many clients are extremely reluctant to report poor-quality service for several reasons. They may fear loss of services or retaliation by the aide, or they may feel a personal loyalty to the aide and not wish to cause trouble with superiors. Social workers also report the converse of this situation, where certain clients or their families are extremely critical of aides and make frequent requests that a new aide be assigned to them.

Applebaum and Phillips (1990) suggested a broad-based strategy (that is, try a little of anything that might work) to monitor the quality of services. It includes educating client and family consumers, conducting random in-home audits of a sample of clients, having supervisory home care staff complete client status reports, and asking case managers to keep a feedback log.

Explicit agreements about the tasks to be performed and the schedule of the in-home aide, the social worker, and the family are one important tool for educating the consumer. The excellent social worker helps the family know what quality of services to expect. Social workers frequently emphasize the need to lay the groundwork for good communication, making sure all parties have similar expectations and working closely with the aide and client during the first few visits.

A careful assessment of the aide's skills and preferences in light of the client's needs and preferences can help ensure quality services. Although it is not possible in all situations, many social workers try to match clients and aides as carefully as possible.

Making unscheduled home visits to check on the quality of services (a form of random in-home audit) is another approach to monitoring in-home services. Caseloads may not permit workers to do this often, so this approach may work most effectively when there have been complaints or problems that have already been identified, rather than as a way to assess a random sample of cases for quality. If the agency considers including random audits as part of its quality assurance program, it should establish a method for choosing cases as well as a detailed protocol or checklist for the social worker (or supervisory auditor) to follow, according to which services were in the plan.

If the adult services program contracts with another agency to provide in-home aides, that agency's supervisory reports on the aide, as well as the client's progress notes, should be a part of the client's status reports made by supervisory home care staff members. In large agencies, similar reports may be made by the in-home aide supervisor and reviewed by the social worker. Regardless of the agency's size, effective social workers will review the notes made by the nurses overseeing personal care clients (see the section "Working with other professionals and agencies" in this chapter). For those working directly with in-home aides, the use of a feedback log, as Applebaum and Phillips (1990) suggested, to record the strengths and problems of individual service providers systematically is one supervisory tool that supports quality assurance.

Many adult services programs require periodic reviews of service plans as the only planned, formal monitoring activity, and often these reviews focus primarily on the continuing need for services, which is a key part of monitoring. However, if this visit is to be the only formal monitoring activity, social workers must do more than monitor the continued need for specific services. They need to measure and document progress toward goals and determine the client's satisfaction or problems with the services provided. Is the client receiving all of the services planned? Is the aide reliable and dependable? Does observation of the environment suggest that the client is receiving quality services? (For example, if the in-home aide is supposed to mop the kitchen once a week, does the kitchen floor look as though it has been mopped within the past week?) This visit is also a time to work with the client to redefine problems and goals or to choose the next problems to work on from the initial problem list.

REASSESSMENT

Adult services programs are bound to differ greatly in their standards and expectations for reassessment. Some will require full reassessments annually or even more frequently. Others will see the process of assessment and reassessment as ongoing activities for the social worker and view formal reassessments at set intervals as unnecessary. This last approach, however, is not consistent with the purpose of reassessment.

The purpose of a formal reassessment is to look at the client with new eyes. It is easy to become so focused on the presenting problem that important life changes and strengths in other domains go unnoticed, especially those that do not have a direct or immediate impact on the presenting problem or the delivery of services. In-home services workers have some advantages in this step—they see the client functioning in the home setting on every visit, and they have the additional "eyes and ears" of the in-home aide and perhaps such other service providers as the person who delivers meals. Still, this familiarity can sometimes make a thorough reassessment more difficult. Because the social worker and aide have been focused on the particular functional problems they began services to address, they may miss subtle changes in other domains. For example, the aide services the client receives may be quite adequate to meet the original needs for a clean house and personal care assistance, but the client may not be eating well or may show other behavioral changes that could signal depression or new health problems. Reassessment in health, social, and mental functioning may reveal that the client has no new health problems but has lost several close friends or family members. Responses to a mental status examination in this case might indicate depression and the possible need for further evaluation, counseling, or medical treatment.

As chapter 3 explains, the purpose of reassessment is not served by the completion of a form alone. If, as sometimes occurs, the reassessment form is filled out by copying information from the previous year's reassessment, the process is useless, because it takes up the social worker's time to write it and the supervisor's time in reading the same information twice. It is useful, however, to compare assessments from one period to another to get an overview of how the client's life is changing. As shown in the diagram of the family assessment and change method (chapter 3), one outcome of reassessment can be termination of the case, but another can lead back to the steps of identifying problems and strengths, setting goals, and planning new activities or services to meet them.

TERMINATION

There are three principal reasons that in-home services are terminated: The client (1) dies, (2) is placed in a long-term-care facility, or (3) no longer needs the services to live at home independently. However, services also may be terminated at the client's request, when the client has difficulty using them effectively, or when their limitations make them ineffective for the client. Local communities may also take the option of responding to funding crises by terminating services to the lowest-priority clients. Other communities may respond to tight resources by reducing the hours of service to most or all clients and putting new clients on a waiting list.

The literature, which teaches termination as a formal set of activities, is predicated on the assumption that clients regain functioning to the point of no longer needing or qualifying for services. In real practice, however, this is unlikely. In the absence of explicit criteria for terminating services on the basis of improved function, only a minority of clients are likely to be terminated on this basis.

Termination based on improved functioning is a positive step that benefits the client and rewards self-determination. Clients take pride in increased independence. Workers must recognize and acknowledge differences among clients in their desire and readiness for independence and outline strategies for tapering or ending services.

Termination is still an important social work function when clients die or are placed out of home. When a client dies there may be family members who need grief counseling or assistance in reorganizing their lives. In addition, the social worker or the aide supervisor may need to help the aide deal with a personal loss, as well as adjusting to a new assignment. When a client needs placement, the ending of in-home services involves helping the client deal with another change in life. Here, too, the aide as well as the family may need help in dealing with feelings of loss and possibly guilt about failing to keep the client at home.

Coordination with Adult Services Functions

Although in-home services social workers need to coordinate their work with that of all other adult services social workers, there are three functions for which coordination is particularly important: (1) the units that handle Medicaid eligibility, (2) adult protective services, and (3) placement services. Knowledge of Medicaid eligibility is essential, because a significant part of state and federal funding for in-home aide services (from adult services or other agencies) comes from this source. Agencies that have other funding sources for clients not eligible for Medicaid will still want to make sure that Medicaid pays for all those who are eligible to stretch scarce funds as far as possible. It is important that workers know enough about Medicaid and other payment sources to provide clients with correct information and point them toward expert help without raising false hopes. Clients and family members can lose respect for social workers if they feel the workers are deliberately withholding information because it is not "part of their job" or, worse yet, do not understand how their own agencies work.

The flow of information and involvement between in-home services and the protective services unit must be in both directions. People who enter the system as APS clients may need in-home services as part of a package to ensure their safety and well-being. Equally, some frail people who are being supported by in-home services, particularly people with cognitive impairments, also may be particularly vulnerable to self-neglect, exploitation, or abuse.

Sometimes the lines between these services may be blurred. For example, when in-home services social workers were asked their opinions about a somewhat ambiguous neglect–self-neglect case involving a client already receiving in-home services, they revealed a wide variety of opinions about how long the case should be handled strictly as an in-home services situation and when it should be referred to APS. Programs can address this directly by asking social workers to hold informal staffings with the APS supervisor, their supervisor, and other social workers before making an ambiguous APS referral, thus reducing unnecessary referrals and also giving social workers a chance to validate their judgments about the safety of continuing to keep the cases in the in-home unit without referring them. In turn, the in-home services social worker needs to participate in deciding whether the aide services available can provide adequate protection for the APS client.

Communication also must flow in both directions between in-home and placement social workers. Placement social workers need to be familiar and comfortable enough with in-home services to avoid cutting short the exploration of this option in preplacement planning. In addition, they commonly need to arrange for in-home services as a stopgap measure while difficult placements are being arranged or located, and in some cases they may need in-home services to support rehabilitated clients who are returning home from a facility. At the same time, in-home social workers need to be able to work with placement social workers to find the best available facility for clients for whom increased disability and dwindling social resources have made placement the most feasible (if sometimes reluctantly chosen) option.

In-home social workers may need to examine their feelings about placement as part of enhancing their relationship with the placement worker. It is easy to internalize the service's overarching goal of avoiding inappropriate out-of-home placement as avoiding out-of-home placement altogether, so that appropriate placements may feel like failures. Such feelings may interfere with the relationship with placement services, as well as with the social worker's ability to support the client and family as they make this difficult choice.

In agencies where community services like adult day care are handled by another worker, unit, or agency, decisions about which is the most appropriate service or how to plan for simultaneous service delivery must be coordinated and turf issues resolved. Communications among social workers with responsibilities for the various program areas may not be a problem in some agencies where the same worker is providing APS, in-home services, and placement, but some of the same sorts of judgments about when to "change hats" from one service to the other may still need to be exercised. Knowing when it is time for a change of services may be harder for the worker who has to "do it all," because he or she may be focused on only one type of solution.

One way to help keep communications open, as well as to take advantage of different viewpoints in bringing about change in difficult cases, is "staffing the case." Agencies will differ in the frequency and formality of staffings, but most who have tried these group meetings to exchange views about a problem case have found them rewarding and productive.

Working with Other Professionals and Agencies

Social workers in this program area often need to coordinate their activities with professionals from other disciplines and with representatives of other public agencies, as well as private–nonprofit and proprietary ones. One of the ways in-home services social workers are highly involved with other agencies occurs when adult services decides to contract for aide services rather than hiring aides directly. Accordingly, this section will discuss choosing and contracting with an agency for services. However, contracting for services is only one example of the interagency coordination that is necessary. There are three stages of the change process during which additional coordination is particularly likely to occur: (1) assessment, (2) implementation, and (3) monitoring.

CONTRACTING FOR IN-HOME AIDES

In choosing agencies from which to contract in-home aide services, social workers or their supervisors will want to look at the same issues that would be relevant to a private consumer selecting an agency. First, they would look at the days and time span that service is offered and then the specific tasks that the aides can and cannot do. Then they would want to know how well prepared the aides are to do their work and how they are supervised. They would gather information about the training and competency testing of aides; the required hours of in-service education; the ratio of aides to supervisors; and the agency's procedure for monitoring the quality of aides' work, including the frequency of aide–supervisor interactions and supervisor's contact with clients. They will look for an agency with a reputation for providing services reliably, as well as a staff sufficient in size to ensure that new clients can begin receiving services in a timely fashion. They also will want to know that there is sufficient staff to supply an emergency replacement when an aide is sick or otherwise unable to keep his or her schedule. (Moore, 1988, mentioned the use of consumers' guides in choosing an agency. One such guide, although written for laypeople rather than experienced social workers, is the American Association of Retired Persons's *A Handbook about Care in the Home: Information on Home Health Services,* 1982.)

Adult services programs in larger communities may have several choices of agency and, for various reasons, may opt to contract with more than one, perhaps because of different levels of services offered, expertise with particular service populations, and ability to serve different parts of the county. Realistically, adult services programs in small communities may have only one choice of agency from which to obtain aide services. In such cases, care in drawing up the contract is particularly important. At a minimum, it should spell out mutual responsibilities and provide mechanisms for routine monitoring and for problem solving when differences arise. The responsibilities described should include the qualifications of aides, the maximum time from the request for an aide to the aide's first visit to the client, and the plan for quality assurance, including how supervision standards will be met. Frequently, one of the advantages of contracting for "hands-on care" is the availability of a registered nurse to assist with clients' assessments and to provide supervision to the aides.

COORDINATED ASSESSMENT

Clients with complex mental or physical health problems may benefit from team assessment. Physical health assessment by a registered nurse is generally required for Medicaid in-home and personal care service and other high-risk clients. Team assessments may be equally useful (although harder to fund) for some other clients. Team members need not necessarily visit the client at the same time. However, to be effective, they must function as a team. This means that they must clarify their separate roles and share both information and their separate professional judgments. When assessment is viewed in a limited way (for example, as a bureaucratic process to be completed rather than as a tool for excellence), the social worker may be tempted to view the contribution of the registered nurse as just sharing the paperwork (and later the supervision of in-home aides), and no real team effort will develop. Similarly, there will be no team if the nurse does not understand and respect the unique contribution of the social worker to the client's well-being. In some cases this may mean that the social worker will need to educate the nurse about the value of the social work function.

To work fully, a multidisciplinary team needs commitment from adult services and other participating agencies (Chafetz, West, & Ebbs, 1987) and good team leadership. This leadership may or may not fall to the social worker. If the social worker is the team leader, he or she will need to communicate well, be proficient at problem solving and stimulate others to do so, understand and be adept in managing group and personal dynamics, and manage the organizational development of the team itself (Balber, 1989). Even if the social worker is not the team leader for specific cases, he or she has important responsibilities, including respecting the differing views of others, keeping discussion of differences open, being able to use all the information gathered from team members, and keeping team goals (such as the welfare of the client) as the first priority. Recognizing the different skills that team members bring to the task and communicating clearly without unnecessary professional jargon also will improve the team (Balber, 1989).

Even when an assessment team is not used, the effective social worker will often use information from other professionals—reading and synthesizing reports from health and mental health providers, discussing the case informally with them, and referring clients to them for specialized evaluation. The latter is especially important when dealing with potentially reversible problems like undiagnosed confusion or urinary incontinence. Early diagnosis and treatment may make the difference between home care and placement and allow functional improvement that will eventually make formal services unnecessary.

COORDINATED IMPLEMENTATION

Because in-home clients often need a variety of services to remain in their homes (for example, durable medical equipment, home repair or renovation, meals, telephone alert, occupational therapy, outpatient mental health services, physical therapy, medical transportation, friendly visiting or caregiver respite, skilled nursing, and other in-home aide and social work services), most in-home social workers will develop care plans that depend in part on services from other agencies. This will likely mean that the social worker must coordinate the activities of different agencies working independently to serve the client. How effective the social worker is may depend on his or her ability to develop informal working relationships with professionals in other agencies, but for standardizing procedures and for coping with widespread problems, the adult services agency also must build formal relationships with other providers through contracts, letters of understanding, and other mechanisms.

COORDINATED MONITORING

In many cases, adult services social workers are overseeing the delivery of one set of services while another agency is providing services simultaneously but independently. When this happens, adult services social workers cannot "monitor" the services of the other agency directly. Still, excellent social workers do notify the other agency of any observed problem with the quality of the service. Tact and previously negotiated procedures will help to prevent concerned workers from appearing to be interfering or officious. However, if a client's life, health, or well-being are compromised, the client must be placed above social niceties.

When social workers acting as case managers have contracted for services to be delivered to their clients, they may have two overlapping but conceptually distinct monitoring tasks to perform: (1) monitoring the contract and (2) monitoring service quality. Monitoring the contract consists of seeing that the agency is providing the number of service hours at the price, level of skill, and times (including backup when regularly scheduled aides are not available) specified. This function may be performed by a supervisor or may be assigned to a social worker. Unless the contracting agency is overtly fraudulent, which the social worker or supervisor will have tried to avoid by careful screening of the agency, this kind of monitoring can be handled by visiting the agency and reviewing client, staff, and fiscal records.

The bulk of monitoring for the quality of services is usually the responsibility of the provider (contract) agency. For example, if adult services contracts with a home health agency to provide in-home aide services, a nurse, social worker, or aide supervisor in that home health agency has principal responsibility for seeing that the aides are performing their assigned tasks correctly. However, the adult services social worker should look for signs of quality during the course of home visits. Is the service meeting the social worker's and the client's expectations? In addition, adult services social workers need to ask themselves the same questions about the services they contract for as for the services that adult services provides: Is this service helping the client to reach his or her goals? Would another service or approach be more effective? Are any changes needed in the way the service is provided?

Working with Paraprofessionals

One of the distinctive features about in-home services social work is the necessity of working closely with aides, who often develop close personal and professional relationships with their clients. Aides may be supervised by the in-home services social worker providing case management, or they may have a team relationship with the social worker but be supervised by someone else in the adult services program or by the contract agency. Developing a strong working relationship between the aide and the social worker and negotiating the other relationships that affect communication can be a challenge to the agency and to the individuals involved. This section covers several aspects of working with in-home aides—supervision and the team relationship, aides' competence and supportive training, problem solving, preventive planning, and the aides' relationships with clients.

SUPERVISION AND THE TEAM RELATIONSHIP

Good supervision of in-home aides fulfills several functions: preparing aides for new clients, monitoring the quality of their work, providing them with information and emotional backup when crises arise, coordinating the requests of several professionals into a coherent work plan, and building on aides' observations to understand the needs of clients. Whether the adult services social worker or supervisor directly supervises aides or works with a contract agency, it is vital to see that all of these functions are fulfilled. One good approach is to include in-home aides as part of the service team.

Moore (1988) wrote, "Even well-trained aides need information about the specific problems of a new client. For instance, while they should have been taught in general about cancer, they need to know how it affects their client and the particular care required in this case" (p. 248). If clients have problems that are likely to result in confusing, annoying, or alarming behavior, the aide needs to be particularly prepared, not only to anticipate the problems but armed with some suggestions about what are and are not effective and acceptable ways to respond to them.

Monitoring the quality of the aide's work may not seem conducive to a team relationship, but it can be so. If it is understood that every team member's work is subject to review (the social worker's by an adult services supervisor, the registered nurse's by a nursing supervisor, and the supervisor's by other administrative personnel) and if this review is given constructively as a basis on which team members can enrich the lives of their clients, it will seem less like policing or "checking up on" the aide. Research showed that, in general, in-home workers perceive supervision as support, and they would like as much or more supervision than they receive (Gilbert, 1988; Haslanger, 1990; Roberts & Sarvela, 1990).

Although in some situations the aide will not be able to contact the supervisor from the client's home, telephone backup—someone to field questions and give reassurance—is an important and required part of supervision. This reliance should be encouraged. Smith (1990) wrote

> We have all seen situations in which home care workers will often shy away from calling their agencies with a problem for fear they will be seen as incapable of carrying out their functions. The message given, be it spoken or not, is "whatever the problem is, handle it." . . . Unfortunately, these workers come to feel isolated and fearful of reaching out to the one place where support should be available for them. (p. 57)

It is equally important that when aides are forced to make a difficult decision on their own, they are given emotional and administrative support for doing so, even if the team decides to deal with similar situations differently in the future.

Support also may be needed in ensuring the safety of the aide. Most of the literature has emphasized the danger of clients being abused or neglected, but Chichin (1991) pointed out that aides face a small but serious danger of verbal, physical, and sexual abuse from clients or their family members. Most aides with any work history can easily give concrete examples from their or other's experience.

Another problem for aides can be receiving different, and sometimes conflicting, instructions from several professionals providing services to the same client. Involving the aide as a member of the team may reduce this potential problem. Nevertheless, the aide's supervisor needs to be able to help translate the concerns of different team members into one clear, coherent picture of the services that the client needs. The team functions best when the aide contributes to the plan rather than merely being expected to execute it.

Including the input from an observant aide in the service plan is one of many contributions the social worker can make to support the client and value the aide better. By the nature of his or her work, the aide sees the client several times each week. The worker is on hand to cheer progress toward a goal, to observe and report changes in any area affecting the client's functioning, and to help the professional staff have a fuller understanding of the client. Part of the social worker's role is to support the aide in the positive things he or she is doing with the client.

AIDES' COMPETENCE AND SUPPORTIVE TRAINING

North Carolina has moved to a new approach to ensure that in-home aides are prepared with the skills and knowledge they will need to perform their jobs and work effectively with clients. The approach gives supervising agencies the responsibility to ensure that each aide is competent to perform the tasks appropriate to the level of service to which he or she is assigned. To carry out the competency-based approach, an appropriate professional observes the aide perform specific knowledge- and skill-based tasks and documents his or her correct completion of them. The tasks for each level of in-home aide services (I through IV) are well identified, and specific protocols for carrying them out are being developed for agencies to use in both preparing aides and competency testing.

Although some aides may have developed competencies through previous experience and learning opportunities, others may need supportive training before they can pass a competency test or review of their skills. The employing agency is responsible for directly or indirectly providing this training. Whether preparing its own training or selecting an agency to provide such training, adult services programs need to think about the most effective training styles. Classes that use creative techniques and hands-on experience but do not skimp on content will be most effective with this group. In addition, some preparation for competency tests is not amiss. However, the adult services social worker or supervisor who selects a training organization should be aware of the difference between training to be a good aide and training to pass the test. When the aide is in a client's home, sometimes without a telephone, a solid core of knowledge about the client's condition, possible behavioral problems, and danger signals to watch for is essential.

Although the primary purpose of training is to prepare the aide to perform his or her work adequately, research indicates that good training has other benefits as well. Workers are less likely to report loneliness, a major occupational hazard of in-home aide work, if they feel that they have been adequately trained for the job (Feldman, Sapienza, & Kane, 1990; Haslanger, 1990).

PROBLEM SOLVING AND CHANGE

Just as good social workers must be creative in helping clients solve problems and bringing about change, they also must be able to help the aides under their supervision solve problems. Absenteeism and tardiness of workers, which can create so many difficulties for clients and social workers alike, often stem from the aides' personal situations. Often they must be supported, enabled, and empowered to do their jobs correctly and reliably. Canalis (1989) suggested six problems that lead to absenteeism among workers:

1. The lack of benefits and poor salary leads aides to work more than one job or for more than one agency. This in turn causes conflicts in scheduling and no-shows.
2. Personal and family problems lead to lost job time and can interfere with job performance.
3. Lack of reliable transportation leads to absenteeism or tardiness.
4. Lack of a sense of commitment or responsibility can mean that workers do not place a high priority on showing up at the expected time.
5. Burnout affects both reliability and job performance.
6. Child care problems lead to lost time.

A skilled social worker will try to build a relationship that permits the aide to share these problems, and the social worker will work with the aide to find other resources and solutions before a crisis arises. This supports the client, but it also enables and empowers the aide.

PREVENTIVE PLANNING

Even the best problem solving cannot prevent occasional times when the aide cannot perform the expected services at the expected time—for example, in cases of illness, bad weather, or death in the family. For these situations, the social worker, client and family, and aide need to develop a contingency plan. In some cases, all might decide that the client can function well enough to simply miss one or two days of service. In others, the family might provide a rotating list of friends and relatives who are willing to provide some care to the client when the aide is prevented from coming. For still others, there needs to be backup coverage from the agency, even if it means temporarily cutting the hours of another client with better resources or ability to function.

Other situations for which preventive plans need to be made with the aide and client include medical emergencies (who should the aide call), fire (evacuation plan), and a plan for the aide if he or she finds herself in a potentially dangerous situation. The aide should have a copy of these contingency plans, but a copy also should be included in the client's record so it can be consulted quickly and easily by anyone who has to deal with the problems in the social worker's absence.

IN-HOME AIDE'S RELATIONSHIP WITH THE CLIENT

The relationship between the in-home aide and the client requires a delicate balance, perhaps even more difficult to maintain than that between social worker and client. A certain sense of intimacy is almost unavoidable, especially if the aide is involved in providing personal care. In fact the opportunity to develop close personal relationships is one of the most attractive and rewarding parts of the job (Chichin, 1992). Lonely clients in particular may begin to think of their aides as friends or even members of the family. Kaye (1986) found that "even the most concrete of home-delivered services are powerfully colored by client expectations for non-instrumental (i.e., affective/emotional) forms of aid" (p. 41), a conclusion that experienced in-home services social workers can validate.

A close relationship between aide and client has positive benefits. It contributes to the client's satisfaction and, in at least one study, was found to be related to job satisfaction for workers as well (Cantor, 1988). Furthermore, the aide who feels a personal bond to the client may be more dependable and may give more conscientious care. However, Eustis and Fisher (1991) pointed out dangers for both aides and clients when their relationships become too personal. Table 14-2 is based on their list, with some additions from North Carolina social workers and supervisors with whom the issue was discussed.

Researchers have not presented useful advice about dealing with these hazards. Eustis and Fisher (1991) wrote

> *The policy implications of linking relationships and quality of care are unclear. How can interpersonal relationships between home care workers and clients be either monitored or regulated? . . . One can argue that a functional and pleasant relationship is a necessary component of accomplishing personal assistance in order for tasks to be performed. But inevitably the cost must be considered. Can socializing be distinguished from a functional and pleasant relationship? Is training for intimate, but bounded, relationships a reimbursable cost?* (p. 455)

The social worker may help teach the aide some of the guidelines about the professional caregiving relationship described in chapters 6 and 7. A strong relationship with the agency staff (social worker, nurse–supervisor, and peers) may help the aide put his or her relationship with the client into perspective. It can also give the support needed to set appropriate limits with the client.

Caseload Size: A Barrier to Excellence

Caseload size is frequently identified as a barrier to quality services. Caseload sizes will vary from state to state and community to community within a state. The data from a 1988 study of adult services social workers in North Carolina (Center for Aging Research and Educational Services, 1990) showed that those social workers with primary responsibility for in-home services, Medicaid waiver, or both averaged larger caseloads than other social workers (59 versus 51 cases per worker), despite a conscientious attempt to give no one worker more than 25 to 30 Medicaid Community Alternatives Program for Disabled Adults (CAP/DA) cases. This average is pretty much in line with the standard of around 60, established as a ceiling for caseloads in other states. However, one-fourth of North Carolina's in-home and CAP/DA social workers had caseloads of 77 or greater, and 5 percent had 108 or more cases. Adult services in-home social work is a demanding and complex job. Reasonable caseloads certainly play a role in determining the quality of such services.

As the demand for in-home services grows for both older and younger adults with disabilities, there will be increasing pressure to respond to that need. Increasingly the response will assume a disability-specific rather than an age-specific approach to service provision (Simon-Rusinowitz & Hofland, 1993). Adult

Table 14-2

POTENTIAL HAZARDS OF THE RELATIONSHIP BETWEEN THE IN-HOME AIDE AND THE CLIENT

For Aides

- Aides may be financially or emotionally exploited if the client and they themselves begin to feel that they have a duty to help beyond the services they are paid to deliver.
- Research by White (1986) suggested that aides may burn out faster than more detached workers.
- Aides may become inappropriately involved in clients' family situations (for example, telling the client's children what they ought to be doing for the client).
- Aides may focus their work around pleasing the client rather than carrying out the plan of care, which may interfere with the client's accomplishing his or her goals (for example, giving inappropriate foods to a client with diabetes or doing tasks for the client rather than assisting the client to do as much as he or she can).
- Aides may be coaxed by the client or family members to do tasks that are beyond their technical capability. This could endanger the client and make both the aide and the agency liable in the event of mishaps.

For Clients

- Clients may be hesitant to voice their needs or be critical of less-than-adequate care because of their feelings about the asymmetry of the relationship—their discomfort because the aide does more for them than they do for the aide. ("It is so nice of her to do all of this for me, I shouldn't complain.")
- Clients may become overly dependent on the aide. For example, they may rely on the aide to perform tasks they could do for themselves or that family members have agreed to do.
- Clients may feel abandoned or betrayed when the aide moves on to another assignment and no longer visits.

Adapted from Eustis, N. N., & Fischer, L. R. (1991). Relationships between home care clients and their workers: Implications for quality of care. *Gerontologist, 31*(4), 447–456.

services programs, unlike most aging network programs, have historically taken a broad and inclusive approach to addressing the in-home service needs of younger and older adults with disabilities—those with developmental disabilities and AIDS as well as those suffering from chronic health problems associated with advancing years. Adult services programs are in a good position to meet these and other challenges in the coming years.

Key Points

Excellent adult services social workers

- balance two seemingly opposite and sometimes overtly conflicting ideas: (1) the goal of supporting, enabling, and empowering the individual client and (2) the need to recognize and support the entire family system
- use the family assessment and change method to assess the client and family; identify areas for change and set goals with them; and plan, implement, monitor, and evaluate the in-home services and activities appropriate for the client
- pay special attention to assessing clients' physical and social environment, because this is both the place where they receive care and services and the work environment for in-home aides and family caregivers
- have a structured service plan that includes all that is necessary to provide for the client's needs at home; this is not limited to services provided by in-home aides but includes other formal services, informal caregiving, and self-care
- accept the primary responsibility for ensuring that the client is receiving quality services
- support the client, the family, and the in-home aide when services are terminated owing to the client's functional improvement or placement and support the family and the aide in the event of the client's death
- coordinate in-home services with other areas of the adult services program, especially the units that handle Medicaid eligibility, APS, and placement services
- work effectively with management, other professional staff (for example, registered nurses), and in-home aides from other agencies, as well as adult services staff members
- build relationships with the aides that permit them to work effectively to deal with problems in their own circumstances that keep them from performing optimally
- work with the client, family, and in-home aide to develop contingency plans for emergencies
- help the aide understand the helping relationship and set limits when the client or family makes inappropriate demands.

Excellent adult services managers

- have clear-cut procedures for identifying emergencies and providing short-term emergency services
- help inform, lead, and support social workers through the practical, ethical, legal, and safety issues that arise when clients need services in potentially dangerous home environments
- use case "staffings" to improve communications between units that have overlapping services, as well as to get fresh viewpoints in problem solving
- support an approach that includes the in-home aide as part of the professional service team

- acknowledge the importance of supervision for in-home aides and give adequate time for and professional recognition to this activity
- recognize that training and testing styles that might be effective for social workers and supervisors may not be appropriate for aides.

Excellent leaders
- develop and find ways to implement workload standards that enable in-home social workers to give excellent service to clients in their homes
- promote the development of sufficient human resources, particularly for aides and social workers, to address the growing need for in-home services in the community.

References

American Association of Retired Persons. (1982). *A handbook about care in the home: Information on home health services.* Washington, DC: Author.

Applebaum, R., & Phillips, P. (1990). Assuring the quality of in-home care: The "other" challenge for long-term care. *Gerontologist, 30*(4), 444–450.

Balber, P. (1989). Interdisciplinary teams. *North Carolina CARES, 1*(1), 3–5.

Benjamin, A. E. (1993). An historical perspective on home care policy. *Milbank Quarterly, 71*(1), 129–166.

Canalis, D. M. (1989). Homemaker–home health aide interruption of services: Methods of prevention and control. *Caring, 8*(9), 52–55.

Cantor, M. (1988, November). *Factors related to strain among home care workers: A comparison of formal and informal caregivers.* Paper presented at the 41st Annual Scientific Meeting of the Gerontological Society of America, San Francisco.

Center for Aging Research and Educational Services. (1990). *Adult services manpower in county departments of social services. Executive summary and full report* (Prepared for the Adult and Family Services Branch of the Division of Social Services and the North Carolina Division of Human Resources). Chapel Hill, NC: Author.

Chafetz, P., West, H., & Ebbs, E. (1987). Overcoming obstacles in cooperation in interdisciplinary long term care teams. *Journal of Gerontological Social Work, 11* (3/4), 131–140.

Chichin, E. R. (1991). The treatment of paraprofessional workers in the home. *PRIDE Institute Journal of Long Term Home Health Care, 10*(1), 26–34.

Chichin, E. R. (1992). Home care is where the heart is: The role of interpersonal relationships in paraprofessional home care. *Home Health Services Quarterly, 13* (1/2), 161–177.

Eustis, N. N., & Fisher, L. R. (1991). Relationships between home care clients and their workers: Implications for quality of care. *Gerontologist, 31*(4), 447–456.

Feldman, P. H., Sapienza, A. M., & Kane, N. M. (1990). *Who cares for them? Workers in the home care industry.* New York: Greenwood Press.

Gilbert, N. J. (1988, November). A study of homemaker–home health aides' perceptions of the work environment. *Caring,* pp. 69–72.

Haslanger, K. (1990). Issues in providing home care services to the protective services population. *PRIDE Institute Journal of Long Term Home Health Care, 9*(2), 31–34.

Kaye, L. W. (1986). Worker views of the intensity of affective expression during the delivery of home care services for the elderly. *Home Health Care Services Quarterly, 7*(2), 41–54.

Kramer, A. M., Shaughnessy, P. W., Bauman, M. K., & Crisler, K. S. (1990). Assessing and assuring the quality of home health care: A conceptual framework. *Milbank Quarterly, 68*(3), 413–443.

Moore, F. M. (1988). *Homemaker–home health aide services: Policies and practices.* Owings Mills, MD: National Health Publishing.

Roberts, D. N., & Sarvela, P. D. (1990). Community care workers in rural southern Illinois: Job satisfaction and implications for employee retention. *Home Health Care Services Quarterly, 10*(3/4), 93–115.

Simon-Rusinowitz, L., & Hofland, B. F. (1993). Adopting a disability approach to home care services for older adults. *Gerontologist, 33*(2), 159–167.

Smith, G. M. (1990). Training aides in caring for persons with dementia. *PRIDE Institute Journal of Long Term Home Health Care, 9*(2), 57–59.

Social Security Act Amendments of 1974. P.L. 93-647, 88 Stat. 2337.

U.S. Department of Health, Education, and Welfare. (1976). *Home health care: Report on the regional public hearings of the Department of Health, Education, and Welfare* (DHEW Publication no. 76-135). Washington, DC: U.S. Government Printing Office.

White, W. L. (1986). *Incest in the organizational family: The ecology of burnout in closed systems.* Bloomington, IL: Lighthouse Training Institute.

CHAPTER 15

Placement

DENNIS W. STREETS

Placement services are designed to assist adults whose impaired functioning makes it necessary for them to move from their current living arrangements—often their own homes—into substitute residences for care and supervision. The adult services social worker who is concerned with the support and empowerment of clients in need of placement has a delicate and important task. Placement is about determining the goodness of fit between clients with disabilities, their environment, and their entire support network as they become more dependent. At a particular point determined by individual and family circumstances, lack of goodness of fit may call for placement in a residential setting, as individual dependencies change in type and intensity (Heumann & Boldy, 1993).

The decision to enter a substitute home, residential health facility, or institutional care setting may represent a serious threat to the client's autonomy. It also will have consequences for the client's family, because placement can be one of life's most difficult decisions. By conceptualizing placement as a dynamic element in a continuum of community support ranging from in-home to skilled residential care and by ensuring continued linkages to family and community networks, the individual can have maximum sense of choice, control, and dignity (Evashwick, 1993).

Because placement produces a major disruption in the lives of clients and their families, there is a growing emphasis in the delivery of public services to discourage placement until it becomes the service plan of choice or necessity (Leutz, Abrahams, & Capitman, 1993). An overriding goal for adult services social workers is to support clients' efforts to remain in their homes for as long as they wish and are able to do so. This translates into doing everything possible to avoid unnecessary or premature placement by strengthening informal caregiving and providing home and community care (Hennessy, 1993).

Not all adults with disabilities can safely remain in their homes or other community settings that provide less than around-the-clock care. Placement in a board-and-care home, nursing facility, rehabilitative hospital, or other group or health care setting is the necessary or desired choice for some. The need for placement services will become more pressing, because people are surviving longer—both younger people with disabilities that previously might have ended their lives early and adults generally, who are living to ages when disabilities are more common.

Agencies may have considerable latitude in determining the scope of placement services—from information and referral to using the family assessment and change method to help clients make this difficult decision and planning other activities to ease the transition. Similarly, agencies may have differing guidelines about eligibility for this service. In North Carolina, county departments of social services are mandated to provide placement services without regard to the means of the client. Services, however, vary from county to county based on county resources and local demand. In other states, placement services may be offered by public agencies only as part of adult protective services (APS). Some additional roles the agency may assume are discussed at the end of this chapter.

How the agency defines its mission and target population determines how social workers provide the service. This chapter reviews placement as an intensive social service from the perspective of the family assessment and change method, rather than as a service that is principally information and referral, using case illustrations to demonstrate the phases of the process and the variety of situations social workers may encounter.

Overview and Case Illustrations

In the past when home and community care services were less available, social workers faced with frail older people, younger adults with disabilities, or people discharged from a state facility moved quickly to put them in group care or institutional settings. This could be why the service came to be named *placement,* a term that connotes a somewhat passive role for the client, who was put in a particular place. The definition of placement found in the third edition of *The Social Work Dictionary* (Barker, 1995) suggests that this is a common view of the service: "Social workers use the term mostly to indicate the assignment of a child or dependent adult to a facility or person who can provide for their needs" (p. 283). Fortunately, there appears to be a growing opportunity to make this care decision using a thoughtful approach based on family assessment, which involves both the person immediately affected and the family.

Placement can occur for a number of reasons. Social workers in adult services find two common scenarios. The first might involve a client already in a group care or an institutional setting who requires transfer to another care setting because of a change in functioning, a payment matter, a serious episode of unacceptable behavior, the stated preference of the client or family, or some similar reason. These situations include transfer from a board-and-care home to a nursing facility and occasionally the reverse; discharge from or entry into state psychiatric hospitals and in-state or out-of-state rehabilitative–specialty hospitals; or transfer among nursing or treatment facilities or board-and-care homes.

A situation related to the first scenario occurs when the client has been residing in a substitute home or facility and returns to live at home or elsewhere in the community. This may be consistent with a planned rehabilitation or made possible by an unexpected improvement in functioning or change in the support system available to the client. It also may result from a change of mind by the client or the family.

The second scenario involves clients residing in the community who reach a point where home and community care are no longer adequate, as determined not only by the functioning of clients but also by the pool of informal and formal caregiving that can be assembled. In a study of long-term-care admissions, Kraus et al. (1976) reported that the reason for applying for placement mentioned most frequently was excessive caregiving burden on family members.

Although placement from the community ideally would occur as a planned transition based on the client's anticipated needs, more frequently this second scenario takes place as part of a situation perceived to be urgent, perhaps even as a result of an APS evaluation. A call for assistance may come from a panicked family member or neighbor or from a hospital social worker seeking assistance in placing a patient for short-term rehabilitative or palliative care or for long-term care of chronic conditions.

The following three cases illustrate a few of the types of clients and situations that come to the attention of the social worker involved with placement.

CASE EXAMPLE 1

Mr. S has been a resident of a state psychiatric hospital for three years. He is 39 years old and has the dual diagnosis of developmental disabilities and chronic mental illness. He entered the hospital after an acute episode when he became overly aggressive in a board-and-care home. The hospital contacted the adult services program nearly 13 months before, requesting assistance in placing him again in a board-and-care facility. Adult services has had an open case since that time but has been unsuccessful in finding placement options. Two reasons frequently given by management of homes for their reluctance to consider Mr. S are his history of aggressive behavior and the fear that the psychiatric hospital would not consider recommitting him if he needed it. His sister is eager to have him return to a facility closer to her home, but she cannot care for him by herself.

CASE EXAMPLE 2

Mrs. J, who is 89 years old, has been living independently. Her granddaughter, who lives out of state, visited her recently and is concerned about Mrs. J's physical and mental state. She reports to adult services that her grandmother can do little for herself and probably needs to be placed in an institution. The granddaughter must return to her home in several days and wants to finalize arrangements for Mrs. J before she leaves.

CASE EXAMPLE 3

Adult services has been providing in-home services to Mrs. T for eight months. She is 59 years old. The last two reassessments have revealed that these services are no longer sufficient to support her continued stay in her home, especially because she is unattended most nights. She has severe diabetes and has had a foot amputated; she also has a chronic heart condition. She refuses even to discuss moving from her home and seems adamant about not moving to "one of those places." Her family and neighbors have contributed significantly to her being able to remain at home this long.

Although certainly not illustrative of all cases that come to the placement worker's attention, these three examples do provide some notion of what makes this field of practice so challenging. They will be used later in this chapter to alert the practitioner to potential pitfalls as well as to potential opportunities. Before looking at practice situations and implications, it is essential to back up and reconsider the general purpose and scope of the placement service and the principles that underlie it. Many of these principles have to do with the relationship of workers with clients and their families.

Purpose, Principles, and Scope

PURPOSE

The placement service involves more than merely moving an adult with disabilities from one place to another. Mr. S, Mrs. J, and Mrs. T are all reportedly in need of residences that will provide appropriate care and supervision. Decisions made with each of them regarding placement will have a major effect on their lives. These decisions should be reached only after careful consideration of their preferences and circumstances and after thoughtfully weighing alternatives. That is why adult services has a special responsibility for understanding the complexity of the role the social worker must assume in assisting with the placement decision.

Placement activities include completing a functional assessment to determine what needs cannot be met currently in the client's environment. If placement becomes part of a service plan that matches the client's and family's goals, the assessment information is used to determine what needs the new environment must meet to provide an optimum setting. The worker provides assistance in locating and securing admission to a setting and level of care that best matches the client's goals. Finally, because placement can generate strong emotional reactions, the worker's next task is supporting the individual and family in this transition.

PRINCIPLES

Some of the more important underlying principles for an effective placement service are that social workers

- encourage clients to participate to the extent of their abilities in making decisions about their care
- solicit and support the participation and assistance of the client's family and friends
- assist clients to remain in their residences so long as their condition warrants and they want to do so
- help and encourage clients to return to the least restrictive living arrangement whenever possible and as soon as appropriate
- respect the client's right to refuse services.

To be effective in assisting with placement, social workers must understand the purpose and scope of the service, seeing its potential as well as its boundaries. They recognize the importance of planned interaction with clients and their families, so as to identify and provide what assistance is needed in terms of case management and counseling.

SCOPE

The social worker's perspective will naturally be affected by the nature of the relationship with the client before placement. For the worker who has had a history with the client that includes arranging for home and community care, placement may be more easily seen as the logical next step when home care is no longer an adequate service plan. On the other hand, the social worker who is newly assigned a case for placement must be assured that alternate care options have been explored. Use of the family assessment and change method will help the worker support and empower clients and their families to make informed decisions.

Using the Family Assessment and Change Method

Essential to providing assistance with placement is the understanding of its beginning and ending points and the realization that it involves a combination of tasks—assessment, case management, and counseling. Within the context of the family assessment and change method, the process of assisting clients begins with intake and establishing a rapport with the client and family. It continues with determining from the intake and screening whether an emergency situation exists that must be addressed first. To help the client and family determine their options, the worker conducts a comprehensive functional assessment to examine the strengths, needs, and preferences of the client and family. The assessment is the starting point for determining the need for initial or continued placement and, if placement is appropriate, the assistance and resources needed (Hennessy, 1993; Leutz et al., 1993). Here, too, the careful assessment of the client's functioning can help clarify whether placement is the best possible service plan. The interaction between the client's need for assistance and the strengths and resources available may make clear that those needs cannot be met in the client's current setting. The thoroughness of this evaluation can support the client and family in making this decision. The needs themselves help in determining what qualities the new setting must have to help the client maintain or restore functioning to the degree possible.

Once the client and family make the decision to seek placement, they may need help in arranging it (case management) and in coping with the prospect of this dramatic change in their lives (counseling). After the client has entered the new living arrangement, the social worker monitors the progress of both the client and family in adjusting to the situation, as well as whether the move to the new setting is meeting the client's need for functional support. The case is closed when adjustment to the placement seems satisfactory and lasting from the perspective of the client, family, facility, and social worker, and when the client's functional goals are being pursued effectively.

Stages in the Placement Process

Against the backdrop of the normal activities of the family assessment and change method, placement activities take place in three stages: (1) preplacement, (2) placement, and (3) postplacement.

PREPLACEMENT STAGE

During preplacement, the worker conducts a comprehensive functional assessment with the client and family to determine what needs changing, to set goals, and to establish an appropriate service plan. At this stage, the social worker offers supportive counseling, assistance with the beginning steps of working through the application and eligibility requirements, and relief of more-immediate problems whose resolution cannot wait for placement.

Careful assessment of the client's functioning in each of the domains—social resources, physical environment, financial situation, physical health and medical needs, mental health, and ability to perform activities of daily living (ADLs) and instrumental activities of daily living (IADLs)—is critical to the provision of placement services. The identification of the preferences, attitudes, and apprehensions of both client and family also have a high priority. Another aspect of the assessment is a study of what community resources, both formal and informal, the client and family have used up to this time and how these resources have met or have failed to meet the client's and family's needs. This includes examining what assistance the family has provided and what it can or cannot continue to provide. The worker is identifying strengths and resources, as well as weaknesses and needs, to be able to engage in a frank discussion with the client and family and subsequently with potential care providers.

The worker's initial contact with the client and family is critical. First impressions can facilitate or inhibit subsequent interaction. Clients and families may struggle with some of the socially distressing or embarrassing issues that have lead to considering placement (Bumagin & Hirn, 1990). Incontinence, wandering, sexually inappropriate behavior, and the onset of dementia are issues that families and clients may try to conceal until they are compelled to face them. For caregivers, the acknowledgment that they can no longer carry the responsibility themselves also may be seen as an admission of failure.

This discussion identifies the problems that the client and family are experiencing and what desired state the client hopes to regain or achieve. In the case of Mr. S, he has presumably reached a point where continued treatment in a controlled psychiatric setting is no longer necessary or valuable. The social worker's obligation to him rests in ensuring that any move made to another care level or setting is based on an informed assessment that involves him and his family.

Effective goals go beyond merely finding a new place to live by addressing the specific functional needs of the client. They might include enhancing the client's ability to perform certain ADLs, improved nutritional status, greater socialization, or a better relationship between the client and family. With goals in mind, the client, family, and worker can then consider options. Although the process should begin with the preferences and potential of clients for remaining in their current living arrangement (when this is the stated desire), the worker has an obligation to introduce the entire range of options. This includes residential and institutional care, which may become appropriate in even the most favorable situations as the client's level of functioning and available resources change.

It also is essential that the social worker respect the client's and family's right to be informed about and decide among care options. Unless the social worker is sensitive to this important issue, the feelings and ideas of Mrs. J, as well as those of the rest of her extended family, could well be overlooked in responding to her granddaughter's sense of urgency. The granddaughter may be right in her evaluation of the situation, but her haste to resolve it cannot be allowed to short-circuit the assessment that may determine some other more suitable alternative. The social worker must slow the pace to ensure Mrs. J's involvement, while trying to sustain and direct the granddaughter's positive interest. Some clients and families will be able to resolve their problems without substantial assistance, whereas others may require considerable time and attention.

Mrs. T is not unusual in her resistance to and apprehension about placement; clients rarely choose placement in a group care setting. Some hold negative views toward long-term-care settings, but the larger issue simply rests on having to leave one's home. Any change is difficult, and this is especially so when all aspects of one's life are altered by a change as dramatic as that of placement. One result of this reluctance, real or assumed, is that placement decisions are often made for and despite the client. This can make it even more difficult for the client to accept the new living arrangement.

Typically, the applicant for placement services is a family member or another agency. It may not be surprising that clients do not often initiate the request for assistance, but this makes it incumbent on the social worker to involve the client in all stages of carrying out the service. Experience in other settings, however, shows that this does not readily happen. Kraus and colleagues (1976) found that applicants for long-term institutional care were involved "very little or not at all" in over 46 percent of the cases. Only part of this could be explained because the person was too confused or too sick to participate. Although this study is old, there is no reason to believe that today's situation is substantially different.

The challenge to the social worker is to balance the need to act efficiently and expeditiously and yet collaborate with the client and family, who surely will need time to consider options and deal with the emotions that come with this type of life transition. The social worker could find it easier to stay focused on the task of locating a bed rather than on developing and maintaining a relationship with the client and family that contributes to their meaningful participation in the process and their coping with emotions and changes in their lives. Although it can be far more expedient to make decisions for others than to assist them in making decisions for themselves, placement should not be a service where something is done "to" the client but rather one where placement assistance is offered to the client and done "with" the client and family. This difference in perception is vital to establishing an honest and trusting relationship. Providing clients and families with reading materials may be a useful means of educating and providing reassurance about the placement decision.

One excellent reference for families struggling with the decision is *When Love Gets Tough* (Manning, 1983). Another useful resource, the chapter "Helping When They Cannot Manage—The Nursing Home Solution" from *You & Your Aging Parent* (Silverstone & Hyman, 1989), suggests ways for the client and family to consider residential and institutional care in a thoughtful manner, rather than as a crisis or haphazardly. Some of the considerations that Silverstone and Hyman discussed were understanding the kinds of care available, understanding how money determines options, and evaluating quality. These references may also be helpful when the client and family are trying to select among group care facilities.

When conducting comprehensive functional assessments, social workers use other resources within the agency and community to assist in gathering and analyzing information. Some of the most effective social work comes from being aware of one's limits and using other expertise effectively. This expertise may include the home health nurse and in-home aides who have been assisting Mrs. T, or it may be Mrs. J's minister and her personal physician. Physicians have an especially important role in determining who gets placed in care facilities. It is often the client's physician who first suggests application for admission to a long-term-care facility. Kraus and colleagues (1976) discovered that physicians were responsible for this in 49 percent of the cases, compared with clients' children in 18 percent of the cases.

A recent study by the American Association of Retired Persons (AARP, 1991) confirmed that physicians are the primary source of information on long-term care for many older adults and their informal caregivers. The study also found that physicians lack a comprehensive understanding of long-term-care options. That physicians hold such an influential position has important implications, because much of their focus is on assessing physical needs, with less attention to psychosocial factors, and their knowledge of community alternatives varies widely. One recommendation from the AARP study was that the social services and medical communities should improve their communication about placement.

Although much of what is needed to improve this communication is beyond the scope of the individual worker, there are still ways to engage the medical community for the benefit of the client. The worker may communicate directly with the client's physician to introduce possible care options and solicit an opinion on their merit. The worker also may interact with a hospital discharge planner or public health nurse who has direct contact with the physician, and the worker may help the client and family prepare for their discussion with the physician. The physician's prominence in decision making cannot be overlooked, because he or she will be responsible for determining the level of care needed by the client.

The preplacement phase is also when to begin assisting the client and family in negotiating the necessary application and eligibility hurdles, both medical and financial. For example, a requirement for nursing home placement is a preadmission screening and resident review evaluation. Eligibility for Medicaid or other third-party payments also must be determined early. In some sense, these activities can be considered part of the assessment.

Another essential element of preplacement is helping the client and family with needs that must be addressed before or until placement. This help can be either emergency or crisis planning, depending on the severity of the client's needs for assistance. These needs may be material, such as food, clothing, or shelter, or social, emotional, or psychological.

Given that placement can take time, periodic monitoring of the client's situation is important. This should focus on any changes in previously identified strengths and resources and weaknesses and needs, as well as on new issues. The preferences and predisposition of the client and family may change over time. When new problems are identified, follow-up is important. The effective social worker seeks to support and stabilize clients in their often fragile environment. This support may entail helping plan and organize a short-term response using not only formal agency services but also what is available from family, friends, neighbors, the church, and others.

The social worker does this for several reasons: to minimize deterioration in the condition of clients and their families, to demonstrate a commitment to their well-being, and to enhance their capacity to assume more responsibility for decision making. Placement workers guard against creating unrealistic expectations and the accompanying dependency while arranging for relief and supporting progress toward achievement of goals. In the case of Mr. S, the placement worker advocates for him to receive the services and support that will at least maintain if not enhance his functioning and ability to return to the community. This might include strengthening his communication skills, helping him manage situations that cause anger, and helping to find ways to comply with his medication regimen.

PLACEMENT STAGE

The placement stage involves assisting clients and their families through case management and counseling. In the case management function, the worker helps the client and family locate a care facility appropriate to the client's functional goals and make arrangements for the move, including finalizing eligibility for any third-party payments or otherwise arranging payments. The counseling function continues the relationship begun during the preplacement phase: It is designed to support decision making by the client and family and to help in managing the changes that accompany placement. This includes helping the client and family deal with their fears, grief, guilt, conflict, and other emotions.

On the basis of the assessment and growing out of the relationship established with the client and family, the social worker assists them to plan and implement the steps necessary for a successful placement. It is important that early on there is an understanding of expectations for the client, family, and worker relative to the service plan. The plan should include specific objectives that spell out who is to do what and when. This is vital to the communication that must take place for achievement of tasks and for the quality of the relationship. The social worker must be sensitive to balancing the perceived urgency that accompanies many cases with the need to develop and support the decision making of the client and family. Excellent placement workers support clients' central position in decision making.

The activities basic to the placement stage are highlighted below. These are discussed as steps in a placement process because they are generally sequential in nature. Not every client and family will require or desire assistance at every step, but some will. The excellent adult services program can respond to the varying needs of clients and families. Some of these steps are supportive in nature. All seek to empower clients and their families. They involve not only the resources of the social worker and the agency but also the strengths and predisposition of the client and family. They draw on what is available in the community, too. The extent to which a worker engages in these activities will depend on the circumstances of each individual case, but this will also be determined by the latitude and support given the worker by management within the adult services program.

Step 1: Information

The most common request for assistance is probably for information about what residential and institutional care is available in the community. As an information and referral activity, this might be handled at intake without a comprehensive assessment. However, whether the assistance is offered by the intake worker or by the placement worker after an assessment, the local adult services program has several levels of responsibility. First, the program should be prepared to provide basic information about residential and institutional care (for example, differences in levels of care, differences in group care settings, and the varying costs and sources of payment) in easy-to-understand terms.

As with any information made available to educate consumers, it is presented best using a variety of methods. For example, the creative social worker may want to produce a pictorial scrapbook showing local homes and their residents engaged in a variety of activities. This could be a project done in collaboration with area facilities and any local nursing and board-and-care home community advisory committees. As previously suggested, having reading materials available to lend to clients and their families is another means of educating and providing reassurance about the placement decision. One useful reference is the 1989 special issue of *Advances in Research,* a newsletter of Duke University, which presented the article "Selecting a Nursing Home: Some Basic Principles Help" (Gwyther, 1989).

Step 2: Consumer Education

After providing information about possible homes and facilities, social workers can assist clients and their families to be better consumers. They begin by ensuring the presence of functional goals for the client. Armed with clear goals, the client and family can begin comparing facilities where there is a choice. To help in decision making, the social worker may want to furnish a checklist of items for consumers to use in comparing facilities. There are a variety of generic checklists prepared by consumer-oriented organizations. Most of these are targeted for nursing facilities, because there is a more universal understanding and acceptance of what to expect of this type of care setting than there is for board-and-care homes.

AARP (1991) has produced several editions of its consumer guide, *Nursing Home Life: A Guide for Residents and Families.* The purpose of this guide is "to provide information that will be of value to consumers as they search for a nursing home, arrange for admission, make sure the nursing home gets to know them, and adjust to life in the home after admission" (p. 3). The guide's checklist encourages the client and family to examine the home's general physical environment; the general social atmosphere and the attitudes of residents and staff members; the home's attention to the safety of residents; the availability of medical, dental, pharmaceutical, and other health services; the quality of its food service, social services, and recreational program; the availability of transportation; and its costs and provisions for assisting residents in managing funds. Many of these questions would also apply to board-and-care homes. Another important area to assess in comparing homes is their handling of issues concerning clients' rights to a natural death, that is, advance directives.

Clients and their families may ask the placement worker to make a recommendation among the homes with available beds. The effective social worker assists the client and family in identifying their needs and preferences and then matching these with the known strengths and disposition of the homes being considered. Mr. S would probably adjust best in a setting where staff members are well trained in managing difficult behaviors while encouraging maximum development of residents' independent functioning. Should Mrs. J be found to benefit from placement in a board-and-care home, it could be that a smaller home with a familylike atmosphere would be one of the more important factors for her. For the worker to feel comfortable in this role, it is important that the adult services program be clear on what it is willing to have social workers say in presenting information about homes.

Step 3: Visiting Prospective Facilities

The effective social worker emphasizes how important it is for the client and family to visit prospective homes. Kraus and colleagues (1976) found that a large percentage of people being placed had not visited the facility before the day of admission. In pursuing excellent placement services, the agency should encourage workers (as time permits) to visit facilities with clients and their families to assist them in dealing with the natural reactions that come with exposure to any group care or institutional setting and to answer questions. The first visit of the client and family to different types of care settings is probably the most important. Accompanying clients on preadmission visits is especially important for those who have no family support available.

Step 4: Logistical Arrangements

Social workers may have to assist clients and their families or guardians in making arrangements for the move to the group home or facility. The social worker also may need to help with payment arrangements and negotiating services to ensure continuity of care and quality of life (for example, participation in sheltered workshop, transportation to a community church, receipt of physical therapy). The social worker may need to participate in the admission process in some instances. In rare instances, the worker's assistance may involve helping the client shop for needed items and pack belongings, tasks with which an in-home aide or other paraprofessional also may be asked to help. A more challenging level of involvement comes when social workers are asked to assist with questions about the disposition of property and possessions.

Step 5: Preparedness of the Facility

The next important activity the social worker undertakes is helping the personnel of the group care facility prepare for the client. This includes clarifying the client's functional goals and sharing other relevant information about the client, with the client's consent. Selected information gathered from a comprehensive functional assessment can be useful in giving the group care home a perspective on the client's needs, strengths, likes, and idiosyncrasies. This helps establish the client as an individual, which is especially important in a group setting. It may be especially important to Mrs. J that she continue to attend her church. If Mrs. T has a goal of improving her ambulation, this is the time to establish a regimen that will support this desire.

Preparing the home can make a great difference to the success of the placement. For example, it would be helpful to share pertinent information about the history of Mr. S's aggressive behavior—what triggers it and how it is best managed. By assuming this type of honest, facilitative role, the social worker is strengthening a positive relationship with the home. Another aspect of this preparation is working with the home, client, and family to ensure that other necessary supportive services are in place. If Mr. S requires some degree of ongoing mental health treatment, this must be arranged with the area mental health program before admission to ensure continuity of care.

Although social workers should take a helping and instructive role in each of the five steps, their ultimate goal is to empower the client and family to assume as much responsibility as possible for arranging or negotiating placement. For some clients and families, the social worker may need to serve as an advocate for the client with physicians, income maintenance caseworkers, home administrators, and other human services agencies. The worker might have to testify, for example, at an appeals hearing about Medicaid eligibility or appropriateness of level of care.

There are cases where the placement worker has to assume a more direct and supportive function. When the client is unable to participate in decision making, the worker must determine who can appropriately act on the client's behalf. It may be the client's family or a legal guardian. Where the local adult services program serves as guardian, the placement worker will likely be the one to perform most of the case management and related functions. Difficult yet important considerations are when and how family members can be counted on to make decisions for clients with impairments informally and when guardianship must be initiated. When the adult services program has legal authority to act on behalf of the client, the social worker tries to identify the best strategy for the client, using what is known about the client's needs and preferences.

One recognized approach to this is decision making based on substituted judgment (chapter 13). Here the worker tries to learn about how the client would have acted if able. Because this judgment is subjective, it is particularly important for workers to be sensitive to their own values and control their actions. They must have a healthy respect for what it means to be placed outside one's home and community, but they also must be able to recognize and manage any of their own anxieties about placement and acknowledge that in some instances it is the most appropriate service plan. Even when guardianship is necessary, though, the effective social worker still attempts to help the client make as many decisions as possible. If nothing more, it may be which items to take from home to the nursing facility.

Coming to grips with one's attitudes is also important to another of the social worker's roles during the placement phase. Workers must see the need to respond to the affective elements of placement and not just the case management tasks. This means assisting clients and their families to cope with the emotions generated as well as helping them with the concrete duties of locating a facility and making the move.

POSTPLACEMENT STYLE

The third stage, postplacement, is what South Carolina's placement program describes as "follow-along," a term presumably used to emphasize the importance of having the worker continue contact with clients and their families after placement. Follow-along implicitly suggests a higher level and more consistent pattern of involvement than follow-up conveys. Of course, the intensity of the social worker's contact with clients and families will vary on a case-by-case basis. Some factors that may influence adjustment to placement, and thus the adult services worker's role, include the presence of a supportive and empowered family, the client's physical and mental condition, and the occurrence of behavioral disorders.

Some principal goals at this juncture are to ensure that clients are adjusting to the new living arrangement, that they are receiving appropriate care, that they have reasonable opportunities to enjoy normal family and community life, that they are assisted with personal problems, that they receive necessary supportive services available in the community (for example, sheltered workshop), and periodically, to review the continued appropriateness of and need for placement. In the postplacement phase, the social worker begins by assessing the client's and family's adjustment to the changes inherent in placement. Depending on what the social worker learns through contacts with the client and family, he or she may need to assist in a variety of ways.

Two examples when group social work as well as individual casework may be effective involve familiarizing clients and their families with their rights under state law and counseling them to develop better ways of sharing their feelings about the changes affecting their lives. Much of the counseling will probably focus on helping clients and their families deal with such feelings as abandonment, isolation, and guilt (Schneewind, 1990). Working with groups of residents and families allows for efficient use of time and creates a network for information sharing and support that extends beyond what the individual social worker can do.

Other examples of ways the social worker can assist during the postplacement phase is by identifying and securing resources needed to help in the client's adjustment; mediating difficult issues among the client, family, and facility; consulting or arranging for the training of the facility's staff members about the client's special needs (for example, sign language, managing behavioral problems); assisting the client in giving proper discharge notice if leaving the facility or reviewing the home's similar notice to a client; and initiating necessary contacts on the client's behalf (for example, notifying the income maintenance staff member of a pending change in placement or contacting an ombudsman or protective services worker if there is some reason to believe that the client's rights have been violated). For intended short stays (for example, short-term, intensive rehabilitation), the social worker also may want to participate in the facility's discharge planning to help the client return more easily to the community. Many of these activities entail working closely with other professionals.

Although there is no foolproof recipe to ensure a successful postplacement phase, there are some rules of thumb. One source for such information is Silverstone and Hyman (1989). This and other resources can provide helpful hints to assist the new resident and family in adjusting to placement. For example, Silverstone and Hyman warned families against early visits home, because this good intention may only make it more difficult for the person trying to adjust to a new living situation. This is not to say that visits to one's family are never a good thing but that careful thought should be given to the pros and cons of actions and, in particular, about how the resident will be affected. Silverstone and Hyman also encouraged families to be patient in the period of adjustment: "Patience and helpful support can go a long way in helping a resident return to his former self. Jumping the gun, taking drastic measures, insisting that another home would be better and moving him, will only put him under further stress and compound his problems" (p. 229).

Postplacement ends and services are terminated when the client's adjustment appears lasting and the level of care appropriate. This is determined with the direct involvement of the client, family, and facility staff. Service should be terminated in such a way that clients and their families feel comfortable in contacting the social worker or someone else in the adult services agency in the event that circumstances change and a new placement or other social services are needed.

Negotiation of Difficult Practice Issues

Not unlike other practice areas, placement cases can present difficult situations for the social worker. Many cases require the social worker's best counseling and mediation skills. Here are some common challenges.

THE RELUCTANT CLIENT

One of the most complicated cases is illustrated by that of Mrs. T, when the worker perceives that placement is best for the client's safety and physical health, but the client prefers to face all risks at home rather than enter residential or institutional care. This situation often becomes further complicated by distressed family members who feel guilty despite doing more than can be reasonably expected. In such instances, counseling the client and family becomes paramount. Does the client understand the consequences of remaining at home, with limits on what the family can continue to do to assist? Do all involved understand the risks inherent in pushing the unwilling client toward placement?

One role for the placement worker may be providing emotional reassurance and helping the family set limits for their involvement when an adult who is frail or disabled but competent refuses placement. Especially in the absence of family, the social worker also has to set limits. For example, assuming that Mrs. J really does require placement, given her caregiving needs, what would happen if she was adamantly against this plan? In the absence of close family, the social worker would have to be careful in the relationship established with her. The relationship could appropriately include helping arrange formal and informal caregiving support in her home, when possible. It would surely involve examining her reluctance to pursue placement and exploring what might be done to overcome her anxiety without jeopardizing her spirit of independence. She may be fearful of confinement; loss of contact with friends, family, and her church; or loss of access to discretionary income. It is important to recognize that many of Mrs. J's fears about loss of autonomy are legitimate but then to consider with her how she could maximize her continued influence in decisions affecting her well-being if she were to accept placement.

At the same time, the placement worker cannot afford to have Mrs. J believe that he or she can substitute for family either in the emotional or caregiving support that is needed. The social worker explains what the client can reasonably expect and then reinforces this through action. The situation changes, of course, when the client's decision-making ability is severely impaired, requiring the worker's intervention to be more directive.

THE RELUCTANT FACILITY

A different situation is one in which distrust and conflict between institutions or agencies develop and then interfere with a client's chance for placement in a more suitable setting. Mr. S might find himself the victim of such a situation if private board-and-care and nursing facilities are anxious about accepting residents discharged from state psychiatric hospitals. The facilities may be worried not only about Mr. S's condition, but also about the extent to which they can expect assistance with follow-up care or readmission, if necessary. Any mistrust compounds the difficulties in placement of someone with a history of behavioral problems.

Social workers can reduce many barriers to placement case by case. The way in which information about Mr. S is presented to prospective facilities can have a major effect on whether they give him serious consideration. A client-centered approach requires that Mr. S be treated as an individual with assets and liabilities, as all people have, and tries to present him this way to those deciding on admissions at prospective facilities. This approach could be described as helping clients sell themselves in a manner similar to using a resume when in search of employment. To be successful at this, the worker must seek an understanding of the motivation of those within facilities making the admitting decisions.

There are innovative ways to help clients present themselves. The examples that follow would apply regardless of where the client is currently residing, but they may be particularly useful when the person is institutionalized or lives out of the area. One way, identified in a case record from North Carolina, involved use of a videotape of an out-of-state client seeking to return to the state. This introduction served to personalize the placement process. The use of a personalized referral packet containing, for example, personal communication from the client is another approach. Such approaches are not intended to frame information in a way that misleads; in fact, it is critical that information provided be relevant and accurate.

Although well-established and trusting relationships between professionals and innovative approaches can overcome many of the obstacles, agencies can facilitate more-permanent solutions through formal letters of understanding or working agreements. An example of this involves efforts to establish interagency councils. Such councils can foster creative problem solving for difficult service issues surrounding placement. Interagency and interdisciplinary councils are effective tools for ensuring quality placements for difficult cases.

OUT-OF-AREA PLACEMENTS

Although adult services programs recognize the value of supporting a client's positive ties with family and community and strive to arrange placements close to home, this is not always possible. A third challenge for workers rests with out-of-area and out-of-state placements. It is difficult to assess, arrange, manage, and follow-along placements when the nature of the contact with clients and their caretakers is by telephone, fax machine, or mail. Essential to casework in all program areas is the personal relationship the worker establishes with clients and their significant others. The worker must overcome geographic barriers by establishing contacts with people who will assume a substitute role in communicating with the client. This includes having a good relationship with other adult services programs, which may need to perform some of the activities at each phase of the placement.

Geography is not the only barrier to good practice. One of the most difficult barriers to overcome relates to the absence of quality choices, especially for those who are considered less-desirable candidates by private homes and facilities. Factors that can create a barrier include financial status, lack of a responsible party, heavy care demands, and behavioral problems. Workers may have the unsatisfying task of helping the client and family arrange for admission to a facility that cannot optimally meet the person's needs. If this happens, the postplacement phase becomes especially important. For clients generally, and particularly for those who experience difficulty in finding suitable residential or institutional care, workers have a responsibility to join with others to advocate for improved options within the community.

OTHER CHALLENGES

There are more challenges to having an effective placement service, for example, working with families who are in substantial disagreement about what should happen to their older member or younger member with disabilities. The social worker's potential counseling role in such situations is discussed in chapter 7.

The responsibility for placement is likely to vary from one adult services program to another. Because of limited staff resources, placement may be only one of several responsibilities assigned to an adult services social worker. For some of these generalists, placement is just one element of a varied caseload where the worker is arranging in-home services for some clients and evaluating others for protective services, as well as assisting with placement. These workers also may handle guardianship and payee duties as well as other services for people receiving placement services.

In states such as North Carolina, another group of social workers directly involved in placement matters are those who are responsible for monitoring board-and-care homes in addition to their work with individual clients. These workers are not only responsible for assisting clients in finding substitute residential care but also monitoring facilities for compliance with licensure requirements.

Although the assignment to placement workers of monitoring duties can give them firsthand familiarity with the quality of care within these homes, it also can present them and their supervisors with some challenges. The social worker who is assisting a difficult-to-place client may face the reality of asking for a "favor" from a board-and-care home or arranging a placement in a less-than-optimal facility. The worker's task is likely to be complicated when he or she is involved both in placing a client and then monitoring the home providing care to the client.

Agency's Role and the Scope of Services

Local adult services programs can play a vital role in assisting people who desire or require placement, but the intensity of services—from information and referral to active assistance in locating a facility and transferring the client—can vary according to the client's level of risk, local demand, and agency resources. Adult services programs must determine what role they should have relative to what can be expected of local hospitals; the area mental health program; home health agencies; the aging network; and other providers of services to adult clients, including agencies involved in out-of-county placements. These and other challenges, though, can be overcome with the collaboration of management, supervisors, and social workers within the adult services program. Although upper management, supported by the agency board, is responsible for determining the commitment that can be made to the placement service, supervisors normally have latitude to mold how placement fits with other agency programs. Beyond the effective support of individual cases, the agency has other vital roles to play in this service area. At the community level, the agency may decide to involve itself in a range of educational, supportive, advocacy, and planning and development activities.

Educational activities might include production of brochures or guides to inform the public about residential and institutional care. The Texas Department of Health (1992) published an attractive and easy-to-use guide for selecting a personal care facility. Sponsorship of community forums to encourage the public's consideration of long-term-care issues and consumer planning for long-term care is another educational approach. The CHOICES project in Catawba County, North Carolina, is an example of such a community forum designed to inform older adults and their families about existing options for care and supervision. One workshop in the project's 1991 forum for "quality living" included a panel discussion by residents of nursing homes and board-and-care homes to provide the perspective of "those who are there now." Among the forum's cosponsors were the local hospital, the community college, a nursing home, and several businesses. Another natural role for adult services is to help train the volunteers who serve on the local board-and-care and nursing home community advisory committees.

As provider of support, adult services might sponsor and develop mutual assistance groups for families undergoing or contemplating placement and train volunteers to help in visiting residents during the postplacement phase. This presents a great opportunity to apply group social work skills for education and support of clients and families.

In addition to education and support directed toward clients and their families, advocacy is another important facet of an effective placement service. Advocacy can occur through letter-writing campaigns to support legislative initiatives addressing inequities in placement options. It is also evident when the local adult services program helps the area mental health center to negotiate agreements between such parties as the state psychiatric institutions and local facilities to increase opportunities for those clients who typically experience difficulty locating suitable placement. Local advocacy also can target state-level policies and practices that affect the placement service.

Helping the community plan and develop suitable options for out-of-home care is another possible and appropriate role for adult services and its placement workers. In most instances, in-county placements are preferred. Who better than the placement worker to be a part of a community effort to assess the need for and help develop specialized facilities or specialized units within existing facilities— for example, specialized programs for victims of Alzheimer's disease (Sandel & Possidenta, 1993–1994) or specialty care units for those with mental health problems (Thompson, Turner, & Wiebe, 1993–1994). To help spread the work and share in the benefit of any new resources, many of these community efforts could be undertaken jointly with neighboring communities.

Given this spectrum of roles, agencies should strive to develop consensus among those in management, supervisory, and practice positions to pursue a plan for developing and maintaining excellence in placement services. An individual worker can be effective one-on-one with a particular client, but enabling and empowering workers, clients, and their families requires a commitment to excellence by the system providing structure and support to the workers.

Key Points

Excellent adult services social workers

- understand the service's beginning and ending points and the nature of its three stages: (1) preplacement, (2) placement, and (3) postplacement
- seek to empower clients and their families by involving them in decisions throughout the process and by supporting the client–family relationship
- apply a family assessment and change method that includes conducting a comprehensive functional assessment and offering an appropriate balance of case management and counseling
- ensure that placement is pursued only when it is the service plan of choice or the most appropriate service option to meet the goals of the client and family
- establish and maintain effective relationships with agencies, organizations, and individuals important to the service
- advocate for improved options for placement.

Excellent adult services managers

- see placement as an integral part of the adult services program and a valued public service
- support development and maintenance of a placement service that involves the three stages—(1) preplacement, (2) placement, and (3) postplacement—and the major service components of assessment, case management, and counseling
- have a systematic way of assessing how effectively the service's intent is being applied by social workers in practice with clients and their families
- support workers in managing challenges
- develop educational, support, advocacy, and planning activities relevant to enhancing the placement service.

Excellent leaders

- acknowledge and support the vital role that local agencies and their social workers assume in assisting younger and older adults with disabilities and their families with placement
- recognize the influence that physicians have in placement decisions and support improved communication and relationship building between the social services and medical communities
- support exploration of improved options for placement, especially for those who experience barriers to suitable residential or institutional care.

References

American Association of Retired Persons. (1991). *Nursing home life: A guide for residents and families.* Washington, DC: Author.

Barker, R. L. (1995). *The social work dictionary* (3rd ed.). Washington, DC: NASW Press.

Bumagin, V. E., & Hirn, K. F. (1990). *Helping the aging family: A guide for professionals.* Glenview, IL: Scott, Foresman.

Evashwick, C. J. (1993). Strategic management of a continuum of care. *Long-Term Care Administration, 21*(3), 13–24.

Gwyther, L. (1989). Selecting a nursing home: Some basic principles help. *Advances in Research, 12*(4), 2–9.

Hennessy, C. H. (1993). Modeling case management decision-making in a consolidated long-term care program. *Gerontologist, 33*(3), 333–341.

Heumann, L. F., & Boldy, D. P. (Eds.). (1993). *Aging in place with dignity.* Westport, CT: Praeger.

Kraus, A. S., Spasoff, R. A., Beattie, E. J., Holden, E.E.W., Lawson, J. S., Rodenburg, M., & Woodcock, G. M. (1976). Elderly applicants to long-term care institutions. II. The application process: Placement and care needs. *Journal of the American Geriatrics Society, 24*(4), 165–172.

Leutz, W., Abrahams, R., & Capitman, J. (1993). The administration of eligibility for community long-term care. *Gerontologist, 33*(1), 92–104.

Manning, D. (1983). *When love gets tough.* Hereford, TX: In-Sight Books.

Sandel, S. L., & Possidenta, E. (1993–1994). The social reengagement model for treating Alzheimer's disease. *Long-Term Care Administration, 21*(4), 17–24.

Schneewind, E. H. (1990). The reaction of the family to the institutionalization of an elderly member. *Journal of Gerontological Social Work, 15*(1/2), 121–136.

Silverstone, B., & Hyman, H. K. (1989). *You & your aging parent.* New York: Pantheon Books.

Texas Department of Health. (1992). *Consumer's guide for selecting a personal care facility.* Austin: Author.

Thompson, K., Turner, L. C., & Wiebe, P. (1993–1994). How specialty care units help residents with mental health problems. *Long-Term Care Administration, 21*(4), 25–29.

CHAPTER 16

Adult Day Care

DENNIS W. STREETS

Adult day care is a relative newcomer in home and community services for adults with physical or mental disabilities. It is viewed by many as a promising long-term-care service option because it provides much-needed regular and reliable respite for caregivers (Conrad, Hanrahan, & Hughes, 1990; Harder, Gornick, & Burt, 1986). It also provides clients with a setting for receiving social support and health services (Weissert et al., 1990).

This chapter provides a history of the development of adult day care services in the United States; a discussion of the major models of adult day care; and a general description of primary target populations, case illustrations, and program coverage issues. Having provided the background and definition of this service, the chapter continues with a look at current and possible roles for adult services programs in the provision of adult day care services. These roles include the certification and monitoring of adult day care, assistance in the provision of adult day care to families, and development of new day care services in communities where those services are unavailable or lacking.

History and Definitions

The history of adult day care in the United States is brief. It is increasingly seen as an important element in home and community care services for those in need of long-term care. In examining the development of community care systems in six states, the National Governors Association (1988) found increasing emphasis on the role of adult day care services for support of family caregivers. In addition to providing much-needed respite, particularly for families caring for people with

Alzheimer's disease and Alzheimer's-type dementia, it also can offer active therapeutic health and social interaction. Adult day care programs are placed in two broad categories—those providing primarily social care and those providing health care.

Adult services programs in Maryland, Wisconsin, and North Carolina play active roles in promoting adult day care services as part of a community-based system of care for adults with disabilities. In North Carolina, adult day care represents "the provision of group care and supervision in a place other than their usual abode on a less than 24-hour basis" (North Carolina General Statute 131D-6(b), 1990) to adults who may be disabled or functionally impaired "to enable them to remain in or return to their own homes" (North Carolina Department of Human Resources, Division of Social Services, 1986, §5110, p. 1).

Despite having a clear purpose for clients and families, adult day care and day health are new services for adults with disabilities. Of the reported 2,100 adult day care programs in the United States in 1989, 40 percent had started operations after 1984 (Wallace, Ingman, Snyder, Planning, & Walker, 1991). As Weissert et al. (1989) observed, adult day care is an area "of particular interest because it represents an entirely different setting for care, apart from the home, outpatient clinic, or institution" (p. 640).

Adult day care had its origin in Great Britain in the 1960s in the form of psychogeriatric day hospitals and community day care centers. It has remained a vital component of that country's health and social services system (Rathbone-McCuan, 1987). In the United States, interest in adult day care emerged in the late 1960s and early 1970s. The National Institute of Adult Day Care had 20 member centers in 1969 (*AGS Newsletter*, 1992). Because adult day care appeared to be a way to reduce institutionalization and thereby control health care costs, a series of research and demonstration projects examined its potential. By 1980 Congress had developed the following definition of adult day care (Rathbone-McCuan, 1987) for the purpose of funding through such programs as Title XX of the Social Security Act (Social Security Act Amendments of 1974) and Title III of the Older Americans Act:

> *[Adult day care services are] services provided on a regular basis, but less than 24 hours per day, to an individual in a multipurpose senior center, intermediate care facility, or agency for the handicapped or other facility licensed by the state, which are provided because such individual is unable to be left alone during the daytime hours but does not require institutionalization. Such services may include (but are not limited to) provision of meals, personal care, recreational and educational activities, physical and vocational rehabilitation, and health care services.* (p. 373)

MODELS OF ADULT DAY CARE

As the service evolved nationally, some day care programs emphasized the provision of rehabilitative and health care services, whereas others focused on providing a safe and stimulating social environment. There have been two models of adult day care—health and social. Their development has been guided by the needs of clients and especially by the availability of funding. There has been a movement toward the health model of day care and, within this model, the delineation of rehabilitative and maintenance goals for older and younger adults with disabilities who have significant levels of functional impairment.

This change in emphasis can be traced to the action taken by Congress in the early 1980s to allow states to establish a plan for use of Medicaid funds for the reimbursement of day health services for participants meeting certain eligibility guidelines. When these plans have included day care, its orientation has naturally been toward the health model. Primarily because the demonstration and research projects have been inconclusive about how day care affects the use of other services (mostly long-term institutional care), it has not realized substantial growth (Rathbone-McCuan, 1987).

In analyzing findings from their national survey of adult day care, Weissert et al. (1990) grouped 62 percent of all programs in the social model, 27 percent into the health model, and 11 percent into a special-purpose model, which includes programs for veterans and for clients with such disabilities as blindness, mental illness, and cerebral palsy. Day health services generally included health assessment, therapeutic diets, physical therapy, occupational therapy, speech therapy, nursing, physician services, and dental care, but most programs routinely offered only nursing services. Programs offering social services provided case management, counseling, transportation, and access to various community support services.

Although adult day care programs offer access to health and social services on or off site, they are primarily a place where clients can go during the day for structured activities to increase social interaction and to receive supervision and a hot meal. Programs typically are open for eight hours a day, but coverage ranges from four to 11 hours. Weissert et al. (1990, p. 15) found the typical morning and afternoon schedule to be

8:30–9:15 A.M.	*Early arrivals/coffee/visiting*
9:15–9:45 A.M.	*More arrivals/reality orientation/current events*
9:45–10:45 A.M.	*Late arrivals/exercise/therapies/health monitoring*
10:45–11:45 A.M.	*Arts and crafts*
11:45 A.M.–1:00 P.M.	*Lunch/rest*
1:00–2:00 P.M.	*Visiting speaker/musician/movie*
2:00–3:00 P.M.	*Games/individual activities/early departure*
3:00–3:30 P.M.	*Snack/departure*

TARGET POPULATION AND COVERAGE

The clientele for adult day care programs is primarily older individuals who are functionally impaired, have low to moderate incomes, and generally live in urban communities and more densely populated sections of the country (Conrad, Hanrahan, & Hughes, 1990). In 1990 the typical adult day care client was 78 years old. Most participants were white unmarried women living with others, generally family members. More than half were functionally dependent and nearly 40 percent experienced some mental impairment. Almost one-third had been hospitalized within the previous year (Weissert et al., 1990). The rural West and the South appear to have the greatest unmet need (Conrad et al., 1990). In 1992 all 11 of North Carolina's most urban counties had adult day care programs, but only 10 of the 56 most rural counties had one and none had more than one program (North Carolina Department of Human Resources, Division of Social Services, 1992).

Weissert et al. (1990) provided two brief case examples to give a more qualitative sense of who adult day care clients are. The first shows a participant in a day health program and the second, a participant attending a social program.

CASE EXAMPLE 1

An elderly widower with a prior hip fracture lives alone. His children visit every two weeks but are not involved in his day-to-day care. Alert and oriented, he walks with an unsteady gait secondary to proximal muscle weakness that developed after his hip fracture. Services provided by adult day care include monitoring his seizure medications, helping him obtain a hearing aid, providing two meals per day, getting him out of the house, providing a sympathetic ear, and giving him a bath (because of mobility problems, he is afraid to bathe at home).

CASE EXAMPLE 2

A 68-year-old woman has osteoarthritis of the spine and hips and weighs 278 pounds. She uses a walker or cane to ambulate, but can perform all activities of daily living (ADL). She lives alone in a high-rise apartment and does her own housework, but tires easily. Hearing, communication, and mental status are good. She identifies the major benefits of adult day care as participating in discussion and exercise groups and socializing with other people.

These case examples typify long-term-care clients who could and do benefit from adult day care programs. In addition, adult day care can be an important noninstitutional strategy that adult protective services (APS) workers may use in cases of suspected or confirmed abuse and neglect (Griffin, 1993).

In APS cases adult day care can provide respite to overburdened family caregivers. It also might be successfully used by caregivers as a time to engage in counseling about the identified issues of abuse and neglect (Kaye & Kirwin, 1990). In outlining principal goals associated with its day care programs, North Carolina (North Carolina Department of Human Resources, Division of Social Services,

1986) made this connection between support for caretakers and assistance in adult abuse or neglect cases:

1. *assist with the economic self-sufficiency of family units by allowing informal caretakers to be gainfully employed*
2. *assist clients with maintaining or regaining personal self-sufficiency in ADL and IADL [instrumental activities of daily living] functioning to avoid such adverse consequences as social isolation, growing dependence, self-abuse or neglect, or institutional placement*
3. *assist in reducing the burden of overwhelmed caretakers that might otherwise lead to abuse, neglect, or exploitation.* (§5110, p. 1)

Adult Services and Adult Day Care

Adult day care as a long-term-care service option or an intervention in a protective services case is an important component of an effective community adult services program. The roles that adult services programs may assume in relation to using adult day care effectively can fall into three areas: (1) certifying or licensing and monitoring adult day care programs for quality and effectiveness; (2) the use of adult day care as an option in planning services with clients and families; and (3) assisting the community to develop new and expanded day care programs for adults with disabilities. The discussion that follows draws on direct experience with North Carolina's adult services programs in county departments of social services, which use all three approaches. These approaches require a combination of activities with clients, families, service providers, and community stakeholders. In working with clients and their families, social workers apply the family assessment and change method introduced in chapter 3. With providers, the role of the local adult services programs includes assisting the state with certification and monitoring, as well as promoting and supporting quality services among programs. Adult services programs also help in assessing, designing, developing, and marketing viable day care options locally.

Most of the responsibilities toward providers rest with the adult day care (ADC) coordinator in local adult services programs, whose responsibilities include "recruitment, study and development of adult day care programs, evaluation and periodic reevaluation to determine if the programs meet the needs of the individuals they serve, and consultation and technical assistance to help day care programs expand and improve the quality of care provided" (North Carolina Department of Human Resources, Division of Social Services, 1986, §5110, p. 1). These functions are interconnected: Clients cannot take advantage of this option for care in the absence of an available service, and a service cannot thrive without clients.

CERTIFICATION, MONITORING, AND PROMOTION OF QUALITY

In North Carolina counties that have ADC centers, staff members from the adult services programs of the county department of social services act to ensure that such programs are operated in a manner consistent with state certification requirements. This function is assigned to at least one adult services social worker in each agency, who serves as ADC coordinator. When activity in a county does not warrant a full-time coordinator, the duties often are assigned to the adult homes specialist, who monitors board-and-care homes, because of the similarity in task (Center for Aging Research and Educational Services [CARES], 1990).

Certification

The ADC consultant in the Adult Services Branch of the North Carolina Division of Social Services has principal responsibility for ensuring that basic certification requirements are met. The consultant works closely with each county's ADC coordinator. The time and effort taken with the initial certification of a program influence its quality of operation. The ADC coordinator's preliminary consultative work with a developing program can help anticipate and avoid problems.

Just as the initial contact with a client affords the caseworker a special opportunity to develop a constructive relationship, the relationship between the ADC coordinator and community ADC programs is equally important to their future work. First, it offers an opportunity to establish credibility, which is critical to the effective monitoring and promotion of quality. Credibility is basically shaped by knowledge and integrity; the effective coordinator is both well informed and well intentioned. Not unlike those who monitor board-and-care homes, the coordinator must have a solid grasp of the rules for certification to interpret them clearly and consistently. Inasmuch as coordinators have some discretion in enforcement, being confident about the intent of the regulations enables them to decide how flexibly regulations can be applied. This prevents coordinators from becoming unreasonably bureaucratic while still protecting their integrity.

For example, adult day health programs in North Carolina are required to have a treatment table on the premises. The effective ADC coordinator understands that the use of a suitable bed, in lieu of a treatment table, is in keeping with the rule's intent. On the other hand, the coordinator recognizes that the staff–participant ratio does not allow such flexibility. A technical but important aspect of this knowledge base is understanding the similarities and differences between adult day care and adult day health care in terms of purpose and requirements.

Although the owner and operator of a developing program will appreciate working with a knowledgeable ADC coordinator, consistency and fairness are other valuable attributes. The effective coordinator can avoid many pitfalls by being reasonable in expectations, careful to apply requirements similarly with all programs, and attentive to what is best for participants. Whether noncompliance with standards results from poor motivation or the inability of personnel to comply with rules, the challenge is to use the same criteria in monitoring programs, regardless of their intent or motivation. "They mean well" cannot be an excuse for a violation of rules or any other compromise in the quality of service.

The initial encounter with a potential operator also affords ADC coordinators the opportunity to set realistic parameters for the relationship. Working in the interest of program participants, effective coordinators make expectations clear from the beginning, both what is required of the operator and what the operator can expect of them. They affirm that compliance with certification requirements is the exclusive responsibility of the day care program staff. Although coordinators can assist staff members to understand the rationale for the rules and offer suggestions on how to apply them within the context of the specific program, it is the program personnel who must demonstrate continuous compliance. To help move the day care program beyond minimum standards, effective coordinators supplement their "good advice" by volunteering consultation and technical assistance. This is discussed later in the section on promotion of quality.

Monitoring

The ADC coordinator role in working with certified day care programs is similar to the adult homes specialist in North Carolina who monitors board-and-care facilities. It is not surprising that a social worker might be responsible for both positions when neither is a full-time duty. Like the adult homes specialist, the coordinator works in the interest of the public adult services program, the community, the state, the service providers, and especially the program participants.

The mission of the coordinator in monitoring is to ensure that participants of ADC programs receive the care, supervision, and enrichment guaranteed them by virtue of their enrollment in a certified program. In assuming this role, the coordinator uses a problem-solving and change approach that involves a comprehensive and thorough assessment and negotiation for correction of deficiencies.

In making a monitoring visit to a day care program at least monthly, the ADC coordinator has an opportunity to become well acquainted with the participants as well as the program personnel. Each contact with a program should be carefully planned, with objectives that include following up previously cited deficiencies, exploring causes of recurring problems, identifying program strengths and areas of improvement, and considering ways to enhance quality of service for participants.

On most occasions, the coordinator will probably learn of at least one problem or concern, and the way in which this discovery and reporting are handled is important to its resolution. First, it is ideal when the program personnel themselves identify and accept responsibility for a problem. This changes the role of the coordinator from whistle-blower to sounding board for problem solving. The effective coordinator builds a relationship in which the program operator is comfortable sharing a substantive problem during the visit or even contacts the coordinator between visits. The coordinator makes clear that a problem violating certification rules will be cited and closely monitored but reaffirms through consultative support the value of the program's openness. The requirement that day care programs evaluate their own operation at regular intervals (at least annually in North

Carolina) further reinforces the worth of self-disclosure and voluntary correction. Second, in those instances where the coordinator identifies the problem, it is vital that the problem be presented in terms understandable to the program personnel. This is an essential part of the due process to which all operators of a closely regulated business are entitled. More basic than this, ensuring comprehension of the problem is necessary if its correction is to be lasting. The program personnel must know whether the problem represents a violation of state rules for certification or a recommendation not directly related to the rules that nonetheless has significance for the quality of the program and the well-being of participants. In either case, how the issue affects participants should be the focus of the problem statement.

A simple example of this might be a citation that "the storage cabinet in the treatment room was found unlocked." Although this is a clear statement of the violation of a rule, a more compelling problem statement would be "The unlocked treatment cabinet, found on [date and time], jeopardizes the health and safety of participants, especially those with dementia, who might mistakenly take some of the medications found there. The cabinet must be kept locked at all times, except when in use and a staff member is in close proximity." This statement not only explains how the problem adversely affects participants but also gives the operator an indication of what is necessary to achieve compliance.

One area in North Carolina's rules for certification that affords the coordinator a particular opportunity to affect the quality of care for participants and their families has to do with monitoring the program's compliance in "planning services for individual participants" and in developing an effective "program plan." The licensing requirements of Maryland (Code of Maryland Regulations, 1994) present a clear picture of what should be expected in a program's assessment of participants and in the associated care planning. Completed within one month of the participant's enrollment, the assessment includes "(a) health status; (b) functioning status; (c) participation in activities; (d) nutritional status; (e) psychosocial status; and (f) home management skills" (04[E] & [F], p. 678-16).

The ADC coordinator can influence how quickly and well problems are corrected by being careful how they are presented to the program personnel. One proven approach is the "P–N–P" style of communication. The coordinator states something positive about the situation, then introduces the negative finding, and concludes with a constructive (positive) remark. This tack leads to open discussion of a problem rather than creating defensiveness.

For example, instead of noting that "You [the program] failed to have the proper paperwork completed for a new participant," the coordinator might say, "You are typically very conscientious about the completeness and timeliness of your participants' records. I was therefore surprised to find that Mrs. J's file was missing a medical examination report and signed authorization for release of confidential information. You have shown in the past your understanding of the importance of this information for planning care for participants and as a form of risk management for the program. When can we expect Mrs. J's records to be completed, and how can you best assure the completeness and timeliness of participants' records in the future?" This invites the program personnel to develop ways to solve and avoid problems, rather than to defend or excuse past actions.

Because this approach encourages the program to use the coordinator's knowledge and skills to assist in problem solving, the coordinator must be careful not to cross the line between facilitation and management. The coordinator must determine whether state and local rules for certification are met and assist in action to require compliance.

In describing a continuum of consultation, Lippitt and Lippitt (1986) showed how this facilitative relationship necessarily varies depending on the specific circumstances. On one end of the continuum, the coordinator is assertive in problem solving. She or he proposes specific changes in how a program operates and then monitors to see that appropriate action is taken. This might be necessary when the management of the day care program is inexperienced, there is reason to question the operator's intent, or the potential effect on participants is great. At the other extreme, the coordinator assumes a more passive relationship: He or she asks questions to spur new ideas that can lead an interested and capable program manager to improve the operation. The delicacy of this relationship is similar to those that social workers must develop with clients and their families, in which the worker must be careful not to cross the line between support and control. The objective in both instances is to support and empower the program or the client toward achieving goals.

The routine monitoring by the coordinator typically culminates each year with the comprehensive review necessary for recertification. This end-of-the-year review should not present any major surprises if the monthly scheduled and unscheduled visits have been conducted effectively. Even with thorough monthly and annual reviews by the coordinator, there is more that can be done to influence the quality of adult day care programs.

Promotion of Quality

Although much can be accomplished through the monitoring process, the responsibility of the adult services program to ensure the quality of adult day care goes beyond this. There are at least three other ways in which quality of service can be affected by the coordinator and the adult services program: (1) promotion of community involvement, (2) support of day care staff members, and (3) case management. These three areas assume that the coordinator is operating as more than a regulatory agent. Building an effective relationship with the day care provider is no less important than building one with clients and their families.

The more involved a community is with a program, the greater the effect on quality of operation, not only because of the resources but also because of the expectations brought to the program. This is why marketing and resource development are so important, as is discussed in the section on service development.

Although community involvement brings outside resources to the program, its internal resources are even more important. The program can only be as good as the capacity of its staff. The ADC coordinator and adult services program therefore have an interest in supporting staff development. This means sharing relevant information about innovative programming, including staff in training sessions on topics pertinent to their work (for example, handling clients with difficult behaviors or dementia), and publicly recognizing their achievements.

There are four aspects to case management. First, the quality of a service increases with a solid match of the needs and preferences of clients with the preparedness and preferences of the day care program. For example, a younger adult with a developmental disability may not be appropriately placed in a center designed for older people with Alzheimer's disease.

Second, quality is related to how well the adult services program can target its limited resources. When day care is an option and there are some public funds available to support participation, the challenge becomes deciding which clients should receive the service. Although program guidelines can identify priority groups for adult day care, the social worker's job is made difficult if there is heavy competition from varied clients for a few available day care slots at centers having discretion about whom they choose to enroll.

It is difficult to establish any criteria in sufficiently definitive terms to make allocation of limited day care resources an easy task. Choosing among priority populations may not be an issue in actual practice unless it interferes with social workers' abilities to help clients make decisions in their best interests. This suggests the importance of having a system for case reviews among adult services social workers. This may be a weekly case staff meeting in larger units or regular meetings between the worker and supervisor in any adult services program. Such analysis of cases is an important feature in a system for quality control, and it will become more essential with the continuing emphasis on ensuring that public funds are used wisely.

Third, the adult services social worker as case manager has an opportunity to affect the quality of care for individual participants by being involved in development and maintenance of the program's care plan for the client and family. The social worker can promote use of the family assessment and change method by the program's personnel, which would include consideration of a comprehensive functional assessment designed to set realistic functional goals for the participant.

Fourth, the adult services social worker must remember that the plan of care, and thus quality of service, for the client and family extend beyond attendance at the program. The quality of care and life during the time the client is not attending the program must be considered as well. How a client is transported to the program or the conditions under which a client lives at home are equally important considerations. The worker is in a position to prompt the client, family, and day care program to consider how the various formal and informal sources of assistance can complement one another.

ADULT DAY CARE AS A SERVICE OPTION

Because the quality of the day care service is affected by the decisions made about who can enroll, the work of adult services programs in assisting clients and their families in considering this care option is vital. When adult day care is available within the client's county of residence or general service area, the adult services social worker has a responsibility to consider it among the appropriate service options. Given that few social workers report having experience with adult day care, adult services programs must ensure that their workers are familiar with this service option. Without an understanding of its purpose, workers may miss opportunities to inform clients and families about how adult day care may be appropriate as a primary source of care and supervision or as part of a multifaceted service plan. The effective social worker will avoid automatically concluding that institutional placement is needed when in-home services are unavailable or inadequate. With the client's and family's collaboration, out-of-home assistance short of 24-hour residential care may ease stresses on family caregivers and provide clients with an alternative that allows them to remain at home.

Social workers must be well acquainted with what the available day care programs can offer to clients. This involves visiting the existing centers to discuss with program staff members their philosophy and capacity for serving a clientele with varying needs. Although most programs have a broad mission to serve enough participants to stay financially viable, each will likely emphasize different aspects of care, based on such factors as the orientation of its financial backers, the professional training of its personnel, and its perception of the community need for service.

Adult day care centers and homes in North Carolina are generally permitted to make their own decisions about whom to serve within the criteria established by the certification rules and within the civil rights of publicly supported clients protected by law. Each program's policies about whom it will enroll must be available in writing. For example, a program might place a limit on the number of people confined to wheelchairs, or it might not accept those who experience intermittent incontinence. One program in which vocational rehabilitation is a priority might welcome a younger disabled adult, whereas another center might have reservations because it serves mostly geriatric clients whose rehabilitation needs relate mostly to ADLs. A program serving mostly younger victims of accidents might not enroll a frail older person who is awaiting placement in a nursing home.

The worker also must have an understanding of potential barriers to effective participation in day care and how these might be overcome. Some questions that workers will want to be prepared to consider with clients and their families include how to pay for participation in the service, what to do to ensure caregiving beyond the center's hours, and how to arrange transportation to and from the center. The responsibility for developing this knowledge rests not only on social workers but is clearly a duty of the adult services supervisor. The supervisor must orient workers to all community service options, including adult day care and day health. This can be part of the orientation process for new workers, in-service training, and case staffings.

As discussed in earlier chapters, adult services workers are responsible for conducting a comprehensive functional assessment with clients and their families as part of the family assessment and change method. From identifying the client's strengths, weaknesses, and preferences, workers can help develop function-oriented goals and a combination of case management and counseling tasks designed to achieve these goals. The aim of social workers' efforts is to support and empower the client and family to manage their affairs, including that part of the day when they receive assistance in the form of day care.

Assessment

Adult day care should not alter how a comprehensive functional assessment is conducted. There are particular areas within the assessment, however, that can help clients and workers determine whether day care is an appropriate service option. One of these areas is the capacity of the informal caregivers. The pressures of informal caregiving are well documented. They can not only affect the financial and emotional well-being of families, but also lead to instances of abuse and neglect. Workers must be sensitive to these pressures and look for them in an assessment. Stress on caregivers may not be evident in initial contacts with clients and families. Adult day care has a clear role in supporting families and other informal caregivers.

Another area important to an assessment is the nature of the client's functional impairments and their consequences for the client and family. Adult day care can be especially useful in cases in which the client's condition may be improved through rehabilitative activities, especially when the modeling or encouragement of others in a group setting motivates the client. The service also has been found particularly useful for people experiencing problems associated with Alzheimer's disease. A recent survey of respite programs found that adult day care "is particularly well suited for some patients with dementia, providing the opportunity to socialize and reconnect to others, as well as for the highly stressed caregivers" (Abrahams, Bishop, & Hernandez, 1991, pp. 23–24).

Because adult day care requires that clients leave their homes during some part of the day, social workers should consider clients' access to transportation and the possible difficulties in readying clients for an activity away from home. Clients and families may need to be educated about the potential benefits of adult day care (Barber, Paton, & Wishnia, 1993). The lack of appropriate transportation is a barrier for some clients and their families. Adequacy of transportation is directly linked to the effectiveness of day care for adults (Abrahams et al., 1991). It is one of four factors Adams (1988) found to be most important to those making the decision to participate in day care. The other three were the program's operating hours, the closeness of the program geographically to the client and family, and the social and economic homogeneity of the clients.

To present a clear analysis of care options, social workers must assess not only clients' needs and limitations but also their strengths and resources. The worker should not underestimate a client's strong will to remain independent or a family's commitment to caregiving. Clients' preferences and apprehensions are also important considerations in helping them and their families identify goals and in identifying what social workers can do to assist. Social workers cannot effectively assess client circumstances, assist with identification of functional goals, or facilitate implementation of a service plan without establishing and maintaining a relationship that fits the needs and interests of clients and families.

Case Management and Counseling

Consistent with the family assessment and change method, after conducting a comprehensive functional assessment, the social worker assists the client and family in identifying the principal issues to be addressed and the goals to be achieved to enhance their lives. Then it is a matter of examining how desired but realistic outcomes can be achieved and developing a plan that likely involves a mix of case management and counseling. The "client" in many cases is both the adult with disabilities and the family, and thus the plan must reflect this.

Among the underlying factors that the effective social worker considers relative to day care is the importance of family. The relationship that a worker establishes with the client and family may sometimes call for the worker to advocate on their behalf, but the worker should also be helping them develop the knowledge, skills, and confidence for self-advocacy. The relationship also may call for negotiation or mediation among the client, family, and day care program staff members and for counseling with the client and family to help each accept the need for this outside assistance.

In cases in which adult day care is identified as an appropriate service option and is available, social workers have several important tasks. The first involves educating the client and family about the service. There is also some indication that among the barriers to its use is a hesitancy or reluctance among clients and their families to use out-of-home care (Abrahams et al., 1991; Hedrick et al., 1991). Although day care is not the same as placement in a board-and-care home or nursing facility, it may conjure up some of the same reservations. This has been a problem especially for day care programs located in or near a nursing or board-and-care home. Social workers may need to acknowledge and help resolve such reservations before any out-of-home assistance can be considered. When clients and families make the decision to try day care they generally give it high marks (Weissert et al., 1989).

Because adult day care is a voluntary service and the client's cooperation is essential, every effort should be made to ensure that the client understands the service. Abrahams et al. (1991) suggested that visiting an operating program can be important to dispel any myths. The term "day care" itself may be responsible for some apprehension, given its common use for children's programs. If a visit is not possible, a videotape and brochure may be an adequate substitute to introduce the service or a particular program to the client and family.

Second, although it is unlikely that a client will have a choice among centers or homes (because few areas have more than one), this does not eliminate the need for an informed consumer. The social worker should help educate the client and family about what they should expect from a day care program and how they should go about getting these expectations met. These expectations should be written in the service plan as specific, measurable goals, against which progress can be gauged. This includes not only logistical considerations such as how many days per week the client will attend and how transportation will be arranged but also functional outcomes for the client, so it is clear why the client is attending. For example, a desired outcome for a client recovering from a stroke might be to increase ability to walk unassisted from 10 feet to 50 feet within six weeks.

A third task for social workers is to encourage the client and family to be actively engaged in the care planning that the program should undertake for each participant. This involvement also allows the participant and family to learn what expectations the program staff may have for them. Effective social workers also contribute to the client's care planning at the day care program. They can evaluate progress and update clients' objectives by communicating regularly with program staff members. Social workers may need to assist clients and families in arranging necessary transportation and for care during times when the clients are not attending the program. The service plan developed by social workers with clients and families should reflect how all these considerations are addressed.

Reassessment and Closure

How well clients adapt to the day care program and how well their needs are being met are the essential objects of the social worker's reassessment. The reassessment should include observing clients both in day care programs and in their home environments. If one objective of the adult services plan is to relieve stressed caregivers, this also should be a focus of the reassessment.

There is no absolute time frame for how long the social worker should keep a day care case open. The case remains open as long as the client needs assistance with achieving goals or until the service plan is no longer valid for some other reason (for example, the client terminates service or his or her condition changes to require a different type of care). Because of the nature of such cases, it may be best to keep the case open as long as this is agreeable with the client and family rather than to close the case and risk a break in communication.

The social worker's role during this continuing phase is more as a problem solver and adviser than monitor, because an objective is to empower clients and families to make decisions and act for themselves. To reassess the adequacy of the service plan, the social worker should have some type of contact with clients and the day care program at least once a quarter and visit the program at least once every six months. The worker may have occasion to observe clients more frequently on other visits to the program and should visit them promptly if there is a substantial change in their conditions or circumstances. The worker should be sensitive to when it is useful to visit clients in their home as part of the reassessment. In an effective adult services program, the worker also receives feedback from others within the agency who have contact with the client at the day care program and in the home.

When adult day care is no longer appropriate for the client, a plan for closure should be developed with the client, family, and day care program. For some, adult day care may present more care and assistance than are needed, and a senior center or congregate meals program may be a better option. Others may require a more intensive or higher level of care.

DEVELOPMENT OF SERVICE

Development may be the most important function for many adult services programs, mainly because adult day care is still largely undeveloped in this country. Because adult day care has proved so useful in many communities and states, local adult services programs may want to take an active part in developing additional programs in their communities. The role of the adult services agency in developing adult day care involves assessing the community's need for out-of-home assistance and determining what type of service response would be most appropriate. It further entails helping develop the resources necessary to implement and sustain a viable program.

Community Assessment

Every social worker can think of clients who could use out-of-home care to remain in the community. For these clients, the assistance that can be provided in their homes may not be adequate or practical for many reasons. Funding may be an issue for some: For those who pay privately and need several hours of daily assistance, the cost of adult day care may be more manageable than the cost of in-home care. Family circumstances also can enter the picture, either when the caregiver needs respite or when the caregiver has a job outside the home. From a systems perspective, there is some logic in centralizing the care of 20 adults with disabilities in a day care program rather than providing each with in-home services. Still, the community's determination of whether to develop a day care program for adults requires more than an impression developed from a few cases.

Much like the comprehensive assessment of a client, the assessment of a community is multifaceted. It involves more than estimating the current number of younger and older adults with disabilities who might benefit from adult day care. The other factors that should be assessed include

- future demographic trends (for example, growth of the older population)
- trends in availability of informal caregivers (for example, women who have traditionally acted as caregivers are now in the workforce in greater numbers)

- indicators of the service system's present capacity to meet needs of clients and families (for example, APS cases, length of in-home services and respite waiting lists)
- attitude of consumers, referral sources, and the general community about institutional, in-home, and community care
- availability of potential sources of funding (targeted and discretionary)
- interest and availability of potential service providers
- the circumstances when care and supervision are most needed (for example, hours and days of the week)
- the location of potential care recipients
- the status of transportation services.

This is not meant to be an exhaustive list; instead it illustrates the types of information to be considered in assessing a community's need, preference, and potential for out-of-home assistance. Without this exercise, a community might miss some of the reasons why adult day care is not further developed, including lack of third-party payers, clients' attitudes, lack of awareness in the community and among service professionals of day care as an option, and transportation problems.

The community assessment should be conducted with the involvement of those who have a major stake in assisting younger and older adults with disabilities. Similar to the assessment of a client, the community assessment should result in the clear identification of strengths, weaknesses, and resources important to considering what must be done to offer out-of-home assistance. This process should be conducted without any preconceived notions about how best to offer out-of-home assistance. A primary objective of this exercise is the discovery of whether there is a need for and support of adult day care, adult day health, or some combination, and whether it is best provided in day care centers or day care homes. As Harder et al. (1986) concluded, "there is as yet no reason to believe that one form [of adult day care] is more appropriate or more effective than another. As long as the health and welfare of clients are not endangered, there is no reason to support the dissemination of a particular model or set of procedures" (p. 438). This outlook gives each community the flexibility to develop an approach to adult day care that is suited best to its needs and resources.

Program Design and Development

Not all communities need or can benefit from adult day care. For this reason it is important to differentiate between physical presence and availability. Although adult day care as a certified service in a center or home may not be viable everywhere, it is hard to imagine that access to out-of-home assistance is not needed. The support of a regional center may be a better option for some communities. The charge to the community, with leadership from the adult services agency, is to determine what type of arrangement is appropriate and pursue strategies to develop it. A community can choose from two options: (1) adult day care and (2) adult day health. And a community can support variations of these two options in terms of size, location, affiliation, service population, and services rendered.

When adult day care or day health is developed, the adult services agency may provide the service directly or arrange for it to be offered otherwise. When the adult services program makes the decision to operate a day care center, it presumably has not only determined the need for this service, but also that it is the most appropriate provider. In most instances, public adult services agencies do not provide the service directly.

Although most adult day care programs are privately owned and operated, the public sector can still influence the character of such programs through funding and general support. For example, a community might choose to encourage and support development of day care homes rather than centers where this is an option. It might emphasize more of a social day care orientation, a health or rehabilitative program, or some combination. It might support targeting of the day care program to serve a special population (for example, people with dementia or with developmental disabilities) or a more general one (for example, people with a certain level of impairment).

A community considering the development of out-of-home assistance for adults with disabilities and their families should start with learning about what other communities have done and their successes and failures. One rural community adapted the concept of out-of-home assistance to its needs and resources by using underoccupied nursing home space for day care at the very low cost of $2.50 per hour (Abrahams et al., 1991). This arrangement was a useful source of respite for the community. In North Carolina and elsewhere, there are examples of effective day care homes as well as centers. There are examples of day care programs located in multipurpose senior centers, hospitals, and nursing homes. There are situations in which several counties support a common program.

Even if the local adult services program does not itself take the initiative to promote development of programs because of its role in their certification, influential people or organizations in the community may seek its consultation. The agency can act as a well-informed consultant, showing an understanding of the benefits and limitations of this service option. The adult services program should be able to attest to the potential value of out-of-home assistance for clients and their families as well as to the factors that might limit its benefit.

In working to develop out-of-home assistance within the community, the adult services program also should be prepared to consult with potential providers about the need for such services and introduce them to the rules for adult day care and adult day health programs. Additional program strategies for facilitating the development of adult day care options also can include activities in the area of marketing, resource development, and program coordination.

Marketing combines education and advocacy. It entails sharing the results of the community assessment with the wide assortment of stakeholders concerned with out-of-home assistance and encouraging their participation in molding an appropriate service response. These stakeholders might include human services agencies, business and religious sectors, and consumers. Marketing also involves continuing promotion of established programs. There is evidence that adult day care is often not a well-recognized service, either in the general community or among potential referral sources (for example, hospital discharge planners and the medical community) (Weissert et al., 1989). To be effective, adult day care requires acceptance and support from referral and funding sources and, most important, from potential users. This acceptance and support comes largely from information and demonstration. People have to know about the service and see that it can be effective.

Resource development strives to generate a fertile environment for the operation of a successful adult day care program. This environment may mean that the business community is willing to include day care in its self-insured health care plans, offer pretax options for employees that cover dependent care, subsidize several day care participant slots, offer technical expertise or physical space, and provide seed money for start-up of a program. In a supportive environment, community churches, synagogues, or other religious institutions also might offer free or low-cost space for programs, assist with transportation, and help organize a volunteer corps. The medical community, in such an environment, could suggest adult day care as an option for patients and donate supplies and equipment. The media could present stories that highlight the contributions day care makes to the community. The local adult services program could explore creative ways to maximize the effect of limited public funding (for example, pay for a portion of a week and the client or family pays privately for additional days). These resource development activities are especially important because, as Wallace et al. (1991) warned, "the adult day care sector faces the risk of losing its emphasis on providing a social good as the costs of providing care rise and sufficient funding becomes harder to obtain" (p. 36).

Coordination ensures that the day care service will be linked effectively with other parts of the continuum of care in the community and with necessary support services. Any agency or organization that undertakes operating a day care program must show the capacity to maintain effective relationships with local health and social services providers. Minimally, this should be demonstrated in letters of support or commitment. Ideally, it would be reflected in a well-defined operational plan that details what support can be expected from others (for example, consultation or referrals). Before others can promise their support, the program must be able to define clearly its expected service emphases.

The purpose of day care must be clear so that individual clients and their families can assess whether it can realistically meet their goals. It is important that the purpose of a day care program is clear so that adult services social workers, acting on behalf of the community, can judge whether the program is meeting the community's needs and expectations.

Summary

Adult services can potentially assume multiple roles vis-à-vis adult day care—provider, community planner and developer, case manager, funder, and monitor and promoter of quality. These roles offer great opportunities, including leading a community to examine the need for and feasibility of such out-of-home assistance. To assume these roles, adult services programs must understand and appreciate the importance of day care as part of the community's continuum of care. As there are increasing demands for assistance from an aging public, from growing numbers of younger people with disabilities, and from informal caregivers facing greater pressure, it is important that adult day care not be overshadowed by other demands for service.

Adult services programs can assess the adequacy of this part of its community's care options by considering how well its social workers can respond to requests for assistance from clients who cannot fully be cared for at home and fall short of needing placement in a group care facility and from families who are overwhelmed with caregiving responsibility. An adult services program that is comfortable with its capacity for responding probably has a well-established adult day care program.

Key Points

Excellent adult services social workers

- understand the potential roles adult service programs can fill with regard to adult day care
- enhance quality day care services through promotion of community involvement, support of day care staff members, and effective performance of case management for clients
- follow the family assessment and change method in working with clients and families
- are sufficiently familiar with adult day care to recognize when it may be an appropriate service option
- understand potential barriers to effective participation in adult day care and explore how they might be overcome
- assist the community in assessing its need and capacity for adult day care, involving the appropriate major stakeholders
- assist in determining the most appropriate type of arrangement for adult day care and in influencing and supporting its development.

Excellent adult services managers

- ensure that at least one professional staff member is knowledgeable about adult day care
- support that staff member in developing relevant knowledge and skills to perform the service development, certification, and monitoring functions effec-

tively

- use case staffings, in-service training, orientation for new workers, and other techniques to develop an awareness among adult services social workers about day care as a service option and how to overcome barriers to its use.

Excellent leaders

- seek to provide additional financial support to make adult day care a more accessible service option.

References

Abrahams, R., Bishop, C., & Hernandez, W. (1991). Respite service delivery: Learning from current programs. *PRIDE Institute Journal of Long Term Home Health Care, 10*(4), 16–28.

Adams, R. (1988). Attitudes of decision makers toward adult day care. *Journal of Applied Gerontology, 7*(1), 37–48.

AGS Newsletter. (1992). Robert Wood Johnson funds adult day care. New York: American Geriatric Society.

Barber, G. M., Paton, R. N., & Wishnia, G. C. (1993). Public's perceived need for adult day care versus actual use. *Home Health Care Services Quarterly, 14*(2–3), 53–71.

Center for Aging Research and Educational Services. (1990). *Manpower in county departments of social services. Executive summary and full report.* Chapel Hill, NC: Author.

Code of Maryland Regulations. (1994, January). *Day care for the elderly and medically handicapped adults.* 10.12.04.

Conrad, K. J., Hanrahan, P., & Hughes, S. L. (1990). Survey of adult day care in the United States. *Research on Aging, 12*(1), 36–55.

Griffin, L. W. (1993). Adult day care centers and adult protective services. *Journal of Gerontological Social Work, 20*(1/2), 115–133.

Harder, W. P., Gornick, J. C., & Burt, M. R. (1986). Adult day care: Substitute or supplement? *Milbank Quarterly, 64*(3), 414–441.

Hedrick, S. C., Rothman, M. L., Chapko, M., Inui, T. S., Kelly, J. R., Ehreth, J., & the Adult Day Health Care Evaluation Group. (1991). Adult day care evaluation study: Methodology and implementation. *Health Service Research, 25*(6), 935–960.

Kaye, L. W., & Kirwin, P. M. (1990). Adult day care services for the elderly and their families: Lessons from the Pennsylvania experience. In A. Monk (Ed.), *Health care of the aged: Needs, policies, and services* (pp. 167–183). New York: Haworth Press.

Lippitt, G., & Lippitt, R. (1986). *The consulting process in action* (2nd ed.). San Diego: University Associates.

National Governors Association. (1988). *State long term care reform.* Washington, DC: Author.

North Carolina Department of Human Resources, Division of Social Services. (1986). Adult day care services. In *Family services manual* (Vol. 1, chap. II). Raleigh: Author.

North Carolina Department of Human Resources, Division of Social Services. (1992). *Adult day care and day health services: Standards for certification.* Raleigh: Author.

Older Americans Act of 1965. P.L. 89-73, 79 Stat. 218.

Rathbone-McCuan, E. (1987). Day centers: Adult. In A. Minahan (Ed.-in-Chief), *Encyclopedia of social work* (18th ed., Vol. 1, pp. 373–376). Silver Spring, MD: National Association of Social Workers.

Social Security Act Amendments of 1974. P.L. 93-647, 88 Stat. 2337.

Wallace, S. P., Ingman, S. R., Snyder, J. L., Planning, M., & Walker, G. K. (1991). The evolving status of adult day care: Evidence from Missouri. *PRIDE Institute Journal of Long Term Care, 10*(4), 30–37.

Weissert, W. G., Elston, J. M., Bolda, E. J., Cready, C. M., Zelman, W. N., Sloane, P. D., Kalsbeek, W. D., Mutran, E., Rice, T. H., & Koch, G. G. (1989). Models of adult day care: Findings from a national survey. *Gerontologist, 29*(5), 640–649.

Weissert, W. G., Elston, J. M., Bolda, E. J., Zelman, W. N., Mutran, E., & Mangum, A. B. (1990). *Adult day care: Findings from a national survey.* Baltimore: Johns Hopkins University Press.

CHAPTER 17

Public Oversight of Board and Care

DENNIS W. STREETS

GARY M. NELSON

Public concern for the care of adults in residential settings has a long, volatile history in the United States. State mental hospitals were established in the early part of the 19th century as a response to the failures and practices of placing destitute and mentally impaired people in local almshouses and jails (Cole, 1987). As a consequence, care of people with mental illness, mental retardation, and cognitive impairments shifted to large, state residential care settings. Not until the 1960s was there a shift away from large institutions to community-based care, including both in-home care and board and care. The development and prescription of psychotropic drugs in the 1950s, mounting evidence of the negative effects and the high costs of institutional care, a civil rights movement that favored treatment in the least restrictive environment, and advances in community-based care triggered a movement toward deinstitutionalization that has not yet abated.

Whether the pendulum will swing back to institutional care in the 1990s as concern for homeless people persists and the cost savings that community-based care was supposed to produce but that failed to materialize is not known. What is known and what has come to be fully appreciated since the 1960s is that the diversity of circumstances among adults with disabilities calls for a diversity of responses, including the full range of options that fall loosely under the heading of board and care. The choices include care and treatment of individuals in their own homes, small (six clients or fewer) private family foster care arrangements, homes for younger and older adults with disabilities, nursing homes, and state hospitals with several hundred residents. These choices should be available to individuals and their families and should reflect the individual's current needs.

This chapter defines terms, discusses the need for and extent of board and care and current regulatory practices in the United States, and suggests roles for adult services programs in ensuring adults with disabilities the option of quality board and care. Roles include those previously outlined in the chapters on placement and case management. In addition, this chapter examines in depth the potential role of public adult services programs in monitoring board-and-care arrangements for adults with disabilities. The chapter concludes with a section on challenges to agencies and social workers.

Definitions and the Need for Board and Care

The term "board and care" is used to capture the broad range of living arrangements to which adults with disabilities resort when they can no longer receive adequate care at home but when their medical status is not such that they need treatment in a nursing home or state hospital. Hawes, Wildfire, and Lux (1993) defined *board and care* "as nonmedical community-based living arrangements that provide shelter (room), board (food), and 24-hour supervision or protective oversight and personal care services to residents (persons not related to the operator)" (p. 3).

Much of the confusion around board and care is reflected in what such substitute care arrangements are called in the various states. For example, in discussing substitute care homes, Talbot (1985) included emergency shelters, boarding homes, domiciliary care facilities, family foster homes, respite homes, group foster homes, and transitional care facilities. Hawes et al. (1993) found that such living arrangements were called by more than 25 different names, with multiple names for the same sort of service within the same state.

For example, a program familiar to many adult services agencies is adult foster care (Center for Aging Research and Educational Services, 1990; Nelson & Streets, 1993), yet the concept of adult foster care and foster families refers to only one of the possible board-and-care settings with which adult services programs concern themselves—the role of private families in providing substitute care. Sherman and Newman (1988) provided an excellent discussion of the history, philosophy, and practice of foster care by private families in the United States.

Board-and-care homes can range from two individuals in a private adult foster care arrangement with a family to 1,000 beds in an institution. In North Carolina, for example, all such substitute living arrangements are licensed under the name of domiciliary care by the state's Division of Facility Services and monitored by adult services programs in county departments of social services. In turn, board-and-care homes (sometimes called domiciliary care programs) fall into three categories: (1) family care homes (two to six adults), (2) homes for the aged and disabled (seven or more adults up to several hundred in one setting), and (3) group homes for adults with developmental disabilities (two to nine people). As of June 1994, North Carolina had 25,650 beds in 1,383 licensed homes, most of which were privately owned and operated (North Carolina Division of Facility Services, Group Care Facilities Branch, Raleigh, personal communication).

It is difficult to determine how great the demand for board and care is nationally because of the question of definition. In a number of states, licensed board-and-care arrangements include assisted living programs, and in others such programs are excluded. Although acknowledging the problem of matching the definitions of care settings across the country, Hawes et al. (1993) estimated that there were 500,000 beds nationally in 32,000 licensed homes. A report prepared for the House of Representatives (U.S. Congress, House Subcommittee on Health and Long-Term Care of the Select Committee on Aging, 1989) estimated that there were 28,000 unlicensed homes in the country with an unknown number of residents. The growth in recent years in the number of licensed board-and-care homes has generally occurred in large facilities (Hawes et al., 1993).

Who lives in board-and-care homes? Nationally, this population contains a mix of ages, types of impairments, and income levels and resources. Many residents experience mental retardation and other developmental disabilities, whereas others have cognitive impairments or histories of mental illness. The most difficult residents to place and serve are those with chronic mental illness, cognitive impairments, and disruptive behaviors. Other residents lack family resources and limited social networks but are not significantly physically or mentally impaired.

Information on the characteristics of current board-and-care residents is sketchy. There is a general concern that the population of board-and-care homes is becoming increasingly impaired (Hawes et al., 1993). In North Carolina, which has one of the largest per capita board-and-care populations in the country, most residents are older than age 65, and many of those are 75 years and older. The proportion of all residents with mental illness, mental retardation, or physical disability is significant (North Carolina Department of Human Resources, Division of Social Services, 1991). A recent study of North Carolina's domiciliary care residents confirmed the significant levels of cognitive and physical impairment. Nearly two-thirds of the residents have moderate to severe cognitive impairment; nearly one in three exhibits one or more behavioral problems; and nearly half have mental health problems in addition to cognitive impairment. One in five receives help with three or more activities of daily living, and nearly 40 percent have urinary incontinence (Research Triangle Institute, 1995).

Incomes for residents and methods for financing board and care vary from community to community and state to state. Some homes operate solely on the resident's monthly Supplemental Security Income (SSI) check. Some states supplement SSI payments with state or county assistance. Some homes serve a population that primarily pays privately, and these charge more than $3,000 per month (Hawes et al., 1993). The majority of residents in board-and-care homes, however, have low incomes.

Regulatory Practices for Board and Care

Unlike nursing homes, whose establishment and regulation have been shaped substantially by the federal requirements for funding available through Medicare and Medicaid, the evolution of board-and-care regulation has been largely a matter left to states and communities. An exception to this lack of federal involvement revolves around the application of the 1976 amendment to the Social Security Act, which called on states and local authorities to set standards "for any category of institutions, foster homes, or group living arrangements in which . . . a significant number of recipients of Supplemental Security Income benefits is residing or is likely to reside" (American Association of Retired Persons, 1985). The impetus for this amendment came from serious fires in board-and-care homes in which a number of residents died. The focus of subsequent standards has been mostly on food, sanitation, basic safety, and civil rights.

The complexity and variety of the board-and-care definitions and operations, the significant heavy private role in ownership, and a limited federal rationale for regulatory involvement has resulted in an equally complex and varied approach to state and local regulation. The unevenness in the quality of board and care—from grim warehouses to innovative programs in assisted living (in Oregon, in particular)—is in part a product of the unevenness in board-and-care regulation. As Dobkin (1989) noted, there is no such thing as a typical board-and-care home. In addition, Hawes et al. (1993) wrote that there is no typical approach to regulation.

Despite a number of studies in the area of board and care, a good deal remains unknown (Beyer, Bulkley, & Hopkins, 1984; Dobkin, 1989; Hawes et al., 1993; U.S. Department of Health and Human Services, 1990). However, some generalizations, with implications for the role of adult services programs, can be drawn in the areas of licensure, monitoring, and enforcement.

LICENSURE

Not all states license the same types of board-and-care arrangements. Some states allow for a largely voluntary process of registration and certification for certain kinds of board and care, and this use of registration and certification for regulation may not include standards, inspections, or provisions for enforcement. For those homes that are licensed, there are some similarities as to what is covered. According to Hawes et al. (1993) most licensing standards address such matters as "fire safety, physical structure, sanitation, the characteristics of residents who can be admitted to homes, and basic safety and services" (p. 28).

Less clear are licensure or regulatory provisions regarding staff-to-resident ratios, staff preparation, residents' rights, and characteristics and regulation of resident populations. Although most states have standards for staff-to-resident ratios, the standards vary. Some states require one staff member for 30 to 60 residents, many with significant impairments, and these minimum standards are insufficient. Staff training is typically insufficient and staff inspections infrequent.

Although most facilities have some provision for residents' rights, none of the states make adherence to those rights a special focus of performance reviews (Hawes et al., 1993).

Little is known about the targeting characteristics for residents in board-and-care homes, especially for those people with high-risk severe impairments. Although most states make some provisions for admission, retention, and staffing patterns according to the level of impairment of the residents, these provisions are varied and unevenly applied. In its foster care program, Oregon makes provision for three levels of impairment to determine staff size and payment levels. Hawes et al. (1993) found that the majority of states acknowledge the risk and special care needs of residents who are bedfast—only five of 62 state licensing officials allowed such residents to be admitted without special provisions for their care.

There is concern regarding the ability of current regulations, including licensure and payment criteria, to ensure adequate care for people who are very impaired. Hawes et al. (1993) suggested that

> there is little evidence that licensure laws will change as the resident case mix changes. In several states, there are different licensure laws for homes that house bedfast residents; however, licensing officials report that the differences tend to revolve around building and fire safety code requirements. Where states have differential staffing requirements, they are largely focused on differences in the size of the home rather than on the care needs of the residents. Where state licensure regulations do attempt to incorporate requirements that are more sensitive to resident needs, they tend to be quite general. For example, the regulations might require that homes have "sufficient staff" to "meet the needs of residents." (p. 33)

A regulatory system is as good as its inspection and enforcement activities. Arizona and Iowa reported that they performed no regular inspections of board-and-care homes (Hawes et al., 1993). In most states, inspections are carried out by a state agency; for others, state *and* local agencies carry out inspections; for a minority, inspection is handled at the local level only. Many of the agencies that conduct inspections rely on social workers, rather than nurses, to carry out this task. Twenty-five of the 62 state licensing officials contacted in the Hawes et al. (1993) study reported using social workers, and 31 reported using a nurse or a team with both a nurse and social worker. Issues regarding placement of and quality of care for residents with multiple chronic illnesses and disabilities point to questions regarding the training and qualifications of nonmedical staff involved in inspections of board and care.

The primary enforcement mechanism for board-and-care homes involves the development and monitoring of a corrective action plan. When the inspecting agency identifies deficiencies or violations, the home must develop a plan for correcting those problems. Regulatory agencies also can issue provisional licenses, revoke licenses, impose fines, or ban admissions and referrals. In the study by

Hawes et al. (1993), only 33 of the 62 agencies engaged in licensing possessed the power to impose fines or ban admissions, although these intermediate steps are viewed as most effective. Corrective action plans, the most frequently used method of responding to shortcomings in the quality of board-and-care homes, rely heavily on the skills of inspectors working directly with the personnel of these homes.

ROLE OF ADULT SERVICES PROGRAMS

The role of adult services programs in ensuring the quality of board-and-care homes for adults with disabilities varies. Some states have active adult foster care programs administered directly by local adult services programs, as in New York and North Carolina. In Oregon, adult foster care involves both local adult services programs and area agencies on aging. In other states, where adult services and aging programs are combined, involvement in board and care occurs through a variety of avenues: information and referral, placement, adult protective services, case management, adult foster care, or state and local long-term-care ombudsman programs.

Either directly or indirectly, because of their concern for adults with physical or mental disabilities, adult services programs are involved with the public oversight of board and care. In examining the roles of adult services for board-and-care homes, this section reviews issues around placement and case management and then elaborates on roles for adult services agencies monitoring this type of care.

Placement

A likely role for an adult services worker in relation to board and care is placement (see chapter 15 for a review of the best practice approaches to this service). Placement services involve performing an assessment to determine the need for temporary or continued placement, assistance to clients and their families in securing a placement in a suitable setting at an appropriate level of care, and supporting the individual and family in making the transfer and in maintaining the placement.

Central to placement is the determination of whether the client needs care of some sort in a residential facility. Problems identifying affordable housing should not be confused with the need for board-and-care services. Clients without impairments in functioning who are having difficulty locating a suitable place to live should be referred to housing services and not considered for placement in a board-and-care home. In the same vein, the lack of a nursing home bed should not be confused with a need for a board-and-care bed. In both cases the worker must assess the individual's need for care, whether or not board-and-care options in the community can best address that need, and if not, help determine what other options are most appropriate.

Case management

Case management has been defined in this book as an intervention strategy to access and coordinate both tangible and intangible resources to address either instrumental or psychological issues affecting the well-being of an individual or family. Case management can pull together concrete resources to support individuals and families and teach more intangible problem-solving and change skills. In the context of providing placement services to a client, an example of the former could be helping locate a suitable facility and helping make application for Medicaid or other assistance. An example of the latter might be coaching the client and family in how to be good consumers (for example, being assertive in getting the client transportation to a favorite weekly meeting). Case management also includes monitoring service interventions to ensure that they are producing the desired outcomes.

Feder, Scanlon, Edwards, and Hoffman (1987) found that residents of board-and-care facilities received fewer services than older people with similar needs who resided in their own homes in the same community. Hawes et al. (1993) found that only half of the 51 local agencies surveyed nationally provided case management services to board-and-care residents. For those involved in providing case management, most agencies focused on placement, with few coordinating needed services in the board-and-care setting and fewer still monitoring the quality of that care and the client's adjustment and progress. Florida was the exception: All residents who received state assistance in paying for board and care also received case management services.

Monitoring

In its narrowest definition, the monitoring of board and care involves ensuring compliance with standards and legal requirements. Many state agencies—whether social services, aging programs, or health departments—limit themselves to this level only. They conduct inspections, develop and implement corrective action plans, and oversee enforcement.

North Carolina's adult services programs in county departments of social services define their responsibilities for monitoring board-and-care homes in somewhat broader terms. In every county with at least one board-and-care facility ("domiciliary care homes" in North Carolina), the local department of social services is required to designate at least one adult homes social worker, whose duties include

- *promoting development of homes based on local needs*
- *providing consultation and technical assistance to home operators*
- *monitoring homes' compliance with standards, residents' rights, and other requirements (for example, civil rights, where applicable)*
- *investigating complaints about the care and treatment of residents in these homes*
- *working closely with others who share some responsibility for assuring resident's well-being.* (North Carolina Department of Human Resources, Division of Social Services, 1991, p. 34)

The charge to adult homes social workers (hereafter referred to as board-and-care social workers) with respect to North Carolina's board-and-care system is comprehensive. At times, however, the tasks seem to be in conflict. On the one hand, board-and-care social workers are asked to provide technical assistance and even help develop new homes where needed; on the other hand, social workers inspect homes for possible violations of rules and regulations. Board-and-care social workers must be knowledgeable and skilled at their work to carry out both these tasks.

The role of board-and-care social workers in North Carolina is only one strategy for monitoring board-and-care homes in the state. The role complements the work of inspectors from the state Division of Facility Services as well as the work of state and local long-term-care ombudsmen, overseen by the state's Division of Aging and the Area Agencies on Aging. Local sanitation and building inspectors also oversee board-and-care homes. This use of personnel from multiple agencies to monitor board and care is not unlike what is found in other states (Hawes et al., 1993). In discussing possible roles for board-and-care social workers, whether in adult services programs or such other oversight agencies as an ombudsman program, this chapter draws heavily on North Carolina's experience.

Values, Knowledge, and Professional Skills for Board-and-Care Social Workers

The role of board-and-care social workers in North Carolina provides a good illustration of the mix of roles that various adult services programs across the country might take in relation to board-and-care homes. Successfully managing the dual roles of inspector and consultant calls for exceptional skills in working with people, knowledge of the service population, and knowledge of the board-and-care industry. This section discusses some of the attributes essential for the effective performance of this role. It also discusses the monitoring tasks of assessment, documentation and reporting, and problem solving and advocacy that mark the day-to-day discharge of this role on behalf of board-and-care residents and their families.

VALUES AND ATTITUDES

One of the most important tasks of the people who oversee board-and-care homes is to recognize what values and beliefs they hold that are relevant to their jobs. All people have predispositions rooted in their value systems that have been reinforced by personal experience, and social workers are no different. Supervisors can help social workers identify and discuss their values and how these might influence the performance of their duties, just as supervisors need to make their values and the values of the agency clear, because these values will shape the nature of practice and outcomes for clients and their families.

Although the values that shape practice are myriad, two deserve some elaboration here. The first is the desirability or appropriateness of residential care compared with community care. Many people in the general public and the professional community have a negative perception of residential care, believing that few, if any, people would choose to live or work in board-and-care homes. The shortcomings of a few homes and individual staff members sometimes overshadow the dedication of the majority of homes and residential care staff. A quality board-

and-care home is a viable and appropriate choice for many people with disabilities. To work effectively, either as monitors of board-and-care homes or as providers of placement services, workers must clarify their values and beliefs regarding residential care.

A second set of values and beliefs falls under the general heading of clients' rights to self-determination and to privacy. Both are reflected in the *Declaration of Residents' Rights,* which applies to residents in long-term-care facilities in North Carolina (North Carolina General Statute 131-21). It is the responsibility of North Carolina's board-and-care social workers and personnel from the state Long-Term Care Ombudsman Program to see that those rights are respected and upheld.

The *Declaration of Residents' Rights* contains 16 articles, among whose provisions are the right to privacy; to receive care and services in keeping with federal and state law; to be free of mental and physical abuse, neglect, and exploitation; to make complaints and suggestions without fear of reprisal; to participate by choice in community activities; and to use social, political, religious, and medical resources or to decline participation. An acceptance and understanding of the values and beliefs reflected in such a declaration of rights is the basis of much of the social worker's advocacy on behalf of board-and-care residents.

KNOWLEDGE OF THE FIELD

The adult services workers dealing with board-and-care homes must know about residents' characteristics, regulations, historical and organizational context, facility operations, and resources. A basic understanding in each is important to the social worker in establishing self-confidence and credibility and in working effectively and efficiently. Social workers must understand the complexity of their tasks and value continuing education opportunities to help them enhance their knowledge and skills.

Knowledge about residents encompasses information about the conditions of people likely to reside in board-and-care homes—people with physical disabilities, developmental disabilities, and severe and persistent mental illness. Because many residents are older adults, workers also must know about aging. Specific information about especially challenging clients such as those with maladaptive behaviors—for example, wandering, sexual inappropriateness, and assaultive behaviors—is also important. Another important area of knowledge is the needs of people with acquired immune deficiency syndrome (AIDS).

Knowledge of regulations calls on the social worker to be well versed in the licensure standards, residents' rights, and other rules that affect board-and-care homes (for example, sanitation and fire safety requirements and civil rights). The worker must know not only how to reference rules but also how to interpret and apply them.

Knowledge of basic facility operations is also essential, particularly as they relate to the state's licensure standards. This may include food service, administration of medications, personal care services, and policies on the use of restraints.

The adult services social worker also must know how laws and rules for APS apply to board-and-care residents and their caregivers. In some instances the social worker also will be the worker responsible for evaluating an APS referral involving a board-and-care resident. The social worker must be careful to differentiate among APS, licensure, and residents' rights in conducting the evaluation, reporting findings, and making recommendations for action. The adult services supervisor has a vital role in ensuring that the board-and-care worker and the APS worker, when different, understand their respective roles and the importance of collaboration.

Some knowledge of the historical and organizational context of board-and-care facilities is vital. This includes knowing something about the history of board and care in the community, state, and nation; how this service has evolved to its present status; and where it might be headed as health care and long-term care are reformed. The effective social worker sees how board and care fits into the continuum of services.

PRACTICAL PROFESSIONAL SKILLS

The work of social workers with board and care, as viewed in the context of the assessment and change process, requires a challenging mix of skills in analysis, negotiation, consultation, diplomacy, and assertiveness. Just as almost every client presents a different scenario to the caseworker, the board-and-care social worker finds that each home's operation shows varying dispositions, strengths, and weaknesses. There are operators committed to complying with rules and solidly interested in enhanced quality of life for residents, but who have limited capacity to achieve these goals. There are others with the capacity, but whose motivations may compromise achievement of these goals. The provision of quality care requires both capacity (an understanding of what is expected and the ability to do what is necessary) and motivation (an interest in and commitment to performing the work as appropriate). Fortunately, many operators have both.

The challenge for the social worker is to work effectively with each home for the benefit of its residents, their families, and the community, taking into account differences in capacity and motivation. Success comes with time and technique. Over time, board-and-care social workers are able to discern the capacity and motivation of the facility's owners, managers and supervisors, and staff members. Here is a brief case example to illustrate effective practice.

CASE EXAMPLE

Licensure rules for board-and-care homes frequently involve oversight of medication practice. During a routine monitoring visit, the social worker discovers that medication practices are not always consistent with the physician's orders. Concerned about the well-being of the residents, the effective social worker works to determine the cause of the inconsistency between medication administration practices and physician orders. Is it the result of the staff members' lack of understanding about medication practices and their relationship to the residents' health and safety? Is there evidence of blatant disregard of physician's orders and their importance? Is the medication system itself poorly designed?

The social worker can begin assessing whether the issue is one of capacity or motivation by asking questions of those involved with all phases of medication administration. On subsequent visits the social worker can assess whether corrective action has been taken to ensure that an effective protocol is in place and that all involved are following it. Although it is the home's responsibility to correct the problem, regardless of its source, the social worker helps achieve compliance by developing insight about the capacity and motivation of the home's management and personnel. The worker's interpersonal skills, assessment and analysis, negotiation, consultation, diplomacy, and assertiveness all come into play in determining social workers' effectiveness in ensuring quality services for board-and-care residents. In all cases involving possible misuse of medications, the worker should consult with the proper medical authorities.

Using the Family Assessment and Change Method as a Basis for Monitoring Board-and-Care Homes

The role of adult services social workers in board-and-care homes can be broad. They often serve as both monitor and consultant. As a monitor, the social worker outlines expectations, watches with a critical eye, measures capacity and commitment, suggests remedial action, uses what means are available to see that it happens, and encourages movement toward higher goals. As a consultant the worker can be a helpful source of information and problem solving for a home. The roles of monitor and consultant reflect a complex and difficult mix of roles and tasks to ensure the well-being of board-and-care residents.

What helps board-and-care social workers avoid tackling an impossible task is being grounded with a clear sense of mission. The social worker's job is to contribute to ensuring quality of life and care for residents of board-and-care homes within the parameters of state laws, rules, and administrative procedures. Their job is not to operate the home but to ensure that its operation meets certain standards designed to protect and promote the interests of the residents.

Because the family assessment and change method presents a commonsense pattern for problem solving, with some modification it can be used as a guide to practice for the board-and-care social worker. The fundamental components of the family assessment and change method are comprehensive assessment; identification of problems, strengths, and corresponding goals; development and implementation of a service plan; and follow-up to ensure compliance. The board-and-care social worker's activities also include prevention of future problems through dissemination of information, training, monitoring, and consultation.

ASSESSMENT

The social worker's assessment of a board-and-care home mirrors in many ways the social worker's comprehensive functional assessment of a client. First and most important, the assessment should have a clear purpose and be organized to achieve this. The social worker visits homes for a variety of reasons. Monthly contacts can monitor and gauge the tenor of life and care for residents and can examine closely one or more areas of the home's operation. Every visit should begin with a walk to observe the home and interactions among residents and staff members. This observation can give the social worker some notion of the quality of care and life for the residents. These periodic visits should be a combination of scheduled and unscheduled contacts. The scheduled visit increases the likelihood of the social worker being able to meet with the home's management. The unscheduled contact can provide a more realistic view of life for residents.

Second, in North Carolina the board-and-care social worker makes an extended annual visit for the purpose of evaluating the home for renewal of its license. In a sense, this represents a cumulative reassessment. It should reflect what the social worker has learned over the course of the periodic visits as well as what this more comprehensive visit reveals.

The third reason for assessing a home is to evaluate a complaint registered about some aspect of the home's service to residents. The timeliness of the social worker's response will depend on the nature of the complaint and whether it might involve protective services or affects residents' rights.

The board-and-care social worker has two principal tools to use in conducting an assessment for any of these reasons: (1) the licensure standards and (2) the residents' bill of rights. The standards present in varying degrees of specificity what is expected of licensed homes. Not surprisingly, standards in such areas as the physical plant and meal service tend to be more exact than those that define the home's responsibilities for residents' psychosocial needs. The bill of rights offers guiding principles that reinforce the view that people should not be asked to sacrifice basic rights simply because they live in a board-and-care setting.

The social worker has several tasks relative to these tools, the most basic of which is to have a solid familiarity with each. Although excellent practice does not require memorization of the standards and rights, it does suggest that the social worker must have a working knowledge of their content and, above all, an appreciation of their intent. Social workers must go through the mental rigors of determining the intent of each rule and right in terms of its perceived benefit for residents.

For instance, many of the rules specifying minimum nutritional requirements are designed for a more sedentary population age 55 and older; logically, the quantity of food should be adjusted in a home of younger, active residents. The board-and-care social worker looks for compliance in relation to the quality of care and life for residents, not just because "that's what the regs call for." The social worker looks for evidence of positive outcomes for residents when conducting an assessment, rather than limiting attention to whether the home achieves minimum compliance with the regulations.

The board-and-care social worker's second task in using the tools to carry out assessments is to organize the work so that it is manageable and systematic. The effective social worker spends some time before visiting the home reviewing the monitoring file and planning the assessment (for example, areas to address and which monitoring approach to use). In North Carolina, the state's Division of Facility Services provides a checklist for monitoring board-and-care homes, a useful tool to promote consistency and thoroughness. An abbreviated example of a guide for monitoring records, adapted from one used by the social workers in Mecklenburg County, North Carolina, appears in Table 17-1.

Just as Mecklenburg's guide indicates that a 10 percent sample of resident records is adequate in certain homes over a certain size, similarly, not all medication administration records must be reviewed to determine whether record keeping meets basic requirements. A social worker can make a reasonable assessment by checking a random sample of records. Similarly, a social worker cannot expect to observe or talk with each resident, especially in larger facilities, but a sample of those engaged in group activities, those staying in their rooms, and those sitting idly in lounge areas can give a balanced perspective of resident life and satisfaction.

The board-and-care social worker's third task is to use all senses in conducting an assessment. An assessment in almost every area of operation involves some combination of reviewing records; observing residents in their daily living and staff members in their performance of duties; interviewing staff members, residents, and their families; and physical inspection. In the food service area, for

Table 17-1

GUIDELINES FOR MONITORING BOARD AND CARE (BASED ON THOSE FOR MECKLENBURG COUNTY, NORTH CAROLINA)

Does each resident in the home have a record in the home's files that contains the following information? (For "homes for the aged and disabled," a 10 percent sample may be drawn.)

a. Form 1865, Resident Register, with a minimum of five specific items recorded
b. Form DFS 4188 or equivalent, Resident Financial Record
c. Form DFS 4190 or equivalent, Report of Health Services to Resident
d. Contracts
e. Form FL-2, Physician's Determination of Need for Services, not over one year old
f. TB test report, not over one year old
g. Personal funds record (if applicable)

example, the social worker can compare the menu with the food being provided to residents; request a test tray to measure the temperature, size of portions, taste, and appearance; interview a sample of residents to learn how satisfied they are with the meals; observe the assistance provided to residents during the meal; and examine the quantity of food left on the trays after residents have finished eating. These are just some of the ways a social worker can assess the home's compliance with the intent of the standards and rights as they relate to the meal service.

A fourth task in conducting an assessment is to set a positive example for the home. For example, the social worker shows respect for residents' privacy by knocking on doors and asking to enter and visit. Another example is taking the time to listen to a resident's concerns and asking permission from residents before examining the orderliness of their rooms. The social worker is careful not to step outside of the monitor's role and thus refrains from assisting with personal care or physically handling residents to assess their condition. If the social worker needs to examine a wound on a resident's upper leg, he or she asks personnel at the home to be present and to assist the resident in showing the wound.

Another reason for setting a positive tone for monitoring is to defuse the concern of some residents and staff members that providing honest feedback will lead to retaliation by coworkers or management. The effective social worker seeks the home's overt acceptance of the value of external monitoring. If the home's management appears to discourage open discussion of problems and concerns, the social worker may need to show greater discretion in how problems are presented and be prepared to advocate on behalf of aggrieved residents.

The social worker may take a concern shared by a resident about the irregular time that dinner is served and systematically explore the extent to which this is an issue. This might be done by asking a number of residents, family members, employees, and managers of the home about when meals are routinely served; by asking managers to have a scheduled mealtime posted and actual time of service recorded for some reasonable period; and by planning an occasional unannounced visit to assess the mealtime firsthand.

A more difficult problem might be one in which a resident alleges that personal mail is routinely opened but is too anxious to complain about this directly or to allow the social worker to investigate further. In this instance the social worker has no alternative but to reemphasize to the home's management how important it is to respect all residents' rights, including the right "to send and receive mail promptly and unopened, unless the resident requests that someone open and read mail" (North Carolina General Statute 131D-21). Management can be asked how this right is reinforced among staff members, and the social worker can ask various residents, including the original complainant, about their receipt of personal mail.

A fifth task is the oral and written communication of findings from the assessment. Timely, clearly stated, and factual written documentation and reporting are critical in following due process. Clearly stated documentation that notifies the administrator of violations and provides an opportunity for negotiating reasonable time frames for correction is fundamental to due process.

In communicating findings, the effective board-and-care social worker takes time to cite both strengths and weaknesses in the home's operation. Although social workers are concerned with identification and correction of problems, they also should recognize in which areas the home is doing well or has made progress. Recording and reporting strengths is a supportive function that encourages continued positive performance and often can be used to spur the home to address a problem area.

In documentation and reporting, the effective social worker differentiates between substantiated violations of rules and recommendations or concerns important to the quality of care and life of residents but not related directly to the licensure rules or residents' rights. This distinction is important because of the leverage the board-and-care social worker has to encourage compliance. Violations of licensure rules and residents' rights can be addressed through the formal corrective action process. Steps to address recommendations and concerns require the home's understanding and acceptance of their importance, so the social worker may need diplomatic skills and persuasiveness to induce the home to make changes.

Whether the problem found by the social worker is a formal violation or an informal concern, the social worker's basic task is the same. The effective social worker, in an enabling role, helps the home understand why the violation or concern is considered a deficiency in performance, why corrective action is needed, and what the possible consequences are for the residents and the home if the problem is not remedied. Whenever possible, this explanation should be framed in terms of how the situation could adversely affect the residents of the home. The goal is for the home's management to acknowledge that a problem exists, which is necessary to ensure appropriate corrective action.

FOSTERING CHANGE

On the basis of the assessment, the social worker has determined whether there are problems that violate standards or rights or that interfere with achievement of quality care and supervision of the residents. When problems exist and change is needed, it is helpful to work closely with the home's administration to set priorities based on the probable effect on residents, identify the probable source of the problems when possible, and identify what the goal of any correction will be. Otherwise there is a strong likelihood of focusing on easy but inconsequential corrections or treating symptoms rather than causes, which make the chance for recurrence high and the risk of serious consequences great.

With the use of food service as an illustration, a board-and-care social worker might find that the meal served is attractive and adequate in portions and nutritional requirements. The social worker notes, though, that the meal is not consistent with the posted menu (that is, substitutions have been made). The social worker also observes that several residents with impairments are not receiving needed assistance in eating and their personal care records document some weight loss over the past two months. Although it would be important for the social worker to cite the home's failure to record substitutions before serving the meal, reemphasize to appropriate personnel the reasons for this requirement, and monitor continued compliance on subsequent visits, the immediate and serious issue is those residents who are not receiving assistance. Is it because of a lack of capacity or motivation on the part of the home's personnel? What will ensure short- and long-term corrections?

In recognition of due process, the social worker provides ample warnings, along with instructions, to assist the home with problem solving and change. The social worker is careful not to overstep and assume any of the operator's responsibility for managing the home. By offering suggestions about how to remedy a problem or by serving as a sounding board for the home's management, the social worker helps empower the home to take decisive action to improve conditions for residents.

Sometimes the principal cause for the problems will be found in a difference in values between the worker and the home's operator or staff. This may be the most challenging of situations for the social worker. Social workers cope with this circumstance by being thorough and fair; by stating their findings objectively in terms of how residents are affected and citing the appropriate references from standards, rights, and other sources; by documenting conclusions and citations in clear and concise terms; by presenting expectations in a timely and understandable manner; and by following up to reassess corrective actions and their effect on residents.

PREVENTION

An important aspect of the board-and-care social worker's role is prevention. Prevention involves a combination of dissemination of information, training, consultation, advocacy, and consistency in performance of the monitoring function. Although the operators of board-and-care homes have the responsibility for staying informed and developing the skills necessary for successful compliance with requirements, local adult services programs can make their job easier by supporting homes in this regard. By taking this approach, these programs demonstrate to the homes and the community their commitment to the quality of care and life for residents.

There are methods adult services programs might use to prevent problems. To disseminate information and training, the program and its social worker could sponsor periodic group meetings with board-and-care administrators to share relevant information about standards and other requirements, demonstrate ways to meet these requirements, and help them solve problems they are experiencing. This gives the adult services program an opportunity to offer training that it believes will most benefit local operators. A newsletter could be another method to share information. Individual consultation offered during visits to the home also can be effective.

A related role that board-and-care social workers can assume involves their advocacy on behalf of homes and residents. Examples of this could be requesting an interpretation of some requirement that is generally causing problems in its application; working with a community college to develop training programs for aides within the homes; or orienting new members of the local long-term-care ombudsman program in a way that contributes not only to their protection of residents' rights but also to the public image of board-and-care homes. Prevention of problems also calls for social workers to be clear with the management of homes and others about their monitoring role and to be consistent in it. Compliance is enhanced when operators know what to expect.

Managing Challenges

Board-and-care issues present some of the most complex challenges to state and local adult services programs. Three areas of particular importance are (1) concerns caused by increasing demographic pressures and the need to control costs, (2) access for residents to case management and community-based services, and (3) training for those who monitor board-and-care homes.

For many people interested in the well-being of board-and-care residents, there is concern that this population is becoming increasingly impaired (Feder et al., 1987; Hawes et al., 1993; Research Triangle Institute, 1995; U.S. Congress, House Subcommittee on Health and Long-Term Care of the Select Committee on Aging, 1989). In addition to demographic pressures—namely the growth of the population age 85 and older, whose members tend to have more impairments—public policies aimed at controlling costs associated with nursing home and hospital care and reducing the institutional placement of people with mental illness and developmental disabilities heighten the risk of inappropriate placements in board-and-care homes. This challenge is best met by clear criteria on placement, a well-trained staff, and careful monitoring by concerned stakeholders.

Board-and-care residents often have multiple chronic needs. There is mounting evidence that some board-and-care residents receive fewer needed services than community-dwelling older people (Feder et al., 1987; Hawes et al., 1993). Local placement workers, case managers, and ombudsmen report that many community-based services were either unavailable or available only in a limited amount to board-and-care residents. Mental health services in particular are largely unavailable to board-and-care residents, which is alarming given the high number of residents who experience some mental impairment (Hawes et al., 1993; Nelson & Streets, 1993).

Finally, many people who are engaged in monitoring board and care lack professional training, yet these workers must meet the challenge of managing complex interorganizational issues around monitoring and individual issues concerning the physical and mental status of residents. Training is essential to the effective performance of their roles. Nelson and Streets (1993) found that adult homes social workers in North Carolina are extremely receptive to continuing education.

Topics of greatest interest include more knowledge about geriatric social work, medical terminology and medications, developmental disabilities, and chronic mental illness.

Summary

Improvement in the quality of care provided to board-and-care residents will require the concerted efforts of many individuals and organizations. Public adult services programs, with their history of commitment to adults with disabilities, can be significant contributors. An appreciation of the role that board and care plays in long-term-care services provided in the community and knowledge about the needs of residents will help to ensure appropriate placements and ongoing access to needed community-based services.

Key Points

Excellent adult services social workers responsible for monitoring board and care

- work in the interest of the local adult services agency, the state, and especially the residents of board-and-care homes
- manage their own values so as not to interfere with the performance of their duties
- are knowledgeable about resident populations, rules, board-and-care context, operating procedures of homes, and pertinent resources
- are skilled in analysis, negotiation, consultation, diplomacy, and assertiveness
- are willing to confer with other resources, including the adult services supervisor and regional and state consultants
- are fully capable of conducting a comprehensive assessment that is purposeful and organized; focuses on licensure standards and residents' rights; is based on the intent of requirements relative to outcomes for residents; involves record reviews, observation, interviews, and physical inspection using all senses; determines degree of concern and differentiates violations from recommendations; includes strengths as well as weaknesses in homes' operations; communicates findings and conclusions in a clear and consistent manner; and is conducted in such a way as to set a positive example for the home
- are effective in managing a process for problem solving and change that sets priorities, identifies probable sources of problems, identifies corrective action needed, ensures compliance over time, and uses community and state resources to provide consultation and technical assistance
- understand the concept of due process and follow procedures consistent with it
- are effective in preventing problems from occurring through dissemination of information, training and consultation, advocacy, and consistency in the monitoring role.

Excellent adult services managers
- select and develop workers with necessary values, knowledge, and skills
- assign compatible duties to social workers when job responsibilities must be broader than board-and-care monitoring
- show appreciation for the difficulty of the social worker's responsibility and exhibit interest in this area
- provide clear expectations to promote consistency among social workers in their performance of duties
- are equally clear about what support the social worker can expect from the agency in their performance of duties, including the recommendation of negative licensure action
- assist the social worker in establishing effective linkages with necessary resources, including the state and local ombudsmen.

Excellent leaders
- develop and operate within a framework for long-term care that clearly delineates the purpose of board and care relative to the continuum of services for adults with disabilities
- emphasize clarity and consistency in monitoring for compliance with requirements
- provide rationales for regulations and timely interpretations to assist social workers in obtaining compliance
- support development of the knowledge and skills of social workers
- enable social workers to stay informed about matters affecting their work with homes and assist them in performance of duties
- empower social workers by supporting their conclusions and actions when accomplished through excellent practice.

References

American Association of Retired Persons. (1985). *Preserving independence, supporting needs: The role of board and care homes.* Washington, DC: Author.

Beyer, J., Bulkley, J., & Hopkins, P. (1984). *A model act regulating board and care homes: Guidelines for states.* Washington, DC: American Bar Association.

Center for Aging Research and Educational Services. (1990). *Manpower in county departments of social services. Executive summary and final report.* Chapel Hill, NC: Author.

Cole, T. R. (1987, Summer). Class, culture, & coercion: A historical perspective on longterm care. *Generations*, pp. 9–15.

Dobkin, L. (1989). *The board and care system: A regulatory jungle.* Washington, DC: American Association of Retired Persons.

Feder, J., Scanlon, W., Edwards, J., & Hoffman, J. (1987). Board and care: Problem or solution? In M. Moon, G. Gaberlavage, & S. Newman (Eds.), *Preserving independence, supporting needs: The role of board and care homes* (pp. 27–39). Washington, DC: American Association of Retired Persons.

Hawes, C., Wildfire, J. B., & Lux, L. J. (1993). *The regulation of board and care homes: Results of a survey in the 50 states and the District of Columbia.* Washington, DC: American Association of Retired Persons.

Nelson, G. M., & Streets, D. W. (1993). Adult foster care home social workers: Roles, responsibilities, and training needs. *Adult Residential Care Journal, 7*(1), 5–16.

North Carolina Department of Human Resources, Division of Social Services. (1991). *The North Carolina social services plan: A road map for change.* Raleigh: Author.

Research Triangle Institute. (1995). *Study of North Carolina domiciliary care home residents* (Prepared for the North Carolina Department of Human Resources and the Division of Facility Services). Research Triangle Park, NC: Author.

Sherman, S. R., & Newman, E. S. (1988). *Foster families for adults: A community alternative in long-term care.* New York: Columbia University Press.

Social Security Act Amendments of 1976. P.L. 94-552, 90 Stat. 2540.

Talbot, J. A. (1985). Community care for the chronically mentally ill. *Psychiatric Clinics of North America, 2,* 437–448.

U.S. Congress, House Subcommittee on Health and Long-Term Care of the Select Committee on Aging. (1989). *Board and care homes in America: A national tragedy.* 101st Congress, Committee Publication No. 101-711 (March). Washington, DC: U.S. Government Printing Office.

U.S. Department of Health and Human Services. (1990). *Board and care.* New York: Author.

PART 4

Leadership and Management

CHAPTER 18

Strategic Planning and Management

DENNIS W. STREETS

Agencies with adult services programs are vital parts of state and community service delivery systems for younger and older adults with disabilities throughout the nation. Whether these programs include a range of services from placement to in-home assistance or focus primarily on protecting adults with disabilities, their leadership is responsible for ensuring effective services and quality outcomes for consumers. The provision of human services to a growing population of adults with disabilities is becoming increasingly demanding and challenging. Policy advocates, planners, and administrators must become increasingly aware of the inter- and intraorganizational complexities of delivering services (Myrtle & Wilber, 1994).

Effective management in adult services requires mastery of a mix of conceptual, human relations, and technical skills to address the needs of consumers and operate in increasingly complex organizational environments (Edwards & Yankey, 1991). In focusing on program planning, this chapter examines the application of many of these skills for planning adult services programs. Planning involves taking charge of the future to improve outcomes for adults with disabilities and their families.

In shaping an approach to program planning for adult services, this chapter draws on planning lessons and concepts from the works of Jenne (1986), Bryson (1988), and Pfeiffer, Goodstein, and Nolan (1989). It also applies concepts concerning the revitalization of government from Osborne and Gaebler (1992) and on effective management from Edwards and Yankey (1991). Some lessons also come from applying planning models to home and community care systems in North Carolina (Center for Aging Research and Educational Services, 1992). The chapter begins by highlighting issues and questions for adult services programs, presents a general community planning model for adult services, and concludes with a discussion of planning issues specific to adult services.

Planning Issues and Questions for Adult Services

Although adult services programs are essential components of home and community care for younger and older adults with disabilities, in many states and communities adult services are but one part of public agencies' larger program and mission. In states where the adult services program is administered through the public welfare agency, agency directors will have to balance competing demands for their attention by child welfare and income maintenance programs with the growing demands for adult services. In states and communities where adult services and aging network programs are jointly administered, a balancing of the interests and demands of the Older Americans Act and adult services programs is in order.

In both cases, compelling reasons exist to be deliberate in considering the future of adult services. The needs of homeless people, of those afflicted by acquired immune deficiency syndrome (AIDS), of those with developmental disabilities and chronic mental illness, and of a growing population of older adults with increasing risk of functional impairments will probably continue to be the responsibility of state, regional, and community adult services programs. With so many competing demands, strategic managers must be willing and able to make decisions in support of excellence in adult services.

Some of these decisions involve the internal workings of the agency or program. Others involve the role of adult services within the community and its relationship with other agencies and organizations. Issues that confront the adult services programs include

- What services for adults should be offered through the community adult services program? Should they be offered directly by agency personnel or provided by others under contract?
- Among the services offered directly by adult services, which should be given priority in terms of social workers' time, access to clerical support, training, and supervision? On what basis is this determination made?
- What is the goal of each of the services offered by adult services? To whom is each service targeted? What are its results for clients and families?
- What personnel are needed to offer these services to clients to achieve the desired goals? What knowledge, skills, attitudes, and work habits are required of these personnel?
- Are there services that adult services programs should help develop within the community but not be directly responsible for operating?
- Are there services that adult services programs are currently offering that could be discontinued or transferred to some other provider?
- What role should adult services assume within the community in influencing the expenditure of public funds for services to adults?

The purpose of this chapter is to encourage managers to think strategically about these questions. It introduces a framework for the strategic manager who leads or participates in community planning. This framework is similar in philosophy and in many particulars to the family assessment and change method discussed throughout this book. It involves collecting and analyzing objective and subjective information for decision making and action. Because most planning takes place within the context of the agency and its adult services program, although in a less formal manner, this chapter examines several features of effective planning important to strategic management within an agency. It is this latter discussion that may have the most immediate relevance to managers of adult services programs, but a familiarity with communitywide planning is also vital.

Communitywide Planning

There are many opportunities for adult services programs to participate in communitywide planning for human services. Some of these initiatives are prompted by decisions made outside the community (for example, the state's development of policy in an area such as home and community care). Many more initiatives develop locally as a result of a demand for action or interest on the part of agencies, organizations, and local government to make the best use of local resources. Interagency councils and coalitions can be found in almost every community, and although they have many purposes, one common purpose is to collaborate for short- and long-range planning to maximize the use of resources to address important needs in the community.

In many communities throughout the nation, adult services programs influence the character of the community's response to the problems faced by adults and their families, especially those with social and economic needs. Adult services programs are frequently unique in the breadth of their contact with diverse client populations and their comprehensive consideration of problems on an individual and community level. This does not mean that adult services programs are or should be principally responsible for meeting all needs but that they have a role in seeing that the community is responsive to those needs. Social services boards in many communities are frequently charged with helping adults with disabilities, which calls for effective planning.

An effective process for such planning is used by several communities in North Carolina to meet the needs of older citizens. These communities have followed a strategic planning approach designed "to assist an organization, community, or other entity to take decisive and feasible action on a few priority issues" (Center for Aging Research and Educational Services, 1990a, p. G-5). In several community planning efforts, adult services agencies provided leadership. On the basis of their experience, these agencies identified the following benefits gained from such community planning:

- improved working relationships among service agencies
- better understanding of the needs of the local population
- avoidance of previous mistakes in strategy design
- expanded view of available resources
- increased community commitment to services.

Another benefit is that participation in community planning can empower adult services staff members. They are able to advocate not only for individual clients but also for changes in the system to benefit groups of clients. The approach these communities used in planning strategically has eight basic steps, reviewed below. Elements of this approach to community planning are drawn from Bryson (1988) and Pfeiffer et al. (1989).

MAKING A COMMITMENT AND ORGANIZING THE PROCESS

At this first stage, those in the position to authorize the community planning process must be willing to accept the risks inherent in planning and change. To feel confident in doing this, there must be a clear purpose to the planning and a sound structure for leadership and participation. Those who will lead the process must think carefully about how to conduct it. Without an effective process, it is unlikely that the plan will be useful, because those responsible for its implementation must understand it and be committed to its success. In organizing the process, the planning group must make decisions about the structure for leadership and participation.

Decisions about the staffing and advisory leadership are among the most important, because those who undertake these activities shoulder the bulk of the day-to-day work associated with planning. Typical chores of staffing leadership are data collection and analysis, correspondence with participants and others, support and clerical duties, and production of written reports, including the plan itself. The advisory leadership has the principal task of establishing an atmosphere conducive to an open exchange of information and ideas in which decisions are made by consensus to the extent possible. Together the staffing and advisory leadership have the responsibility of directing the process so that it remains focused and on schedule.

CLARIFYING VALUES AND FORMULATING A MISSION

One of the first important tasks of the planning leadership is to establish a climate for the free exchange of ideas and concerns among participants. This includes reaching agreement on ground rules to guide the resolution of disagreements and the process for decision making. It also involves bringing to the surface participants' assumptions, values, and beliefs that influence their perspectives about priority issues and possible solutions.

The time spent developing or refining a mission statement is another aspect of this early stage of planning that requires leadership and benefits from different perspectives. Formulation of a mission statement forces participants to reach general agreement on what should be done, for whom, and how. This statement is the touchstone for the remainder of the process.

SCANNING THE ENVIRONMENT

A critical step in the planning process is the environmental scan, which involves collecting information to identify major risks to and opportunities for realizing the mission. The environmental scan looks at factors inside and outside the community that will affect clients and their families and the capacity of the human services system to assist them. It is similar to the assessment phase in the family assessment and change method for social work practice.

The scan helps bridge the gap in knowledge and experience among the planning participants by giving them common information to make a collective decision on what are the most important issues. How much time is spent in scanning the environment will depend on what is already known and available for study. Sources of information for the scan include clients' demographics, census data, and opinions of key informants. The process of collecting information affords another valuable opportunity to involve stakeholders. Stakeholders are individuals and groups that have a vested interest or stake in the issue under consideration. They are people or organizations that can either be affected by decisions made or can influence decision making. Planning involves understanding competing interests, politics, and power (Pfeffer, 1992).

SELECTING KEY ISSUES AND SETTING GOALS

With a scan in hand, the next task is the identification of a few priority issues and the development of corresponding goals. The issues should be selected because there would be serious consequences if nothing is done, because there is an absence of other leadership or intervention, or because a substantial change for the better can be realized. Both the issues and goal statements should be client- and family-centered, because the success of the plan is measured by its positive effect on human conditions or circumstances. This approach mirrors that taken by social workers identifying problems and strengths and setting goals with clients and families.

An issue statement is a statement of a problem, need, or opportunity that relates to clients; it is not a solution. Although the work that goes into identifying issues may later help with strategies, this is not the time to develop them. The goal statement for each issue is a global description of a long-range condition toward which efforts will be directed. Although this state may not be fully achievable, it does inspire action.

CONDUCTING A SWOT ANALYSIS

When the planners have identified a priority problem or circumstance and a related goal, the stage is set for looking more critically at the issue. Salient questions include the following:

- What are the reasons this issue is a problem, concern, or interest?
- What are the strengths and weaknesses in how the matter is currently being addressed?
- What are the outside opportunities and threats that could affect achievement of the related goal?

In the planning literature, this phase is referred to as the SWOT (strengths, weaknesses, opportunities, and threats) analysis.

By its nature, this is a stage of questioning and discovery designed to establish objectives and identify strategies for their accomplishment. The identification of objectives gives greater substance to the goals. The objectives state specifically what will change in the condition or circumstance of adult services clients and families as a result of strategic actions. If done correctly, anything and everything is subject to being questioned during this phase, and thus it is a somewhat risky time for those who have a stake in the outcome. For example, in considering the effectiveness of an existing adult services program, the SWOT analysis could produce findings that suggest that a different approach or provider might be more appropriate, a conclusion affecting those now offering the service. Therefore, the process for conducting the analysis should be carefully planned along with the method for considering the results. Questions to consider about how to conduct the analysis include

- Will information be gathered through the organization's self-questioning and data gathering?
- How will disputes about information and conclusions be resolved?
- How and with whom will findings be shared?

This is another stage in the process that offers an opportunity for involving stakeholders.

SELECTING STRATEGIES AND DEVELOPING THE ACTION PLAN

With an understanding of what may enable or inhibit achievement of objectives, the planning participants finally return to the area where they usually want to begin—identifying solutions. This stage should begin creatively, allowing participants to brainstorm as many different strategies as possible. Participants build on what currently exists and think of new approaches to achieve the objectives. The time spent in conducting a SWOT analysis should aid in the identification and then selection of the best strategic option or combination of options.

The final selection of a strategic approach should be based on criteria determined ahead of time by the planning participants. These criteria would include compatibility with the goal, immediate and long-range benefits, acceptability to intended audience and authorizing body (for example, local social services board, county commission), political feasibility, and affordability. Other criteria for selection of a strategy might be the ease with which it can be operationalized with existing resources, lack of disruption to existing service systems, or independence from outside support or interference.

Because the goal of planning is action rather than good intentions, the planning process does not end with recommendations. Instead, the strategies are transformed into operational statements that specify who does what, when, and how. This becomes the strategic action plan used to marshal the resources necessary to achieve the identified goals for clients and their families.

IMPLEMENTATION

Because the planning process is designed to include the appropriate stakeholders at each critical juncture, implementation of the plan should represent a natural continuation of effort rather than a distinct activity. This is the time to put into operation what the planners and stakeholders have agreed on and committed themselves to doing. There are several key elements to effective implementation. First and foremost is securing the commitment of stakeholders. A second element important to successful implementation is marketing. The initial presentation of the plan should be highly publicized to reinforce messages that should have been shared with the public and community stakeholders throughout the process. Any changes in purpose or direction should not come as a surprise during implementation. Third, continuing communication about the progress of implementation is also important. New and unexpected barriers to implementation will undoubtedly emerge, and so the planning group will probably need to encourage continued support for the plan and advocate on its behalf to counteract or overcome obstacles.

MONITORING AND UPDATING

The process cannot end with the production of a plan and movement toward its implementation. As Jenne (1986) advised, "No matter how well the strategies are planned, carrying them out will be as hard as any collective activity the community has undertaken, and someone must be a patron and a leader to rekindle the fire of enthusiasm when progress is slow or resistance is high" (p. 41).

The responsibility for monitoring implementation of the plan should not rest entirely on those who are assigned to carry it out. Some individual or group should provide oversight and recommend corrective measures that will keep the plan on course and modify it to respond to any significant changes. This means that the oversight body must have access to information to evaluate progress in implementation.

Community planning projects require considerable support. With the assistance of outside funding and participants volunteering their time and energy, many such efforts will take from 12 to 18 months of group work to complete. The availability of staff members with the necessary skills and temperament is vital to such projects. A local community planning process requires the time and energy of capable personnel, clerical and material support for their work, access to vital information, and the dedicated effort of all important stakeholders.

Although successful community planning benefits from a thoughtful, step-by-step approach, unforeseen contingencies will arise. Effective administrators must be flexible, capable of regrouping, and able to respecify issues when necessary. The "ready, fire, aim!" perspective on strategic planning recognizes that events and circumstances may sometimes call on planners to jump and then look, or at least jump and look simultaneously, to ensure that the program comes down in an acceptable position (Gummer, 1992). Planning, like the lives of many adult services clients and families, is not always a tidy affair.

Planning for Adult Services

The experience of community planning and service efforts in North Carolina and elsewhere (American Public Welfare Association and the National Association of State Units on Aging, 1988, 1989) proved invaluable in revealing some "dos and don'ts" that should be useful for all adult services programs to consider. Some considerations are particularly important to the strategic manager responsible for planning adult social services.

Some community adult services programs will have the need and the resources to undertake planning at the same level as communitywide projects. Although those who have engaged in such extensive planning frequently believe it is worth the investment of time, energy, and other expense, not all adult services programs may need or desire to undertake planning at this level of detail and sophistication. However, all programs engage in planning of some sort, and strategic planning is a process that applies equally well to organizations and communities.

Planning takes place in a variety of forms and at different levels within a community adult services program. There are work plans developed for program areas and for the individual staff members within these areas. The agency's development of a budget is by itself a planning exercise. The extent to which the budget is linked to program goals and objectives varies among agencies, but in all cases, decisions about where to direct funds represent a plan.

Work plans and budgets are essential tools of the agency in administering programs and managing resources, but in the absence of a mission they are less likely to be effective for clients and families. Many work plans and budgets are self-perpetuating (new ones are developed as a continuation of current activities without serious questioning of purpose or priority). Strategic managers encourage questioning to provide renewed vigor to work plans, budgets, and the personnel and programs they govern. In this sense, the strategic manager is a planner. The effective human services manager recognizes that planning must be oriented to the future rather than to the status quo, that it should focus on outcomes for clients, that it is influenced by values and assumptions that are part of the agency culture, that stakeholders should be identified and involved in the process, that it involves setting clear priorities based on resources and mission, and most of all that it is a continuous process.

ORIENTATION TO THE FUTURE

Every adult services program has two possible futures: the one its personnel would like to see occur and the one that will occur if events are simply allowed to take their course. Those people who are serious about planning see their role as helping to "steer" adult services toward the desired future, as opposed to "rowing" aimlessly or staying fixed on a predetermined route that is no longer appropriate (Osborne & Gaebler, 1992). Whether excellence in adult services is achieved will largely depend on the commitment made to questioning the present and planning for the future. As Robert Kennedy remarked, "We cannot stand idly by and expect our dreams to come true under their own power. The future is not a gift. It is an achievement" (Wortman & Rhodes, 1969, pp. 51, 53). A responsibility of management is determining how adult services programs must change and what should remain the same in light of the program's mission, what is known about emerging needs of clients and families, shifting expectations within the community, and trends in the availability of resources.

Planning at its best is not designed to help an organization out of a crisis but to avoid one (Edmondson, 1990). Planning calls for anticipating the future and constantly reevaluating the system in a changing environment. Planning, like leadership, demands continuous alertness, curiosity, and impatience in pursuit of a mission that is constantly in focus (Bennis, 1991). In constructing the future, the capabilities of individuals within organizations and communities must be merged to respond effectively to the needs of adults with disabilities and their families.

Chapter 2 emphasizes the importance of having a mission statement for the adult services program that is consistent with the mission for the agency. Developing this mission encourages taking time to think about the special characteristics and forces that drive the program and the agency. It is the chance to step back from urgent and routine matters to consider the future character of the adult services program. This statement of mission is a critical frame of reference for all other decisions to be made about the program. The presence of a mission empowers workers to perform their duties.

FOCUS ON CLIENTS

The worth of adult services programs is measured by their ability to maintain or improve the functioning and quality of life of adult services clients. Services must be continually examined in the context of community needs and administrative structure and service delivery operations to make them more responsive to the individual, family, and community.

It is easy to assume that programs operate in the best interest of clients, but without testing this assumption one cannot be sure. The following are questions for strategic managers to consider in assessing whether their planning for adult services is client and family centered:

- Does the adult services program have a mission statement that is clear about the social needs of clients and families that adult services is striving to address?
- Is it clear who is to benefit from each service (for example, in-home or adult day care) and are resources targeted accordingly?
- Is the program willing to ask what it can do to improve the conditions or circumstances of adult clients and their families?
- Are decisions about allocation of resources determined primarily by the needs of clients and family members rather than the needs and preferences of staff and other interests?

Programs that plan with a focus on clients and families

- collect and manage data to identify unmet needs of clients and families and evaluate current services in terms of outcomes for clients and families
- offer clients and their families opportunities to share ideas and concerns about the services provided
- make use of training opportunities, the professional literature, and other sources of continuing education in search of improved ways to address clients' needs.

VALUES AND ASSUMPTIONS

All people have biases and predispositions that affect their decisions and actions. These attitudes and beliefs are largely based on knowledge, experience, and surroundings. Those who work in adult services programs are not any different in this regard. This book has discussed the importance of acknowledging the values and assumptions of social workers in their practice with clients and families. Similarly, the strategic manager recognizes that values and assumptions have a lot to do with the character of the adult services program. One of the most important tasks of the effective manager is understanding the assumptions and values under which the agency and program operate, whether by design or habit.

The effect of values and assumptions is especially significant when difficult choices must be made. Is it better to provide a little care to a large number of clients or an adequate amount to a few? Should a program change its approach to service delivery when it is in the clients' best interest but could adversely affect existing staff members? Should the agency stay silent when it recognizes a glaring need (for example, housing and supportive services for people with AIDS) if there is little community support and ample work in other areas?

The strategic manager is not only willing to consider the effect of values and assumptions but makes a conscious effort to bring them to the surface in the context of identifying a set of principles to guide decision making for the adult services program. Some questions to consider include

- Should the future of the adult services program be influenced more by the interests and skills of current staff members, the leadership of the agency, local politics, decisions made at the state level, or the needs of clients?
- Is this a time to be proactive or cautious?
- Should ideas and initiatives be driven by clients' needs or the availability of resources?
- What should receive greater emphasis—quality or quantity of service?

Who decides these guiding principles is as important as what they are. The principles must be accepted by the adult services personnel, the administration (for example, director and board), and the community. For this to happen, there must be an open discussion in which these stakeholders are represented.

An example of why it is important to recognize and consider various perspectives is found in the results of the 1988 study of personnel in North Carolina's county adult services programs (Center for Aging Research and Educational

Services, 1990b). Asked about the availability of 25 home and community-based services for adults, social workers and supervisors rated two as least adequate: (1) intermediate nursing care (mentioned by 56 percent of social workers and 69 percent of supervisors) and (2) respite services (50 percent and 68 percent, respectively). On the other hand, intermediate care was not among the services mentioned most often by administrators, of whom only 41 percent rated the supply as inadequate. Administrators rated recreation for individuals with physical disabilities, transportation, and respite services (64.2 percent, 55.6 percent, and 55.3 percent, respectively) as being the services least available. In contrast, 43.3 percent of supervisors and 47.3 percent of social workers rated recreation for individuals with physical disabilities as inadequate, and the percentages for transportation were 51.1 percent of supervisors and 40.2 percent of social workers. One cannot draw conclusions about who is right and who is wrong in their presumptions about the adequacy of services. The important point is that such differences of opinion exist among those in positions that can influence service options available to clients.

Another example of this was evident in the response of these three groups to a question about 18 potential problems faced in the delivery of adult services. Although "insufficient funding to meet clients' needs," topped the list for all three, there was no general agreement about whether "not reaching clients who need services" is a priority issue. Although it was the second most frequently mentioned problem among supervisors and administrators, it was eighth for social workers.

These examples illustrate that one cannot assume that all people in a position to influence the future of adult services will share the same perspective. This is because people have different depth or breadth of knowledge or experience and possess different values. The strategic manager is interested in providing all people involved with a common set of information to help bridge gaps in knowledge and experience. This may mean inviting the adult services manager or supervisor to case staffings (unit meetings where a worker presents a case situation and solicits comments from his or her peers) or social services board members to accompany social workers on visits with clients. An annual forum or retreat may provide another vehicle for sharing perspectives on adult services. Effective planning is about learning, experimentation, and adaptation (Senge, 1990).

INTERNAL AND EXTERNAL INFLUENCES

There is a story in the planning literature about how frogs, being cold-blooded, adapt readily to changes in temperature. However, if a frog is placed in a pan of water that is slowly heated, it may adapt so well to its changing environment that it boils rather than jumps out (Pfeiffer et al., 1989). Although there is much to be said for being adaptable, it is also essential to be aware of changing circumstances and be ready for action to avoid threats and to take advantage of opportunities. Adult services is experiencing great change for a variety of reasons, some of which are within the control of the community adult services program, many of which are not. Some result from structural changes in the health and social services systems (for example, expansion of rural hospitals into community services, new cost-sharing provisions, and the influence of resource management), others result from the character and circumstance of clients and their families (for example, a higher proportion of older women living alone and more potential informal caregivers having to work outside the home). The responsibility of community adult services administration is to ensure the presence of leadership to manage this change for the benefit of the agency, its workers, clients, and the community to which it is accountable. The strategic manager is aware of the importance of planning within the adult services program, the agency, and the community. Effective planning must occur at each of these levels for optimum effect for clients, but especially in the absence of communitywide planning for adult services, the adult services program within a local agency must consider community influences.

The strategic manager understands that the dynamics of both the internal and external environments of the adult services program are vital to planning. An adult services unit or program within a community agency does not exist in isolation. It is affected by other areas within the agency, interests in the community, and influences at the state and federal levels. External factors compel as well as enable action; other forces inhibit or prevent change.

In examining any issue relevant to adult services, the strategic manager considers the issue from a number of different perspectives. Some potential areas for analysis include

- the agency's and community's current awareness and interest in the particular issue
- the magnitude and characteristics of the issue in terms of the client population (for example, how many people are affected, and how substantial is the impact on them?)
- the factors that have precipitated the need for change and those that otherwise influence the ability to take action
- the quality of leadership and level of commitment within the agency and the community
- the current and potential capacity of adult services and the community to respond to this issue
- any successes and failures of other adult services programs and communities in their efforts to address this or similar issues
- any salient fiscal considerations
- any state and federal initiatives or constraints that may affect the capacity of the agency and community to respond.

INVOLVING STAKEHOLDERS

The strategic manager recognizes that many different entities have a stake in the future of the adult services program. These stakeholders, as noted before, are either affected by decisions made about the program or can influence decision making. Chapter 19 defines a *stakeholder* as any distinguishable group or person with an actual or potential interest in or impact on the adult services program. It reviews four categories of stakeholders—contributing or sponsoring, internal, agent, and consumer—and considers how their interest and influence vary.

These stakeholders must be figured into planning for adult services. Strategic managers find ways to include stakeholders in shaping the future of the program and still maintain an effective process for making decisions. The most obvious and interested stakeholders probably are the program's present clientele and staff. The strategic manager empowers staff members by involving them in program planning and by seeking consensus in decisions affecting their work.

Outside spheres of influence include the state and local human services systems; other related public and private agencies; and the political, economic, religious, and media sectors. Each of these community interests can affect the success of an adult services program. The human services system includes numerous agencies and organizations covering the entire continuum of care—from nursing and board-and-care homes, hospices, and hospitals to councils or departments on aging, senior centers, area mental health programs, local health departments, and housing authorities. Related public and private agencies might include such planning and coordination bodies as interagency councils, transportation development planners, state units and area agencies on aging, and professional groups such as the legal and medical communities. In the political sphere, obvious influences include the members of the county commission, the county manager, and the local social services board. The attitude of the general public, as the electorate, represents a political force too. Planning is a political process of negotiating public and private visions, garnering resources to realize those visions, and implementing them (Pfeffer, 1992).

It is important to recognize and involve stakeholders in identifying issues, setting goals, and selecting strategies. For example, if an adult services program proposes to change some aspect of its operation that will significantly affect other programs within the human services system, the endorsement or acceptance of those affected cannot be assumed at the time of implementation. The planners must consider the interests of those most likely to be affected and obtain their participation and consent as the plan is developed.

That there is such an assortment of stakeholders does not mean that all have a direct role to assume in planning for the adult services program. The strategic manager finds appropriate ways to involve others within the agency and the community who will either be affected by decisions made for the adult services program or can influence its capacity for change. One mechanism for linking the adult services program with critical stakeholders within the agency and community is the use of a steering or advisory committee. If the manager establishes such a committee, selection of participants and its advisory leadership are important tasks. A possible chairperson for the committee might be a member of another local human services agency or a community spokesperson (for example, a business executive or the head of the ministerial association) who is recognized and respected by other stakeholders. Ideally, those on the committee should be capable of considering information objectively and be relatively free of hidden agendas.

ESTABLISHING PRIORITIES

In his work with local governments, Jenne (1988) found that "the most effective organizations define the results they seek, develop plans to accomplish them, and then tailor their everyday actions and decisions to be consistent with those plans" (p. 33). The strategic manager agrees that it is important to be focused. In practice, this means targeting the program's attention and resources to matters the planning group has established as most important to the successful functioning of the program.

The effective adult services manager is clear about what must be done to achieve a few priority goals that are significant, needed, and achievable. To be significant, there must be some noticeable adverse consequence or missed opportunity if the program does not act. Action is needed when the program or other community agencies have nothing else in progress or planned to address the problem. What can be achieved is determined by the availability of, or possibility of obtaining, required resources.

The strategic manager operates with a plan that is more than a series of recommendations. An effective plan details who is to do what, when, for whom, how, and at what cost. Its objectives are stated as relevant, attainable, and measurable outcomes for clients. This plan provides the basis for accountability and the means for monitoring progress. Planning strategically is time well spent when it helps put into operation specific roles and service strategies that benefit present and future clients by guiding the allocation and management of resources through work plans and budgets.

PLANNING AS A CONTINUOUS PROCESS

Adult services are in a state of flux that probably will continue. Factors contributing to change include demographics, competing demands for resources, state and federal initiatives, and increased expectations on the part of consumers. More specifically, the aging of the population and the anticipated demand for services by those at the highest risk of needing assistance are important influences. For example, an increase in reported cases of abuse, neglect, and exploitation, the possible results of added pressures on informal caregivers, might be expected.

Other factors weighing on the future of adult services include emerging demands from a larger population of younger adults with disabilities. As the need for services is likely to increase, the competition for limited public funding will probably increase too. One can assume there will be greater competition for funds among adult services and other needed social programs. This proposition suggests the value of strategic management at the agency level to consider priorities across program areas and ensure effective targeting and coordination of resources.

The strategic manager believes that a community adult services program can be active in setting its agenda instead of merely reacting to the mandate of others. The public social services system historically has had the dual roles of implementing existing local, state, and federal policies and programs and of pioneering new ones in response to human needs. Although there are legal mandates and state and federal administrative policies that influence the work of the local adult services program, the program still retains significant discretion in deciding where to place its emphasis. Community planning, organizational leadership and initiative, and local politics account for many of the decisions about what services a community adult services program offers.

Summary

Those who agree that the adult services system should be client and family centered, that the field of adult social services is undergoing substantial change, and that community adult services programs have at least some control over their work agenda search for ways to better manage their future. This chapter has presented some concepts to help the strategic manager take the lead in controlling the future of the adult services program. Effective managers are those who can build a shared vision, challenge prevailing ways of doing things, and foster more systematic ways of bringing about action that benefits adults with disabilities and their families.

Key Points

Excellent adult services social workers
- support and participate in planning
- accept the risks inherent in questioning and change.

Excellent adult services managers
- value planning for the future
- use responsibility for contributing to community social planning as an opportunity to make a positive difference for clients and families
- have an interest in and skills for communitywide planning
- act as strategic managers who "steer" rather than "row," develop and use a mission statement as a frame of reference for decision making, focus on clients and their families, recognize and consider the effect of values and assumptions, establish guiding principles and bridge gaps in knowledge and experience among planning participants, are sensitive to changes and influences in the program's internal and external environments, recognize and involve the various stakeholders, target the program's attention and resources to priority areas, operate with a plan that allows for accountability and monitoring progress, ensure that work plans and budgets reflect planning decisions about purpose and priority, and see planning as an ongoing responsibility.

Excellent leaders

- support local planning initiatives with information, expertise, and resources
- empower local decisions by being open to new approaches to addressing clients' needs
- involve communities in state planning for adult services.

References

American Public Welfare Association and the National Association of State Units on Aging. (1988). *Social services for the elderly. Phase I report: State-level relationships.* Washington, DC: Author.

American Public Welfare Association and the National Association of State Units on Aging. (1989). *Social services for the elderly. Phase II report: Local-level relationships.* Washington, DC: Author.

Bennis, W. (1991). *Why leaders can't lead.* San Francisco: Jossey-Bass.

Bryson, J. M. (1988). *Strategic planning for public and nonprofit organizations.* San Francisco: Jossey-Bass.

Center for Aging Research and Educational Services. (1990a). *Guidelines for strategic planning in the counties.* Chapel Hill, NC: Author.

Center for Aging Research and Educational Services. (1990b). *Manpower in county departments of social services. Executive summary and full report.* Chapel Hill, NC: Author.

Center for Aging Research and Educational Services. (1992). *Strategic planning for aging: Final report on demonstration projects in Cleveland, Durham, Pamlico, and Surry counties.* Chapel Hill, NC: Author.

Edmondson, C. (1990). Evaluating the effectiveness of strategic planning for communities. *Economic Development Review, 8*(3), 27–29.

Edwards, R. L., & Yankey, J. A. (Eds.). (1991). *Skills for effective human services management.* Silver Spring, MD: NASW Press.

Gummer, B. (1992). Ready, fire, aim! Current perspectives on strategic planning. *Administration in Social Work, 16*(1), 89–106.

Jenne, K. (1986, Spring). Strategic planning: Taking charge of the future. *Popular Government,* pp. 36–43.

Jenne, K. (1988, Summer). From vision to reality: Effective planning by the governing board. *Popular Government,* pp. 33–38.

Myrtle, R. C., & Wilber, K. H. (1994). Designing service delivery systems: Lessons from the development of community-based systems of care for the elderly. *Public Administration Review, 54*(3), 245–252.

Older Americans Act of 1965. P.L. 89-73, 79 Stat. 218.

Osborne, D., & Gaebler, T. (1992). *Reinventing government.* New York: Addison-Wesley.

Pfeffer, J. (1992, Winter). Understanding power in organizations. *California Management Review*, pp. 29–50.

Pfeiffer, J. W., Goodstein, L. D., & Nolan, T. M. (1989). *Shaping strategic planning: Frogs, dragons, bees, and turkey tails.* San Diego: University Associates.

Senge, P. M. (1990, Fall). The leader's new work: Building learning organizations. *Sloan Management Review*, pp. 7–23.

Wortman, A., & Rhodes, R. (Eds.). (1969). *Robert F. Kennedy: Promises to keep.* Kansas City, MO: Hallmark Cards.

CHAPTER 19

Program Development

GARY M. NELSON

LANE G. COOKE

The duties, responsibilities, and tasks of program managers and supervisors in adult services are broad and varied. In addition to supporting and facilitating the work of related staff members, most program managers and supervisors perform other functions, such as representing the agency in the community; negotiating with groups and organizations; and planning, designing, budgeting, and evaluating ongoing and new programs.

These managers have different formal and informal titles depending on the size of the agency, its organizational structure, and its personnel policies. To avoid any confusion this may cause about the responsibilities of this group, all staff members in adult services management positions, including directors, service directors, program managers, and line supervisors, are identified as managers.

This chapter examines the competencies and roles of managers within a philosophy of empowerment for line social workers in the adult services agency. These competencies and roles fall into two broad and overlapping areas: (1) program development and (2) staff development. Chapter 20 considers staff development, whereas this chapter addresses program development; management competencies and roles; empowerment in the areas of planning and budgeting, resource development, and fostering self-evaluating systems; and central dilemmas for adult services managers.

Management Competencies and Roles

As leaders, the chief function of adult services managers is to help steer the agency, its staff, and the various community stakeholders through the process of change.

The object of this change is to achieve the agency's vision of improved outcomes for its clientele—older and younger adults with disabilities. In collaboration with the agency's staff and community stakeholders, managers must demonstrate a range of competencies to perform roles and responsibilities necessary to achieve the agency's mission.

COMPETENCIES

To achieve their mission and goals, adult services managers must effectively engineer a fit between financial and material resources in the organization and community and the talents and capabilities of the agency's staff. Managerial competencies—that is, the knowledge and skills that a manager needs—fall into six principal areas, which may be grouped under the headings of program or staff development (see Table 19-1).

The competencies necessary for effective program development include knowledge and skills in program planning and budgeting, resource development, and the creation of self-evaluating organizations. The competencies necessary for staff development include knowledge and skills to support and enhance effective social work practice, foster self-direction in daily activities, and stimulate motivation for best practice.

ROLES

It is not easy to define how adult services managers do what they do. Although competencies are the skills and knowledge managers use, roles are the ways they exercise these competencies to steer the organization toward realizing its mission. Mintzberg (1973) identified 10 roles, grouped in the categories "interpersonal," "informational," and "decisional," that capture many of the parts that managers play in effecting change (see Table 19-2). More colloquially, Handy (1993) called these roles leading, administering, and fixing.

This complex mixture of activities captures the variety and what may at times appear to be the fragmentation of leadership in adult services and social work as a whole. These roles require the manager's purposeful use of self to steer the organization as it pursues its vision. Not unlike social workers interacting with

Table 19-1

MANAGEMENT COMPETENCIES FOR ADULT SERVICES

Program Development
- Planning and budgeting
- Resource development
- Self-evaluation capabilities

Staff Development
- Facilitating adult services practice
- Fostering self-directing behaviors
- Motivating for excellence

Table 19-2 ———————————————

ROLES OF MANAGERS

Interpersonal roles (leading)	Figurehead Leader Liaison
Informational roles (administering)	Monitor Disseminator Spokesperson
Decisional roles (fixing)	Entrepreneur Disturbance handler Resource allocator Negotiator

clients and families, the challenge for the effective adult services manager is to keep in check the chaotic feeling of "just doing one confounding thing after another" and to develop the capacity to see how use of self in the roles can help steer the process of change.

Management and Empowerment

Before examining the specifics of program development or staff development, it is important to reconsider some of the major principles of empowerment as they influence interactions between adult services managers and line workers and, in a parallel process, between social workers and clients and their families. Particularly important here are the principles of partnership and responsibility.

PARTNERSHIP

Many people in adult services know what they do not like about the current management paradigm but are less clear about what they want to put in its place. The definition of the word *manage* in *Webster's Ninth New Collegiate Dictionary* provides us with some notion of what we want to move away from: "1: to handle or direct with a degree of skill or address as: a: to make and keep submissive . . . 2: to alter by manipulation" (Mish, 1990, p. 722). Mirroring this generally hierarchical approach to management based on command and control, Kadushin (1985) defined social work managers and supervisors as "agency administrative staff members to whom authority is delegated to direct, coordinate, enhance, and evaluate the on-the-job performance of the supervisees for whose work they are held accountable" (p. 24). The prevailing management principle here is that responsibility for the direction and work of the organization flows from the top down rather than from the bottom up.

The concept of partnership, a principle of empowerment, offers an alternative to this approach. Partnership is about joint responsibility for creating and realizing a vision. Managers who act in accordance with this principle exist primarily to contribute to and support the people doing the agency's primary work, not to simply plan, watch, control, or evaluate their actions (Block, 1993). Partnership involves line workers and community stakeholders working collaboratively to achieve a vision.

RESPONSIBILITY

With the right to shape and help implement an organizational vision comes responsibility. Most traditional notions of empowerment stress the rights of the unempowered, whether worker or client, with little or no notion of a corresponding responsibility for the successful or unsuccessful exercise of those rights (Hasenfeld & Chesler, 1989; Staub-Bernasconi, 1991). The price of empowerment and the freedom to exercise choices and to help shape a change process is responsibility for the current situation and for achieving the desired outcomes. Each party—manager, line worker, community stakeholder, client, and family—is jointly responsible and accountable for the success and failure of the enterprise (Block, 1993).

The responsibility of managers working under these principles is to help create the social architecture and practices that support partnership and mutual accountability. In this paradigm, managers are responsible for helping set the vision and providing access to the knowledge and skills that are essential for all those involved in direct work with clients and families to be successful. In this paradigm, managers create an organizational environment in which more authority and decision making are placed where the work gets done.

Program Development in Adult Services Agencies

How do the various management competencies and roles, as well as notions of empowerment, translate in the everyday life of an adult services manager? First, in thinking about the day-to-day reality of a manager, there must be a distinction between the hectic, varied demands placed on a typical adult services manager and the feelings of many managers that they are helpless to organize or control the demands on their time. The issue is not the pace or demands, which actually attract many individuals to this type of job, but control.

Managers who work as partners with their staff and others in the community understand that a fundamental paradox of effective management is that in order to achieve control you have to give up control. Everybody manages. Everybody needs to be in control and accountable, although some will have a wider perspective and a longer view than others (Block, 1993). Another point is that effective management is not a full-time management job. Managers do more than direct and control the behavior of others. Sometimes adult services managers lead, sometimes they administer (make decisions), and other times they engage in fixing problems. This approach to management plays itself out in planning and budgeting, resource development, and evaluation.

PLANNING AND BUDGETING
Planning

Planning in an adult services program can be broad (for example, shaping the direction and thrust of the program for adults with disabilities) or very narrow (for example, planning a specialized program to serve people with acquired immune deficiency syndrome [AIDS] in the community). Regardless of the scope, planning efforts require similar approaches. Chapter 18 described a process for communitywide planning. Planning as a management activity in an adult services program is a cyclical process, probably carried out yearly, of assessing resources— number, talents, and expertise of staff, or available funding—to obtain specific quality outcomes for clients and families within a reasonable time.

Upchurch (1991) identified seven specific ingredients that should go into a self-assessment of how organizational resources, capacity, and utilization figure in the delivery of quality services:

1. *Determine why you do what you do (develop your mission).*
2. *Determine what you will do to accomplish your mission (service delivery).*
3. *Determine how you want to do what you do (job designs).*
4. *Determine how much it's reasonable to expect people to do (workload).*
5. *Determine how much (staff, materials, and money) is needed to do what you want to do and to achieve the quantity you think is reasonable.*
6. *Determine how well you are doing (quality) what you decided to do.*
7. *Determine what is a reasonable time frame for people to do what you want them to do (timeliness), in the amount you expect (quantity), and with the quality you want.* (p. 3)

These parallel to some degree the steps for communitywide planning mentioned in chapter 18, but they are more specific to the areas of concern to a human services agency.

Creating a resource development and utilization plan is the first part of a planning-directed change process. The second part involves turning it into a dynamic learning process. In doing this it is important not to think of developing a plan and then implementing it as two distinct phases, that is, "ready, aim, fire!" In human services planning and program development, sometimes it will be "ready, fire, aim!" (Gummer, 1992). Planning and program implementation are part of the same dynamic ongoing learning process (Jacobs, 1994).

The steps in planning, both in the community and in the organization, are interdependent and ongoing elements of an approach to change. Planning and change are both cyclical, feedback processes. To learn and to improve outcomes, the agency must embrace the elements of the scientific method. Deming refers to improving outcomes as a continual learning process in which one specifies what it is one wants to do (plan), produces outcomes (do), inspects what one has done with respect to quality and desired outcomes (study), and standardizes the processes based on theory about what has transpired (act)—the PDSA process (cited in Delavigne & Robertson, 1994). To give a more concrete example, one might plan a support program for people with AIDS, do what is necessary to produce outcomes, study what has been accomplished with respect to clients and families, and act to standardize those elements that contribute to the best outcomes. In the midst of this process, it is imperative to keep the mission in sight; to paraphrase Walt Kelly's cartoon character Pogo, having lost sight of our objectives, it will not help to re-double our efforts.

Budgeting

What is the clearest way to see the agency's mission? Look at the budget. What-ever the agency may say its mission and priorities are, how it spends its money tells the tale. According to Miringoff (1980) the budget is an agency's statement of

> *goals, values, priorities, political trade-offs, decisions, authority structures, and as such, is probably the single most revealing document about how an organization functions. The major question regarding budgeting becomes: How can the resources of a human service organization be dispersed in such a way as to be both efficient and to maximize the organization's service capability and effectiveness? (p. 115)*

Budgeting for adult services programs is a complex technical task. It is also a complex sociopolitical undertaking. Budgeting reveals the philosophy behind and importance of issues of governance, control, and empowerment in the organi-zation. Allocation of money is the universal litmus test for service systems. Al-though it does not capture all of an agency's professed values and concerns, it provides a common language for expressing promises made within and between agencies and to constituents, and it tells us something about how well those prom-ises have been fulfilled (Block, 1993).

On the technical side of budgeting and program development, there are issues involving the adult services manager's understanding of different federal, state, and local funding sources, as well as the varied eligibility guidelines and reporting requirements. With constantly changing guidelines and requirements, the challenge to stay current is daunting.

Key federal sources of funding for adult services programs include, but are not limited to, the Social Services Block Grant (SSBG), Medicaid, Supplemental Security Income (SSI), Medicare, the Older Americans Act, and veterans' benefits. State and local funding initiatives are equally varied and complex. Adult services managers, particularly at the state and local level, have an opportunity to shape legislative appropriations as well as to secure foundation and private nonprofit agency support for their mission.

Another technical aspect of budgeting is the choice of method. Managers may need to master various types of budgets, according to the needs of their com-munity and organization. Although there are many possibilities and little space here to describe them, four common methods—line item, functional, zero-based, and program budgets (Rapp & Poertner, 1992)—are contrasted here.

In a line item budget, each line reflects a particular expense category. It is one of the least flexible, bureaucratically controlled types of budgets. In contrast, functional budgets offer more discretion by breaking budgeting categories into at least two areas, administrative services and program services. Zero-based budgets theoretically wipe the slate clean each budget cycle and call for a thorough reassessment of all budget decisions from the previous year. Although it can help avoid knee-jerk responses characterized by simply funding what was funded the year before, the staff time required to prepare such budgets can undermine its theoretical intent. By shifting the attention away from a strict line item and overly broad categories such as services and administrative overhead, program budgets attempt to link budgeting to specific program missions, goals, and outcomes.

Although adult services managers frequently find themselves struggling and caught up in the details of complex financing issues, no issue is more central to empowerment than control of the budget. Few things capture our philosophy, beliefs, and fears more clearly than the procedures we establish to control money, and few things reveal empowerment more clearly than control over the resources necessary to one's well-being or work. Many adult services managers may not even consider budgeting as part of the overall agency planning and development process or view it in the context of their own empowerment or lack of empowerment. Some do not participate directly in the budgeting process, often because they are not invited to.

CASE EXAMPLE

In 1993, 14 adult services supervisors or program managers from North Carolina's county departments of social services (about 10 percent of mid-level managers in the state) were polled by telephone regarding their understanding and involvement in their agencies' budgeting process. Nine said that their agencies have a line item budget; one, that the agency used a zero-based budget; and four did not know what kind of budget their agency had. Seven of the managers were able to describe the budgeting process in their agency, and seven could not. Of the nine managers whose agencies used the line item budget, six said that they had no control over allocations for the items they were responsible for. Four were able to make recommendations or provide justifications for requests for expenditures, they were responsible for not overspending, or both. Managers expressed varying feelings about involvement in or responsibility for budgeting. Some saw it as an opportunity, others as a challenge, and still others as a mystery.

Block (1993) identified the processes by which the agency approves expenditures, budgets resources, and discloses budget information as central to our notions of partnership and empowerment. Osborne and Gaebler (1992), in addressing this point, proposed a new type of budget for responsive government services systems, a mission-driven budget.

Traditionally in adult services, and in public human services generally, the mission of the organization as judged by the budget is meeting the client's reimbursable needs. Financing, not mission, goals, or performance, drives many programs. Creative adult services managers, to achieve more flexibility and increase performance, struggle to make program budgets respond to the dynamic nature of human services problems and the varied community contexts in which they operate.

Mission-driven budgets, which provide managers with the flexibility to move funds from one item or category to another in support of outcomes, provide incentives for creativity and improve accountability. Mission-driven budgets can heighten performance by freeing resources to test new ideas, give managers greater autonomy and motivation for responding to changing circumstances and needs, create more predictability in unstable environments, simplify the budget process, and save money that can be reinvested in new prevention or treatment programs (Osborne & Gaebler, 1992). In North Carolina, a home and community care block grant that combines SSBG, Older Americans Act funds, and state resources in a common fund dedicated to maintaining individuals in their homes provides community agencies with a measure of flexibility that is not often present in more categorical programs.

Returning to the case example, the words of the supervisors and program managers eloquently illustrate the empowerment supported by involvement in the process of budgeting: "Being involved shows you the big picture." "It captures a lot of information." "You get a handle on what you've done, and how it compares to previous years." "It's creative." "It encourages you to advocate, give input, and ask questions." "It allows you to look at helping as many folks as possible." "It's truly enjoyable to justify the need and to work with staff to help them understand." Although there are drawbacks to such involvement—it can be tedious, frustrating, and uncomfortable for those who lack training and experience in budgeting procedures—in the long run, it is empowering.

DEVELOPING NEW RESOURCES

In addition to providing leadership, making decisions, and fixing problems in the areas of planning and budgeting, adult services managers frequently have the opportunity to advocate for the development of new resources and programs. Among other things, effective resource development turns on effective networking, the artful use of public relations and community education, and kindling the entrepreneurial spirit.

The isolated adult services manager may be afflicted with the feeling that they alone in the community are interested in the welfare of adults with disabilities. However, many citizens' organizations and community groups have an interest in the well-being of adult services clients. These are the stakeholders. Effective resource development in large measure involves identifying, clarifying, and capitalizing on a common mission and interest among a diverse group of stakeholders to produce new resources or to retarget those that exist already.

To tap the political, moral, and technical support of a diverse set of community stakeholders effectively, adult services managers must first understand what a stakeholder is and the different kinds of roles that stakeholders play. For an adult services program, a stakeholder is any distinguishable group or person with an actual or potential interest in or impact on the well-being of the program's clientele.

Contributing or sponsoring stakeholders provide sanction, support, resources, or regulations that affect the operation of adult services programs—for example, elected officials, boards of directors, licensing or regulatory agencies, and upper management within the agency where the adult services program is housed. Contributing stakeholders also include the array of human services agencies whose missions overlap with that of adult services—for example, councils or departments on aging, public health departments, hospice and home health agencies, mental health centers, hospitals, public housing authorities, family services agencies, and private nonprofit agencies such as the United Way or the YMCA. To network effectively, adult services programs must take care to collaborate with other agencies that are perceived to be competitors for the same area of service. Clients and their families benefit from collaborative approaches on the part of agencies and lose in situations marked by competition and turf battles.

Internal stakeholders are within the adult services program: line workers, supervisors, paraprofessional staff members, and fiscal officers. Too frequently, programs overlook or take for granted the support and talent they already have when formulating resource development strategies.

Agent stakeholders are formal or informal publicists for the adult services program who actually take the message to the general public or a funding source. They articulate the adult services mission and program development strategy to others, either through disinterested benevolence or self-interest. Finally, consumer stakeholders are adult services clients and their families, who benefit directly from the agency's activities.

Two of the chief tools that adult services managers have at their disposal when fostering collaborative networks and initiating program development strategies are public relations and community education. Many managers view public relations with discomfort and suspicion or fear. The discomfort and suspicion may lie in the belief that marketing or "selling" the mission of a public service program is somehow unworthy or in hesitation about being able to deliver on promises in an uncertain economic or political climate. Fear may arise from having to acknowledge failures or shortcomings publicly or from worries about how others may judge the actions of the agency. Whether one uses the term marketing or public relations or community education to describe this part of program development, it is critical that all the types of stakeholders defined previously are continually informed about the adult services program, and this effort must extend to detractors as well as supporters of the program.

Jones (1991) outlined 10 commandments of media relations for human services agencies that are relevant whether the audience is the news media, the chamber of commerce, local elected officials, or foundation directors. With some modification, they apply more broadly to community education, networking, and media relations:

1. *Always appear open and cooperative; never lie. Conspiracy theories seldom pan out, be open with information and cooperate.*
2. *Personalize the organization. Who are you? What do you do? How do you benefit clients and their families?*
3. *Develop media contacts. Include such nontraditional sources as business association newsletters and foundations, as well as traditional print, radio and television sources.*
4. *Take good stories to the reporters and your network. Share and publicize success in your organization.*
5. *Respond quickly. If your organization is under attack, respond quickly. If you experience a significant success, publicize it quickly.*
6. *Never say, "No comment." Be cooperative, reveal as much information as you can and explain what information you can't reveal and why.*
7. *It is okay to say, "I don't know." If you don't know something, say so and then find the answer and get back to them.*
8. *If you make a mistake, confess and repent.*
9. *Use the big dump. If there is bad news to dump, dump it all at once.*
10. *Prepare. Be fully knowledgeable about your program, you are one of its best representatives.* (pp. 109–111)

In communicating with the broader community network, including the media, language is important. For example, the slogan, "Let's stop the hurting," was very successfully used by North Carolina's adult protective services initiative to publicize its mission. The slogan is personal and understandable. Human services language is often impersonal and not understood by the broader public. The concepts "Pay me now or pay me later" and "smart investment" can be effectively used to market the importance of in-home services for older adults and adults with disabilities as an alternative to expensive nursing home or hospital care. Managers must be attuned to the language of their network constituents and be able to speak to those constituencies in a language that they understand and can relate to. The artful use of language and varied networks is an effective outreach tool for adult services programs to reach into neighborhoods and communities that might be traditionally overlooked.

Adult services managers are among the principal voices clarifying the agency's mission for both internal stakeholders and the broader community. They articulate need, report on successes, and acknowledge failures. They also must be able to communicate realistically what the agency can and cannot deliver. When the agency's response is limited (for example, insufficient funding to provide enough in-home aide services to meet demand), the manager must articulate the constraints with which the program operates. If the community does not understand the values and benefits of adult services programs, as well as the constraints, and if staff members are unable to understand and articulate those values, benefits, and constraints, adult services programs are doomed to remain underdeveloped and undersupported. Line workers, as well as managers, must be empowered to carry the message of adult services to the broader community. Adults with disabilities lose out when the community is unaware of the agency's role and mission.

An important outcome of effective networking and public relations is an increase in both initiatives inside and outside the agency. For outside initiatives, adult services managers may choose to help develop a support program for people with AIDS, a community awareness campaign on abuse of elderly people, or a church- and agency-based project for homeless people. Within the agency, the manager might help develop a risk-screening unit to identify adult clients unnecessarily at risk of placement or assemble a specialized team to work with older adults with developmental disabilities living in the community.

This freedom of enterprise is the essence of empowerment for adult services managers: the right and authority to make localized, decentralized choices regarding their work. In empowered organizations, "everyone uses his or her intelligence to find problems to address, to do work in ways that make the most of everyone's talents, education, and experience" (Pinchot & Pinchot, 1993, pp. 65–66). In forming new initiatives and organizations to improve the quality of life for adults with disabilities, adult services managers will rely less on hierarchy for direction and more on common vision, less on rules and more on choice, and less on command and more on initiative. In bringing these new initiatives to life both in the community and in the organization, adult services managers also will rely more on result-focused teams and collaborative partnership between external and internal stakeholders.

SELF-EVALUATING ORGANIZATIONS

Historically, few adult services programs conduct any ongoing evaluation of client and family outcomes. Most adult services information systems focus on process evaluation: how many adult day care slots are supported or in-home services provided. They seldom are designed to capture on an ongoing basis such things as whether the burden on family caregivers is reduced as a result of a particular service intervention or whether the service has improved the quality of the client's life—perhaps by deferring placement through services in the home or community. Reporting systems are designed to meet the requirements of external funding sources, and these often focus on more readily obtainable information: numbers of clients served, telephone calls received, and home visits made. Although such information is necessary to measure outcomes, agencies seldom collect the sort of information that can be used to measure and provide the basis for direct outcomes for adult services clients and their families.

Managers know that in private business or in human services, "What gets measured gets attention, particularly when rewards are tied to the measures" (Eccles, 1991, p. 131). Currently, what is measured and rewarded is the volume of services delivered and the funds expended. In a system driven by mission and outcomes, however, measurement and reward should focus on outcomes achieved for clients and their families (Kettner & Martin, 1993; Monkman, 1991).

The decision to evaluate adult services on the basis of outcomes stems from the vision and core organizational values that shape the behaviors of adult services managers and staff. Chief among these values is the belief that superior performance depends on superior learning (Senge, 1990). Superior learning, in turn, stems from continuous feedback and experimentation. The fitness of an adult services program is measured by its ability to add value to the lives of clients and their families through constantly adapting its approaches. The impulse to become self-evaluating—to create a continuous learning cycle—must come from within the program (Austin et al., 1982). A self-evaluating work unit can be empowered through continuous assessment and reassessment of its strengths and weaknesses relative to client and family outcomes and by initiating improvements without being required to do so by outside evaluators. A self-evaluating entity, whether system, program, work unit, or employee, has little to fear from outside evaluators.

Information is the lifeblood of a self-evaluating adult services program. Austin et al. (1982) pointed to three measurements essential to self-evaluating organizations: (1) information on effort, (2) effectiveness, and (3) efficiency. Measuring effort captures time spent by the staff on activities, the agency's resources, and the services devoted to achieving a particular outcome. Measuring effectiveness addresses whether effort has produced the outcomes foreseen for clients and families: Are they better off for having come in contact with adult services? Have they achieved their own goals? Finally, measures of efficiency compare the cost of achieving these outcomes, relative to the cost of alternative approaches, to the same problem or alternative uses of the resources altogether.

For example, an outreach program designed to decrease abuse of older adults through extensive community networking, public forums, and meetings might be compared with a similar campaign focusing entirely on public education through the media. The quality of the referrals, subsequent reductions (or increases) in the number of adults being abused, and costs would all have to be compared to decide which approach was more effective. This approach in turn might be compared with a second approach that focuses on preventing abuse of older adults through targeting support services to family caregiving situations that might produce abuse or neglect.

Adult services managers can help cultivate learning organizations and communities by providing leadership for self-evaluation. Translating a broad vision into measurable standards for line workers, unit supervisors, program managers, and community leaders and arranging for the technical support to gather and evaluate information is the collective task of adult services management. Managers are responsible for developing organizational and social architecture to support a culture of continual learning and self-evaluation to give purposeful and meaningful direction to program development activities.

Management Dilemmas

Most management dilemmas stem from how managers deal with the imbalance in demands, constraints, and choices that characterize and give texture to their jobs. Two factors that shape managers' responses to the situations that arise in the course of their work include organizational culture and issues of trust and control between managers and agency personnel and managers and the community.

DEMANDS, CONSTRAINTS, AND CHOICES

Management jobs differ in the balance of demands, constraints, and choices they place on individual managers (Stewart, 1983). The configuration of these three elements will vary among adult services managers within the same program; among managers across programs in the same agency (for example, in-home services versus APS); and among programs in the community, state, and nation. How adult services managers respond to these elements of their work will determine their overall effectiveness.

Adult services managers frequently find themselves in situations in which demands include required responses, accountability but vague and uncertain criteria for performance, and the necessity to make decisions in an organizational climate that operates on principles of command and control. Constraints may include limited resources, physical location (building, community, and culture), and the attitudes and expectations of others. Choices include what work is done and how it is carried out (Stewart, 1983).

The way of achieving a workable balance within the demands, constraints, and choices that characterize management positions is paradoxical. The way to balance, control, and independence lies in living with ambiguity, giving up control, and interdependence. Imbalance tells us that something about the way we currently do business is not working. The usual response to feeling out of control is to try to exert more control. Frequently, the results are lower levels of individual and organizational performance and higher levels of staff burnout and turnover.

Paradoxically, when managers feel out of balance, it is time to open up to new approaches and explore new partnerships for doing the work of adult services—time to give up some control. Periods of imbalance mark the time for renegotiating partnerships and fostering greater interdependence to restore balance. Only by relinquishing control can the demands, constraints, and choices be renegotiated.

Unclear accountability might be addressed by involving consumers in helping to evaluate and provide feedback on agency programs. Constraints in resources might be addressed by new public–private partnerships among nonprofit organizations, volunteers, foundations, and adult services programs. Choices for service interventions are increased by the growth in public–private partnerships. Certainly, changes in accountability and the forging of new partnerships to increase resources will reconfigure how the work of adult services programs and program managers is done.

TRUST AND CONTROL

Many of the dilemmas of adult services managers and the imbalances among demands, constraints, and choices center on broader issues of trust among managers, agency personnel, and the community. Issues of trust are at the center of increased demands for collaboration in adult services. The call for greater collaboration is "a mine field filled with unexpected problems, unexpressed differences of opinion, and unanticipated outcomes" (Wimpfheimer, Bloom, & Kramer, 1990, p. 90). However, calls for greater collaboration and interdependence, whether in adult services or the private business sector, reflect a growing awareness of the multicausal nature of problems in general and the need for collaborative partnership to resolve them.

To address problems effectively and bring some balance to their work, it is clear that adult services managers must nurture increased cooperation and collaboration, both in the agency and the community. In providing this leadership, managers will come to recognize that, to gain more control, power, and choice in dealing effectively with the problems of clients and families, they must give up more control to workers and to collaborating programs that also are engaged in this mutual enterprise. Giving up a measure of control by calling on others to join in creating and implementing problem-solving strategies will engender trust.

Key Points

Excellent adult services managers

- build competencies in all three areas of program management: (1) planning, (2) program evaluation, and (3) community resource support
- identify what is necessary to make their adult services program successful, that is, develop a vision of success as a first step to empowering themselves and creating an environment where social workers can become empowered
- provide the leadership to develop a structured planning process within their work units, including developing a mission for adult services and a clear definition of the target populations, with the participation of their social workers
- provide leadership and participation in the community process of planning in the fullest way possible
- understand general concepts about the budgeting process and have knowledge about adult services funding sources to be an effective member of the agency and community planning team
- seek creative ways to enhance and supplement current program funding
- identify the products of adult services and teach stakeholders about the importance of those products to build a base of support in the community for needed resources
- model cooperation within the agency and in the community toward other organizations and groups
- develop self-evaluation in work units that measures effectiveness and efficiency as well as effort.

References

Austin, M. J., Cox, G., Gottlieb, N., Hawkins, J. D., Kruzich, J. M., & Rauch, R. (1982). *Evaluating your agency's programs.* Beverly Hills, CA: Sage Publications.

Block, P. (1993). *Stewardship: Choosing service over self-interest.* San Francisco: Berrett-Koehler.

Delavigne, K. T., & Robertson, J. D. (1994). *Deming's profound changes.* Englewood Cliffs, NJ: Prentice Hall.

Eccles, R. G. (1991, January–February). The performance measurement manifesto. *Harvard Business Review,* pp. 131–137.

Gummer, B. (1992). Ready, fire, aim! Current perspectives on strategic planning. *Administration in Social Work, 16*(1), 89–106.

Handy, C. (1993). *Understanding organizations.* New York: Oxford University Press.

Hasenfeld, Y., & Chesler, M. A. (1989). Client empowerment in the human services: Personal and professional agenda. *Journal of Applied Behavioral Sciences, 25*(4), 499–521.

Jacobs, R. (1994). *Real time strategic change.* San Francisco: Berrett-Koehler.

Jones, C. (1991). Developing strategic media relationships. In R. L. Edwards & J. A. Yankey (Eds.), *Skills for effective human services management* (pp. 103–142). Silver Spring, MD: NASW Press.

Kadushin, A. (1985). *Supervision in social work* (2nd ed.). New York: Columbia University Press.

Kettner, P. M., & Martin, L. L. (1993). Performance, accountability, and purchase of service contracting. *Administration in Social Work, 17*(1), 61–79.

Mintzberg, H. (1973). *The nature of managerial work.* New York: Harper & Row.

Miringoff, M. L. (1980). *Management in human services agencies.* New York: Macmillan.

Mish, F. C. (Ed.-in-Chief). (1990). *Webster's ninth new collegiate dictionary.* Springfield, MA: Merriam-Webster.

Monkman, M. M. (1991). Outcome objectives in social work practice: Person and environment. *Social Work, 36,* 253–258.

Older Americans Act of 1965. P.L. 89-73, 79 Stat. 218.

Osborne, D., & Gaebler, T. (1992). *Reinventing government.* Reading, MA: Addison-Wesley.

Pinchot, G., & Pinchot, E. (1993). *The end of bureaucracy and the rise of the intelligent organization.* San Francisco: Berrett-Koehler.

Rapp, C. A., & Poertner, J. (1992). *Social administration: A client-centered approach.* New York: Longman.

Senge, P. M. (1990, Fall). The leader's new work: Building a learning organization. *Sloan Management Review*, pp. 7–23.

Staub-Bernasconi, S. (1991). Social action, empowerment and social work. *Social Work with Groups, 14*(3/4), 35–51.

Stewart, R. (1983). *Choices for the manager.* New York: McGraw-Hill.

Upchurch, W. (1991). *Resource management: A prescription for change.* Raleigh: North Carolina Department of Social Services.

Wimpfheimer, R., Bloom, M., & Kramer, M. (1990). Inter-agency collaboration: Some working principles. *Administration in Social Work, 14*(4), 89–102.

CHAPTER 20

Staff Development

LANE G. COOKE

This chapter discusses how adult services managers provide leadership and foster an organizational culture that maximizes the effective use of human resources. Chapter 1 identified human resources as people first, not positions or roles, whose individual and collective ideas, skills, and abilities can enhance the well-being of adults with disabilities. Adult services managers are the people most responsible for nurturing and enhancing their staff members' capabilities and assisting them to make the best use of their talents.

Chapter 1 also pointed out that the quality of services provided to clients is conceptually and practically linked to the culture of the agency and how employees at all levels experience that culture and its effect. If workers are empowered to do their best and to assume responsibility for outcomes associated with their practice, they will in turn be able to help their clients become empowered. Kadushin (1985) called this phenomenon *parallel process*, which means that behaviors, attitudes, and patterns tend to repeat at all levels of a system. If agency directors and community decision makers adopt a supportive, enabling, and empowering approach toward adult services managers, managers will tend to adopt the same approach with social workers, and workers with clients. The reverse is also true. If managers do not extend themselves to help their staff members, then the staff members may repeat this behavior in indifference to their clients (Kadushin, 1985).

As a supervisor, the adult services manager has the greatest opportunity to shape the experience of line workers, help them master the skills of social work, develop positive working relationships with colleagues, and establish positive helping relationships with clients. Effective management is the effective use of management or supervisory relationships to support individual learning and increased effectiveness (Shulman, 1993).

In examining the link between management, staff development, and effective adult services programs, this chapter discusses the adult services manager's role as a steward in developing staff; in creating and supporting a learning, self-evaluating community; and in teaching and motivating workers to help clients achieve quality outcomes. Staff development, as used in this chapter, designates the adult services manager's primary role in enhancing staff competencies and effectiveness. An awareness and understanding of cultural diversity is also a necessary condition for achieving quality outcomes. (For a discussion of this topic, see chapter 11.) Beyond this, the role of adult services managers includes managing performance through promoting self-evaluation and responsibility for outcomes through careful deployment of human resources and coaching.

Management as Stewardship

An adult services manager is the leader and steward of a work unit. The literature describes leadership as "a process of influencing others to act in a way that will accomplish the objectives of the leader or the organization" (Preston & Zummerer, 1976, p. 100). Block (1993) used the term "stewardship" to capture the willingness of managers to be accountable for results without resorting to a controlling or caretaking relationship with the staff. Stewardship reflects an approach to governance and management that emphasizes partnership, interdependence, and empowerment as the most effective ways of producing high-quality programs. Block's philosophy of stewardship provided the concept of leadership used in this chapter and book.

For adult services managers, "the leader is a team builder who empowers individuals in the organization and passionately 'lives the vision,' thereby serving as a mentor and example for those whose efforts are necessary to make the vision become reality" (Nanus, 1992, p. 14). Leadership and opportunities for distributed leadership are the foundation on which excellent management rests.

Leadership for adult services managers and others is a philosophy and set of practices, both of which can be learned. Kouzes and Posner (1987) characterized leaders as practicing five common approaches to bringing about change:

1. Leaders challenge the process. They are innovators who look for new ways of accomplishing goals and improving the work unit. They treat mistakes as chances to learn, and they always search for opportunities, experiment, and take risks.
2. Leaders inspire their coworkers to share a vision of success for the organization. Leaders hold a positive and hopeful vision of what can be accomplished. Through skilled and thoughtful communication, they enlist the support of their work unit to meet a common purpose.

3. Leaders enable others to act. They purposefully involve the work unit in envisioning the future and planning for it. They help workers feel strong and capable. They value and support collaboration.
4. Leaders model behaviors they want to see their staff members copy. Leaders have clear beliefs and values, and they demonstrate them in their behaviors. They break projects down into achievable steps to give their workers the chance to experience "small wins." They set an example by focusing on priorities.
5. Leaders "encourage the heart." Leaders let staff members know how much their efforts are appreciated and show their pride in the team's contributions to achieving the vision. Leaders look for ways to celebrate achievements. They nurture team spirit that enables staff members to continue their efforts to meet goals.

Developing and Sustaining a Learning Community

Adult services managers typically assume full responsibility for the performance of their work unit, but they often have only limited authority to make things happen. There are few things that a manager can do alone; accomplishments usually depend on the support, cooperation, or approval of others in the work group or in the agency. They accomplish their goals by helping to establish an organizational culture that promotes continuous learning and experimentation, that facilitates relationships based on learning and self-evaluation, and that exercises leadership by modeling.

To provide the kind of leadership that supports social workers, the manager must create and nurture a work environment that many adult services administrators call a "team environment." Weinbach (1990) specified some of the characteristics of a work and learning "climate" that produces good team efforts, outlined here.

RESPECT

A climate of mutual respect is one in which the manager demonstrates trust and confidence in social workers' abilities and does not use any unnecessary reminders that a power differential exists. In as many ways as possible, the manager should respect and treat workers as colleagues rather than as subordinates.

UNDERSTANDING

A climate of understanding is one in which each member of the team appreciates the other members' roles. Social workers must understand why the manager makes certain decisions. Learning the basis for decision making is valuable to social workers because it helps them understand how the work unit fits in the larger system. Understanding the "big picture" often makes change easier for those who must implement it. Managers in turn must consult with and listen to their staff members and reflect their concerns and opinions in decisions.

A climate of understanding means that the manager who has been a line social worker in the past actively tries to remember the rewards, stresses, and difficulties of that position. The manager who has never held one of the positions he or she supervises should make an effort to understand what it is like. It is also easy for a manager to forget the pressures and anxieties of a new worker. A climate of understanding also values cultural awareness and celebrates cultural and personal differences.

ADVOCACY

A climate of advocacy is one in which the middle manager champions the rights and privileges of the line staff, even if it invites the temporary disfavor of superiors. Although managers may find it easier to court the favor of administrators who evaluate their performance and reward them for not making waves, managers who do not protect and defend their staff members' interests will eventually lose their respect and confidence. If the manager has stood up to superiors for a just cause, then most of those superiors will eventually recognize that advocacy is part of the supervisor's job and gain respect for that supervisor's willingness to fight for an unpopular cause. The supervisor also is modeling for the social workers how to advocate on their clients' behalf.

AUTONOMY

A climate of autonomy is one in which the goals of the manager are to foster independence and creative decision making in workers to the full extent the system will allow. As Weinbach (1990) put it, "As long as a decision or behavior is within policies and guidelines, staff members should be able to assume that they will be supported, even if things go wrong" (p. 269). Decision making and the authority behind those decisions should be placed right where the work is done—by line staff in adult services agencies.

OPEN COMMUNICATION

A climate of open communication is one in which line social workers trust that it is acceptable to share bad news, such as a failure with a client, as well as good news. Managers also should demonstrate a belief that communication will not be used for control and manipulation of staff. To this end, managers do not have confidants among the people they supervise and do not withhold information selectively from other staff members. Managers give constructive feedback to the workers, which makes it safe for workers to share problems and concerns. Finally, workers must be able to trust that managers will pass on information to others only when appropriate (Weinbach, 1990).

Supporting Adult Services Social Work Practice

Social work practice, as outlined in the previous chapters, is both art and science. The successful social worker must be effective in both aspects. To further social workers' professional development, managers teach, coach, and act as sounding boards for decision making.

As stated in earlier chapters, the activities of line workers focus on the two principal tasks of the family assessment and change method: (1) case management, including advocacy, and (2) counseling. Counseling and case management both depend on the worker's ability to build a professional caring relationship with a client. This relationship is neither a friendship nor simply a supportive, nonconfrontive interaction. Rather, because it has a purpose and is focused on achieving certain goals, to attain them it may need carefully managed confrontation.

The manager's ability to support social workers' practice begins with his or her values regarding adult clients and belief in the need for workers to develop skills in case management and counseling. Establishing professional caring relationships is a practice skill that workers can learn and managers can teach, but the manager must believe that all the components identified in the family assessment and change method are critical to workers' effectiveness. If the manager does agree, then all of his or her tasks with workers center on supporting and nurturing these skills.

When a sample of adult services managers in North Carolina were asked in 1991 about the values underlying their programs, many of them emphasized autonomy and empowerment of clients (telephone and personal interviews conducted by the Center for Aging Research and Educational Services, 1991). Translating this value into guidelines for their work, they stressed the importance of showing respect for clients, seeing them as individuals, discovering and building on their strengths, acknowledging that people can and do change, enabling clients to do as much as they can for themselves, and allowing them to determine their own fate whenever possible.

Adult services managers in a rural program in Catawba County, North Carolina, used several formal phrases to stress the client-centeredness of their philosophy. They identified the "client as king" and spoke of a "senior partnership" with the client in case planning. One manager noted how essential it is to involve those closest to the client in decision making. Other values identified by managers as important to high-quality practice were maintaining confidentiality, being honest and nonjudgmental, and making it easy for clients to ask for help. Adult services managers must ensure that clients and their families are treated with respect.

How well the values of the manager get translated to and accepted by social workers is critical to the success of the adult services program. Managers translate their values to workers through their expectations of those workers. If a manager values discovering and building on clients' strengths, he or she will teach workers to make functional assessments of clients to discover strengths and see that these assessments are documented in the case record. The manager also will model assessment skills during reviews of workers' job performance, helping workers identify areas of strength, as well as deficiencies, and strategies for improving effectiveness. If a manager values allowing clients to decide their own fate whenever possible, he or she will teach workers how to use case management and counseling skills in such a way that clients can gain empowerment. The manager also will serve as a mentor to help workers develop their own judgment of how to practice effectively.

If a manager values the right to self-determination and autonomy, he or she will help the worker know when advocacy for clients is appropriate and demonstrate methods for doing it, perhaps through advocating on behalf of the work unit.

Teaching and Motivating Social Workers

Managers may not think of themselves as teachers, but in fact they teach every day. Just as every contact between social worker and client can be an effective intervention, every contact between adult services manager and social worker is a teaching opportunity. The manager's educational responsibility is to create and manage a learning environment to help workers learn governing policies and procedures, help them develop effective social work practice skills, influence their attitudes, help them apply what they have learned to their everyday job activities, and reinforce learning from peers, which leads to empowerment.

The manager fulfills this supervisory responsibility by such direct methods as individual case conferences, unit meetings, and group case staffings and also indirectly through arranging and facilitating training opportunities. The manager is the social worker's primary teacher and staff developer. In being effective teachers, adult services managers must be aware of central principles of learning, learning styles, methods for assessing learning needs and forming learning contracts, planning learning experiences, and motivating staff.

PRINCIPLES OF ADULT LEARNING

Because teaching adults is such an important role, it is crucial for managers to know the principles of helping adults learn and the processes adults go through to learn new things. According to Kadushin (1985) learning is most effective when five conditions are present:

1. When the content is relevant to the learner's needs. For most continuing professional education, learners will prefer training whose content is immediately useful and that addresses current problems in their work. When teaching workers about the family assessment and change method, the manager should link that training to actual cases in their caseload and show them how a functional assessment or goal setting will make planning services for their clients simpler. New information that has an immediate application usually motivates adult learners, who can perfect their skills while doing their jobs.

2. When learners can devote most of their energies to learning. If the learner feels guilty, fears failure, or does not know what to expect, these emotions take energy from learning. The manager must establish an atmosphere of safety and a framework of security in which the worker can admit failure or ignorance and get the manager's help. It is hard for a worker to say to a manager, "It didn't go well."

3. When learning is successful and rewarding. Adult learners seek to repeat what has been satisfying and avoid what is painful. Managers should pay attention when a worker has learned something new and give the worker the opportunity to show it off. Managers should seek out opportunities to praise eager learners.

4. When the learner is actively involved in the learning process. Adults generally know what they need and want to learn to be more successful at any task. Continuing professional education should offer and encourage choice on the part of the learners.

5. If the manager considers the learner's unique method of learning and abilities. Workers have different learning styles and life experiences. Managers should perform an educational diagnosis with each worker to find out what the worker already knows well, needs to learn, and wants to learn, as well as how the worker learns most effectively.

LEARNING STYLES

The first step in doing an educational diagnosis of a worker's learning needs is to assess the worker's learning style. Kolb (Kolb, Rubin, & McIntyre, 1984) developed an experiential learning model to describe how people learn, which can form the theoretical basis for the way social work supervisors teach social work practice. Kolb identified a four-stage learning cycle (Figure 20-1).

Concrete experience is participation in the event, for example, a social worker's interview with and assessment of a client. Formulating *observations and reflections* is often accomplished through a process Kolb called "publication," which involves sharing observations, feelings, or other reactions generated by the experience. Summarizing the assessment with the client belongs to this stage in the learning process, but discussing a difficult case with the manager and the process of writing the case record also may figure in accomplishing this task. *Formation of abstract concepts and generalizations* is the systematic examination of the patterns and dynamics of the concrete experience that gives meaning to the experienced event. This, too, is part of any summary process—not only recounting facts or events but considering their meaning. During this process, clients, workers, and managers may identify patterns of behavior and their causes and form hypotheses about what

Figure 20-1

THE LEARNING CYCLE

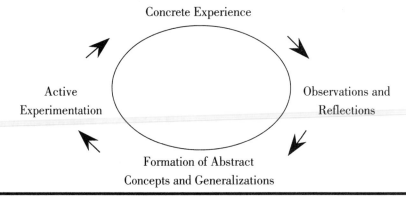

Adapted by permission from Kolb, D. A., Rubin, I. M., & McIntyre, J. M. (1984). Preface. In *Organizational psychology: Readings on human behavior in organizations* (p. xiv). Englewood Cliffs, NJ: Prentice Hall.

might change them and the implications of making a change. They might generalize to other situations and speculate whether the same strategies can be used in other circumstances. Finally, *active experimentation* is when the client, worker, or manager actually tries the strategies, at which point the cycle begins again, with experience of the new situation (Kolb, Rubin, & McIntyre, 1984).

Kolb claimed that learners move through all four stages in every learning situation, but he noted that they may enter the process at different places. This is because all learners have a preferred learning style. For example, social workers whose preferred learning style is abstract conceptualization may want to read something about the helping interview before trying it. Those who prefer observation and reflection may want to watch some interviews before trying one. Those preferring active experimentation may wish to risk trying several strategies first. For those who begin with concrete experience, they learn first through contacts with clients.

Historically, the teaching of social work has its roots in the apprenticeship model, that is, "learning by doing" or concrete experience. However, not all social workers prefer this learning method. Therefore, managers will find it helpful to assess their workers' preferred learning styles to understand what training methods work best for them. Because learning is a process for workers and because they may enter at different points of the cycle and must progress through each stage, it is important that managers provide social workers with the opportunity to follow the process through to have a complete learning experience.

Because managers themselves have preferred learning styles, they also will likely have a teaching style that corresponds to their own preferences. It may be hard for managers to understand and respect a worker's preferred learning style if it is different from their own. For instance, the manager who learns through abstract conceptualization might have a hard time understanding why a worker has no interest in reading about something before trying it. Equally, a manager might not understand a worker's willingness to experiment with a strategy before discussing or observing it. The manager must adapt his or her teaching style to correspond to each worker's learning style. Wolfe and Kolb's (1984) studies of the preferred styles of different professional groups showed that more social workers prefer concrete experience over the other three learning styles. This means that an abstract conceptualizer might have a hard time in a hands-on practice work unit.

ASSESSING LEARNING NEEDS AND MAKING CONTRACTS

In addition to identifying the learning styles of each social worker, managers also may find it helpful to make individual learning needs assessments. Figure 20-2 shows a sample tool that may be used to evaluate a worker's learning needs and a chart to record what must be learned. The areas cover life and work experiences, the skills and knowledge the worker brings to the position, what competencies are required to perform the tasks in the position or program, and what the worker's learning needs are.

After the manager and social worker have made the assessment together, they decide on how the worker will meet the learning goals. One possible way to structure this plan is to develop a learning contract that spells out what the worker will learn, how the worker will learn it, what the target date for completion is, and how the worker and manager will know that the worker has learned it. This plan bears more than a passing resemblance to the process of developing plans for services with clients. As with clients, this learning plan is framed as a contract to suggest that both manager and worker have a responsibility to see that it is fulfilled.

The learning needs assessment and the learning contract are part of an ongoing process in which new needs and new strategies for learning are identified throughout social workers' careers. This process enables them to continue setting goals for professional growth no matter how long they spend in any given job qualification. The assessment and contract also can be used as an additional tool to help the manager evaluate performance.

PLANNING LEARNING EXPERIENCES

Adult services managers are not the source of all learning for the worker, but they plan learning experiences with the worker on the basis of the worker's learning style, the learning contract, and available resources. As appropriate learning experiences are selected, the manager has three tasks to help workers get the most out of those opportunities: (1) The manager prepares the worker by discussing the learning objective, specifying what the worker should expect, and clarifying the worker's role in the learning experience. (2) The manager monitors how the learning is progressing. (3) The manager debriefs the worker, allowing him or her to process the experience emotionally and intellectually and to draw conclusions from it.

There are many places in which learning experiences for the worker can take place and many methods that the manager can use. The following list contains nine suggestions:

1. Using a learning case. A learning case is one selected jointly by manager and social worker as an opportunity for the worker to develop the particular knowledge or skill identified in the worker's learning contract. For example, Mr. and Mrs. O are a couple in their eighties who are part of the worker's caseload. Mrs. O is confused and Mr. O is physically frail. They are attempting to manage at home, but it is a dangerous and unhealthy situation because Mrs. O often leaves stove burners on when she tries to cook a meal. Mrs. O is suspicious and does not want anyone else in the house. Mr. O is trying to take care of Mrs. O. The clients need relief from the danger of a house fire that could result from Mrs. O's behavior and support for Mr. O in his efforts to care for himself and his wife. The learning need for the worker is to understand and use the strengths of the couple, and to know which counseling, client advocacy, and case management skills could be used.

Figure 20-2 _____

A LEARNING CONTRACT

What are you going to learn? (objectives)	How are you going to learn it? (resources and strategies)	Target date for completion	How are you going to know that you learned it? (evidence)	How are you going to prove that you learned it? (verification by judges)

Source: Knowles, M. S. (1978). *The adult learner: A neglected species.* Houston: Gulf Publishing. Copyright © 1978 by Gulf Publishing Company, Houston, TX. Used with permission. All rights reserved.

2. Holding unit meetings. These are appropriate for teaching content needed by most or all workers. For example, in teaching about new policy or forms, the use of case examples and a discussion of how to apply the policy is helpful for the workers whose learning styles favor concrete experience.
3. "Staffing" a case. In a unit meeting, one of the workers presents a case situation and solicits comments from his or her peers. Discussing practice-related issues in a group draws on the experience and knowledge of the group's members.
4. Practicing role play. Practicing an anticipated interaction with a client can help a new worker or a worker who is learning a new behavior—for example, confrontation—become more confident and skillful. The role play can be spontaneous and informal in a supervisory conference, or with a coworker, or alone with a tape recorder.

5. Using resource materials. Written materials, audiotapes, and other audiovisual media can be useful. With this method of learning, managers will need to prepare the worker by discussing objectives and debriefing the worker at the end. Reading, listening, or watching with a goal in mind helps the learner focus attention, and making a report afterward helps summarize the material.

6. Observing. Observing community meetings such as an adult services board meeting or a district court session can be a valuable learning experience. The objectives of this sort of participation may relate to learning about resources, community politics, or how to understand situations from another point of view. A social worker who goes with a client to observe him or her dealing with a landlord, for example, sees a different view of what the client experiences. Again, the learning is enhanced if the manager prepares the worker about what to observe and if the debriefing afterward allows the worker to question the manager.

7. Modeling. Managers teach by modeling, whether they intend to or not. The manager can talk about involving the client in the service plan but demonstrates it by involving the worker in the learning plan. Attitudes of acceptance and respect for people are "caught" by the worker more than they are consciously taught by the manager. Learning from other workers' actions is also natural, and here the manager can plan specific experiences. New workers or workers learning a new phase of work can benefit by spending time with a more skilled worker and watching as he or she performs the tasks involved in the job. When the focus is on a specific task—for example, interviewing skills—scheduled participation in that area may be useful. Here, especially, managers must prepare workers for the experience and debrief them individually and together.

8. Holding individual supervisory conferences. Planned, regular conferences between workers and managers are perhaps the single most important learning method. Managers provide the continuity in the process, they reinforce new knowledge, and they explain or prompt workers to discover how to transfer it to new situations. Their guidance moves workers toward competent independence. Documentation of the process, that is, recording progress in meeting learning objectives, becomes the basis for an objective analysis of performance and motivates the continuing cycle of professional growth and learning. In the individual conference, privacy and freedom from interruption are important, and scheduling of conferences should be flexible, according to the needs of workers. For example, newer workers or workers experiencing problems might need conferences scheduled more frequently. These conferences require planning and preparation by the manager and the worker. There should be continuity; at each conference they should agree on goals for the next conference. The individual conference enables the worker to depend on having the manager's undivided attention on a regularly scheduled basis.

9. Using the "spot" or "pop" conference. This sort of conference is held "on the run," sometimes in an emergency, when the worker usually is asking for immediate

advice on how to handle a situation. The spot or pop conference meets a real need, but relying on this type of learning experience has many hazards for manager and worker alike. Managers should work hard to avoid falling into this style of interaction. The first hazard is that if workers have access to the manager only in a crisis, all of their problems may become crises and they may become overdependent rather than self-reliant. The manager's responsibility to help workers develop their knowledge and decision-making skills is undercut, because no systematic practice planning or evaluation of the worker's learning comes from spot conferences. The worker's learning experience is not being managed. The second hazard is that managers forced to make split-second decisions are more likely to make bad ones that a little reflection would change. Additionally, living in a perpetual state of crisis is wearing on everybody and produces burnout. Finally, managers who have a steady stream of spot conferences lose control of their day. They become reactive instead of proactive. They are modeling a crisis environment for their whole staff. Supervisors who pride themselves on their open-door policy should examine whether they are in control of at least some of their work time and whether they have sufficient time for program management tasks such as planning and evaluation. Do they allow unending case consultation because they feel more comfortable and competent with those tasks than they do with program management? The scheduling of regular supervisory conferences and unit meetings gives the manager control of his or her day and promotes better learning experiences for workers. Emergency consultations are necessary, but the manager should take care to revisit those cases during the regular conference to help the worker determine if and how the worker could have handled the situation independently.

All the methods supervisors use to teach their staff members are, with some modification, parallel to methods social workers use with clients in helping them effect change. The "case" most clients use will be their own, but it may help to get clients to look for solutions they have used in the past for difficult problems or to see how others solve similar problems. Unit meetings have parallels in informational meetings clients may attend to learn new things. Case staffings are echoed by participation in multidisciplinary assessment teams, family conferences, and self-help groups. Social workers can use role playing to help clients prepare for a new activity—for example, a job interview, a discussion with a family member, or interaction with an agency or organization. Some clients are willing and able to use media resources to find information, whereas others benefit from demonstrations of new ways of doing things. Through interactions with clients, social workers model effective ways of behaving to produce desired ends. Finally, all monitoring visits with clients and families help them assess progress toward goals. For this reason, in the course of teaching staff members, supervisors are teaching methods as well, which should be made plain to social workers.

MOTIVATING STAFF MEMBERS

To keep workers motivated, managers must create and maintain environments that reward initiative, self-reliance, and careful performance of duties. Most employees are motivated to work well when they are supported and empowered by their managers. Because social workers are professionals, most take pride in doing their job well, which is often reward enough. Nonetheless, most people need acknowledgment from their supervisors and peers to continue to perform well at difficult tasks.

Some adult services programs recognize excellent performance through formal reward systems. Specific examples might include certificates of achievement, recognition by peers, special privileges such as a convenient parking space at work or recognition by community decision makers such as the mayor or board of county commissioners. However, such efforts are not enough.

Informal, intangible rewards are likely to have the most meaning for managers and employees in adult services. Chief among these is empowerment—the opportunity to be creative and stretch oneself as far as talent will allow. The ability and opportunity to exercise choice about what to undertake, how to undertake it, and how to manage one's time is frequently more motivating than any tangible reward. For example, if the social worker who has a special interest in developmental disabilities is given the opportunity to take leadership on developing a special community initiative in this area, that opportunity is both empowering and motivating.

Performance Management: Directing Daily Activities

Kadushin (1985) called day-to-day organization and monitoring of work the administrative function of human resources management. It is "getting the work done," and it includes seeing that agency policies and procedures are carried out while delivering services; accounting for the quantity, timeliness, and quality of the work being done; controlling the work flow to staff members; making proper use of staff resources; and evaluating the performance of workers.

RESOURCE MANAGEMENT

Resource management concerns the effective and efficient use of the adult services system's resources to achieve positive outcomes for adults with disabilities. Chapter 19 provided a discussion of elements of resource management pertaining to the effective and efficient use of materials and money (Rapp & Poertner, 1992). Resource management with respect to adult services personnel concerns itself with staffing levels, workloads, training, job qualifications, and the means for evaluating the performance of workers (Upchurch, 1991). Increasingly, programs are turning automation and information system tools and technologies to the evaluation of workers' performance and effectiveness. For some agencies, this will mean automated scheduling and assignment protocols for services such as transportation and in-home care or vacancies in nursing homes and board-and-care homes.

Other agencies are experimenting with automated case management methods to keep track of service interventions and costs and, in some cases, to evaluate outcomes for clients and families.

SELF-EVALUATION

A major responsibility of many adult services managers is to appraise the performance of personnel. Of the tasks required, performance appraisals make adult services managers the most uncomfortable. Reasons for disliking this function include feelings of walking a tightrope, awkwardness, and pressure because the manager knows the workers so well. Many managers feel that performance appraisals are too subjective and have a negative impact on team efforts because it is difficult to sort out individual contributions.

Block (1993) argued that traditional performance appraisals are counterproductive because they undermine the spirit of partnership and empowerment. He suggested that if organizations insist on performance appraisals, they should let employees be appraised by their customers or let them be responsible for self-appraisal. Another approach is to tie performance appraisals to individual learning contracts, so the focus is shifted to helping individuals to succeed, accomplish goals, assess their results, correct their course if necessary, and celebrate successes. Appraisals should be an ongoing process of establishing learning and performance objectives and measuring progress toward them. Automated case management methods that incorporate measurement of outcomes for clients and families provide a promising avenue for self-evaluation and performance appraisals.

COACHING AND RESOURCE MANAGEMENT

The approach to management of human resources and to performance appraisal is linked to the philosophy of administrative direction and control that produces it. A manager who gives primacy to the empowerment of workers assumes that their behaviors and competencies can be identified and associated with outcomes for clients and families. The use of coaching as a principal strategy, rather than sanction, recognizes that the "control-order-prescription" (COP) philosophy that underlies much of present-day personnel resource management practices runs counter to principles of empowerment that stress continuous learning, partnership, and collaborative approaches to change (Evered & Selman, 1989).

Coaching is concerned with improving the performance of staff members through a relationship whose primary objective is not to convey technical information (although some may be conveyed), address personal or psychological issues, or be a friend. Rather, it is to facilitate the staff member's critical self-assessment of performance to improve it. The source of change and improvement lies within each employee, and these things emerge from a process of self-evaluation and self-reorganization, not from external assessments, judgments, and prescriptions. Evered and Selman (1989) suggested 10 of the central qualities of coaching:

1. *partnership, mutuality, relationship*
2. *commitment to producing a result and enacting a vision*

3. *compassion, generosity, nonjudgmental acceptance, love*
4. *speaking and listening for action*
5. *responsiveness of the player to the coach's interpretation*
6. *honoring the uniqueness of each player, relationship, and situation*
7. *practice and preparation*
8. *willingness to coach and to be coached*
9. *sensitivity to "team" as well as to individuals*
10. *willingness to go beyond what's already been achieved.* (pp. 23–24)

Summary

Excellent adult services management and supervision empowers social workers and facilitates quality service to clients. Adult services managers in state, regional, and local agencies are leaders, teachers, mentors, advocates, resource developers, and coaches. Successful adult services managers are both artists and scientists, and their accomplishments come through two areas: (1) the art and science of management, which includes program planning and budgeting, program evaluation, and resource development, and (2) the art and science of supervision, which includes supporting social work practice, facilitating excellent performance, and teaching, coaching, and motivating staff members.

Key Points

Excellent adult services managers

- model a supportive, enabling, and empowering approach for social workers and other staff members
- build their competencies in supporting excellent social work practice, teaching and motivating staff members, and directing daily work unit activities, including performance management
- practice and refine leadership skills to create and maintain a collaborative environment
- support and enable the social worker to build skills and knowledge in the areas of case management, counseling, and client advocacy
- create and manage a learning environment in which the needs of adult learners are understood and respected
- make an educational diagnosis of each staff member that includes an assessment of preferred learning style, learning needs, and development of a learning contract
- plan learning experiences for workers based on their learning styles, objectives, and available resources
- schedule and hold regular individual conferences with each social worker
- value and celebrate cultural and personal diversity and help their employees do so as well

- create and maintain a motivational environment, including both formal and informal reward systems
- implement a performance management system in which both positive and negative feedback is given to workers on an ongoing daily basis
- review with workers their learning and performance objectives, identifying which have been accomplished and which remain and set new objectives as needed during the year; use self-evaluation performance appraisals as part of the ongoing process of professional development and learning.

References

Bennis, W., & Nanus, B. (1985). *The strategies of taking charge.* New York: Harper & Row.

Block, P. (1993). *Stewardship: Choosing service over self-interest.* San Francisco: Berrett-Koehler.

Center for Aging Research and Educational Services. (1991). *National telephone survey of state adult services programs.* Unpublished data. Chapel Hill, NC.

Evered, R. D., & Selman, J. C. (1989, Autumn). Coaching and the art of management. *Organizational Dynamics,* 16–33.

Kadushin, A. (1985). *Supervision in social work* (2nd ed.). New York: Columbia University Press.

Kolb, D. A., Rubin, I. M., & McIntyre, J. M. (1984). Preface. In D. A. Kolb, I. M. Rubin, & J. M. McIntyre (Eds.), *Organizational psychology: Readings on human behavior in organizations* (pp. xiii–xiv). Englewood Cliffs, NJ: Prentice Hall.

Kouzes, J., & Posner, B. (1987). *The leadership challenge.* San Francisco: Jossey-Bass.

Nanus, B. (1992). *Visionary leadership: Creating a compelling sense of direction for your organization.* San Francisco: Jossey-Bass.

Preston, P., & Zummerer, T. W. (1976). *Management for supervisors.* Englewood Cliffs, NJ: Prentice Hall.

Rapp, C. A., & Poertner, J. (1992). *Social administration: A client-centered approach.* New York: Longman.

Shulman, L. (1993). *Interactional supervision.* Washington, DC: NASW Press.

Upchurch, W. (1991). *Resource management: A prescription for change.* Raleigh: North Carolina Department of Social Services.

Weinbach, R. W. (1990). *The social worker as manager.* New York: Longman.

Wolfe, D. M., & Kolb, D. A. (1984). Career development, personal growth, and experiential learning. In D. A. Kolb, I. M. Rubin, & J. M. McIntyre (Eds.), *Organizational psychology: Readings on human behavior in organizations* (pp. 124–152). Englewood Cliffs, NJ: Prentice Hall.

INDEX

Strengths assessment, 36, 40, 83, 114, 221–223

Stress management, 183–184

Subjective, objective, assessment, plan format, 153

Substance abuse. *See* Drug abuse

Suicide counseling, 186–187

Suncoast Gerontology Center, 81

Supervision, 266–268

Supplemental Security Income, 8, 319, 320, 361

Support groups, 124

Sustenance goals, 45

SWOT (strengths, weaknesses, opportunities, and threats analysis), 343–344

Symptoms approach, 79, 80

T

Tatara, T., 216, 218

Team building, 27, 71, 84, 374–375

Technology, 163. *See also* Data identification; Databases

10 commandments for media relations, 364–366

Terminating services, 47–48, 115–116, 225, 244, 261

Texas Department of Health guide, 292

Timeliness, 14, 95

Title XX, 7–8, 10, 24, 89, 250. *See also* Social Security Act

Transfer summary, 151

Transitional care facilities. *See* Board and care

Transportation services, 10

Truisms, 28

Tuckerman, Joseph, 89

U

U.S. Department of Commerce workforce report, 74

U.S. House Select Committee on Aging, 215

Unified model adult services program, 13

University of Hawaii School of Social Work, 228

Unrealistic expectations, 171–172

V

Values
 cultural, 199–200
 multicultural, 208
 supporting personnel, 21–23

Veteran's benefits, 8

Viorst, Judith, 36

Vision statement, 26

Visual EcoScan, 76

W

Wickenden, Elizabeth, 6, 7

Work environment, 23, 142–143

World Health Organization health risk factors, 79

Written records, 150

Y

Yesavage and Brink's geriatric depression scale, 78

ABOUT THE EDITORS

Ann C. Eller, MSW, is the Adult Prevention and Placement Services Coordinator of the North Carolina Division of Social Services. She was coordinator in the division for developing *A Model for Excellence in Adult Services Administration and Social Work Practice* and a supporting record-keeping system, on which this book is based. She has provided leadership in developing a family-centered approach for use by adult services social workers in public social services agencies in North Carolina. She has extensive experience as a social work consultant, trainer, and practitioner in the full range of adult, family, and children's services in the division and in a local public social services agency.

Margaret L. Morse, PhD, is the publications coordinator for Family Forum at the School of Social Work, University of North Carolina–Chapel Hill, and since 1989 has edited, designed, and produced many of the Center for Aging Research and Educational Services's (CARES's) contract publications for the North Carolina Divisions of Social Services and Aging. She is a graduate of University of North Carolina–Chapel Hill's Curriculum on Comparative Literature.

Gary M. Nelson, DSW, is associate professor and director of the Family Forum Program and CARES at the School of Social Work at the University of North Carolina–Chapel Hill. He has had a long career working with aging people, focusing on adult services, care for aging individuals in rural areas, long-term care, and the role of the family. He has been a member of NASW's Subcommittee on Aging and the Family and is a fellow of the Gerontological Society of America. He is currently involved in research, teaching, and consultation on social intervention theory and practice, public services work force issues, long-term care, and organizational culture.

Dennis W. Streets, MPH, MAT, LNHA, is a clinical instructor at the School of Social Work, University of North Carolina–Chapel Hill and associate director of the Family Forum Program, of which CARES is a part. Since 1978 he has worked as a human services planner and trainer, program manager, consultant, and agency administrator, mostly in the field of adult and aging services. He has worked with one of North Carolina's Area Agencies on Aging; the state Division of Social Services; Blue Cross and Blue Shield of North Carolina; and the Evergreens, a nonprofit long-term-care organization.

ABOUT THE CONTRIBUTORS

Vickie L. Atkinson, MSW, CCSW, is a clinical instructor in the School of Social Work, University of North Carolina–Chapel Hill and mental health specialist in the school's Center for Aging Research and Educational Services (CARES).

Lane G. Cooke, MSW, is a clinical instructor in the School of Social Work, University of North Carolina–Chapel Hill and program coordinator of the school's Family and Children's Resource Program.

Robert Leibson Hawkins, MPA, is a clinical instructor in the School of Social Work, University of North Carolina–Chapel Hill and human resources planner in the school's Family Forum.

Mary Anne P. Salmon, PhD, is a clinical instructor in the School of Social Work, University of North Carolina–Chapel Hill, aging research specialist in CARES, and research fellow of the Cecil G. Sheps Center for Health Services Research.

Anna Scheyett, MSW, CCSW, is a clinical instructor in the School of Social Work, University of North Carolina–Chapel Hill and program coordinator in the school's Mental Health Resource Program.

The Field of Adult Services: Social Work Practice and Administration

Designed by Anne Masters Design, Inc.

Composed by Patricia D. Wolf, Wolf Publications, Inc., in Bodoni and Futura.

Printed by Boyd Printing Company on 60# Windsor.

Books on Adult and Gerontological Practice from the NASW Press

The Field of Adult Services: Social Work Practice and Administration, *Gary M. Nelson, Ann C. Eller, Dennis W. Streets, and Margaret L. Morse, editors.* Presents a clear model for the field by combining an overview of key skills with a framework for excellence in adult services practice. Chapters are written to stand alone, with cross-references to aid the reader in making comparisons across service areas. A useful text for students, supervisors, managers, and administrators in state and area agencies on aging.
ISBN: 0-87101-250-2. Item #2502. $34.95.

Gerontology for Health Professionals: A Practice Guide, *Florence Safford and George I. Krell, editors.* Offers an interdisciplinary look at the knowledge, skills, and attitudes required of gerontological practitioners.
ISBN: 0-87101-218-9. Item #2189. $22.95.

Caring Families: Supports and Interventions, *by Deborah S. Bass.* Identifies the stress factors and rewards that affect caregiving families and family members and presents techniques to help the professional support them.
ISBN: 0-87101-185-9. Item #1859. $21.95.

(order form on reverse side)

ORDER FORM

	Title	Item #	Price	Total
___	The Field of Adult Services	Item 2502	$34.95	_____
___	Gerontology for Health Professionals	Item 2189	$22.95	_____
___	Caring Families	Item 1859	$21.95	_____
		+ 10% postage and handling		_____
			Total	_____

❑ I've enclosed my check or money order for $ _____.

❑ Please charge my ❑ NASW Visa* ❑ Other Visa ❑ MasterCard

_____ _____

Credit Card Number   Expiration Date

Signature _____

Use of this card generates funds in support of the social work profession.

Name _____

Address _____

City _____ State/Province _____

Country _____ Zip _____

Phone _____ _____

NASW Member # (if applicable)

(Please make checks payable to NASW Press. Prices are subject to change.)

NASW PRESS

NASW Distribution Center
P.O. Box 431
Annapolis, MD 20701
USA

Credit card orders call
1-800-227-3590
(In the Metro Wash., DC, area, call 301-317-8688)
Or fax your order to 301-206-7989

*FASz 6/95